A Publication Sponsored by
the Center for Negotiation
and Conflict Resolution
at Rutgers, the State University
of New Jersey

Mediation Research

Kenneth Kressel
Dean G. Pruitt
and Associates

Mediation Research

The Process and Effectiveness
of Third-Party Intervention

 Jossey-Bass Publishers
San Francisco   •   London   •   1989

MEDIATION RESEARCH
The Process and Effectiveness of Third-Party Intervention
by Kenneth Kressel, Dean G. Pruitt, and Associates

Copyright © 1989 by: Jossey-Bass Inc., Publishers
350 Sansome Street
San Francisco, California 94104
&
Jossey-Bass Limited
28 Banner Street
London EC1Y 8QE

Library of Congress Cataloging-in-Publication Data

Kressel, Kenneth.
    Mediation research : the process and effectiveness of third-party
intervention / Kenneth Kressel, Dean G. Pruitt, and associates —
1st ed.
      p. cm. — (Jossey-Bass social and behavioral science series)
(Jossey-Bass management series)
    Bibliographies
    Includes index.
    ISBN 1-55542-162-8 (alk. paper)
    1. Mediation.   2. Mediation and conciliation, Industrial.
I. Pruitt, Dean G. II. Title. III. Series. IV. Series: Jossey-
Bass management series.
HM136.K75   1989
303.6′9 — dc20   89-8211
                                  CIP

Manufactured in the United States of America

The paper in this book meets the guidelines for
permanence and durability of the Committee on
Production Guidelines for Book Longevity of the
Council on Library Resources.

JACKET DESIGN BY WILLI BAUM

FIRST EDITION

Code 8936

A joint publication
in
The Jossey-Bass
Social and Behavioral Science Series
and
The Jossey-Bass Management Series

Contents

Foreword

Dispute resolution is a field in which research is hurrying to catch up with practice. Developments on the legislative, executive, and judicial fronts are generally occurring faster than the research can advance to offer guidance and direction.

Mediation is the dispute resolution process that has gained the most attention of late, although it is not the only one. During the last decade, experimentation with mediation as an alternative or complementary process for resolving conflict has been increasing. Institutional support for mediation programs has come from many sources, including foundations, government agencies, and the judiciary. These initiatives have arisen from the perception that confrontational and adversarial approaches often make things worse, rather than better, and from the quest of a beleaguered court system for less costly, more efficient mechanisms for resolving conflict.

Because of the vigorous growth of mediation programs and the increasing sums being spent on them, the dearth of research on the mediation process has become a subject of concern among policy makers and judicial and other administrators. This book will not answer all their questions, but it is a highly significant step in the right direction.

All the contributors are acknowledged leaders in their respective domains of research, and the chapters they have written summarize some of the most significant empirical work in the mediation area. If there is one single place to go for a "read out" on the current state of mediation research, this must surely be it.

As the editors make clear in their incisive concluding chapter, the collective implication of the extant empirical literature is that mediation works, in the sense that public satisfaction with the process is generally high and that constructive agreements are frequently reached under its auspices. Kressel and Pruitt make it equally clear that the research enterprise is still very young. Much remains to be learned about the dynamics of the mediation process and the conditions under which it is most likely to be effective. In this connection *Mediation Research* also promises to invigorate the collaboration between researchers and practitioners and to entice new researchers into the mediation arena.

The Center for Negotiation and Conflict Resolution at Rutgers University has enthusiastically supported this undertaking as part of its own commitment to aid in constructing theory, to inform policy development, and to guide practice. As readable as they are insightful, these chapters are an important contribution in all these areas. Accordingly, we commend the book to policy makers and mediators as well as to scholars and teachers.

June 1989   Sanford M. Jaffe
                                              Director, Center for Negotiation
                                              and Conflict Resolution
                                              Rutgers, the State University
                                              of New Jersey, Newark

Preface

This book is intended to provide the most up-to-date information on the mediation process and its effects currently available in a single volume. Most of the chapters were commissioned expressly for this book. The names of the contributors will be instantly recognizable to anybody familiar with the last decade of mediation research—a signal decade because it is the first sustained period of empirical scrutiny of the mediation process. We know of no other volume that contains contributions by so many of the influential researchers from this crucial formative period and of no other in which nearly all the major projects are discussed.

As the principal authors of *Mediation Research*, we have several specific purposes. First, we wish to summarize what has been learned about the mediation process. Although we are a long way from definitive answers to many of the most vexing questions that confront us in the field, we are on much firmer empirical ground than we were only a few short years ago.

Second, we want the volume to contribute to a sense of shared discourse in a field with extremely heterogeneous intellectual roots. Mediation researchers draw upon the methods and intellectual traditions of law, psychology, sociology, industrial relations, anthropology, political science, communications, social work, and public policy. These diverse origins are a source of strength, but they can also retard communication and formation of a sense of common purpose. This collection testifies to the many questions and methods that the mediation research community has come to share.

Finally, we hope that the book will play a part in shaping the future research agenda. While much progress is being made, it is evident that mediation research is still in its toddlerhood. Major conceptual and methodological issues confronting mediators are set out here in virtually every chapter.

Audience

Mediation Research will be particularly useful to social scientists studying mediation or social and interpersonal conflict. It will serve them as a compendium of findings about the dynamics and effects of mediation, as a casebook of research methods, and as a spur to critical thinking in the design of their own projects.

Practicing mediators—those mediating community, divorce, environmental, public policy, small claims, and organizational conflicts—will also find the book relevant. Practitioners often wonder if there is any "scientific" evidence that what they do works; here they will find reassurance on that score. They will also find that, while empirical answers are not available to many of their most pressing questions about how and when to intervene most effectively, researchers are actively joining in the quest for such knowledge.

The book should also be useful to teachers, particularly in courses where the aim is to prepare students to do research or to develop in them a critical appreciation of the research literature on conflict and conflict management.

Overview of the Contents

To reflect the research focus of the book, we have organized its chapters according to research method, research objectives, or both. This is not an infallible organizing principle, given that there is much overlap among chapters in both method and purpose, but certain major methodological and conceptual similarities in theme seemed to bind some chapters together more than others.

Our brief introductory chapter is intended to set the stage by providing an overview of the research history of the field. It is followed by Part One, on evaluation research. The three chapters assembled in this part are united by a common concern: bringing empirical data to bear on the broad and sometimes heated controversy about whether and in what ways mediation may be a better way to resolve disputes than exclusive reliance on the adversary legal system. This part includes Pearson and Thoennes's summary of their influential ten-year study of divorce mediation; Roehl and Cook's integrative analysis of empirical assessments of mediation programs primarily inspired by the federal government's "neighborhood justice" initiative; and the report by McEwen and Maiman on their signal project on small claims mediation.

The second part of the book illustrates the use of case study methodology. Despite their diverse data sources, all of the chapters in this part use case analyses to describe how the wider social or cultural context affects the shape and scope of the mediation process. Merry's chapter presents a classic anthropological view of this theme, demonstrating how the differences between mediation in nonindustrial societies and that in industrial societies are rooted in broader cultural contrasts. Kolb's chapter, building on her pathbreaking account of labor mediators, describes how mediators' conceptions of their role in formal organizations is tied to the immediate organizational culture in which they function. Touval and Zartman demonstrate how the culture of power politics shapes the role—and creates many of the headaches—of the international mediator. Brock and Cormick use case study method to identify the political, practical, and psychological factors that determine the success or failure of efforts to institutionalize negotiations and mediation in the public sector.

In Part Three we have grouped those research programs that use aggregate data to explore what factors influence the process and outcome of mediation. These chapters have much

in common with those in Part One, but they are less concerned
with the general efficacy of mediation than with the conditions
that determine efficacy. With the exception of Chapter Thirteen, which uses archival sources to analyze international mediation, these chapters also share an exclusive reliance on interviews or questionnaires.

Three major issues are addressed by the chapters in this
part: (1) which factors determine whether a potential mediator
will choose to assume the mediation role (Chapters Eight and
Nine); (2) how mediation strategies and tactics can be classified
and in what circumstances different mediator interventions are
most likely to be effective (Chapters Nine, Ten, and Eleven); and
(3) which dispute and disputant characteristics are likely to
foster successful mediation (Chapters Ten, Eleven, Twelve, and
Thirteen).

In Part Four we have included four chapters based on
observation and experimentation. The use of such methods is a
relatively recent development in mediation research and, in our
view, a promising and important one. Chapter Fourteen makes
partial use of experimentation to explore how one disputant's
desire for retribution—or a belief in the appropriateness of
retributive action by those in a position to refer people to
mediation—affects the likelihood that mediation will occur and
the prospects that it will succeed.

In understanding the mediation process there is ultimately no substitute for direct and systematic observation of
mediators at work. The remaining chapters in this section are
important illustrations of this point. From Donohue's analysis of
the transcripts of mediation sessions (Chapter Fifteen), we learn
which patterns of mediator activity distinguish divorce mediations that reach settlement from those that do not. Chapter
Sixteen employs the classic laboratory experiment to test a
theory about how the mediator's perceptions and motivations
affect that person's tactical choices during mediation. In Chapter Seventeen Pruitt, McGillicuddy, Welton, and Fry, working in
a community mediation setting, report on how mediators' authority to arbitrate—or lack thereof—affects problem solving
and cooperation. The authors also discuss the nature and func-

tion of the caucus, as well as the mediator behaviors associated with different stages of mediation. Their work illustrates the power of the randomized field experiment to shed empirical light on polemical discussions about managing conflict.

Most of these chapters represent entirely new works written for this book by researchers in the forefront of their various fields of inquiry. In a few cases we have published pieces of special significance in revised form (Chapters One, Two, Four, Six, and Thirteen).

It is a notorious weakness of edited volumes of this type that the reader is often left with a jumble of poorly organized facts and findings, and with little sense of any overall coherence or meaning. We believe that the creative function of editors is to prevent such malaise. To that end we have concluded the book with its longest single chapter: our own extended effort at an integrative and critical assessment of the state of the art in mediation research.

Since our initial foray into the domain of mediation research (as coeditors of a special issue on mediation for the *Journal of Social Issues*), the field has expanded into new areas, experimented with a growing range of methods, and introduced new theoretical perspectives. Our concluding chapter reflects on these many new developments and tries to place them in a comprehensible framework. The chapter concentrates heavily on the studies contained in this book but also draws on other literature in mediation and related fields. In it we summarize what is currently known about the strengths and limitations of mediation as a means of conflict management, identify the convergent findings on the conditions under which it has been found most useful and on the most effective interventions, and draw conclusions about the topics and methods most in need of further exploration.

Acknowledgments

The organization and structure of this book have benefited greatly from astute readings of the manuscript by Jeffrey Z. Rubin and Tom R. Tyler. The Center for Negotiation and Conflict Resolution at Rutgers University has provided editorial and production support, for which we are grateful. Our warmest appreciation goes to our good colleague, George Levinger, who, during his tenure as editor-in-chief of *The Journal of Social Issues*, first suggested that we work together and gave us our topic.

June 1989   Kenneth Kressel
                                                         Newark, New Jersey

                                                         Dean G. Pruitt
                                                         Buffalo, New York

The Authors

Kenneth Kressel is associate professor of psychology at Rutgers, the State University of New Jersey, Newark. He received both his B.A. degree (1964) from Queens College of the City University of New York and his Ph.D. degree (1973) from Columbia University, in psychology. He has done research on labor mediation, international mediation, divorce mediation, and family and marital therapy and has published widely on these topics. He is the author of *The Process of Divorce: How Professionals and Couples Negotiate Settlements* (1985), and the coeditor (with D. G. Pruitt) of *The Mediation of Social Conflict*, an issue of *The Journal of Social Issues* (1985). He is on the editorial advisory boards of *Mediation Quarterly*, *The Negotiation Journal*, and *The Journal of Divorce* and is a fellow of the American Psychological Association.

Dean G. Pruitt is professor of psychology at the State University of New York, Buffalo. He received his A.B. degree (1952) from Oberlin College and his M.S. degree (1954) and Ph.D. degree (1957) from Yale University, all in psychology. He did postdoctoral work in psychology at the University of Michigan and in international relations at Northwestern University. He is a fellow of Divisions 8 and 9 of the American Psychological Association and has held a Guggenheim Fellowship. He specializes in the psychology of social conflict and does laboratory and field research on negotiation and mediation. He is the author of *Theory and Research on the Causes of War* (1959, with R. C. Snyder), *Negotiation Behavior* (1981), and *Social Conflict: Escalation, Stalemate and Settlement* (1986, with J. Z. Rubin), and the coeditor (with K. Kressel) of *The Mediation of Social Conflict*, an issue of *The Journal of Social Issues*.

Jacob Bercovitch is a senior lecturer in international relations at the University of Canterbury in Christchurch, New Zealand. He received his B.A. degree (1971) from Lancaster University, England, in politics, and his Ph.D. degree (1980) from the London School of Economics in international relations. Bercovitch's main research activities have been in the field of international conflict resolution and international mediation. He is the author of *Social Conflict and Third Parties* (1984), editor of *ANZUS in Crisis* (1988), and coeditor of *Superpowers and Client States* (1989) and *Mediation in International Relations* (forthcoming).

Kathryn Blumenfeld-Jones is a research associate in organizational behavior at the Fuqua School of Business, Duke University. She received her B.S. degree (1967) from the University of Kentucky in agriculture.

Jonathan Brock is an associate professor in the Graduate School of Public Affairs at the University of Washington, Seattle. He holds an A.B. degree (1971) from Franklin and Marshall College in economics and an M.B.A. degree (1973) from the Harvard University Graduate School of Business Administration. He has served in government at the Department of Labor, the Cost of Living Council, and on detail in the Executive Office of the President. Brock was a faculty member at the John F. Kennedy School of Government, Harvard University. He now serves as a consultant and adviser to major public and nonprofit agencies and is the author of *Managing People in Public Agencies* (1984) and *Bargaining Beyond Impasse* (1982).

Peter J. D. Carnevale is assistant professor of psychology and industrial relations at the University of Illinois, Urbana-

Champaign. He received his B.A. degree (1977) from the University of Delaware in psychology and his Ph.D. degree (1982) from the State University of New York, Buffalo, in social-organizational psychology.

Donald E. Conlon is a graduate student in the organizational behavior group of the Department of Business Administration at the University of Illinois, Urbana-Champaign. He received his B.A. degree (1983) from the University of Illinois, Urbana-Champaign, in psychology.

Royer F. Cook is president of the Institute for Social Analysis in Washington, D.C. His primary research activities are in the areas of drug and alcohol abuse prevention, criminal justice, and dispute resolution. Cook received his B.S. degree (1963) from Pennsylvania State University in psychology, and his M.A. (1966) and Ph.D. (1968) degrees from Kansas State University in experimental/industrial psychology.

Gerald W. Cormick is research associate professor in the Graduate School of Public Affairs at the University of Washington and founder of the Mediation Institute. He was a pioneer in the application of negotiation and mediation techniques to community, racial, environmental, regulatory, and public policy conflicts. His research and practice center on improving dispute settlement. Cormick serves on several editorial boards and has written widely on the process and ethics of negotiation and mediation. He received his B.Comm. degree (1964) from the University of British Columbia and his M.B.A. degree (1965) and Ph.D. degree (1971) in organizational behavior and labor relations, both from the University of Michigan.

William A. Donohue is associate professor of communication in the Department of Communication at Michigan State University. He received his B.A. degree (1972) from Bowling Green State University and his M.A. (1974) and Ph.D. (1976) degrees from Ohio State University, all in communication. Donohue's research interests focus on the strategies that mediators and negotiators use to manage intense conflict situations.

William Rick Fry is associate professor of psychology at Youngstown State University. He received his B.S. degree (1972) from Western Illinois University in psychology and both his M.A. (1976) and Ph.D. (1979) degrees from Wayne State University in social psychology.

Lynn L. Gigy is research psychologist at the Northern California Mediation Center, and interim coordinator of research and statistics with the Administrative Office of the Courts, Family Court Services for the State of California. She received her B.A. degree (1967) in sociology and her M.A. degree (1976) in research psychology, both from San Francisco State University, and her Ph.D. degree (1982) from the University of California, San Francisco, in human development and aging.

Kathy A. Hanisch is a graduate student in the Department of Psychology at the University of Illinois, Urbana-Champaign. She received her B.A. degree (1985) from the University of Northern Iowa in psychology and her M.A. degree (1987) from the University of Illinois, Urbana-Champaign, in industrial and organizational psychology.

Karen L. Harris is a graduate student in the Department of Psychology at the University of Illinois, Urbana-Champaign. She received her B.S. degree (1985) from Northern Illinois University in psychology and her M.A. degree (1987) from the University of Illinois, Urbana-Champaign, in industrial and organizational psychology.

Jean Marie Hiltrop is professor and director of the Master of Business Administration Program at the University of Leuven in Belgium. He received both his B.A. degree (1976) in general psychology and his M.A. degree (1978) in organizational psychology from the Free University of Brussels, his M.B.A. degree (1982) from Bradford University (U.K.), and his Ph.D. degree

(1982) from Tufts University in general and experimental psychology. He has taught personnel management and industrial relations at leading business schools and universities in Britain, France, Belgium, and China. He has done research on mediation, negotiation, and organizational behavior and currently serves as management consultant to a variety of companies throughout Europe and the Far East.

Joan B. Kelly is executive director of the Northern California Mediation Center, where she is principal investigator with the Divorce and Mediation Project, a divorce and family mediator, and director of training. An assistant clinical professor in the Department of Psychiatry, University of California, San Francisco, she is president of the Academy of Family Mediators and serves on the editorial board of *Mediation Quarterly* and *Conciliation Courts Review*. She received her B.A. degree (1961) from Bucknell University in psychology and sociology and her M.S. (1963) and Ph.D. (1965) degrees from Yale University in child development and clinical psychology.

Deborah M. Kolb is professor of management at the Simmons College Graduate School of Management and associate director of the Program on Negotiation at Harvard Law School. She holds a B.A. degree (1965) from Vassar in history, an M.B.A. degree (1973) from the University of Colorado, and a Ph.D. degree (1981) from the Sloan School of Management at the Massachusetts Institute of Technology in organizational behavior and industrial relations. Kolb is the author of *The Mediators* (1983), an ethnographic study of labor mediators. Currently, she is engaged in a multidisciplinary project on comparative mediation, conducted under the auspices of the Program on Negotiation.

Rodney G. Lim is a Ph.D. candidate in the department of psychology at the University of Illinois, Urbana-Champaign. He received his B.A. degree (1985) from the University of California, Berkeley, in psychology, and his M.A. degree (1988) from the

University of Illinois, Urbana-Champaign, in industrial and organizational psychology.

Craig A. McEwen is professor of sociology at Bowdoin College. He received his B.A. degree (1967) from Oberlin College in sociology and his M.A. (1969) and Ph.D. (1975) degrees from Harvard University in sociology.

Neil B. McGillicuddy is currently a program manager at the Research Institute on Alcoholism in Buffalo, New York. His current research involves the comparison of substance abuse prevention programs for the mentally retarded. His other research interests are in social conflict, mediation, and problems related to substance abuse. He received his B.A. (1982) and M.A. (1986) degrees from the State University of New York, Buffalo, in psychology and will soon receive his Ph.D. in social psychology from the same institution.

Mary E. McLaughlin is an assistant professor of psychology at San Diego State University. She received her B.A. degree (1983) from the University of Arizona in psychology and both her M.A. (1986) and Ph.D. (1988) degrees from the University of Illinois, Urbana-Champaign, in industrial and organizational psychology.

Richard J. Maiman is professor of political science and public policy at the University of Southern Maine. He received his B.A. degree (1967) from Lake Forest College in government and his Ph.D. degree (1972) from Brown University in political science.

Sally Engle Merry is associate professor of anthropology at Wellesley College. She received her B.A. degree (1966) from Wellesley College, her M.A. degree (1968) from Yale University, and her Ph.D. degree (1978) from Brandeis University, all in anthropology. She is on the editorial advisory board of the *Law & Society Review* and is the treasurer of the Society for Urban Anthropology. She is the author of a monograph on urban crime, *Urban Danger: Life in a Neighborhood of Strangers* (1981), and has written numerous articles on mediation, neighborhood social organization, working-class conceptions of the law, and environmental design and social conflict, including an article on crowding and neighborhood regulation in I. Altman and A. Wandersman (eds.), *Neighborhood and Community Environments* (forthcoming).

Dean E. Peachey is the national staff coordinator of the Network for Community Justice and Conflict Resolution in Canada and adjunct assistant professor of peace and conflict studies at Conrad Grebel College in Ontario. He has served as the director of a community mediation program and is coauthor (with B. Snyder and A. Teichroeb) of *Mediation Primer: A Training Guide for Mediators in the Criminal Justice System* (1983). He received his B.A. degree (1976) from Eastern Mennonite College in psychology and his M.A. (1982) and Ph.D. (1986) degrees from the University of Waterloo in social psychology.

Jessica Pearson received her B.A. degree from Sarah Lawrence College (1970) in sociology and her M.A. (1972) and Ph.D. (1974) degrees from Princeton in sociology. She currently codirects the Center for Policy Research and the Research Unit of the Association of Family Conciliation Courts. She has served as the principal investigator on numerous research projects related to alternative dispute resolution and recently completed a fellowship at the Socio-Legal Centre at Oxford University in Oxford, England (1987–88).

Janice A. Roehl is vice-president of the Institute for Social Analysis in Washington, D.C., where she is engaged in research on alternative dispute resolution, crime and arson prevention, and other criminal justice topics. She received her B.A. degree (1973) from the University of California, Davis, in psychology, and her Ph.D. degree (1988) from George Washington University in social psychology.

Jonelle Roth is a doctoral candidate in organizational behavior at the Fuqua School of Business, Duke University. Her research interests include institutionalization, socialization, and third-party intervention in conflict resolution. She earned her B.S. degree (1985) at the University of Illinois in industrial psychology.

Dale E. Rude is assistant professor of management in the College of Business and Public Administration, University of Missouri. He received both his B.S. degree (1975) in engineering operations and his M.S. degree (1978) in psychology from Iowa State University, and his Ph.D. degree (1984) from the University of Iowa in organizational behavior.

Blair H. Sheppard is associate professor, organizational behavior, at the Fuqua School of Business, Duke University, and director of the Center for the Study of Human Resource Management. He received his B.A. (1976) and M.A. (1977) degrees from the University of Western Ontario in psychology and his Ph.D. degree (1980) from the University of Illinois, Champaign-Urbana, in social psychology. His research interests include negotiation, conflict management, motivation, and group performance. He has published articles on all of these topics in a range of business and psychology journals and is coeditor of an annual series entitled *Research on Negotiation in Organizations*.

Nancy Thoennes completed her B.A. (1976) and M.A. (1977) degrees at the University of Colorado in sociology and received her Ph.D. degree (1981) from the University of Denver in sociology. She currently co-directs the Center for Policy Research and the Research Unit of the Association of Family and Conciliation Courts. Her research has included work in the field of alternative dispute resolution, child custody and child support, and domestic violence, especially child sexual abuse.

Saadia Touval is professor of political science at Tel Aviv University. During the preparation of the material for this book, he was visiting scholar at the Center for International Affairs at Harvard University and visiting professor of political science at the Graduate Center, City University of New York. He is the author of *The Peace Brokers: Mediators in the Arab-Israeli Conflict, 1948–1979* (1982), and, together with I. W. Zartman, he is a contributor to and coeditor of *International Mediation in Theory and Practice* (1985). He received both his A.B. (1957) and Ph.D. (1960) degrees from Harvard University in government.

James A. Wall, Jr., is professor of management in the College of Business and Public Administration, University of Missouri, and senior fellow at the Center for the Study of Dispute Resolution at the Missouri School of Law. He received his A.B. degree (1967) from Davidson College in economics and his M.B.A. degree (1967) and Ph.D. degree (1972) in organizational behavior from the University of North Carolina.

Gary L. Welton is visiting assistant professor of psychology at the University of Missouri, Columbia, where he conducts research on mediation, negotiation, and social dilemmas. He received his B.A. degree (1979) from Cedarville College in psychology, an M.A. degree (1982) from Slippery Rock University in counseling, and M.A. (1986) and Ph.D. (1987) degrees from the State University of New York, Buffalo, in social and organizational psychology.

I. William Zartman is professor of international politics at Johns Hopkins University, School of Advanced International Studies. He received his M.A. degree (1952) from Johns Hopkins University in political science, a diploma (1953) from the University of Copenhagen in international relations, and his Ph.D. degree (1956) from Yale University in international relations. He is the author of *Ripe for Resolution: Conflict and Intervention in Africa* (2nd ed., 1989), *The Practical Negotiator* (1981, with M. Berman), *International Mediation in Theory and Practice* (1984, with S. Touval), and *The Negotiation Process*, among other works. He is director of the Conflict Management Program at the School of Advanced International Studies and a member of the Council on Foreign Relations.

Mediation Research

Introduction:
An Overview
of Mediation Research

Dean G. Pruitt
Kenneth Kressel

When people are in conflict, they can take various approaches. They can launch a struggle in an effort to win; they can concede unilaterally, giving the other party a victory; or they can seek a mutually agreeable solution by means of problem solving. There is much to be said for the last approach, especially when the conflict is deadlocked or the parties must rely on each other in the future. Yet problem solving is not always easy. Hostile relations and inadequate communication often get in the way. When this happens, mediation may be the answer.

Mediation is third-party assistance to people who are trying to reach agreement in a controversy. There are hundreds of things a mediator can do to help, ranging from simply being present at a joint discussion to thinking up new ideas and arguing for them vigorously. Mediation is one of the oldest and most common forms of conflict resolution, emerging informally whenever there are three people who rely on one another and two of them quarrel. Formal mediation has been practiced for many years in two arenas: international relations and labor-management relations.

In the past ten years, there has been a quiet revolution in the field, and formal mediation now plays an increasing role in virtually every significant area of social conflict. Some of the most prominent new developments involve family and divorce settlements, small-claims cases, neighborhood feuds, controversies between landlords and tenants, decisions about the siting of dams and offshore oil rigs, and civil cases. More than three hundred mediation centers have been established around the country where citizens can obtain inexpensive third-party services.

Research in mediation has developed in tandem with this emerging field of practice. The earliest theoretical and empirical pieces concerned mediation in international settings (Burton, 1969; Doob, 1970; Fisher and Ury, 1978; Hill, 1982; Jackson, 1952; Kelman and Cohen, 1979; Rubin, 1981; Stenelo, 1972; Touval, 1975; Young, 1967, 1972) and labor-management settings (Blake, Shepard and Mouton, 1964; Douglas, 1962; Kerr, 1954; Kochan and Jick, 1978; Kolb, 1983; Kressel, 1972; Landsberger, 1955a, b; Peters, 1952, 1955; Rehmus, 1965; Simkin, 1971; Stevens, 1963; Walton, 1969). Many of the ideas were later refined in laboratory experiments involving simulated mediation tasks (Bartunek, Benton, and Keys, 1975; Bigoness, 1976; Harnett and Wall, 1983; Hiltrop and Rubin, 1982; Johnson and Pruitt, 1972; Johnson and Tullar, 1972; Podell and Knapp, 1969; Pruitt and Johnson, 1970; Vidmar, 1971).

The most recent research period began with the development of manuals (for example, Kessler, 1978; Underhill, 1981) and books of advice to community and divorce mediators (Coogler, 1978; Haynes, 1981; Beer, 1986; Moore, 1986). A polemical literature also appeared, directed toward championing (Wahrhaftig, 1981, 1982) or criticizing (Tomasic, 1982) the rapidly developing mediation movement. Two new journals directed toward practitioners were also developed, the *Mediation*

Quarterly and the *Negotiation Journal.* Empirical work in this period was mainly evaluative (see Chapter Two), often contrasting mediation with courtroom settlements. These studies usually found that mediation, though still largely unknown by the general public, gets very high marks from its users and that mediated agreements tend to stick. In most of these studies, mediation fares better than the courts on both dimensions.

More recently, there has been a resurgence of theoretically oriented empirical projects. Reports on several of these projects were gathered together in a special issue of the *Journal of Social Issues*, which we edited (Kressel and Pruitt, 1985a). The questions raised in these investigations go well beyond those of the earlier evaluation studies, with hypotheses based on theory developed in other branches of the social sciences. An interest in general theory can also be seen in a number of reviews of the literature that look at mediation as a whole (Bercovitch, 1984; Fisher, 1983; Kressel and Pruitt, 1985b; Pruitt, 1981; Rubin, 1980; Wall, 1981).

Another feature of the recent period is the availability of funds earmarked for research on mediation. In 1983, the National Institute for Dispute Resolution, a private granting agency, was established with support from various foundations. Among other programs, it has given grants for pilot mediation projects and for research on the techniques and practice of dispute resolution. Funds for research on alternative dispute resolution are also available from the Law and Social Sciences Program of the National Science Foundation. The Hewlett Foundation has recently funded twelve university-based centers for research on conflict resolution, with a heavy focus on mediation. One of these centers, at Rutgers University, is the sponsor of this volume. Even more recently, the Ford Foundation has appropriated $3 million for research on various ways our society handles disputes, including mediation.

In spite of these developments, it is clear that the field of mediation research is still in its very formative stages. This contrasts markedly with the study of psychotherapy, another domain of research in which meliorative social influence is the target of inquiry. In that area it is taken for granted that the

subject under investigation constitutes an enduring and worthwhile social activity. Although other disciplines contribute, the
field is dominated by the methods, intellectual agendas, and
academic infrastructure of psychology and psychiatry. While
controversy abounds, the major issues and research paradigms
are well staked out.

In comparison, scholars planning to devote themselves to
the study of mediation are on much less certain ground. In some
quarters serious questions have been raised about the survival of
the entire subject: Is the interest in mediation a durable phenomenon or just a temporary and unrealistic utopian spasm
that will shortly subside? If interest does continue, from whence
will mediation researchers draw intellectual and career suste-
nance, when a myriad of intellectual traditions vie with equal
claims for preeminence and there is as yet no obvious discipline
to be called home?

We cannot answer such questions with any certainty. However, this volume is evidence that matters are moving in a
positive direction. The initial doubts about the value of mediation as a social activity have not disappeared completely, but
there is firm and generally favorable evidence (some of the most
cogent of which appears in the first section of this book) that the
mediation process has genuine merit, in spite of the fact that
practitioners are still largely inexperienced.

No single discipline, or combination of disciplines, can
claim hegemony, but there is evidence that we are beginning to
see agreement on certain key themes as targets for study: the efficacy of mediator behavior as a function of the nature and stage
of the dispute and the characteristics of the disputants; the importance of studying not only formal mediation but the informal mediation of everyday relationships; the effect of the wider
social context in which conflict is embedded; and the stressful
and complex nature of the mediator's role. No consensus on
research paradigms has emerged either—which is natural and
desirable at this stage of the game—but the array of methods is
expanding and becoming more sophisticated and the systematic observation of mediators at work is no longer a rarity.

All these developments are set forth in detail in the chapters that follow, and we trace their implications in more detail in our closing chapter. Their general import is that we have moved into a more mature and self-conscious stage of work. It is our hope that this book will have a significant formative influence on the stage that follows.

References

Bartunek, J. M., Benton, A. A., and Keys, C. B. "Third Party Intervention in the Bargaining Behavior of Group Representatives." *Journal of Conflict Resolution*, 1975, *19*, 532–557.

Beer, J. E. *Peacemaking in Your Neighborhood*. Philadelphia: New Society Publishers, 1986.

Bercovitch, J. *Social Conflicts and Third Parties: Strategies of Conflict Resolution*. Boulder, Colo.: Westview, 1984.

Bigoness, W. J. "The Impact of Initial Bargaining Position and Alternative Modes of Third Party Intervention in Resolving Bargaining Impasses." *Organizational Behavior and Human Performance*, 1976, *17*, 185–198.

Blake, R. R., Shepard, H. A., and Mouton, J. S. *Managing Intergroup Conflict in Industry*. Houston, Tex.: Gulf, 1964.

Burton, J. W. *Conflict and Communication: The Use of Controlled Communication in International Relations*. London: Macmillan, 1969.

Coogler, O. J. *Structured Mediation in Divorce Settlement*. Lexington, Mass.: Heath, 1978.

Doob, L. W. *Resolving Conflict in America: The Fermeda Workshop*. New Haven, Conn.: Yale University Press, 1970.

Douglas, A. *Industrial Peacemaking*. New York: Columbia University Press, 1962.

Fisher, R. J. "Third Party Consultation as a Method of Intergroup Conflict Resolution." *Journal of Conflict Resolution*, 1983, *27*, 301–334.

Fisher, R. J., and Ury, W. *International Mediation: Ideas for the Practitioner*. New York: International Peace Academy, 1978.

Harnett, D. L., and Wall, J. A., Jr. "Aspiration/Competitive Effects on the Mediation of Bargaining." In R. Tietz (ed.), *Aspiration*

Levels in Bargaining and Economic Decision Making. Berlin: Springer-Verlag, 1983.

Haynes, J. M. *Divorce Mediation: A Practical Guide for Therapists and Counselors.* New York: Springer-Verlag, 1981.

Hill, B. J. "An Analysis of Conflict Resolution Techniques: From Problem-Solving Workshops to Theory." *Journal of Conflict Resolution*, 1982, *26*, 109–138.

Hiltrop, J. M., and Rubin, J. Z. "Effects of Intervention Conflict of Interest on Dispute Resolution." *Journal of Personality and Social Psychology*, 1982, *42*, 665–672.

Jackson, E. *The Meeting of Minds: A Way to Peace Through Mediation.* New York: McGraw-Hill, 1952.

Johnson, D. F., and Pruitt, D. G. "Preintervention Effects of Mediation Versus Arbitration." *Journal of Applied Psychology*, 1972, *56*, 1–10.

Johnson, D. F., and Tullar, W. L. "Style of Third Party Intervention, Face-Saving and Bargaining Behavior." *Journal of Experimental Social Psychology*, 1972, *8*, 319–330.

Kelman, H. C., and Cohen, S. P. "Reduction of International Conflict: An Interactional Approach." In W. G. Austin and S. Worchel (eds.), *The Social Psychology of Intergroup Relations.* Monterey, Calif.: Brooks/Cole, 1979.

Kerr, C. "Industrial Conflict and Its Mediation." *American Journal of Sociology*, 1954, *60*, 230–245.

Kessler, S. *Creative Conflict Resolution: Mediation.* Atlanta, Ga.: Society of Professionals, 1978.

Kochan, T. A., and Jick, T. "The Public Sector Mediation Process: A Theory and Empirical Examinations." *Journal of Conflict Resolution*, 1978, *22*, 209–240.

Kolb, D. M. *The Mediators.* Cambridge, Mass.: MIT Press, 1983.

Kressel, K. *Labor Mediation: An Exploratory Survey.* Albany, N.Y.: Association of Labor Mediation Agencies, 1972.

Kressel, K., and Pruitt, D. G. "The Mediation of Social Conflict." A special issue of the *Journal of Social Issues*, 1985a, *41* (2).

Kressel, K., and Pruitt, D. G. "Themes in the Mediation of Social Conflict." *Journal of Social Issues*, 1985b, *41*, 179–198.

Landsberger, H. A. "Interaction Process Analysis of Professional Behavior: A Study of Labor Mediators in Twelve Labor-

Management Disputes." *American Sociological Review*, 1955a, *20*, 566–575.

Landsberger, H. A. "Interaction Process Analysis of the Mediation of Labor-Management Disputes." *Journal of Abnormal and Social Psychology*, 1955b, *51*, 552–559.

Moore, C. W. *The Mediation Process: Practical Strategies for Resolving Conflict*. San Francisco: Jossey-Bass, 1986.

Peters, E. *Conciliation in Action*. New London, Conn.: National Foremen's Institute, 1952.

Peters, E. *Strategy and Tactics in Labor Negotiations*. New London, Conn.: National Foremen's Institute, 1955.

Podell, J. E., and Knapp, W. M. "The Effect of Mediation on the Perceived Firmness of the Opponent." *Journal of Conflict Resolution*, 1969, *13*, 511–520.

Pruitt, D. G. *Negotiation Behavior*. Orlando, Fla.: Academic Press, 1981.

Pruitt, D. G., and Johnson, D. F. "Mediation as an Aid to Face Saving in Negotiation." *Journal of Personality and Social Psychology*, 1970, *14*, 239–246.

Rehmus, C. M. "The Mediation of Industrial Conflict: A Note on the Literature." *Journal of Conflict Resolution*, 1965, *9*, 118–126.

Rubin, J. Z. "Experimental Research on Third-Party Intervention in Conflict: Toward Some Generalizations." *Psychological Bulletin*, 1980, *87*, 379–391.

Rubin, J. Z. (ed.). *Dynamics of Third Party Intervention: Kissinger in the Middle East*. New York: Praeger, 1981.

Simkin, W. E. *Mediation and the Dynamics of Collective Bargaining*. Washington, D.C.: Bureau of National Affairs, 1971.

Stenelo, L.-G. *Mediation in International Negotiations*. Malmo, Sweden: Studentlitteratur, 1972.

Stevens, C. M. *Strategy and Collective Bargaining Negotiation*. New York: McGraw-Hill, 1963.

Tomasic, R. "Mediation as an Alternative to Adjudication: Rhetoric and Reality in the Neighborhood Justice Movement." In R. Tomasic and M. Feeley (eds.), *Neighborhood Justice: An Assessment of an Emerging Idea*. New York: Longman, 1982.

Touval, S. "Biased Intermediaries: Theoretical and Historical

Considerations." *Jerusalem Journal of International Relations*, 1975, *1*, 51–69.

Underhill, C. I. *A Manual for Community Dispute Settlement*. Buffalo, N.Y.: Better Business Bureau of Western New York, 1981.

Vidmar, N. "Effects of Representational Roles and Mediators on Negotiation Effectiveness." *Journal of Personality and Social Psychology*, 1971, *17*, 48–58.

Wahrhaftig, P. "Dispute Resolution Retrospective." *Crime and Delinquency*, 1981, *27*, 99–105.

Wahrhaftig, P. "An Overview of Community-Oriented Citizen Dispute Resolution Programs in the United States." In R. Abel (ed.), *The Politics of Informal Justice: The American Experience.* Vol. 1. Orlando, Fla.: Academic Press, 1982.

Wall, J. A., Jr. "Mediation: An Analysis, Review and Proposed Research." *Journal of Conflict Resolution*, 1981, *25*, 157–180.

Walton, R. E. *Interpersonal Peacemaking: Confrontations and Third Party Consultation*. Reading, Mass.: Addison-Wesley, 1969.

Young, O. R. *The Intermediaries: Third Parties in International Crises*. Princeton, N.J.: Princeton University Press, 1967.

Young, O. R. "Intermediaries: Additional Thoughts on Third Parties." *Journal of Conflict Resolution*, 1972, *16*, 51–65.

ONE

Divorce Mediation:
Reflections on a Decade
of Research

Jessica Pearson
Nancy Thoennes

In 1978, lawyers and mental health professionals serving on a subcommittee of the Colorado Bar Association met to discuss alternatives to litigation in contested child custody and visitation disputes. One committee member had heard about experimental efforts to negotiate with disputing parents in Minnesota and Los Angeles. The nonadversarial approach intrigued the committee. As veterans of the adjudicatory system, most committee members were convinced that a new approach was needed.

Three Projects

In subsequent months, we secured foundation support for a demonstration mediation project, including a longitudinal evaluation comparing the effects of conventional litigation with the experimental nonadversarial approach. The result was the Denver Custody Mediation Project (CMP). During 1979–1981, the CMP provided mediation services to 160 couples contesting child custody or visitation arrangements. During the evaluation process, three sets of interviews were conducted with 217 mediation clients, 113 who rejected an offer of mediation, and 89 others with custody and visitation disputes who used traditional adversarial methods to resolve their disagreements.

A second research study—the Divorce Mediation Research Project (DMRP)—began in 1981, with an award from the Administration for Children, Youth and Families to evaluate court-based mediation services involving custody and visitation disputes. Through observations, interviews, and analysis of mediation tapes, we collected data at three sites: the Los Angeles Conciliation Court, the Family Relations Division of the Connecticut Superior Court, and the Domestic Relations Division of the Hennepin County (Minneapolis) Family Court. In addition, at three time points we administered questionnaires to approximately 450 mediation clients, each of whom entered mediation with a custody or visitation problem. In Colorado, where court-based mediation was not available, we conducted a similar series of interviews with 100 individuals using the traditional adversarial approach and 100 divorcing, but noncontesting, individuals.

In 1984 we initiated a third major study of divorce mediation. This project assessed a program that mediates child support matters in the Family Court of the state of Delaware. Delaware is the only state to mandate mediation in the development of new and modified child support orders. It has also pioneered the development of a mathematical formula (the Melson formula) to guide the establishment and modification of child support. The study compared support order levels generated in mediation with those generated in adjudicatory forums, and compared the orders produced in each with the level predicted by the formula.

The research focus in the three projects was largely dictated by the newness of the mediation phenomenon. Basic questions begged to be addressed. Who chooses mediation? Who prefers to adjudicate? How long is the mediation session? What actors participate in the mediation sessions? What techniques are used? How effective is the procedure in producing agreements? What types of agreements are generated? What characteristics of the dispute or disputant are associated with settlements? What are the reactions of users? How do reactions differ for men versus women? How do they compare to reactions to adjudication? What is the impact of mediation on children? Does mediation affect compliance and relitigation behaviors? Does it translate into savings in time and money for litigants or courts?

The balance of this chapter describes the major findings from our research in divorce mediation. We focus on the decision to mediate, mediation strategies, the effectiveness of the intervention, and factors affecting outcomes. Although we rely primarily on data from the CMP and DMRP studies, the results of the Delaware evaluation are also noted when relevant.

Research Methods

Both the CMP and the DMRP were longitudinal studies involving telephone (and sometimes in-person) interviews with parents experiencing conflicts over custody or visitation. In the CMP, couples contesting child custody or visitation arrangements were flagged by Colorado courts and referred to the project for random assignment to the experimental mediation or control groups. Interviews with respondents in both categories, as well as those who rejected the offer to mediate, were conducted at three time points: upon referral to the project, after final orders were issued, and approximately six months after the second interview. In addition, court files for all respondents were reviewed approximately seventeen months after promulgation of the final orders. This review assessed the incidence of relitigation, modification, and punitive legal activity.

Data were collected in the DMRP from clients in three states who used court-based mediation services. They completed questionnaires at three time points: before mediation started, approximately fifteen weeks after the first contact, and thirteen to fifteen months after the initial interview. In Colorado, we interviewed adjudicating and noncontesting parties at comparable time points. We generated audio tapes of eighty-one mediations at the three sites. Finally, to gain a longer perspective, we interviewed (by phone) a sample of people at each site who had litigated or mediated child custody approximately five years earlier, in 1978 and 1979.

In both studies, the questionnaires elicited information on socioeconomic and demographic characteristics, marital and divorce history, problems in coping with divorce, acceptance of the divorce, the mutuality of the divorce decision, parenting patterns, ability to communicate and cooperate, visitation problems, magnitude and duration of the dispute, and sources of satisfaction and dissatisfaction with the court. The second and third interviews included detailed questions on outcomes, experiences, and reactions to mediation and adjudication, including user satisfaction, perceived equity and justice, compliance with child- and financial-related agreements, punitive legal activity, modification behaviors, and relitigation. Child adjustment in the CMP was gauged with a parental report checklist developed by Achenbach and Edelbrock (1981).

The Delaware evaluation relied on a sample of 320 child support cases filed between January 1983 and December 1984. In all cases both parents resided in the state and the court files included a calculation of the support guideline level derived from the Melson formula. The analysis compared child support amounts generated in three ways — mediation, judicial hearings, and master's hearings — to one another and to the levels predicted by the formula. Subsequent compliance and relitigation patterns were also noted. In addition, via telephone interviews we asked fifty people who had used mediation their impressions of the process. Most respondents had also attended a master's hearing, either to review the mediation agreement or to resolve a problem with support, and their impressions of court were also recorded. Finally, we conducted qualitative, in-depth interviews with lawyers, judges, masters, and mediators.

Major Findings

Choosing or Rejecting Mediation

Approximately one-third of the individuals who were offered free services through the CMP refused the offer of mediation. Most typically, one parent was willing to try but the other could not be persuaded to participate. Although males and females were equally likely to refuse the mediation offer, their reasons differed. Women most commonly cited mistrust, fear, or a desire to avoid an ex-spouse. When men rejected mediation, they typically explained that they could win in the legal process or were skeptical that mediation would work.

Looking at individuals who agreed to mediate and those who rejected the opportunity, we can learn more about the factors that promote acceptance. Mediation candidates scored higher than their rejecting counterparts on traditional socioeconomic indicators. For instance, 72 percent of the men and 55 percent of the women who preferred mediation had at least a college education, whereas fewer — 58 percent of the men and 48 percent of the women — among those who rejected mediation had a college education. Men who favored mediation also held higher-status occupations; only 18 percent were in semiskilled jobs, compared to 31 percent of those who rejected mediation. Finally, people who accepted the offer had higher incomes both before and after the divorce.

In addition to socioeconomic differences, those interested in mediation reported better spousal communication patterns. Whereas 60 percent of the men who rejected mediation reported that they currently did not communicate at all with their former spouse, only 15 percent of men who accepted mediation reported this. For women, the patterns were similar: 43 percent of those who refused mediation reported no current communication, compared to 14 percent of those who accepted the offer.

Reactions to the legal process also appear to have been a factor. Women who preferred mediation viewed it as less remote and impersonal than the court system. Although they rated their chances of winning in court at least as highly as their rejecting counterparts, they felt that courts were impersonal and inappropriate for resolving child custody disputes. They were also more likely to have attorneys who encouraged them to try mediation. More than 72 percent of the women who wanted to mediate, but only 18 percent of the rejecting women, reported lawyer encouragement.

In some respects the factors influencing the decision to mediate were similar for men. Like women, men responded to the reactions of their attorneys: 69 percent of those preferring mediation, but only 32 percent of those declining, reported that their lawyers were enthusiastic about mediation. Men who selected mediation also expressed more dissatisfaction with the court and believed that judges discriminate against men. Unlike women, however, mediation-minded men gave themselves only slim chances of winning in court while men who rejected mediation rated their chances in court more favorably.

These patterns suggest that as long as it remains a voluntary procedure, mediation will be most widely used by couples with relatively high socioeconomic standing and some degree of ongoing communication, particularly when their attorneys support mediation and when the parents themselves have misgivings about the traditional court process.

However, mediation is not always voluntary. To reach a broader cross section of the population, numerous courts have mandated mediation in disputed divorces. Compulsory mediation generates some controversy because it appears to contradict the notion of free choice, which is basic to mediation ideology (Danzig and Lowy, 1975). Data from the DMRP, however, suggest strong user support for mandatory mediation. We find that 60 to 70 percent of our respondents who used court-based mediation services in Los Angeles, Minnesota, and Connecticut in 1978 and 1979 favor the mandatory mediation of child custody and visitation disputes. Among those who mediated agreements in 1982, 85 to 90 percent favored a mandatory system, and about two-thirds of those who failed to settle in mediation would still favor a mandatory attempt.

Voluntary participation does not appear to be a key to

producing mediated settlements. Approximately 60 percent of those who mediated voluntarily in the course of the CMP ultimately were able to reach a full or partial settlement. In the DMRP, the clearest example of a mandatory program was that offered at the Conciliation Court in Los Angeles, where all disputants were ordered into mediation; about 60 percent of them also produced a full or partial agreement. In Connecticut and Minneapolis, judges selectively referred parties to mediation; as in other locations, 60 and 70 percent of users, respectively, reached full or partial agreement.

Nor did we find evidence that the question of voluntary versus mandatory is related to user satisfaction. In all three DMRP sites, and in the CMP, about 80 percent of those who attempted mediation said they would probably recommend it to a friend. Similarly, at the final interview, about three-quarters of all those who used mediation through either project reported that they were glad they tried the process. Also, both mediation clients in the purely voluntary CMP program and those in more mandatory programs believed that mediators pressured parties to produce an agreement. Thus, a mandated attempt to mediate does not appear to affect the settlement rate, general user satisfaction, or the perceived coerciveness of the outcome.

Strategies and Tactics of Intervention

Mediation intervention differs in scope and duration in the public and private sectors. Public-sector interventions generally involve fewer sessions of shorter duration and focus on custody and visitation issues rather than financial disputes. However, public-sector programs also vary in scope and format. For example, in Delaware, child support mediations were conducted in a single session, generally sixty to ninety minutes long. In the DMRP, custody and visitation cases mediated in Minnesota, Connecticut, and Los Angeles took an average of 1.5 to 3.3 sessions and 2.3 to 4.3 hours. Only 21 percent of the respondents in Minnesota, 57 percent in Los Angeles, and 65 percent in Connecticut reported having attended just a single mediation session. Although all three courts officially permit a

larger number of hours or sessions, cases were usually terminated, with or without a resolution, before the upper limit was
reached.

Participation of children and attorneys also differed.
While 75 percent of the Los Angeles respondents reported that
their lawyers were seen by the mediators, this was noted by only
16 percent of the Minneapolis and 11 percent of the Connecticut respondents. Children were most likely to have been seen by
mediators in Minneapolis (66 percent) and in far fewer of the
Los Angeles (28 percent) and Connecticut (15 percent) cases. In
other differences, mediations in Connecticut were routinely
conducted by teams comprising one man and one woman;
California and Minnesota sessions were most commonly conducted by one mediator, who might be either male or female. In
Connecticut and Minneapolis, mediation sessions were scheduled in advance using an appointment system; in California
families typically moved directly to mediation from a preliminary court appearance.

The variation in scope, format, and duration belies a
more basic similarity in technique. In both the DMRP and the
CMP, the mediation process involved building rapport, identifying issues, and making the agreement. Although mediation
ideology stresses the notion of self-determination, there was
evidence that most mediators were active and directive, playing
a major role in structuring the process and even in suggesting
the terms of the agreement.

Detailed analysis of tapes from eighty-one cases in the
DMRP showed more about the behavior of both mediators and
disputants. Mediators seemed to do most of the questioning in a
mediation session. Requests for information took about a
quarter of their speaking time, but only 10 percent of the
disputants' time. Neutrality also characterized mediators' verbal
behavior. Fully 80 percent of their statements were offered in
neutral or positive voice tones while negative tones were common in the statements made by husbands (55 percent) and wives
(60 percent).

Mediators, understandably, devoted time to orienting
spouses to the process and facilitating discussions between

them. Almost 13 percent of mediators' statements were to explain what mediation is and is not, and another 13 percent were devoted to "process" communications: establishing the agenda, returning the conversation to relevant topics, suggesting ways for the parties to negotiate, and positively or negatively reinforcing the negotiating behavior of one or both spouses. Another 8 percent of mediator talk time was devoted to facilitating communication by summarizing and paraphrasing disputant remarks.

In contrast, spouses offered information about themselves, their children, or their spouses, and revealed opinions or attitudes. Another common verbal behavior was "mind reading." About 20 percent of the statements made by parents were attributions about the attitudes, motives, and behaviors of others — typically the other parent. Mediators engaged in only about half as many of these attribution statements.

One final type of verbal behavior dealt with agreement making. Gulliver (1979) has noted that mediator behaviors range widely from "passive" (the mediator merely encourages communication and negotiation) to "leader" (the mediator makes suggestions and recommendations). Mediators in the DMRP were clearly oriented to more active and directive roles and were responsible for making most of the proposed solutions. About 20 percent of mediator talk time involved identifying solutions and creating agreements, compared to only about 12 percent of the spouses'.

Mediation tapes were also analyzed to determine what, if any, spousal and mediator behaviors were associated with success — that is, with the production of an agreement. We learned that in successful cases mediators spent more time discussing possible solutions and brainstorming options; for their part, spouses spent more time exhibiting empathetic understanding of the other point of view.

Subsequent studies of these mediation tapes generated in the DMRP by other researchers suggest that mediators in successful cases were able to recognize when couples were beginning to demonstrate trust and to encourage this behavior (Donohue, Allen, and Burrell, 1985). They were also more in control of the interaction and used reframing and other clarifying interventions to move the disputants toward agreement. These findings underscore the important role successful mediators play in eliciting options and creating proposals for disputants.

The Effects and Effectiveness of Mediation

In general, our interviews with mediating and adjudicating respondents have revealed that mediation was effective in generating agreements on custody and visitation issues, that these agreements normally involved mutual compromise, that user satisfaction was high, and that mediated agreements were no less stable than agreements generated in lawyer negotiations or court hearings. The following discussion provides details on each of these findings and also considers the limited ability of mediation to achieve other effects, such as easing child adjustment to divorce or improving spousal relationships.

Agreement Rates and Terms. The highest agreement rates were in Delaware child support mediation cases; nearly 80 percent of the cases that used mediation were successful in reaching a settlement. Approximately 40 percent of the mediating disputants in the DMRP and CMP projects reached full agreements on custody and visitation and an additional 20 percent reached partial agreements.

Most couples in the CMP with mediated agreements chose joint legal custody, an arrangement rarely arrived at by those who were exposed only to the adversarial process. In mediated agreements calling for sole custody, noncustodians received more visitation than was commonly found in nonmediated agreements. In the DMRP study, joint custody was also more common among mediated than adjudicated arrangements, but there was no evidence of greater visitation for noncustodians.

Findings in the Delaware study show no greater sharing of resources as a result of mediation. In fact, support established through mediation falls below the levels ordered by masters or judges for families of comparable economic standing. Thus, in the Delaware child support program the compromise created through mediation is likely to take the form of reduced support levels.

User Reactions. More than three-fourths of the CMP and DMRP mediation clients expressed extreme satisfaction with the process and would recommend it to others. In contrast, only 40 percent of the CMP respondents were satisfied with the court process, and only about 30 percent of the DMRP sample.

Several factors were cited frequently. The majority (69 percent) in both studies agreed that mediation helped them to focus on the needs of the children and felt that this was beneficial. In the words of one Connecticut mother, "It made me feel more considerate toward the kids and their feelings." Another benefit was the opportunity to air grievances. Seventy to 90 percent of the respondents at each of the DMRP sites agreed with the statement "Mediation gave me a chance to express my own point of view."

Other positive features of mediation cited by users included its ability to identify the real issues in a dispute (63 percent), and the less rushed and superficial nature of mediation compared to the courtroom (72 percent). Over half (65 percent) agreed that mediation was "certainly better than going to court." As one father put it, "The mediators brought up things, [visitation] options, that I hadn't even considered. We ended up compromising. . . . I got a chance to present everything that I wanted to present. It helped us understand each other."

However, negative reactions to mediation were also voiced. About half of the DMRP respondents reported that the sessions were tension-filled and unpleasant, and that they stimulated feelings of anger and defensiveness. The source of these perceptions is unknown. If they spring from the emotional nature of the dispute or apprehensions about dealing with an ex-spouse, possibly no dispute resolution forum would have been entirely satisfactory.

Still other respondents may have felt displeased as a result of faulty expectations. At each DMRP site 20 to 40 percent of the respondents agreed with the statement "mediation was confusing," and in-depth interviews with respondents often revealed profound misconceptions about the goals of mediation. For example, many people were under the impression that the process was designed to save the marriage. Those who had no interest in reconciling began the session feeling annoyed, while those hoping for a reconciliation were upset that the process did not stress ways to save the marriage. Other common erroneous beliefs were that the mediator would make the final custody decision and that mediation was merely another variety of counseling.

Finally, between a quarter and a third of all DMRP respondents felt that the mediation process was rushed and should be given more time. For some, the short duration created anger and perceptions of assembly-line treatment.

Still, despite the confusion and unpleasantness sometimes associated with mediation, evaluations of the legal system are almost uniformly less favorable. Fully half of those who had custody investigations conducted felt dissatisfied with the service and thought it was unfair. Equally as many expressed general dissatisfaction with the legal system. The principal objection noted by DMRP respondents was the treatment of private family issues in a public forum. Many remarked that a court appearance seemed to suggest criminal behavior. The impersonality of the experience and the degree of control exercised by lawyers and judges seemed shocking to many.

However, the sharp contrast in perceptions of mediation and the courts is not shared by users of the child support mediation program in the Family Court of Delaware. The quest for a more personalized, individual treatment probably helps to explain why user satisfaction was lowest here. Although mediators varied in the extent to which they permitted couples to negotiate about the issues of child support, in most cases the brief intervention relied largely on a calculation of the guideline formula with little discussion of visitation or other ancillary issues. Although it was an informal process, it lacked many of the communicative, therapeutic, and bargaining features usually associated with mediation.

Unlike the DMRP and CMP samples, few Delaware respondents (18 percent) indicated that mediation "brought issues, problems and feelings out into the open." Nearly all perceived it to be a rushed experience that should have been given more time (94 percent). While a majority felt that the mediator seemed to understand the problem (60 percent), a substantial proportion felt that the mediator was biased and took the side of the mother (25 percent) or the father (36 percent). Finally, when asked to compare mediation sessions with hearings by judges or masters, about half (56 percent) disagreed that "mediation was better than a hearing with a master or judge."

Thus, although the Delaware intervention clearly expedited the processing of child support matters, it did not provide disputants with a forum that was substantially more responsive or caring than traditional adjudicatory settings.

Compliance and Relitigation. There is mixed evidence on the compliance and relitigation patterns associated with mediated and adjudicated agreements. At the final CMP interview approximately 80 percent of people with mediated agreements reported their spouses were complying with all the terms of the agreement, compared to more than 60 percent of adversarial respondents. Also, more than a third of the adversarial group, but less than 10 percent of successful mediation clients, reported serious disagreements over the settlement.

In the DMRP study, the successful mediation clients also reported more compliance than the adversarial group respondents, although the differences were not always so pronounced. For example, among those respondents awarded child support, about a third of the successful mediation clients reported irregular or absent payments, compared to more than half of those who adjudicated the custody arrangement. Reports by those parents who were awarded visitation rights reveal that none of the noncustodians with mediated settlements reported infrequent visitation, but 30 percent of adversarial group noncustodians said they rarely saw their children.

When we consider subsequent relitigation, the positive outcomes associated with mediation versus litigation generally continue, but there are exceptions. There is less relitigation among successful mediation clients in the CMP: 13 percent returned to court within two years whereas 35 percent of the adversarial group did so. Mediation is less dramatically associated with reduced relitigation in the DMRP. By the final interview, 21 percent of those who had resolved the custody dispute in mediation returned to court to file contempt charges, to take out temporary restraining orders, or to modify custody, visitation, or child support. Among unsuccessful mediation clients and the adversarial group, 31 percent and 36 percent, respectively, had returned to court. Indeed, among the adversarial group, 13 percent had been back at least twice, but only 6 percent of those settling in mediation returned to court this often.

In contrast, we found no differences in relitigation patterns among the DMRP respondents who mediated and those who used the adversarial process in 1978. In the ensuing five years, about a quarter of each group had returned to court on custody or visitation matters. Similarly, in the Delaware study we found identical proportions of mediated and adjudicated cases involved in subsequent motions to modify child support, have wages withheld, or initiate contempt citations for nonpayment of child support.

Given the contradictory findings across these studies and samples, it may be safest to conclude that while mediation may not always be more effective than adjudication in preventing relitigation, it certainly does not produce a rash of such activity. Mediated agreements are no less stable than those originating from court orders or lawyer-conducted negotiations. This is especially noteworthy given that, unlike other civil cases, divorce mediation involves parties with lengthy, intimate, and problem-ridden histories and deeply established behavioral patterns. Furthermore, these couples can expect to engage in many transactions after mediation. Visitation, child support payments, and child-care arrangements are complex, emotional issues that require couples to be involved with each other for years to come. In short, in a mediated agreement, no less than a court-mandated one, there are many opportunities for noncompliance.

Relationships with Former Spouses. Disputants consider mediation less damaging than the traditional courtroom proceeding. In the DMRP, 30 percent of those with mediated agreements felt the process had improved their relationships. In contrast, very few (15 percent) of those exposed to court felt that the legal system improved their relationship with a former spouse. In fact, almost half indicated that adjudication had detrimental effects on their relationship.

Nevertheless, mediation appears to have a very limited ability to alter basic relationship patterns or promote cooperation between divorcing parties. For example, in the DMRP final interview the proportions of respondents with multiple problems surrounding visitation were nearly identical (30 to 40 percent) for those mediating and adjudicating their disputes. The respondents reporting the least troubled relationships were those who never contested custody. Clearly postdivorce relations remain fraught with a fair amount of conflict regardless of whether the parties were exposed to mediation.

Child Adjustment Patterns. In the DMRP, parents rated the adjustment of eight- to eleven-year-olds on the Achenbach-Edelbrock Behavior Checklist, a 112-item, three-point behavior rating scale. Taken as a whole, these ratings revealed no statistically significant differences between the mediation and adversarial groups. Children whose parents successfully mediated did have the best rating on most of the Achenbach-Edelbrock scales; however, this was attributable to better ratings on indicators of family dynamics and parent-child relationships.

The factors contributing most to successful child adjustment were: (1) the child's age, with younger children rated as better adjusted; (2) the absence of physical violence during the marriage; (3) high levels of parental cooperation at the final interview; (4) a minimal number of recent changes in the child's life, such as moving, changing schools, being held back a grade; (5) agreement between parents on basic child-rearing practices; (6) less awareness of the anger between parents; (7) close physical proximity between the child's and the noncustodian's residences, and (8) frequent visitation at the time of the first interview.

Factors Affecting Mediation Outcomes. Mediation outcomes were affected by three elements: the skill and behavior of the mediator, the characteristics of the disputants, and the nature of their disagreements. To determine how each contributed to mediation outcomes, we used dispute, disputant, and mediator characteristics as independent variables in a discriminant analysis of the DMRP data. Two outcome measures were considered: settlement and satisfaction with the process. Cases were divided according to whether complete agreement or no agreement was produced, and whether the respondent was willing or unwilling to recommend mediation.

We found that the following two measures were best able to predict both settlement and willingness to recommend the process: users' perceptions of the mediator's ability to provide insights into their own feelings, and the mediator's ability to aid disputants in understanding the feelings of their children and ex-spouses. These findings underscore the importance of open communication, empathy, and self-insight, and are consistent with the work of other researchers. For example, Hochberg and Kressel (1983) found that couples who were apprehensive about communicating during divorce and whose attorneys did not adopt a counseling orientation were subsequently more dissatisfied with the divorce experience and less cooperative with each other than more communicative couples.

The preexisting characteristics of disputants that best defined those who did and did not settle and those who would and would not recommend the process were the duration of the custody dispute, the intensity of the dispute, and the quality of the relationship with the ex-spouse. More recent and less severe disputes were most likely to be resolved, as were disputes between parties with at least a modest degree of communication and cooperation. Again, this parallels the findings of Hochberg and Kressel that postdivorce cooperation is associated in part with limited differences over the terms of the divorce agreement and with a cooperative orientation during the divorce process.

Predictors of mediation outcome derived from DMRP respondents are similar in many respects to those that come from analyzing the audio tapes generated during the project. From the tapes we identified certain mediator behaviors associated with success: substantial time devoted to discussions of the final settlement terms, less time spent explaining the mediation process or comparing it to other settlement forums, less time coaching spouses on how to negotiate, and fewer attributions by the mediator about the attitudes of others.

A number of spousal behaviors also differentiated cases that settled from those that did not. In unsuccessful cases, parties made more statements of fact about their spouses or themselves as a couple and more attributions about past, present, or future behaviors and motives. In successful cases, on the other hand, there were more empathetic statements between spouses, more statements of simple assent, and more offers or proposals.

One plausible interpretation is that unsuccessful cases involved spouses with poor communication skills. Certainly their communication behavior seemed decidedly less than direct and cooperative. Quite possibly parties who communicated inefficiently required more help from mediators to negotiate. In the absence of clear communication, mediators may have begun assuming or attributing behaviors. Given the limited time allotted for mediation, the fact that a disproportionate amount of time was spent on basic communication skills may have meant that the session could not otherwise progress to real problem solving and agreement making.

Disputant Characteristics. Our findings suggest that certain disputant characteristics help to differentiate individuals who voluntarily choose to mediate from those who do not, and certain characteristics are associated with settlement or lack of it. In light of these findings, it might be argued that any beneficial outcomes noted for successful mediation clients are in fact the result of these preexisting characteristics. For example, do successful mediation clients, compared to those who adjudicate or fail to settle in mediation, actually reach more compromise agreements, express greater satisfaction with the dispute resolution forum, and better comply with settlement terms principally because they begin as more cooperative, communicative couples with less severe disputes?

Research studies that employ random assignment to mediation or litigation are rare. However, in the CMP and DMRP studies it is possible to explore outcomes while statistically controlling for key background characteristics. In past analyses (see, for example, Pearson and Thoennes, 1984) we have compared compliance patterns, perceptions of equity, and satisfaction with the settlement for those who settle in mediation, those who unsuccessfully mediate, and litigants never exposed to mediation, while statistically controlling for the following: reported magnitude of the custody or visitation dispute, the level of parental cooperation before mediation or litigation, and the type of custody arrangement ultimately adopted or ordered.

These analyses continue to show generally more favorable outcomes for parents who settle in mediation. However, they also suggest that certain people are most likely to experience the benefits of nonadversarial dispute resolution. Specifically, parents who initially indicated that they were "not on speaking terms" were ultimately quite similar on most outcome measures, regardless of whether the settlement was litigated or mediated. However, where some level of communication existed, even if cooperation was described as very difficult, we find more positive outcomes for successful mediation clients. Background characteristics are not irrelevant, but they do not entirely explain away the beneficial effects that have been reported for mediation.

The Findings: Strengths and Weaknesses of Mediation

Our research has identified some of the limitations of divorce mediation, as well as its strengths. For example, despite professional enthusiasm for divorce mediation and the recent proliferation of public and private mediation services, journals, and professional associations, voluntary programs are typically refused by large numbers of clients. A recent national survey on divorce and divorce forums eliminated the mediation category when pretesting failed to reveal significant use (National Opinion Research Corporation, 1986). Although divorce mediation is somewhat more attractive to better-educated individuals, who are traditionally more receptive to new ideas, the use of divorce mediation programs is also tied to the attitudes of the legal community. People whose attorneys are ambivalent or opposed to mediation are very reluctant to try it.

Compulsory mediation programs, on the other hand, appear to handle a much larger volume of cases and in some settings have been found to be highly cost effective and helpful to courts. Mandatory mediation in all cases of contested child custody and visitation has been introduced by statute in California and by local court rules in Fort Lauderdale, Honolulu, Reno, and elsewhere.

We also find only limited evidence that mediation will reduce disputant animosity or later relitigation, although it certainly does not generate excessive litigation or simply defer inevitable litigation. Similarly, while mediation cannot address the deep-rooted emotional and social causes of divorce disputes or alter relationships between former spouses, it is typically perceived by users as a less damaging intervention than adjudication and it permits a more complete airing of grievances, which is widely appreciated by litigants.

Perhaps the most noteworthy positive finding is the high level of user satisfaction with custody or visitation mediation services. Impressive levels of satisfaction are consistent with previous research in the field. For example, Felstiner and Williams (1979–1980) reported that eight to fourteen months after mediating issues of assault, battery, and harassment in the Community Mediation Program in Dorchester, Massachusetts, most people were glad that they tried mediation (78 percent), thought that it had helped their situation (50 percent), and felt that they had an opportunity to air their complaints (70 percent). An average of 88 percent of all respondents at the Neighborhood Justice Centers were enthusiastic about mediation (Cook, Roehl, and Sheppard, 1980), and McEwen found that 66.6 percent of disputants were satisfied with small claims mediation (McEwen and Maiman, 1981).

By contrast, our studies found that parents with custody or visitation disputes were largely dissatisfied with the adversarial legal system. In similar findings the National Center for State Courts, in its evaluation of the public image of the courts, noted that 40 to 50 percent of respondents who had been to any court, whether as defendants, plaintiffs, or witnesses, held an unfavorable view of the experience (Yankelovich, Skelly, and White, Inc., 1978).

The relative attractions and drawbacks to mediating and adjudicating are numerous and complex; however, the perceived impersonality and inaccessibility of the legal system seem to operate in favor of mediation. Respondents are distressed by the perfunctory nature of court procedures and hunger for a forum that is more humane. Thus, it is understandable that women who chose to mediate in the CMP did so because it promised to be a "warmer way of disputing," and that mediation users praised the process because it gave them a chance to express their own point of view.

Given the brevity of the typical mediation intervention, it is impressive that mediation is perceived by users to be satisfactory and its effects are perceptible even after statistically controlling for the initial level of cooperation. A national survey of public- and private-sector divorce mediation services concluded that in the public sector, the average case required 6.3 hours and nearly 40 percent were handled in four hours or less (Pearson, Ring, and Milne, 1983). (In our court-based sample, most cases were handled in no more than three hours.)

Although it is valuable, our findings suggest that mediation has limited capacity to produce changes in the basic economic and psychological profile of participants. The mediation intervention is, after all, a brief episode in a long history of interaction involving deeply established behavior patterns. After the hearing, there are many opportunities for the agreement to come apart.

In assessing our findings, we must caution that there is little evidence that mediation and adjudication are absolutely distinct approaches. Some mediators structure the process, offer opinions, and advocate for agreements that they regard as fair and beneficial. At times, judges clearly mediate and most cases filed for litigation are resolved in bargaining and settlement of some kind (Trubek and others, 1983) with lawyers who display a range of styles extending from conciliatory to highly adversarial (Kressel, 1985).

Going beyond variations in personal style, it appears that the degree of disputant participation may be the key distinction between mediation and adjudication. Although judges sometimes mediate and mediators sometimes judge, in mediation, disputants retain the opportunity to shape settlements and to accept or reject them. The active participation of the mediator need not reduce the participation of the parties. Nor does a court order to attempt mediation limit the disputants' ability to consent to or reject an agreement.

Like other researchers, we find that parties who mediate tend to view the process as equitable. For example, disputants who used Maine's small claims mediation service were more likely (67 percent) to view the settlements as fair than those who went to court (59 percent) (McEwen and Maiman, 1981). However, serious questions remain. In the divorce arena, there are concerns that mediation compromises the long-term financial interests of women and children. Mediation has also been accused of generating joint custody agreements that undermine the legal status of women vis-à-vis their children and render them vulnerable (Fineman, 1987; Fineman and Opie, 1986; Avner and Heiman, 1984). To date, the debate is largely hortatory; expert assessment of the equity of mediated versus adjudicated outcomes is sorely needed.

References

Achenbach, T. M., and Edelbrock, C. S. "Behavioral Problems and Competencies Reported by Parents of Normal and Disturbed Children Aged 4 through 16." *Monograph of the Society for Research in Child Development*, 1981, *46*, 1–83.

Avner, J., and Heiman, S. *Divorce Mediation: A Guide for Women.* Washington, D.C.: NOW Legal Defense and Education Fund, 1984.

Cook, R. F., Roehl, J. A., and Sheppard, D. *Neighborhood Justice Centers Field Test: Final Evaluation Report.* Washington, D.C.: U.S. Department of Justice, 1980.

Danzig, R., and Lowy, M. "Everyday Disputes and Mediation in the United States: A Reply to Professor Felstiner." *Law and Society Review*, 1975, *9*, 675–694.

Donohue, W. A., Allen, M., and Burrell, N. "Communication Strategies in Mediation." *Mediation Quarterly*, 1985, *10*, 75–89.

Felstiner, W.L.F., and Williams, L. A. *Community Mediation in Dorchester, MA: Final Report*. Los Angeles: University of Southern California, Social Science Research Institute, 1979–1980.

Fineman, M. L. *Dominant Discourse: The Professional Appropriation of Child Custody Decision-Making*. Madison, Wisc.: Institute for Legal Studies, 1987.

Fineman, M. L., and Opie, A. *The Uses of Social Science Data in Legal Policy Making: Custody Determinations at Divorce*. Madison, Wisc.: Institute for Legal Studies, 1986.

Gulliver, P. H. *Disputes and Negotiation: A Cross-Cultural Perspective*. Orlando, Fla.: Academic Press, 1979.

Hochberg, A. M., and Kressel, K. "Determinants of Successful and Unsuccessful Divorce Settlement Negotiation." Presented at the American Psychological Association annual meeting, Anaheim, California, Aug. 1983.

Kressel, K. *The Process of Divorce: How Professionals and Couples Negotiate Settlements*. New York: Basic Books, 1985.

McEwen, C. A., and Maiman, R. J. "Small Claims Mediation in Maine: An Empirical Assessment." *Maine Law Review*, 1981, *33*, 237–268.

National Opinion Research Corporation. *National Longitudinal Study of the Class of 1972 Fifth Follow-up Questionnaire*. Chicago: National Opinion Research Corp., 1986.

Pearson, J., Ring, M., and Milne, A. "A Portrait of Divorce Mediation Services in the Public and Private Sector." *Conciliation Courts Review*, 1983, *21*, 1–24.

Pearson, J., and Thoennes, N. "Mediating and Litigating Custody Disputes: A Longitudinal Evaluation." *Family Law Quarterly*, 1984, *17*, 497–524.

Trubek, D., and others. "The Costs of Ordinary Litigation." *UCLA Law Review*, 1983, *31*, 72–172.

Yankelovich, Skelly, and White, Inc. *The Public Image of the Courts: Highlights of a National Survey of the General Public, Judges, Lawyers, and Community Leaders*. Williamsburg, VA: National Center for State Courts, 1978.

TWO

Mediation in
Interpersonal Disputes:
Effectiveness and Limitations

Janice A. Roehl
Royer F. Cook

The rapid growth of mediation programs in the past decade has been accompanied by substantial research and critical interest. Although most studies of mediation find it effective and satisfying for resolving disputes outside the courts, questions remain about its processes, effectiveness, and broad impact.

We believe that the central question underlying these debates should be whether mediation, as practiced in the past decade, is a valuable mechanism for resolving disputes in U.S. society. Included in this broad question are specific issues: (1) the appropriateness of mediation for different types of disputes, considering both the probability of resolution and the possible exploitation of weaker disputants; (2) the pros and cons of affiliating mediation programs with government agencies as opposed to local communities; (3) the impact on court case loads and on neighborhoods; (4) coercion of disputants; (5) the public's knowledge about and use of dispute resolution mechanisms; and (6) fears that mediation programs may become instruments of state control.

Mediation should first be judged on how well it resolves disputes between conflicting parties. Only after we have carefully examined the immediate effects of the mechanism itself — do people find it satisfactory? are agreements durable? — should we look beyond to potential broader effects. Much confusion and criticism of mediation have resulted when these priorities are reversed (sometimes inadvertently). The implicit perspective of many critics seems to be that mediation must first be weighed on the grand scale — its capacity to build cohesive, more empowered neighborhoods or its ultimate compatibility with contemporary Western social structures and dynamics.

Let us therefore look first at the elements of the basic process, focusing on how people who have been in mediation evaluate the experience and whether mediated agreements are durable. Then we can discuss possible larger roles for mediation, and analyze the fears and concerns surrounding its increased use.

This broad look at mediation is based on the research conducted on the early programs, which handled primarily minor disputes of all types — neighborhood disputes, assaults among family or friends, small claims, and divorce cases — and the commentary that accompanied that research. These programs offered classic mediation: disputants voluntarily participated in a dispute resolution process facilitated by a neutral third party with no power to impose a settlement. The desired outcome was an agreement mutually reached and viewed as fair by both parties. Our personal knowledge and views of mediation stem from our evaluation studies of the original Neighborhood Justice Centers (NJCs) in Atlanta, Kansas City, and Los Angeles; the second-generation NJCs in Houston, Honolulu, and the District of Columbia; and the seven community-based dispute settlement projects in the Urban Crime Prevention Program.

Does Mediation Work?

In different settings and locales, under different sponsors and philosophies, a high proportion of mediation cases have consistently ended in agreements satisfactory to the parties involved and upheld by both. The main deficiencies seem to be in processes that occur before mediation; approximately half of all cases that come to the attention of mediation programs never reach a hearing (either mediation or conciliation). Once a case reaches a hearing, though, the likelihood of effective resolution is high.

Disputing parties typically hold positive views of mediation; they feel satisfied with the process and would return if a dispute arose in the future. Cook, Roehl, and Sheppard (1980) found that 80 to 89 percent of disputants in diverse criminal and civil disputes were satisfied with the mediator, the terms of agreement, and the mediation process. Similar or slightly lower satisfaction rates were found by Davis, Tichane, and Grayson (1980), Felstiner and Williams (1980), Florida's Dispute Resolution Alternatives Committee (1979), and Schwartzkoff and Morgan (1982). The specific issue of perceived fairness, rather than satisfaction, has also been explored. Several studies of mediation involving different settings and types of disputes—Davis, Tichane, and Grayson (1980) on felony criminal cases, Pearson and Thoennes (1982, 1983) on divorce and child custody, and McEwen and Maiman (1981) on small claims—found that disputants perceived the outcomes of mediation hearings to be significantly fairer than those of court proceedings. Although McEwen and Maiman found that one's perception of a "fair" outcome was related to one's victory or loss, this association was considerably weaker in mediated than in court cases.

Speed is another measure of effectiveness. Mediation hearings for minor disputes are typically held within a week or two of intake, considerably faster than the usual time required for final court disposition. Many small claims courts hold day-of-trial mediations, in which hearings are conducted outside the courtroom for cases on that morning's docket. Critics who report that mediation is *not* faster than adjudication tend to use a spurious basis of comparison (Tomasic, 1982). The time between intake and mediation is compared to the speed of *dismissal* of a case in court (which may occur within days or a few weeks of the initiation of prosecution), and not to the time required for a case to come to trial.

How solid and lasting is a mediated agreement? It is true that no significant differences have been found in recidivism rates (actual arrest of either party for a crime against the other) between mediated cases and those processed by the court (Davis, Tichane, and Grayson, 1980). However, compliance with the decision is greater in mediated versus adjudicated cases in two areas: small claims (McEwen and Maiman, 1981), and divorce and custody (Pearson and Thoennes, 1982; Pearson, Thoennes, and Vanderkooi, 1982). McEwen and Maiman found that 71 percent of mediated settlements versus 34 percent of adjudicated judgments were paid in full. Pearson and Thoennes found that, after mediation, couples report higher compliance with divorce decrees involving children and financial terms than do couples in adjudication. Self-reported information from disputants indicates that the majority of agreements are kept by both parties for months after the mediation hearing. Follow-up interviews with hundreds of disputants attending mediation sessions at the Neighborhood Justice Centers found that 67 to 87 percent of agreements were fully kept and an additional 3 to 12 percent were partially upheld (Cook, Roehl, and Sheppard, 1980). Similar results were found in other major evaluation studies. Disputants also report improvements in their relationships with the other parties (Block and Kreger, 1982), better communication, alleviated anger and frustration (Pearson and Thoennes, 1982), and improved behavior (Davis, Tichane, and Grayson, 1980).

Although the promise of mediation has been that it can deal with the problems underlying disputes, it is clear that one hearing cannot resolve serious, longstanding problems such as alcoholism or unemployment, nor should it be expected to do so. However, mediation can address the underlying issues and the history of a dispute in ways that the courts cannot. In mediation, discussions of past incidents related to the problem at hand, as well as future relations between the parties, are part of the dispute-solving process; the courts focus on the specific charge before the bench.

Mediation does not function equally well with all types of cases. Studies of programs that handle a wide variety of disputes found that the likelihood of mediation and the stability of agreements vary among different types of cases (Cook, Roehl, and Sheppard, 1980; Felstiner and Williams, 1980). Certain cases — more serious, ongoing disputes between people with a continuing relationship — are likely to be mediated, but are also prone to agreement breakdown and to future problems. In contrast, civil disputes involving disagreements over money and property, particularly in landlord-tenant and consumer-merchant relationships, are difficult to get to a mediation hearing (although about a quarter are conciliated without a hearing taking place). Once mediated or conciliated, however, they are likely to result in agreements upheld over time. In the landlord-tenant group, the parties tend to have sustained relationships and an entrenched pattern of hostilities, so their potential for continuing conflict is substantial. Their agreements are often vague, require behavior changes difficult to document, and tend to be easy to reach but hard to keep (Felstiner and Williams, 1980). On the other hand, disputes over money or property often result in concrete agreements involving a one-time payment or exchange of property and the disputants are apt to have infrequent contact, making future problems unlikely.

All the researchers cited above have advocated sustained intervention for cases least amenable to mediation; that is, mediation followed by counseling or multiple mediation hearings. Agreements in interpersonal disputes often include provisions for counseling for one or both parties, and a referral for such assistance may be provided by the mediator or staff. However, only a small proportion of disputants actually follow through with referrals for additional assistance. Recent research has identified promising approaches to resolving complex interpersonal disputes through mediation by offering more than the standard single hearing. Block and Kreger (1982) reported on the mediation of PINS ("persons in need of supervision," that is, children out of parental control) cases. The PINS mediation program involved four or five mediation hearings with the parents and child; it was shown to be more successful than court intervention on several indices, particularly when mediation was followed by counseling. Similarly, the divorce and child custody program studied by Pearson and Thoennes (1982) indicates that the complex problems of divorcing couples can be effectively handled through a series of mediation hearings.

In summary, the evidence consistently shows that the basic mechanism of mediation can be effective in resolving a wide variety of disputes in a lasting manner, to the satisfaction of disputants. Mediation has been applied to straightforward monetary claims, complex interpersonal disputes involving minor infractions, criminal cases involving serious assault charges, longstanding problems between intimates, and one-time automobile accidents involving strangers. It is not a panacea for every legal and nonlegal case, and its adequacy differs among programs, mediators, and case types, but mediation appears to be an increasingly attractive alternative to either court processing or avoiding disputes.

Our positive conclusion is muted somewhat by the methodological problems that plague comparisons between mediation and court processing. Problems in achieving random assignment and comparable control groups make it difficult to conclude unequivocally that mediation is more effective than adjudication. Several studies have found a self-selection bias among mediated cases that inflates the degree of success. Vidmar (1984, 1985) found that cases in which respondents conceded partial liability were successful in small claims mediation. However, the self-selection bias accounted for only part of the success of mediation in Vidmar's study. When Davis, Tichane, and Grayson (1980) controlled for the self-selection problem through a random assignment design, higher satisfaction and perceptions of improved behavior were reported by disputants in mediation than by those who entered adjudication.

One goal of the new Multi-Door Dispute Resolution Centers is the development of a typology of cases to aid in screening and resolving disputes (Sander 1976a, 1976b). The Multi-Door Centers, sponsored by the American Bar Association's Committee on Dispute Resolution, are designed to be centralized intake and diagnostic centers for disputes, to screen cases with an eye to their obvious and underlying characteristics, and to refer cases to appropriate resolution mechanisms (Roehl, 1986).

The first funded Multi-Door Centers, in Tulsa, Houston, and the District of Columbia, handle a wide variety of disputes and refer them to scores of dispute resolution agencies and agents. Referral decisions — "fitting the forum to the fuss" — are based on the intake specialists' view of the match between dispute and dispute resolution forum characteristics, the complaining party's desires, and the criteria imposed by the agency housing the intake service. Developing a typology for fitting the forum to the fuss has proceeded slowly. Rigorous experimental designs involving random assignment of cases to forums and a wide variety of case types and resolution processes are needed to provide definitive answers on which mechanisms are best for which types of disputes. Because of intake criteria and constraints, referrals in the Multi-Door programs have followed expected paths — assault cases are referred to prosecutors, neighborhood problems are referred to mediation, and so on.

Larger Roles of Mediation

Having reviewed the evidence for mediation's general efficacy, we now turn to the larger roles mediation may play in our society. At the outset, however, we caution that these potential larger roles should not be construed as claims or concrete goals of mediation; they are not to be viewed as benchmarks against which mediation should be measured. In particular, adherents of community-based mediation programs (Wahrhaftig, 1981, 1982; Shonholtz, 1983) have been especially grandiose in their statements of the potential impact of mediation on neighborhoods and communities, thereby inviting much criticism.

Mediation has been identified with two larger roles: (1) having some larger, ultimate impact on our system of justice, and (2) being a major force for helping neighborhoods and communities become less alienated, more empowered, and more cohesive.

Mediation's Role in the Justice System. Let us first consider how mediation holds promise for improving our established system of justice. This issue is germane to the vast majority of mediation programs that may be called justice-system models. A justice-system model may be court sponsored or independent; in either case, it has strong referral ties to the court, receiving many cases from prosecutors, court clerks, and judges. Does mediation in justice-system models contribute positively to the *operational* effectiveness (as opposed to ultimate social justice) of our established system of justice? Some advocates have hoped that mediation programs would reduce court case loads and judicial delays. Until recently, there has been little evidence that any substantial reductions have occurred. Mediation programs with large case loads (for example, the Houston NJC, which handles about 3,600 cases each year) and close connections to the courts still account for only a small portion of the courts' case load. Many of the cases referred to mediation are those dismissed or dropped very early in the court process, and thus mediation as currently practiced offers relief to citizens but has little impact on court backlogs. Although they have not played a major role in relieving court congestion and delay, mediation programs do appear to remove certain types of cases from court dockets (neighborhood and domestic disputes, for example), enabling judges to spend more time on other cases (Cook, Roehl, and Sheppard, 1980; McEwen and Maiman, 1981, 1982).

Recent changes in state laws and statutes (Freedman and Ray, 1982) may enable mediation programs to meet the early expectations of positive impact on court case loads and delays. Mandatory mediation and arbitration programs are becoming more commonplace, particularly for family matters and small claims. These mandatory processes may handle substantially more cases than those less officially connected to the courts. In New York City, Summons Court intake functions have been taken over by the Institute for Mediation and Conflict Resolution (IMCR) (Whipple, 1982). As a result, approximately 2,500 cases each month (close to 90 percent of all cases appearing at the Summons Court intake) are referred to IMCR or the Victims Service Agency for mediation. While mediation is not mandatory in the New York City system, current procedures make initiating prosecution very difficult except in certain nonmediable cases.

The increasingly widespread use of divorce mediation also appears to hold promise for relieving the divorce court case loads. California legislation requires the use of mediation for property settlement and custody and visitation issues in divorce cases prior to court processing (McIssac, 1981). Small claims mediation is another burgeoning area. Many small claims court systems (for example, the District of Columbia, New Jersey, and Maine) offer day-of-trial mediation services for disputes on the court docket. These types of services can divert 50 percent or more of small claims cases from the court docket (Vidmar, 1985).

It was also hoped that the cost of mediation programs such as the NJCs would compare favorably to court processing of similar disputes. Reliable analytical data, particularly comprehensive cost-benefit analyses, are still unavailable, and court costs are notoriously difficult to construct. The NJC evaluation, however, concluded that mediation mechanisms can well become less expensive on a per-case basis than courts, particularly as mediation case loads grow without concomitant increases in staff and resources. Accurate cost estimates of present procedures are needed.

As we move from the mechanics of the established system toward concerns for the quality of justice, we see greater promise that mediation will assist in promoting justice. For example, most of the research on the mediation process indicates that participants feel that they are treated with dignity, that the process and product are satisfactory overall, and that they are able to maintain some control over the dispute resolution process. The strengths of mediation become especially evident in this qualitative domain.

Dispute resolution processes must be judged on the basis of their perceived procedural justice (the parties' perceptions that they have been dealt with fairly) as well as their perceived

distributive justice (the parties' perceptions that the final decisions are fair). Most procedural-justice research has been concentrated on adjudication, but there is some empirical evidence
that mediation processes are viewed as procedurally just (Lind,
Lissak, and Conlon, 1983).

Sander (1983) has delineated three positive qualities of
mediation: (1) the solutions that it can reach are more flexible
than those of the other mechanisms; (2) mediation avoids the
winner-loser syndrome; and (3) the mediation process involves a
wide-ranging inquiry into what the interested parties want to
talk about—it is not dominated by what the judge wants to hear
about. Sander cites evidence that mediation gives an enhanced
sense of participation to the disputants: the process is specifically geared to them, and they therefore have a strong commitment to the resolution reached.

Mediation and the Community. The notion that mediation-
based dispute resolution can help build cohesive, more empowered neighborhoods and communities has served as both a
rallying point for certain proponents of mediation and a target
for critics. The largest and best-known community program is
the San Francisco Community Boards Program created in 1977
under the leadership of Raymond Shonholtz. Other community
models include mediation programs that operate independently of the courts and aim to serve a target neighborhood,
and mediation services sponsored by grass-roots community
organizations.

The leading proponents of the community-based model
(Wahrhaftig, 1981, 1982; Shonholtz, 1983) posit that this type of
mediation can help bring about neighborhood empowerment,
social change, equal distribution of power among citizens, and
reductions in reliance on services provided by government.
Wahrhaftig believes that the appropriate goal of dispute resolution programs is "to promote a just society in which power is
more evenly distributed, and that we ought to judge dispute
resolution projects in terms of how well they promote this goal"
(1981, p. 101). Moreover, he favors "collective" action over "individual" bargaining, citizen empowerment over the resolution of
a particular individual dispute, and forms of community orga-

nizing (essentially) over mediation per se. In the community model, mediation is offered as a means for neighborhood residents to resolve their own disputes without recourse to the state, and, as the theory goes, this internal capability will strengthen the neighborhood over time by building leadership, training citizens in resolution skills, and increasing cohesiveness and autonomy (Merry, 1982).

Adherents of community models of dispute resolution tend to criticize the justice-system model harshly. Wahrhaftig is concerned that justice-system models of dispute resolution may perpetuate citizens' reliance on the services of the state. A frequent complaint of community proponents is that the justice-system models overemphasize case-load size and that assessments of mediation rely too heavily on case-load criteria.

What can be said in response to these lofty goals held by community mediation proponents and their criticisms of the mainstream mediation movement? If community-based mediation is to have the sweeping impact desired by its proponents, it must first offer helpful, effective services to neighborhood residents. Quality of justice (perceptions of procedural fairness, outcomes that lead to effective resolutions, and so on) should be the foremost concern of a mediation program, whether it aims to serve the community or the justice system. The Neighborhood Justice Centers (the three original centers roughly represented the justice system, agency, and community models) produced a high quality of justice for individuals, as did the small community dispute settlement projects we have studied (Cook, Roehl, and Sheppard, 1980; Roehl and Cook, 1983). Their scale has been radically different, however. Court-connected centers have helped thousands of citizens, while community-based programs have served far fewer. The Urban Crime Prevention Program dispute settlement projects handled an average of five cases a month, and mediation hearings were rare events (Roehl and Cook, 1983).

Underutilization is a problem common to most mediation programs (Edelman, 1984). Most programs could handle more cases without compromising the quality of services or substantially increasing staff or resources, due to the reliance on a large cadre of volunteer or minimally paid mediators. Citizens rarely bring disputes to mediation programs on their own initiative, as illustrated by the low case loads of community-based programs and the relatively few walk-ins of programs with eclectic referral sources. In particular, citizens appear hesitant to bring interpersonal disputes to mediation; rather, they tend to bring housing, consumer, and neighborhood problems (Cook, Roehl, and Sheppard, 1980; Wahrhaftig, 1982).

McEwen and Maiman (1984) concluded that the under-utilization of voluntary mediation services was the result of the consensual process and limited circumstances under which these services operate. Parties who feel they have the advantage in a dispute have little incentive to negotiate. McEwen and Maiman (p. 46) concluded that "informal community justice is unlikely to serve many disputants unless it is intimately connected to some formal legal agency" that can impose costs on the advantaged party, to induce negotiation.

The community perspective seems to view the state and, in particular, the justice system as alien to the people; it does not recognize that citizens may view the state as a source of services rather than a ubiquitous oppressor. Although we see nothing inherently incompatible about the use of mediation by both neighborhood-based organizations and the court system, the proponents of the community-based models seem to reject the notion that mediation can help humanize the established system of justice. Finally, Wahrhaftig (1982) proposes that mediation is the central approach to be used by community programs to bring about neighborhood empowerment and social change. However, the San Francisco Community Boards Program — the "best example" of the grass-roots community model — actually appears to depend much more on organizing techniques than on mediation. This is, of course, entirely appropriate, since its chief goal is neighborhood empowerment and social change, not the resolution of individual citizen disputes. Unlike community organizing and other social-change strategies, mediation does not appear to be a central vehicle for achieving the ends that Merry, Wahrhaftig, and Shonholtz seek.

In summary, mediation-based dispute resolution does

not seem to be the appropriate way to foster collective action in pursuit of citizen empowerment and social change. The most effective tools for such a task are community organizing, political action, and so on. This is not to suggest that mediation does not belong in community organizations or that it cannot be used for collective disputes. Rather, it would seem that the proper role for mediation at the grass-roots level is as part of a community-based program that uses citizen organizing and other similar approaches to empower citizens and the neighborhood, not as the central vehicle for social change and empowerment.

Fears About Mediation

A number of legal scholars have expressed fears about mediation and its potential for violating the rights of citizens. These serious concerns include the possible exploitation of less-powerful individuals (Hofrichter, 1977; Singer, 1979); use of coercion (Shonholtz, 1983; Snyder, 1978; Tomasic, 1982); expansion of state control into private lives and the denial of due process (Abel, 1982a, 1982b; Hofrichter, 1977, 1982; Tomasic and Feeley, 1982); and hindrance of social change and the resolution of collective grievances (Abel, 1982a, 1982b; Wahrhaftig, 1981). These areas of concern are not mutually exclusive; in the aggregate, they form a viewpoint that postulates mediation as second-class justice. What do these fears mean when viewed in the context of the concrete practice of mediation?

Power Disparity. Power differentials between disputing parties may result in the more powerful party refusing to participate in mediation or dominating a hearing to the point of intimidating the less-powerful party into a potentially inequitable agreement. People with considerable resources, such as corporate representatives, landlords, merchants, and employers, often refuse to participate in mediation. Power imbalances (exhibited within the mediation hearing), which may leave the weaker party in a disadvantaged position, are of great concern in parent-child and domestic violence cases (Lerman, 1981; Woolley, 1978).

Power disparity between parties is a serious concern, yet little research has been conducted on its effects. In judicial settings, formal procedures protect the weaker party by obliging the more powerful party to attend court hearings, following rules of evidence, and prohibiting the use of violence and coercion. Such safeguards are absent in mediation. In regard to mediating individual disputes, more information is needed on the interpersonal dynamics of a hearing, and the extent to which power imbalances hinder success or place the weaker party at a disadvantage.

Although we know power differentials exist, the vast majority of disputants report that they are satisfied with the agreement terms or feel the agreement was fair. There is evidence, however, that some disputants may agree to terms they later consider unsatisfactory. McEwen and Maiman (1981) found that some disputants agreed to mediated settlements they later claimed to be unfair because of mediator (or internal) pressure to settle. Special policies and procedures have been suggested and implemented to protect less-powerful parties in these and other types of cases. For example, under Massachusetts law, immediate protection is provided in domestic violence cases by coupling mediation with court protection orders (Orenstein, 1982). The protection orders are designed to place the power of the law behind the woman and provide her parity with the abuser in the bargaining process.

The arguments about power disparity and second-class justice hinge partly on the fact that many mediation programs serve mainly groups that are low-income and otherwise disadvantaged. However, middle- and upper-income citizens have participated in mediation, as have corporate respondents (Cook, Roehl, and Sheppard, 1980). The growth of court-sponsored and court-mandated alternative forms of dispute resolution (including mediation, arbitration, minitrials, and summary jury trials) will further increase the numbers of middle- and upper-income citizens, corporations, and public agencies using such alternatives (Susskind and Madigan, 1984).

Substantial attention has been placed on mediator training, credentials, and standards (see for example Lincoln, 1983), in part to address power disparity concerns. Mediators are taught to balance power, to be nonjudgmental, to help parties communicate, and to improve problem solving, but their methods and capabilities in these areas have not been rigorously assessed. The professionalization of mediation is in its infancy, but is a primary concern of associations representing neutral third parties (Hay, Carnevale, and Sinicropi, 1984) and the alternative dispute resolution movement's watchdogs.

Coercion. Coercion can enter the mediation process in several ways. Explicit coercion may be used to persuade a reluctant disputant to agree to mediation by implying that prosecution will be initiated if mediation is not. Implicit coercion is evident in referrals by judges who agree to dismiss the court case if successful mediation takes place, and it appears in communications from prosecutors, police officers, and mediation program staff. Another form of coercion may enter the hearing itself when mediators pressure disputants to come to an agreement or to agree to certain terms (Felstiner and Williams, 1978; McEwen and Maiman, 1981; Snyder, 1978). Mediation/arbitration arrangements — an arbitration award is made if mediation fails — may also have this impact.

Although "intake coercion" is a concern, most individuals do not seem to feel terribly coerced by the threat of prosecution. This is indicated by high dropout rates (about 50 percent) in the majority of programs. Indeed, less than a third of the cases referred to NJCs by prosecutors, court clerks, and police officers had mediation hearings. Even in the New York City court, where rigid diversion procedures are practiced, one or both parties fail to appear in nearly two-thirds of the cases scheduled for mediation (Whipple, 1982). We tend to agree with Sander (1983) that as long as disputants are fully informed about the mediation process and alternatives, and can exit the process at will, intake coercion by judges, court rules, and the like is not abhorrent but necessary, at least until public awareness and acceptance grow.

The issue of coercion bears watching and further study,

particularly in situations where the voluntary nature of mediation is promoted but in word only. Recent research indicates some benefits of mediator directiveness (see Pruitt, Chapter Seventeen) and few harmful, measurable effects from compulsory mediation (see Chapter One).

State Control and the Resolution of Collective Grievances. The danger of expanding state control has been expressed in several ways. Abel (1982a) fears that government sponsorship of the mediation of interpersonal disputes extends state control into the private lives of citizens. Wahrhaftig (1981) fears that if disputes are handled at an individual level rather than through collective bargaining (for example, mediating a landlord-tenant problem versus pursuing a bad landlord through a class-action suit or collective grievance procedure), citizen rights will be ignored and social change circumvented. Because mediation programs handle cases often dismissed by the court (typically because of the complainant's reluctance to continue) or never brought to court, it is feared the state is intervening in heretofore private areas. Borderline criminal cases and intrafamily disputes, for example, which may violate social norms but not laws, may be mediated, and thus subjected to scrutiny and sanctions; in the past, such situations have remained private.

Mediation is not individualistic per se; its format depends on its purpose and setting. The Harvard Negotiation Project, for example, uses mediation to further citizen involvement in shaping public policy: environmental disputes over land use, nuclear power, and budget allocations have been mediated (Susskind, 1983; Susskind and Ozawa, 1985). Individuals have resolved disputes with institutions through mediation processes in schools, prisons, universities, local government agencies, and other diverse settings. Neighborhood justice centers are capable of identifying collective problems through staff attention to recurring similar cases (Schwartzkoff and Morgan, 1982). With their stake in neighborhood concerns, community-based programs may be more capable of promoting collective action than justice-system models.

Fears that mediation expands state control and subsequently denies due process appear to stem from individuals' political philosophy rather than empirical evidence. Thus, while Abel (1982a, 1982b) states that mediation tends to extend state control, McIssac, in reporting California's mandatory mediation of contested custody judgments, believes it "takes government out of the lives of families" (1981, p. 76). Abel himself comments on the ambiguous nature of informal justice and its potential for liberation as well as exploitation. With appropriate safeguards of confidentiality, decision control, and the right to turn to the courts if necessary, undue state expansion appears to be a minimal risk.

Implications for the Future

Although the evidence is not unequivocal, it is remarkably consistent: mediation works fairly well across a variety of disputes and settings, and citizens like it. Its main strength continues to be its humanizing force, its treatment of citizens with concern and dignity, and its satisfactory resolution of disputes while leaving relationships intact. Although its record in solving disputes to the satisfaction of both parties is respectable, the tradition of holding single mediation sessions in most cases needs to be questioned. Recent research has shown the value of multiple mediation hearings coupled with ancillary services and good follow-up for dealing with complex situations.

The field needs to be careful about its claims. Mediation was oversold by early proponents and then roundly criticized for not achieving the profound impact hoped for. Mediation is only now showing its potential for reducing court case loads and spearheading court reform efforts, and there is scant evidence that it can be a central force in strengthening neighborhoods. Indeed, we would suggest that in the same vein that court-connected programs enhance the justice system, mediation may best serve the community as a complement to existing mechanisms rather than as a stand-alone service. New experiments such as the Multi-Door program hold promise for increasing awareness and acceptance of alternative dispute resolution services. In the realms of both the justice system and the community, mediation and other dispute resolution processes will be increasingly viewed as valuable, complementary services.

Although progress has been made, there is still a need for public education about the existence, purpose, and benefits of mediation. Concerns about the dangers of mediation are legitimate, but the field appears capable of monitoring itself through standards promoted by professional associations, legislation, educational efforts in law schools and other institutions, and the oversight activities of interested groups and individuals. Interdisciplinary research on issues such as the ones discussed here is needed. Other issues should also be closely scrutinized in the future: mediator training and accreditation; ethical issues of confidentiality, neutrality, and public responsibility; and statutory protections, such as upholding the principle of mediators' privileged communication.

References

Abel, R. "Introduction." In R. Abel (ed.), *The Politics of Informal Justice: The American Experience*. Vol. 1. Orlando, Fla.: Academic Press, 1982a.

Abel, R. "The Contradictions of Informal Justice." In R. Abel (ed.), *The Politics of Informal Justice: The American Experience*. Vol. 1. Orlando, Fla.: Academic Press, 1982b.

Block, J., and Kreger, B. *Mediation: An Alternative for PINS*. New York: Children's Aid Society, 1982.

Cook, R. F., Roehl, J. A., and Sheppard, D. *Neighborhood Justice Centers Field Test: Final Evaluation Report*. Washington, D.C.: Government Printing Office, 1980.

Davis, R., Tichane, M., and Grayson, D. *Mediation and Arbitration as Alternatives to Prosecution in Felony Arrest Cases: An Evaluation of the Brooklyn Dispute Resolution Center*. New York: Vera Institute of Justice, 1980.

Dispute Resolution Alternatives Committee. *The Citizen Dispute Settlement Process in Florida: A Study of Five Programs*. Tallahassee, Fla.: Office of the State Court Administrator, Supreme Court of the State of Florida, 1979.

Edelman, P. B. "Institutionalizing Dispute Resolution Alternatives." *The Justice System Journal*, 1984, *9* (2), 134–150.

Felstiner, W. L. F., and Williams, L. A. "Mediation as an Alternative to Criminal Prosecution: Ideology and Limitations." *Law and Human Behavior*, 1978, *2* (3), 223–244.

Felstiner, W. L. F., and Williams, L. A. *Community Mediation in Dorchester, Massachusetts*. Washington, D.C.: U.S. Government Printing Office, 1980.

Freedman, L., and Ray, L. *State Legislation on Dispute Resolution*. Special Committee on Alternative Means of Dispute Resolution, Monograph Series Number 1. Washington, D.C.: American Bar Association, 1982.

Hay, L. I., Carnevale, C. M., and Sinicropi, H. "Professionalization: Selected Ethical Issues in Dispute Resolution." *The Justice System Journal*, 1984, *9* (2), 228–244.

Hofrichter, R. "Justice Centers Raise Basic Questions." *New Directions in Legal Services*, 1977, *2* (6), 168–172.

Hofrichter, R. "Neighborhood Justice and the Social Control Problems of American Capitalism: A Perspective." In R. Abel (ed.), *The Politics of Informal Justice: The American Experience*. Vol. 1. Orlando, Fla.: Academic Press, 1982.

Lerman, L. G. *Prosecution of Spouse Abuse: Innovations in Criminal Justice Response*. Washington, D.C.: Center for Women Policy Studies, 1981.

Lincoln, W. F. "Ethical Considerations in Dispute Resolution." Panel presented at the Society of Professionals in Dispute Resolution, Eleventh International Conference, Philadelphia, Oct. 1983.

Lind, E. A., Lissak, R. I., and Conlon, D. E. "Decision Control and Process Control Effects on Procedural Fairness Judgments." *Journal of Applied Social Psychology*, 1983, *13* (4), 338–350.

McEwen, C. A., and Maiman, R. J. "Small Claims Mediation in Maine: An Empirical Assessment." *Maine Law Review*, 1981, *33*, 237–268.

McEwen, C. A., and Maiman, R. J. "Mediation and Arbitration: Their Promise and Performance as Alternatives to Courts." In P. L. Dubois (ed.), *The Analysis of Judicial Reform*. Lexington, Mass.: Lexington Books, 1982.

McEwen, C. A., and Maiman, R. J. "Mediation in Small Claims Court: Achieving Compliance Through Consent." *Law & Society Review*, 1984, *18* (1), 11–50.

McIssac, H. "Mandatory Conciliation Custody/Visitation Matters: California's Bold Stroke." *Conciliation Courts Review*, 1981, *19* (2), 73–81.

Merry, S. E. "Defining Success in the Neighborhood Justice Movement." In R. Tomasic and M. Feeley (eds.), *Neighborhood Justice: An Assessment of an Emerging Idea*. New York: Longman, 1982.

Orenstein, S. G. "The Role of Mediation in Domestic Violence Cases." In H. Davidson, L. Ray, and R. Horowitz (eds.), *Alternative Means of Family Dispute Resolution*. Washington, D.C.: American Bar Association, 1982.

Pearson, J., and Thoennes, N. "Mediation and Divorce: The Benefits Outweigh the Costs." *The Family Advocate*, 1982, *4* (3), 26, 28–32.

Pearson, J., and Thoennes, N. "Divorce Mediation: Strengths and Weaknesses Over Time." In H. Davidson, L. Ray, and R. Horowitz (eds.), *Alternative Means of Family Dispute Resolution*. Washington, D.C.: American Bar Association, 1983.

Pearson, J. Thoennes, N., and Vanderkooi, L. "Mediation of Contested Child Custody Disputes." *The Colorado Lawyer*, 1982, *11*, 336–355.

Roehl, J. *The Multi-Door Dispute Resolution Centers, Phase I: Intake and Referral Assessment: Executive Summary*. Washington, D.C.: Institute for Social Analysis, 1986.

Roehl, J., and Cook, R. F. "The Neighborhood Justice Centers Field Test." In R. Tomasic and M. Feeley (eds.), *Neighborhood Justice: Assessment of an Emerging Idea*. New York: Longman, 1982.

Roehl, J., and Cook, R. F. *Evaluation of the Urban Crime Prevention Program: Executive Summary*. Washington, D.C.: National Institute of Justice, U.S. Department of Justice, 1983.

Sander, F. "Varieties of Dispute Processing." *Federal Rules Decision*, 1976a, *10*, 111.

Sander, F. "The Multi-door Courthouse: Settling Disputes in the Year 2000." *The Barrister*, 1976b, *3* (3), 18–21, 40–42.

Sander, F. "Family Mediation: Problems and Prospects." *Mediation Quarterly*, 1983, *2*, 3–12.

Schwartzkoff, J., and Morgan, J. *Community Justice Centers: A Report on the New South Wales Pilot Project, 1979–81.* Sydney, Australia: The Law Foundation of New South Wales, 1982.

Shonholtz, R. "New Justice Theories and Practice." Paper presented at the Law and Society Association Annual Meeting, Denver, Colorado, June 1983.

Singer, L. R. *The Growth of Non-judicial Dispute Resolution: Speculations on the Effects of Justice for the Poor and on the Role of Legal Services.* Washington, D.C.: Legal Services Corporation, 1979.

Snyder, F. E. "Crime and Community Mediation—The Boston Experience: A Preliminary Report on the Dorchester Urban Court Program." *Wisconsin Law Review*, 1978, *2*, 737–791.

Susskind, L. "Public Interest and Mediation Values." Panel presentation at the Society of Professionals in Dispute Resolution, Eleventh International Conference, Philadelphia, Oct. 1983.

Susskind, L., and Madigan, D. "New Approaches to Resolving Disputes in the Public Sector." *The Justice System Journal*, 1984, *9* (2), 179–203.

Susskind, L., and Ozawa, C. "Mediating Public Disputes: Obstacles and Possibilities. *Journal of Social Issues*, 1985, *41* (2), 145–159.

Thibaut, J. W., and Walker, L. *Procedural Justice: A Psychological Analysis.* Hillsdale, N.J.: Erlbaum, 1975.

Tomasic, R. "Mediation as an Alternative to Adjudication: Rhetoric and Reality in the Neighborhood Justice Movement." In R. Tomasic and M. Feeley (eds.), *Neighborhood Justice: An Assessment of an Emerging Idea.* New York: Longman, 1982.

Tomasic, R., and Feeley, M. M. "Introduction." In R. Tomasic and M. Feeley (eds.), *Neighborhood Justice: Assessment of an Emerging Idea.* New York: Longman, 1982.

Vidmar, N. "The Small Claims Court: A Reconceptualization of Disputes and an Empirical Investigation." *Law and Society Review*, 1984, *18* (4), 515–550.

Vidmar, N. "An Assessment of Mediation in a Small Claims Court." *Journal of Social Issues*, 1985, *41* (2), 127–144.

Wahrhaftig, P. "Dispute Resolution Retrospective." *Crime and Delinquency*, 1981, 27 (1), 99–105.

Wahrhaftig, P. "An Overview of Community-Oriented Citizen Dispute Resolution Programs in the United States." In R. Abel (ed.), *The Politics of Informal Justice: The American Experience*. Vol. 1. Orlando, Florida: Academic Press, 1982.

Whipple, C. T. *The Mediation of Citizen Disputes in New York City: A Comparative Assessment of the IMCR and VSA Mediation Centers*. New York: Criminal Justice Coordinating Council, 1982.

Woolley, S. F. *Battered Women: A Summary*. Washington: Women's Equity Action League, 1978.

THREE

Mediation in
Small Claims Court:
Consensual Processes
and Outcomes

Craig A. McEwen
Richard J. Maiman

Our research began in 1978, shortly after mediation was introduced in Maine's busiest small claims court. One of us was
working part time in the program as a mediator and the other
was being trained to mediate by observing mediation sessions.
As mediators will do, we spent much of our time between
sessions comparing notes and talking shop. As social scientists
will do, we traded informal theories about mediation. Soon we

Note: Research for this article was supported by grants from the Law and
Social Sciences Program of the National Science Foundation (SES-7908872,
SES-8310393, and SES-8310451). The opinions and points of view are those
of the authors and do not necessarily reflect the position of the National
Science Foundation.

realized that if our curiosity about mediation could be brought to bear on the growing volume of data at our fingertips, we could address some of the questions that we, and an increasing number of others, were asking about mediation in the new settings where it was then appearing. Although considerable writing had been done about labor mediation by the late 1970s, much of the work on mediation in other contexts consisted of encomiums asserting its superiority over adjudication in achieving cost-effective, high-quality justice. By recasting these enthusiastic but unsupported claims as neutral hypotheses, we had the beginnings of a workable, if formidable, research project.

At the same time, we discovered, many advocates and critics of mediation shared a fundamental assumption that its applicability and utility rested on its capacity to work on cases of conflict in continuing relationships based in well-defined, tight-knit communities (Fuller, 1971; Danzig and Lowy, 1975; Felstiner, 1974; Witty, 1980). In the world of practice, we found that many of the proliferating neighborhood dispute resolution centers required a continuing relationship between disputing parties as an intake qualification (Felstiner and Williams, 1980; Cook, Roehl, and Sheppard, 1980; Davis, Tichane, and Grayson, 1980).

Maine's growing program of small claims mediation provided a fascinating arena in which to test the validity of these assumptions about community and continuing relationships. Since these elements were typically lacking in the small claims setting, we wondered whether mediation could still succeed. This meant that we had to join the struggle to define measures of success. However, in doing so we wanted not just to focus on outcomes but to identify what, if anything, distinguished mediation as a dispute resolution process from other processes and made it particularly successful or unsuccessful.

These were the general questions that launched us on the most exhaustive study of small claims mediation in the United States. Our work was supported by several generous grants from the National Science Foundation, supplemented by sabbatical leaves and grants from our academic institutions. At about the same time Neil Vidmar (1984) launched a parallel study of small

claims mediation in Ontario, which both challenged and reinforced our findings and interpretations. Despite the breadth of
our separate inquiries and analyses, we both came to focus on
some striking and unanticipated findings about one particular
dimension of dispute resolution processes — to what extent they
produce compliance with their outcomes, and how.

Methodology

We began our study of small claims mediation in 1979
after a year of preparation and pilot study. The first round of
research, which continued until fall 1980, produced data about
some 400 mediated and nonmediated cases. A total of 700
interviews were conducted with plaintiffs and defendants in
small claims cases. We also conducted open-ended interviews
with all of Maine's small claims mediators as well as several of the
district court judges who were most heavily involved with small
claims. In 1983 we conducted another 140 interviews with a
random sample of small claims defendants, looking primarily
for information on reasons for compliance and noncompliance
with small claims settlements and judgments. We also gathered
additional data on some 300 mediated and adjudicated cases.

In addition to these data sources, this chapter also draws
on observational data from 20 small claims hearings, transcripts
of more than 60 mediation sessions, and coded data from court
records of more than 20,000 small claims cases. Further details
about the methodology of our research can be found in prior
publications (McEwen and Maiman, 1981, 1984).

Compliance and Consent

Not long after starting to analyze our data in 1981, we
began to discover remarkable differences in the likelihood of
compliance with agreements arrived at through mediation and
judgments imposed after a court hearing. We found and reported (McEwen and Maiman, 1984) that 81 percent of mediated cases resulted in full compliance by defendants, compared
to only 48 percent of adjudicated cases. Furthermore, there was

at least partial compliance in 93 percent of mediated as compared to 67 percent of adjudicated cases. These striking differences in the reactions of defendants to mediation and adjudication left us with much explaining to do.

Some Inadequate Explanations. We considered a number of
possible explanations for these findings. One was that they were
simply a statistical fluke caused by our sampling of cases. We
were able to check that possibility in two different ways. First, we
undertook a smaller-scale research project to learn more about
patterns of compliance. We found similar rates of compliance
for mediated cases in this new sample (89 percent with at least
partial compliance), although rates of compliance after adjudication were higher (now 87 percent) as a consequence of
legal changes by the courts that increased compulsion to pay
(McEwen and Maiman, 1988). This second study helped convince us that our original findings about compliance with mediated outcomes were accurate.

At the same time Neil Vidmar was publishing the results
of his study of mediation in small claims court in Ontario (1984).
His strikingly similar data about compliance patterns provided
further independent support for the validity of our findings on
compliance (McEwen and Maiman, 1986). Confident, then, that
our data were reasonably accurate, we resumed our search for
an explanation for differential compliance rates.

Could the answer lie in a pattern of self-selection of cases
into mediation and adjudication? If certain kinds of parties
were more likely than others to choose mediation, then the
characteristics of the disputants rather than of the processes
might account for the differences in compliance.

The first disputant characteristic that we examined was
the presence or absence of a past or continuing relationship
between disputants. Earlier work in New York small claims court
(Sarat, 1976) had shown a tendency for parties with continuing
relationships to opt more frequently for informal arbitration. In
fact, however, only 12 percent of our respondents reported
having a relationship with the other party that predated their
dispute or continued beyond it. Traffic accidents, consumer
disputes, and private sales were the staples of the small claims

case load. Moreover, we found no evidence in Maine that litigants with a past or continuing relationship were any more likely to choose or succeed in mediation than were parties without such ties.

Could the observed differences in compliance rates nonetheless be attributed to self-selection with regard to other variables? For example, might those parties who agree to mediation be inherently more cooperative or compliant than those who take their cases to trial? Observations of small claims court proceedings suggest that many litigants have little or no choice about mediation. Under rules applied during the period of our study, judges encouraged informal resolutions by the parties, or even required that they try mediation before the case could be heard in court. Even before these rules were adopted, judges frequently exerted pressures on litigants to try mediation. The most common tactic was to make adjudication costly in terms of lost time. For example, one judge typically told litigants: "Would either of you be willing to discuss this with a mediator? This is voluntary. If you want a contested hearing you will have to come back next month. If you are able to settle this by mediation, you will have a judgment today."

At other times, the judge assigned all contested cases to mediation without giving the parties any choice at all. Even when parties were given choices, they were not always completely free or fully informed. For example, after providing assembled litigants with a clouded introduction using the words *mediation* and *arbitration* interchangeably, one judge called the first case:

Judge: "Approach the bench, please. Is there any chance of arbitrating this?"

Defendant: "As far as I'm concerned, there is."

Judge: (To plaintiff) "And you?"

Plaintiff: (Apparently does not understand.)

Judge: "You sit down in a comfortable room, listen to both sides and if you reach an agreement you submit it to me for approval."

Plaintiff: "Can you come back?"

Judge: "Yes, if you can't agree you have a hearing."

Given such practices, it is not surprising that about half of the small claims litigants interviewed remembered being given little choice about whether to go to mediation or to trial. This included some litigants who, because of the unavailability of mediators, were scheduled for trials despite their willingness to try mediation first. Ultimately, we found that rates of compliance were virtually identical for those cases where parties felt they had chosen the forum and those where they felt it had been imposed on them (McEwen and Maiman, 1984, p. 28). Thus, we concluded that self-selection of disputants into mediation or adjudication had no impact on compliance.

Vidmar (1984) argued that still another kind of self-selection was at least partially responsible for the higher rates of compliance observed in mediation. He showed that mediation was more likely to achieve an agreement in disputes where the defendant had conceded some debt. In these cases, he pointed out, defendants had already shown a commitment to paying the debt. He concluded that it was that prior attitude of commitment rather than the mediation process that produced compliance. However, we have shown elsewhere (McEwen and Maiman, 1986) that Vidmar's conclusion was not entirely supported by his data. The characteristic of "admitted liability" was less important as an explanation of compliance than were the qualities of the forum in which the dispute was resolved. In particular, mediation is more sensitive than adjudication to the defendant's admission of partial liability and better able to mobilize litigant attitudes on behalf of compliance.

Some Possible Explanations. If the observed differential rates of compliance between mediated and adjudicated cases do not result from any of these factors, to what *can* they be attributed? Advocates of mediation have long claimed that the process leaves participants with a greater sense of satisfaction and that mediation participants are more likely than those who have gone to trial to feel that the outcome was fair. There is empirical evidence to support both of these assertions. In our Maine sample, about 67 percent of those whose cases were mediated indicated that they were completely or mostly satisfied with the overall experience, compared to 54 percent of those whose cases were adjudicated. A more significant difference occurred on the dimension of fairness: 52 percent of the mediation defendants perceived the outcome as fair, compared to 32 percent of the adjudication defendants. Both feelings of satisfaction and perceptions of fairness were positively correlated with compliance, though not so strongly as to completely account for the difference in rates of compliance.

Another possible explanation lies in the case outcomes themselves, which are different for mediated and adjudicated cases in several important ways. Mediated small claims settlements were, we found, on average, smaller than adjudicated judgments; they also tended to represent a smaller proportion of the original claim than did adjudicated outcomes. Elsewhere we have reported the unstartling finding that smaller settlements are more likely to be paid than larger ones (McEwen and Maiman, 1984, p. 37).

Another factor that we found to be related to compliance was the arrangement of immediate payment or the setting of a time payment schedule. In our study, such arrangements were more frequent in mediated (65 percent) than in adjudicated (24 percent) outcomes. Concerned with preserving the "dignity of the court," judges, unlike mediators, often were reluctant to make specific arrangements for payment of debts.

These differences in litigant perceptions and case outcomes still were not sufficient to explain all the differences between rates of compliance. Our statistical analysis (see McEwen and Maiman, 1984) indicated that even in the most unpromising circumstances—cases where defendants had to pay all or most of the claim against them and believed the outcome to be unfair—compliance was more likely after mediation than after adjudication. The tantalizing question thus remained: what is it about the mediation process that helps produce these higher levels of commitment?

Consensual Aspects of Mediation. We have come to believe

that the *consensual* aspect of mediation is the most significant force behind the parties' sense of obligation to abide by outcomes. Social psychological theory and research suggest why this should be the case.

The theory of cognitive dissonance describes the tension that people tend to feel when they recognize that their actions are inconsistent with one another (Brehm, 1966; Feldman, 1966). People strive for consistency to prevent this tension. Thus, when parties to a dispute commit themselves orally and by signing a mediation agreement to behave in a particular way, they experience internal pressure to abide by that commitment. For them, obedience is not just an impersonal obligation to follow laws but also a test of their sense of themselves as truthful and honorable human beings (Lempert, 1972). Through its reliance on consent, mediation more than adjudication activates a personal sense of responsibility for the implementation of the outcome.

The mediation process activates this sense of responsibility in part by giving room for discussion of general moral and interpersonal obligations as well as legal obligations. The fact that mediators are free from the judicial obligation to decide cases allows them to explore with the parties a wider range of moral and practical standards for arriving at outcomes. Even in the informal hearing setting of the small claims court, the responsibility for issuing a binding judgment based on a legal principle encourages judges to focus attention on potentially decisive legal principles and information relevant to them. Mediation, by contrast, involves widening the consideration of applicable principles and evidence and acknowledging varying views of obligations and past events. Mediators, more easily than judges, can help the parties to understand another point of view, to identify a range of competing but relevant values for decisions, to recognize the pressures bearing on them and the alternatives they face, and to help them justify to themselves a consensual resolution.

These consensual resolutions are not always embraced enthusiastically by the parties, however. As a result, we observed that mediators deployed a variety of tactics, both moral and practical, to encourage parties to reach an agreement.

Many mediators, although holding to their initial promise not "to judge" the case, were not reluctant to tell the parties what they thought of some of their claims and counterclaims. Such a moral judgment was clear in the following example.

Mediator: "Well, what we should talk about is, is there any way we can accommodate this thing, so that neither one of you gets hurt an awful lot? As it stands now, I guess you're [the plaintiff] the one being hurt. You haven't received any rent for that month. And at the same time, you're [the defendant] not of course being hurt."

Defendant (interrupts): "I feel I am."

Mediator: "How do you feel—"

Defendant (interrupts): "Because my husband hasn't worked since January."

Mediator: "Well, that has nothing to do with this situation."

Defendant: "What do you mean it has nothing to do with it? I think it does."

Mediator: "Well, well, how does this situation affect that? Why . . . why would that necessarily mean that you haven't hurt [the plaintiff] by—?"

Defendant (interrupts): "I just really don't feel, honestly, right inside, I really don't feel I have."

Mediator: "Isn't it true that you did sign a lease? And made a commitment, and then went back on the commitment, and doesn't that in effect hurt the landlord since it takes one month's rent away from the landlord?"

Defendant: "I still don't feel I did."

Mediator: "Well, it's your privilege to feel that way."

Although unsuccessful here, a mediator's challenges to the position of one of the parties can be a powerful device for inducing compromise and settlement.

In addition to challenging the moral position of one of the parties, Maine mediators sometimes challenged both parties equally, emphasizing that they shared blame and responsibility, as in the following case involving an unpaid cleaning bill:

Mediator: "From what I hear, I don't see that either one of you . . . I could go either way on it. I just don't know. I just think you [the defendant] were a little bit wrong. You got this bill and just let the three months go by and never did anything about it. And I think, you know, if the statement was made that the rust would be removed or else they wouldn't have to pay, okay, you [the plaintiff] are admitting that statement was made although you don't really know. As you say, the rust is still there. You have no way of knowing because you didn't have the occasion to go check it, really. So, you know, maybe the bill wasn't paid right away or maybe you should have become more personally involved in what was said. I don't know. So maybe there's a little bit of wrong on both sides here."

Thus, in addition to providing opportunities for both parties to win, mediators sometimes pressed for a distribution of losses appropriately among the parties as a way to achieve a settlement.

Despite the effectiveness of such moral pressures, it was far more common for mediators to lead parties toward consent by highlighting the practical advantages of settling their dispute without having to return to court. Especially in the later stages of a session, Maine small claims mediators tended to emphasize either the riskiness of adjudication, the problems of collection, or the delay involved in getting before a judge.

Often the mediator would remind both parties of the difficulty of predicting a result once the case is handed to a judge. That risk is compounded by the myth of the "all or nothing" character of judicial decision making, a myth that mediators perpetuate. Although empirical evidence shows that judges can and often do render accommodative decisions in small claims cases (McEwen and Maiman, 1981; Vidmar, 1984), it remains true that the parties abandon responsibility for and control over the decision when they go to adjudication.

Much less frequently, however, the mediator predicted to one party, often in a caucus, that he or she was almost certain to lose if the case went back to the courtroom. In the following illustrative case, the defendant had argued throughout the session that the repair bill he had received from an automobile body shop should have been sent instead to the person responsible for his accident. The mediator made it clear that he did not agree:

Plaintiff: "Let me ask you a question. You don't think this is your bill?"

Defendant: "Under the circumstances I think it's vague."

Plaintiff: "Why is that?"

Defendant: "Because of the agreement that I made [with the responsible party]."

Mediator: "But the agreement doesn't say that they'll collect the money from him."

Defendant: "When I brought my car in there, like I said, it seemed like everything was all fine and good between [the responsible party] and the person who was the sales manager."

Mediator: "Yeah, but you're going to lose everything. I'm almost certain of it. I'm not the judge and I'm not a lawyer. But I'm . . . based on the experience of a few cases here within the last few years . . . and I think if you would reach some sort of figure which you would pay and then if you want to sue [the responsible party], why, that's your business. And that would be the best way out for you."

Another negative aspect of adjudication, at least from the standpoint of the prevailing party, is the difficulty of collecting a court judgment. Mediators occasionally mentioned this problem to the plaintiff, though by doing so they ran the risk of calling it to the attention of the defendant as well. In the following case, which also illustrates the "certainty of loss" argument discussed above, the mediator discreetly reminded the plaintiff's lawyer of what lay ahead if the case went back to court:

Mediator: "Mr. ———, you're the plaintiff here. I really think it's up to you to decide. You've got the job, I think a hard job, to convince the judge that this was a loan rather than a partnership. Now, you can try to do that or you can continue the case, because of his statement of goodwill that he'll pay when he can. You're not going to get your money. All you're going to get is a judgment, and then there'll be a disclosure, and that isn't going to get you your money."

Plaintiff's lawyer: "Well, I've had enough of those. I've had some other judgments that never go anywhere."

Warnings like this one were fairly rare, however. It was more common for mediators to point out the advantages of the flexible payment arrangements that were often included in mediated settlements. While there is no reason in theory why adjudicated judgments cannot contain such arrangements, in Maine, as elsewhere, judges typically paid little attention to the issue of payment. To the defendant, the mediator stressed the obvious: a payment plan would take some of the sting out of paying the debt. For the plaintiff, the advantage was perhaps less obvious but certainly no less real: the more comfortable the defendant felt about the plan, the more likely he or she would abide by it. Moreover, the mediator might be able to arrange for the defendant to make an immediate down payment on the debt, thus guaranteeing the plaintiff at least part of the amount.

If all else failed, mediators often resorted to the argument that failure to settle their dispute through mediation would necessitate a further investment of the disputants' time. This could be a compelling argument, particularly if the parties had already devoted several hours to waiting for the judge, and then for the mediator, and finally to the mediation session itself.

The impact of such pressures for settlement is illustrated by this sampling of litigants' reasons for agreeing to mediated settlements that they later came to regard as unfair:

Plaintiff: "I thought it was better than nothing."

Plaintiff: "By then I was worn down; I was tired of it. I wanted to finish and get out of there, to get away from them."

Defendant: "Time factor. I'd been there all afternoon. For me it was easier to pay $20. I didn't like the principle of paying because it was like admitting guilt."

Plaintiff: "I felt I'd accomplished my goal. I'd let her know that she couldn't get away with it."

Plaintiff: "I felt we still were going nowhere — the mediator, actually. I felt the mediator leaned toward them and the judge would have done the same."

Defendant: "Because it was proved I was partially wrong. I wanted to get it off my back."

In light of such pressures, is it indeed accurate to speak of consensual settlement at all? Our interview data show that while many mediating parties feel that they were subjected to pressures to settle, and some even agreed to outcomes that they subsequently viewed as unfair, the overwhelming majority believed that they could have chosen to reject the settlement. And in about one-third of the mediated cases we studied, one or both of the parties did precisely that. Operationally, then, consent should not be defined as the total absence of constraints and pressures on decisions, but, rather as the parties' belief that they have the capacity to say no to a proposed outcome. Thus, paradoxically, the presence of a reasonable proportion of failed mediations — ones in which one or both parties exercised this option to reject a settlement — should be seen as a significant measure of program success in promoting a truly consensual process.

Conclusion

Our study of small claims mediation in Maine emphasizes some of the special features of mediation that set it apart from even informal adjudication, and that highlight the power of the consensual process. Even in the absence of strong community pressures and those imposed by continuing relationships and mutual obligations, small claims mediation still succeeds in producing agreements and encouraging compliance. The kinds of outcomes encouraged by mediation make compliance more probable. But the consensual quality of the mediation process also powerfully promotes compliance by implicating the parties in enforcing agreements upon themselves. By consenting to outcomes that they had some part in achieving, parties to a settlement enlist their own sense of honor and need for psychological consistency on behalf of compliance.

At the same time we also know that many parties who agree to an outcome do so not simply out of conviction that a settlement is the best and fairest available. They may do so because they are tired of the struggle, fear the alternatives, or simply want to get it over with. Both the inherent power of consent and the wide array of pressures that help produce it underscore the ethical obligation of mediators to act wisely and fairly.

References

Brehm, J. W. *A Theory of Psychological Reactance.* Orlando, Fla.: Academic Press, 1966.

Cook, R. F., Roehl, J. A., and Sheppard, D. I. *Neighborhood Justice Centers Field Test: Final Evaluation Report.* Washington, D.C. Government Printing Office, 1980.

Danzig, R., and Lowy, M. J. "Everyday Disputes and Mediation in the United States: A Reply to Professor Felstiner." *Law & Society Review,* 1975, *9,* 675–694.

Davis, R. C., Tichane, M., and Grayson, D. *Mediation and Arbitration as Alternatives to Prosecution in Felony Arrest Cases: An Evalua-*

tion of the Brooklyn Dispute Resolution Center (First Year). New York: Vera Institute of Justice, 1980.

Feldman, S. (ed.) *Cognitive Consistency: Motivational Antecedents and Behavioral Consequents*. Orlando, Fla.: Academic Press, 1966.

Felstiner, W. L. F. "Influences of Social Organization in Dispute Processing." *Law & Society Review*, 1974, *9*, 63–94.

Felstiner, W. L. F., and Williams, L. A. *Community Mediation in Dorchester, Massachusetts*. Washington, D.C. Government Printing Office, 1980.

Fuller, L. L. "Mediation: Its Forms and Functions." *Southern California Law Review*, 1971, *84*, 305–339.

Lempert, R. O. "Norm-Making in Social Exchange: A Contract Law Model." *Law & Society Review*, 1972, 7, 1–32.

McEwen, C. A., and Maiman, R. J. "Small Claims Mediation in Maine: An Empirical Assessment." *Maine Law Review*, 1981, *33*, 237–268.

McEwen, C. A., and Maiman, R. J. "Mediation in Small Claims Court: Achieving Compliance Through Consent." *Law & Society Review*, 1984, *18*, 11–50.

McEwen, C. A., and Maiman, R. J. "The Relative Significance of Disputing Forum and Dispute Characteristics for Outcome and Compliance." *Law & Society Review*, 1986, *20*, 439–447.

McEwen, C. A., and Maiman, R. J. "Coercion and Consent: A Tale of Two Court Reforms." *Law and Policy*, 1988, *10*, 3–24.

Sarat, A. "Alternatives in Dispute Processing: Litigation in a Small Claims Court." *Law & Society Review*, 1976, *10*, 339–375.

Vidmar, N. "The Small Claims Court: A Reconceptualization of Disputes and an Empirical Investigation." *Law & Society Review*, 1984, *18*, 515–550.

Witty, C. J. *Mediation and Society: Conflict Management in Lebanon*. Orlando, Fla.: Academic Press, 1980.

FOUR

Mediation in
Nonindustrial Societies

Sally Engle Merry

Mediation is an important mode of settling disputes in many small, nonindustrial societies. There are some similarities between this form of mediation and that which occurs in American community mediation. But there are also some profound differences, which cast doubt on the claims of some American mediators to be spiritual descendants of nonindustrial mediators. This chapter describes in detail mediation in four societies and uses these descriptions and other material to paint a broad

Note: Funding for the research described in this paper was provided by the Law and Social Sciences Program of the National Science Foundation to Sally Engle Merry (SES-8606023), and to Sally Engle Merry and Susan Silbey (SES-8012034). I am grateful for comments and suggestions by Richard Abel, Kenneth Kressel, and Dean Pruitt on earlier drafts, although the present errors remain my own. This chapter is adapted from "The Social Organization of Mediation in Nonindustrial Societies: Implications for Informal Community Justice in America" by Sally Engle Merry in THE POLITICS OF INFORMAL JUSTICE, Volume 2, edited by Richard L. Abel. Copyright © 1982 by Academic Press, Inc. Reprinted by permission of the publishers.

picture of the nature of nonindustrial mediation. It ends with a comparison between nonindustrial and American mediation.

Nonindustrial societies range from horticultural and pastoral peoples, whose political institutions are coterminous with their kinship systems, to peasant villages incorporated into nation-states. Disputants in societies of the first type turn to mediation as an alternative to violence, feud, or warfare; those in the second choose it in preference to violence or court. At one extreme are the peoples of highland New Guinea, for whom mediation only occasionally replaces vengeance (Koch, 1974; Meggit, 1977). At the other are the peasant villagers of China, whose culture mandates mediation and who use it in virtually all disputes within the village, despite the availability of a national court system, albeit one that is remote (Cohen, 1966; Crockett and Gleicher, 1978; Lubman, 1967; Yang, 1945).

Mediation in Four Societies

These four societies are described in detail: the Nuer (Sudanese pastoralists), the Ifugao (Philippine agriculturalists), the Waigali of Afghanistan, and the Zinacantecos of Mexico. The first two lack centralized political organization and courts, whereas the others are peasant villagers incorporated into nation-states that outlaw the use of violence within the village and provide a judicial alternative.

In addition, the process and organization of mediation in the following societies are incorporated in the overall analysis: the Arusha and Ndendeuli (Tanzanian horticulturalists; Gulliver, 1963; 1969); the Tiv (Nigerian farmers; Bohannan, 1957); the Tonga (Zambian farmers; Colson, 1953); the Cheyenne (North American Indian hunters; Llewellyn and Hoebel, 1941); the Swat Pathan and Sardinian shepherds (Ruffini, 1978); and peasant villagers in Liberia (Gibbs, 1963), Lebanon (Ayoub, 1965; Rothenberger, 1978; Witty, 1978), Zambia (Canter, 1978), Taiwan (Gallin, 1966), Italy (Brogger, 1968), and Japan (Kawashima, 1973).

The analysis is inevitably tentative since I have not exhausted the ethnographic literature on mediation. Yet the patterns that emerge are sufficiently consistent and represent such a wide geographical range that I believe they justify an effort to formulate a general model of the social organization of mediation in nonindustrial societies. Descriptions are couched in the ethnographic present.

The Nuer. The Nuer are pastoral nomads, herding cattle across the barren flatlands of Ethiopia and the Sudan. Studied by Evans-Pritchard (1940) in the 1930s, soon after their final conquest by the British, the Nuer were still a proud and independent society of 200,000 people who recognized no central government and had neither courts nor formal political offices. Although Evans-Pritchard makes a few fleeting references to the use of government courts, his analysis assumes that Nuer society is still unaffected by the outside world (an assumption that may have been unwarranted; see Howell, 1954; Kuper, 1973). The political system is based on kinship, organized around an elaborate structure of lineages in which smaller segments are nested within larger, more inclusive segments. Lineage membership varies with the level of segmentation that is relevant to a particular situation.

The Nuer are contentious and fight frequently over issues such as cattle theft, cattle trespass, adultery, watering rights in the dry season, pasture rights, or borrowing without permission (Evans-Pritchard, 1940, p. 151). A Nuer responds to any infringement of his rights by an immediate challenge to a duel, and children are taught early to settle disputes by fighting. Almost the only way Nuer achieve redress for wrongs is through force or the threat of force (p. 162).

In some situations, however, Nuer are willing to mediate disputes rather than pursue vengeance. The close agnates of a murdered man (males related to him through other males) are expected to avenge his death by killing the slayer or one of his agnates, but the aggrieved lineage can instead accept damages (bloodwealth) of about forty to fifty cattle. Disputants choose to mediate homicide disputes when they are close kin, when they or their kin live close together, or when marriage links the two kin groups. The existence of such crosscutting ties poses several problems if disputes are not settled. There is the constant dan-

ger of revenge if the villages of murderer and victim are close by
or if agnates of the latter live in the village of the former. If
members of the slayer's kin group eat or drink with the dead
man's kin group, or even use the same utensils, the former
believe they will die (Evans-Pritchard, 1940, p. 154). Consequently, the lineage of the slayer will quickly call in a mediator to
arrange the payment of damages. If the disputants are only
distantly related, however, and crosscutting ties are weak or
nonexistent, they feel less need to submit to mediation since
they have fewer social contacts (p. 157).

The Nuer have institutionalized the role of mediator in
the leopardskin chief. He has no secular power, only ritual
(however, see Gruel, 1971; Haight, 1972; Howell, 1954, p. 28). He
can mediate a dispute only if the parties wish to settle and
cannot prevent their recourse to violence if negotiations break
down. His sole power is the ability to curse the intransigent
disputant who refuses to accept a reasonable settlement, with
the threat that supernatural forces will aid his enemies if he
continues to seek vengeance. Although Evans-Pritchard never
witnessed a leopardskin chief's curse, he saw the threat of a
curse act as a deterrent (1940, p. 172). In homicide cases, the
leopardskin chief provides sanctuary to the slayer while bloodwealth negotiations progress, to prevent the opposing kin group
from taking vengeance in anger. The chief acts as a mediator
between the two groups, assessing what the killer's lineage can
pay and pressuring the victim's lineage to accept it.

The mediator is expected to be impartial and belongs to
neither of the disputing groups. The settlement he produces
must be mutually acceptable and thus must take into account
the status of the man killed—his social importance and position
in the lineage structure—as well as the power of his kin group to
extract damages (Howell, 1954, p. 60). Although the chief receives a small payment, it is unclear whether this must be spent
in the ritual of reconciliation or belongs to him (see Gruel, 1971;
Haight, 1972). The leopardskin chief also mediates disputes
concerning seizure of cows that are owed, adultery, or sexual
relations with an unmarried woman, but tradition specifies

particular damages for particular wrongs, and these can be collected only by force or the threat of force.

Mediation among the Nuer suggests a number of general characteristics of the process. First, the mediator is a respected and influential leader with expertise in settling disputes. His authority rests on his control over supernatural power: the ability to curse. Second, mediation occurs only when the disputants are linked to one another through a network of social relationships that renders a feud between their families disruptive and dangerous. Third, the mediator settles the dispute by negotiating an exchange of goods sanctioned by tradition: his role is to arrange the payment of damages. Fourth, the mediated settlement relies on heavy social pressure. Disputants are pressured both to negotiate and to accept the settlement recommended by the leopardskin chief and lineage elders. The sanctions are public opinion, the threat of the chief's curse, and the real possibility of vengeance killings if the dispute cannot be resolved by payment of damages. Fifth, the settlement is not justified in terms of Western liberal notions of equality before the law but reflects the relative importance and strength of the disputants. Bloodwealth varies according to the status of the dead man. The leopardskin chief, lacking a monopoly of force, can only arrange a settlement that both parties find mutually acceptable. Inevitably, such a settlement must reflect what the stronger is willing to concede and the weaker can successfully demand.

The Ifugao. The Ifugao are wet-rice farmers who own elaborate terraces climbing the steep hills around their small villages in the mountainous regions of the Philippines. When studied in the early twentieth century by Barton, they had neither government nor courts, but they did have a highly institutionalized mediator role and an elaborate set of customs for settling disputes (Barton, [1919] 1969; Hoebel, 1954). At that time, the Ifugao were essentially unaffected by the colonial courts.

Disputes commonly involve debt, breach of contract, adultery, slander, sorcery, murder, and other injuries against persons, property, and reputation. The plaintiff seeks a mediator, or *monkalun*, to assist him. The *monkalun*, however, is not an advocate for the plaintiff but represents the interests of the community at large in restoring peace and equilibrium (Barton, [1919] 1969, pp. 94–95). He therefore must not be too closely related to either side.

The *monkalun* works as a go-between, shuttling back and forth between the disputing parties with messages and proposals he can reinterpret and elaborate. If one side appears intransigent, he adds dire warnings about the other side's readiness to abandon negotiations and fight, replete with descriptions of sharpened spears, talk of violence, and so forth. To maintain his honor, a defendant must initially resist any suggestion that he accept payment rather than exact vengeance, but the *monkalun* gradually pressures him to settle. If a deadlock occurs, the *monkalun* withdraws, leaving the plaintiff with the option of finding another *monkalun* or simply ambushing the defendant. If the defendant is generally thought to be unreasonable and stubborn in the case, public opinion will support such violence (Barton, [1919] 1969, p. 100).

The *monkalun* has no authority to make binding decisions, but he does wield considerable influence. He is a member of the highest stratum and has achieved the highest title through his wealth and genealogical connections. A string of satisfactory settlements builds prestige as a mediator, attracts more cases, and provides fees in the form of pigs and other valuables. The opinions of the *monkalun* carry added weight because of his own reputation for violence and his social, economic, and political standing. An additional source of coercion is the threat of violence by the other side if negotiations fail. In Ifugao society, according to Barton, "the lance is back of every demand of importance, and sometimes it seems hungry" (p. 94).

The *monkalun* negotiates payments, whose amount varies with the nature of the offense, the relative class position of plaintiff and defendant, the strength and geographical proximity of their kin groups, and their individual personalities and reputations (Barton, [1919] 1969, pp. 61–69; Hoebel, 1954, pp. 116–117). Those in higher strata both pay and receive higher damages. Offenses such as rape, adultery, slander, sorcery, and even murder are seen not as crimes against society but as of-

fenses against particular individuals, to be settled through payment of damages.

As with the Nuer, quarrels between residents of the same
small valley are likely to end in mediation and settlement,
whereas disputes between individuals who live farther away
generally lead to violence and feud. In moderately remote areas,
efforts at mediation are perfunctory, and in more distant locations no legal procedures are used at all.

Thus in this society, too, the mediator is an influential
individual with rank, important kinship connections, wealth,
and a reputation for violence. He enhances this position
through his skill at mediation. Individuals agree to mediate
disputes and pay damages only where they are involved in
ongoing social relationships and have to deal with one another
in the future. Those who are more distant eschew settlements.
Mediators arrange the payment of damages, negotiating economic exchanges. Although the settlements must be mutually
acceptable and are not imposed by the mediator, mediation
itself is virtually compulsory since an individual risks the violence of his enraged adversary if he refuses to negotiate.

The Waigali. A third society, in the remote mountains of
Afghanistan, relies on mediation as the predominant mode of
handling disputes but, starting in the 1960s, began to submit
some conflicts to the national courts. The process closely resembles that already described but has been influenced by the
availability of courts.

The Waigali are herdsmen of goats and farmers of millet
and maize who live in small villages in the valleys of the Hindu
Kush, between Pakistan and Afghanistan. When studied by
Jones in the 1960s, they retained considerable independence
from the Afghan government by virtue of their location, but
Afghan courts were available to disputants who chose to trek
down the mountain to the nearby town and deal with officials of
that culturally and linguistically alien world (Jones, 1974). Each
of the nine villages occupying the Waigal Valley is politically
autonomous, but they share cultural bonds and may cooperate
or compete. Within each village, power is held by lineage elders
who derive their authority from their wealth and family posi-

tions. In the absence of formal government and courts within the village, the segmentary lineage system forms the backbone of the political structure.

Disputes occur over the theft of goats, trespass on pastureland, premature harvesting of walnuts or grapes, assault, extramarital sexual relations, and homicide. The Waigali are highly competitive over social status. They are quarrelsome and prompt to defend their rights, proud of ancestors who were warriors, and eager to appear fearless and decisive. Although they do not value reconciliation or compromise, villagers do endeavor to prevent conflicts within a village that divide and weaken it (Jones, 1974, p. 78). Disputes over serious offenses such as murder must be settled by either payment of damages or vengeance. When a dispute erupts within a village, it must be resolved quickly or violence and bloodshed will further split the village.

When such a dispute develops, the plaintiff usually appeals to one or more respected village elders to mediate. Those who regularly serve as mediators, *du-wrai*, include members of the landowning class and others with a reputation for being honest, forthright, skilled in formulating arguments, and clever in debate. Often they are also members of important lineages and have had many years of experience in village affairs. According to the Waigali, the most important trait is the ability to be objective: to focus on the problem, not the people (Jones, 1974, pp. 62–62). The *du-wrai* are carefully selected in terms of their kin relationships to the disputants: they belong to the largest kin group of which both are members but to the subgroups of neither plaintiff nor defendant. They are thus equally close to both parties. Since they are leaders of villages containing no more than 300 families, they are very familiar with the history of relationships between the disputants and with their families and personal reputations. The *du-wrai* have no power to enforce a legal decision.

The *du-wrai* function as go-betweens, visiting the house of the plaintiff and then that of the defendant, carrying messages back and forth and seeking to determine what will be mutually agreeable. At the same time, they gather evidence, present proposals, and even leave a "silent mediator" in each house as an informer to see what each side is really prepared to accept (Jones, 1974, pp. 74–78).

Like the Nuer, Waigali demand the maximum and do not want to acquiesce to a settlement too readily. Both sides are supposed to refrain from violence while the mediators are working, and they therefore conduct round-the-clock negotiations, some napping while others continue to shuttle from one party to the other, in order to forestall violence or a hardening of positions. Since each visit of the *du-wrai* demands lavish hospitality—meat, honey, and wheat bread (the most desirable foods), in an escalating pattern of competitive feasting—the costs of continued negotiation quickly mount. Furthermore, uninterrupted negotiation is probably intended to wear down the disputants. If the *du-wrai* are unable to find a mutually acceptable settlement, they can threaten to call in more *du-wrai*, often from other villages, which has the double disadvantage of increasing the cost of hospitality and advertising to the larger society that the village is unable to maintain harmony.

The mediators deal with each side separately and caucus by themselves to formulate proposals, a strategy that seems effective because the disputants are really lineages and not individuals. The offender's kin group is collectively responsible for his debt, and the plaintiff's kin will all share the damages. If the particular offender or victim is intransigent, his own kinsmen may pressure him to compromise.

The settlement reached by the mediators takes into account both village norms and the status and relationships of the disputants. The *du-wrai* must consider previous conflicts, the total social personalities of the persons involved (including the importance of their lineages and their individual statuses), and the nature and extent of the affront (Jones, 1974, pp. 78–82). An important man will hold out for higher damages, which both reflect and demonstrate his rank (p. 82).

Although disputants rarely turn to the Afghan courts, any case can be taken there directly. The availability of this alternative influences settlements even when it is not used. In one case, for example, the plaintiff wanted to kill the defendant but was deterred by the argument that a murder would involve the Afghan authorities, who impose long prison sentences (Jones, 1974, pp. 83–91). Two kinds of cases are taken to the government court: those involving outsiders, such as Afghans, in disputes over the theft of goats, trespass on pasturage, homicide, debt, and boundaries; and those lodged by the subordinate social caste against the dominant, landowning caste.

Roughly 10 percent of the villagers belong to a castelike social group with severely restricted rights, separate living quarters, segregated eating, and endogamy. Because the Afghan court does not accept the legitimacy of this subordinate status, its members frequently bring cases against their superordinates concerning land, property, and especially women, whom the landlords molest (Jones, 1974, p. 240). Knowing they will get no satisfaction within the village, whose mediators simply reflect existing social inequalities, they appeal to a court endowed with coercive power and a more egalitarian ideology. In this social setting, therefore, mediation tends to reinforce and perpetuate social inequalities, whereas adjudication exerts its authority to counteract them.

Zinacantecos. A fourth case suggests the role mediation plays in a peasant society with a more complex political organization that offers the alternatives of a state court and a local official with limited judicial authority.

Zinacantan is a Mayan Indian community located high in the mountains of Chiapas in southern Mexico. The Zinacantecos are maize farmers, eking a poor living out of patches of land on steep mountain sides and increasingly working as migrant farmers in the lowland valleys. At the time of Collier's study in the 1960s, contact with the Mexican state was increasing, a few villagers spoke Spanish in addition to Tzotzil, and local leaders were learning about the power of the Mexican court located in a neighboring valley (Collier, 1973). Although Zinacantecos did not use the court frequently (only three to seven times a year), knowledge about it was widespread, and predictions about the action it would take significantly affected the settlements reached by local mediators.

Collier analyzes three levels of dispute settlement. First,

leaders in each residential area, or hamlet, mediate disputes between neighbors and kinsmen who live within the hamlet and are involved in ongoing relationships, aiming at conciliation and compromise (1973, pp. 66–68). Second, cases can be taken to the town hall, where they are heard by the political leader of the village, the *presidente*, who has the power to make a decision enforced by a fine or up to three days in jail. In fact, the *presidente* also seeks to mediate disputes. Third, cases can be taken to the Mexican court, although this is expensive for both plaintiff and defendant, each of whom must hire a lawyer. The court imposes a zero-sum outcome that may include a steep fine or long jail sentence for the defendant, so that recourse to court is regarded as a serious step.

Mediators are hamlet elders, known for their wisdom, who have sufficient authority to persuade the defendant to appear. Some are politically powerful, and all enhance their reputations through successful mediation. Although they lack coercive power, they can encourage disputants to settle by threatening to send the case to the town hall court, which will consume additional time, expose them to the shame of a public hearing, and may lead to a fine or jail sentence (Collier, 1973, pp. 26–28). A mediator may even threaten to take a case to the Mexican authorities.

Another potent form of pressure is the fear that anger in the heart of a dissatisfied disputant will call down the wrath of the ancestral gods and lead to the illness or death of his opponent. The mediator seeks to cool the anger in the heart of the plaintiff by satisfying his demands at the same time that he seeks to avoid infuriating the defendant with unreasonable requests for compensation. Since sickness is ever-present, it is common for a disputant or one of his kinsmen to fall ill after angering an adversary, thereby confirming this belief (Collier, 1973, pp. 123–124). The mediator seeks to arrive at a settlement as quickly as possible, summoning the defendant as soon as a case is brought to him.

Because settlement through compromise is paramount, the outcome does not necessarily uphold social norms. Thus here, as in the other societies described above, mediation occurs between individuals whose ongoing relationship leads them to seek reconciliation, yet they are simultaneously coerced into settlements by the authority of the mediator and the sanctions he or she wields, both secular and supernatural.

Characteristics of Mediation in Nonindustrial Societies

These and other case studies suggest some general features of process, social organization, and outcome in mediated settlements. Many of these features recur in Cuban Popular Tribunals (Berman, 1969; Cantor, 1974), Chinese People's Mediation Committees (Lubman, 1967), Chilean neighborhood courts (Spence, 1982), and "courts" in American ethnic communities (Jaffe, 1972; Doo, 1973).

Cuban Popular Tribunals, for example, serve 4,000–5,000 residents each, conduct informal public hearings no more than two months after the incident, focus on restitutive and rehabilitative settlements, award concrete damages, frequently give moral lectures and public admonitions, and disqualify a judge as biased only if he is a friend or enemy of the disputants, not just because he knows them. Judges are laymen, elected by the local residents, and receive three weeks of training in law (Berman, 1969; Cantor, 1974). People's Mediation Committees in China were created in 1954 in each area or street in the city and in districts containing several villages in the countryside (Lubman, 1967). Mediators are elected by representatives of the residents and should be "politically upright." They mediate only when the parties agree. They also conduct propaganda and educate the people about national policies and laws. Urban mediators tend to be politically active housewives; in organizations and rural areas they are closely linked to the administration. Since they are part of the mechanism for constructing a socialist society, they operate within a clear moral system and often deliver harangues on moral virtue and new ways of thought. The mediators can invoke sanctions either through the police and other cadres in the urban neighborhoods or through work supervision in factories and communes (Lubman, 1967, p. 1349). Individuals from peasant or worker backgrounds fare

better than those whose families were bourgeois, reflecting communist values (pp. 1346–1347).

The Process of Mediation. Mediation is prompt. Ideally, it
occurs immediately after the incident, before the disputants
have time to harden their positions or, as the Waigali say, before
they can "think about their ancestors"—their pride and social
positions. The process is time consuming, taking hours or days,
as long as is necessary to reach a settlement. Arusha disputes
may be mediated for months (Gulliver, 1963). Negotiations are
often conducted in public forums where neighbors and
kinsmen can offer opinions and condemn the behavior of unreasonable disputants. Even when the mediator is a go-between
who meets with the parties privately, the wider public often
knows the nature of the discussions through its kin ties to both
sides.

Mediators arrange the payment of damages. Their function is usuallly to negotiate an outcome that will satisfy both
parties through an exchange of property, the demarcation of a
new boundary line, or the rendering of a public apology; vague
promises of improved behavior in the future are not sufficient.
Injuries such as insult, adultery, assault, and even homicide are
generally perceived as reparable through gifts of cattle, sheep,
or other valuables in amounts specified by custom.

The mediation process usually ends with immediate con-
summation of the agreement. When it is necessary to postpone
the final settlement—for instance, while one disputant finds
enough sheep—the assembly will often reconvene to observe the
exchange. In societies that lack written contracts, such an immediate exchange is the only guarantee of performance (Gulliver,
1963). However, when debts are not paid promptly they often
remain unsatisfied, offering fertile soil for future disputes. The
last step in the mediation process is typically a ritual of reconciliation, whether drinking coffee together in a Lebanese village
or a massive village feast financed by the loser as a public
apology, as in prerevolutionary China (Yang, 1945).

The Nature of the Mediator. Mediators are respected, influential community members with experience and acknowledged
expertise in settling disputes. They derive their authority to

intervene from their positions in kinship networks, their wealth, their political power, their religious merit, and their past successes at mediation. Successful settlements enhance their prestige and political prominence and often earn them some form of payment from the disputing parties. Among the Ifugao and Waigali, only titled members of the elite can become mediators, whereas among the Jale (Koch, 1978), Zinacantecos, and Arusha individuals become mediators by virtue of their positions within the lineage system or kin network. Mediators often have special religious status, as in Nuer and Swat Pathan society.

The reputation mediators earn for skillful negotiation, expertise in community norms and genealogies, and fairness and impartiality brings them more cases and political influence. However, their position as a mediator rarely rests on successful mediation alone. Instead it depends on a range of factors such as kinship connections, religious merit, wealth, the strength of supporters, and the possession of traditional offices. Mediators are usually of higher social status than the disputants. Where disputes involve members of higher social strata, outsiders are often needed. In prerevolutionary China, for example, disputes between village leaders were mediated by gentry from neighboring villages (Yang, 1945, p. 185). Baumgartner notes a similar reluctance among judges in colonial New Haven to adjudicate cases involving their social equals (1978, pp. 163–169).

Mediators represent the norms and values of their communities, often attaining their postions by virtue of their expertise in moral issues. They advocate a settlement that accords with commonly accepted notions of justice, couched in terms of custom, virtue, and fairness, and reflecting community judgments about appropriate behavior. To flout such a settlement is to defy the moral order of the community. Mediators often deliver moral lectures to one or both disputants. Finally, they are experts in village social relationships and genealogy, bringing to the conflict a vast store of knowledge about how individuals are expected to behave toward one another in general as well as about the reputations and social identities of the particular disputants. Mediators build on their past experience with sim-

ilar cases and their knowledge of local customs regarding such
disputes, manipulating these rules to justify their opinions.

Mediators are generally neutral, but they are rarely disinterested; nor are they complete strangers to the disputants.
Their impartiality is secured by crosscutting ties that link them
to both sides. Waigali mediators, for example, have close ties to
the lineages of both disputants but never belong to either. Jale
mediators have important exchange relationships with both
sides (Koch, 1974, pp. 140–141). A mediator's neutrality is also
enhanced by his or her position as representative of an entire
village or community or of an important component such as a
lineage or age group. The mediator represents this group's
interest in peace. She may be an outsider, not intimately connected to either party, or an expert summoned because of her
extensive knowledge of the substance of the dispute (Gulliver,
1977, pp. 36–40). Like a labor arbitrator, she seeks settlements
that seem fair to both sides in order to enhance her reputation
and attract more cases (Fuller, 1971). But mediators may pressure one side or another. If one side appears stubborn and
unreasonable, the mediator may cast his weight on the other
side in an effort to arrive at a settlement—a pattern observed
among the Ifugao, the Zinacantecos, and the Swat Pathans.

Receptivity to Mediation. Mediation is most likely to succeed
between disputants whose various residential and kinship ties
require them to deal with one another in the future. In other
words, it is a phenomenon of communities. When social relationships are enduring, disputants need to find a settlement to
continue to live together amicably. In societies without states
and courts, the alternative to a mediated settlement is usually
vengeance, which exposes the close kin of the offender to constant danger. Studies of such societies vividly document the role
of the offender's kinsmen in pressing for payment of damages,
particularly when these kinsmen have married into the victim's
lineage (Colson, 1953; Evans-Pritchard, 1940; Gluckman, 1960).

Similarly, in peasant villages, where courts, as well as
violence, offer alternatives to mediation, disputants agree to
settle only when they belong to the same village or subgroup
and feel the need to maintain amicable relationships. Several

village studies indicate that members refrain from pressing their claims against covillagers in court for fear of disrupting important social relationships (Bohannan, 1957, p. 210; Rothenberger, 1978; Witty, 1978, pp. 307–311; Yngvesson, 1976). Yet, where urbanization and social change break down this cohesion and mutual dependence, villagers seem more willing to use the courts (Ayoub, 1965; Fried, 1966, p. 298; Gallin, 1966; Kawashima, 1973, p. 73). They are no longer so dependent on their neighbors for support nor are their neighbors so central to their social lives, since they can always move from the village to the city or to another neighborhood in the city if tensions run too high. Moving away from conflict is far more difficult in villages.

The Nature of Mediated Settlements. Mediated settlements are backed by a variety of social pressures. Although the mediator lacks authority to impose a judgment, he is always able to exert influence and social pressure to persuade an intransigent party to accept some settlement and, often, to accept the settlement the mediator advocates. The community also exerts social pressure on disputants to settle and to abide by their agreement. Supernatural sanctions are often important as well.

Since mediators are usually powerful and influential, loss of their goodwill is itself a cause for concern. Some simply facilitate dyadic negotiations (Koch, 1974), whereas others practically adjudicate, backing their decisions with armed force. In the Swat valley in Pakistan, for example, "saints" serve as mediators by virtue of their religious positions but occasionally call on their followers to reinforce religious authority with military might (Barth, 1959; Bailey, 1972, pp. 28ff.). One saint, for example, arrived at a negotiating session where the disputants had agreed to appear unarmed only to find one party and his armed followers about to massacre the unarmed opponent. The saint whistled, calling out his own armed men hiding behind the bushes, thus quickly shifting his position from mediator to arbitrator (Barth, 1959, pp. 98–99). Similarly, the Ifugao *monkalun* acts as a go-between, but in the event of a failure to reach an agreement, his reputation as a headhunter becomes salient, and he threatens violence against the stubborn party. A mediator's

opinions are often backed by the economic and political power
of his kin group.

The community itself exerts pressure to settle. Recalcitrant disputants become the objects of gossip and scandal.
In Chinese villages they lose face for failing to behave in a
reasonable, conciliatory manner (Yang, 1945). Swat Pathans who
refuse to settle lose general support and gain a reputation for
ungodliness (Barth, 1959, p. 98). Witchcraft and supernatural
beliefs about illness also serve as a powerful incentive to restoring amicable relations. Zinacantecos believe that the anger in
the heart of a dissatisfied party causes sickness in its object
(Collier, 1973); those who refuse to act in a manner perceived as
fair in a Chinese village open themselves to attacks by witchcraft
(Yang, 1945).

One further form of coercion and social pressure is the
need to maintain peaceful relations with the other party. Terminating relations may be damaging to political, economic, or
kinship transactions; threats of violence or court action raise the
specter of protracted, ruinous litigation or a bloody feud. Inso-
far as they seek to avoid these disasters, disputing parties are
coerced to settle. Nevertheless, in no case is a mediator's decision
backed by institutionalized force, and parties are always free to
reject mediation and face the consequences.

Mediated settlements between unequals are unequal.
With few exceptions, a mediated settlement reflects the status
inequalities between the disputants. Payments for homicide
among the Sudanese Nuer and the Enga of New Guinea (Meggit,
1977) depend on the social status of the dead man; Ifugao
compensation varies according to the status of both plaintiff
and defendant. The amount of damages a Waigali receives reflects his total social personality (Jones, 1974, p. 82). A Swat
Pathan landlord who is pronounced loser in a conflict with a
weaker adversary often simply refuses to abide by the agreement
(Barth, 1959, p. 98). In prerevolutionary China, mediated settlements between families or individuals of equal prestige or
wealth reflected community norms, but those between wealthy,
educated families and the village poor often did not (Cohen,

1966, p. 1224) and were unjust (Yang, 1945, p. 242; see also Lubman, 1967, p. 1295).

Since a mediator lacks the ability to enforce his decisions, he must find an outcome both parties will accept. A mutually acceptable solution tends to be one in which the less powerful gives up more (Gulliver, 1963, pp. 2–3; see also Ruffini, 1978, p. 236). The greater the power of the mediator, the more leverage he has to impose a solution that disregards the inequality of the parties. The judge by contrast, at least in theory, adjudicates the legal rights of the disputants; he does not weigh their total social personalities.

Conclusions: The Contrast with American Mediation

Nonindustrial mediation is dissimilar to American community mediation in many important ways. Nonindustrial mediators are generally known by the disputants and often have high community status and considerable power. American mediators are almost always strangers to the disputants and tend to be low-power court officials or community volunteers. Mediators in nonindustrial societies bring to the mediation session considerable knowledge of the events in the dispute and the character of the disputants. American mediators typically lack this knowledge, and must struggle to develop a coherent account from conflicting and ambiguous stories and to assess the characters of both parties on the basis of their talk and presentation in the mediation session itself. Nonindustrial mediators are often quite directive, advocating settlements that accord with notions of justice commonly accepted in their societies. American mediators are generally less forceful and are more concerned about achieving a lasting settlement than about enforcing societal norms. The broader community, in nonindustrial society, often exerts pressure on the disputants to settle and abide by the settlement. In American society, such pressures, if they exist at all, come mainly from the court.

In nonindustrial societies, the authority to intervene in conflict situations rests on kinship connections, political position, religious merit, previous experience, and knowledge of customs and community. American mediators base their intervention on their training and expertise in the process of mediation. Indeed, a close examination of patterns of using mediators in three programs suggests the gradual emergence of a group of core mediators who are viewed by program staff as the most competent and who are invited to mediate cases most often (Harrington and Merry, 1988). These core mediators are people who are most successful in maintaining the detached stance toward the conflict and the values expected of mediators. The respected American mediator is one who can remain outside the struggle, asserting expertise and a commitment only to the values of the process itself—to negotiation and compromise rather than fighting (Silbey and Merry, 1986). Thus, the American mediator to some extent replicates the stance of the judge, as an expert in ideas, an intellectual, a person above the fray (Foucault, 1980).

One reason mediation in the United States differs from that in nonindustrial societies is the cultural dominance of the judicial form and the power of judicial institutions to infiltrate and take over alternative, informal forms of dispute resolution—a process that Auerbach has described over the course of American history (1983). Just as the mediator comes to resemble the judge in stance and claims to authority, so the process of mediation itself acquires some of the symbolic and formal structure of the court. Mediation adopts the form of the court in its use of official documents, its rituals of signing and funding, its self-definition as official, and its construction around the metaphor of the contract. American mediators negotiate contractual agreements with something for each side to which both parties consent, then sign, in the form of an official-looking document. Parties themselves tend to interpret the event as quasi-legal, in our observations, sometimes describing mediation as a "cock-eyed court" or a "kind of court" and expressing uncertainty about exactly how much and what kind of authority the mediators exercise (see Silbey and Merry, 1986, 1987).

As this exploration of mediation in other societies indicates, the process is open and flexible, shaped by the culture and institutions within which it operates. American mediation is also an open process, shaped by and infused with the pervasive legal ideology of American society and the powerful image of judicial dispute resolution embedded in American culture.

References

Auerbach, J. *Justice Without Law?* New York: Oxford University Press, 1983.

Ayoub, V. F. "Conflict Resolution and Social Reorganization in a Lebanese Village." *Human Organization,* 1965, *24,* 11.

Bailey, F. G. "Conceptual Systems in the Study of Politics." In R. Antoun and I. Harick (eds.), *Rural Politics and Social Change in the Middle East.* Bloomington: Indiana University Press, 1972.

Barth, F. *Political Leadership Among the Swat Pathans.* London: London School of Economics (monograph no. 19), 1959.

Barton, R. F. *Ifugao Law.* Berkeley: University of California Press (University of California Publications in American Archaeology and Ethnology No. 15), 1969. (Originally published 1919.)

Baumgartner, M. P. "Law and Social Status in Colonial New Haven. 1639–1665." *Research in Law and Sociology,* 1978, *1,* 153.

Berman, J. "The Cuban Popular Tribunals." *Columbia Law Review,* 1969, *69,* 1317.

Bohannan, P. *Justice and Judgement Among the Tiv.* London: Oxford University Press, 1957.

Brogger, J. "Conflict Resolution and the Role of the Bandit in Peasant Society." *Anthropological Quarterly,* 1968, *41,* 228.

Canter, R. S. "Dispute Settlement and Dispute Processing in Zambia: Individual Choice versus Societal Constraints." In L. Nader and H. F. Todd, Jr. (eds.), *The Disputing Process in Ten Societies.* New York: Columbia University Press, 1978.

Cantor, R. "Law Without Lawyers: Cuba's Popular Tribunals." *Juris Doctor,* 1974, *4,* 24.

Cohen, J. A. "Chinese Mediation on the Eve of Modernization." *California Law Review,* 1966, *54,* 1201.

Collier, J. *Law and Social Change Among the Zinacantan.* Palo Alto, Calif.: Stanford University Press, 1973.

Colson, E. "Social Control and Vengeance in Plateau Tonga Society." *Africa*, 1953, *23*, 199.

Crockett, G. W., and Gleicher, M. "Teaching Criminals a Lesson: A Report on Justice in China." *Judicature*, 1978, *61*, 278.

Doo, L.-W. "Dispute Settlement in Chinese-American Communities." *American Journal of Comparative Law*, 1973, *21*, 627.

Evans-Pritchard, E. E. *The Nuer*. London: Oxford University Press, 1940.

Foucault, M. *Power/Knowledge*. New York: Pantheon, 1980.

Fried, M. "Some Political Aspects of Clanship in a Modern Chinese City." In M. Swartz, V. Turner, and A. Tuden (eds.), *Political Anthropology*. Hawthorne, N.Y.: Aldine, 1966.

Fuller, L. "Mediation: Its Forms and Functions." *Southern California Law Review*, 1971, *44*, 305–339.

Gallin, B. "Conflict Resolution in Changing Chinese Society: A Taiwanese Study." In M. Swartz, V. Turner, and A. Tuden (eds.), *Political Anthropology*. Chicago: Aldine, 1966.

Gibbs, J. L., Jr. "The Kpelle Moot." *Africa*, 1963, *33*, 1.

Gluckman, M. *Custom and Conflict in Africa*. Oxford: Blackwells, 1960.

Gruel, P. J. "The Leopard-Skin Chief: An Examination of Political Power among the Nuer." *American Anthropologist*, 1971, *73*, 1115.

Gulliver, P. H. *Social Control in an African Society*. Boston: Boston University Press, 1963.

Gulliver, P. H. "Dispute Settlement Without Courts: The Ndendeuli of Southern Tanzania." In L. Nader (ed.), *Law in Culture and Society*. Hawthorne, N.Y.: Aldine, 1969.

Gulliver, P. H. "On Mediators." In I. Hamnet (ed.), *Social Anthropology and Law*. London: Academic Press (Association of Social Anthropologists Monograph No. 14), 1977.

Haight, B. "A Note on the Leopard-Skin Chief." *American Anthropologist*, 1972, *74*, 1313.

Harrington, C., and Merry, S. E. "Ideological Production: The Making of Community Mediation." *Law & Society Review*, 1988, *22*, 709–737.

Hoebel, E. A. *The Law of Primitive Man: A Study in Comparative*

Legal Dynamics. Cambridge, Mass.: Harvard University Press, 1954.

Howell, P. P. *A Manual of Nuer Law.* London: Oxford University Press, 1954.

Jaffe, J. *So Sue Me! The Story of a Community Court.* New York: Saturday Review Press, 1972.

Jones, S. *Men of Influence in Nuristan: A Study of Social Control and Dispute Settlement in Waigal Valley, Afghanistan.* London: Seminar Press, 1974.

Kawashima, T. "Dispute Settlement in Japan." In D. Black and M. Mileski (eds.), *The Social Organization of Law.* New York: Seminar Press, 1973.

Koch, K.-F. *War and Peace in Jalemo: The Management of Conflict in Highland New Guinea.* Cambridge, Mass.: Harvard University Press, 1974.

Koch, K.-F. "Pigs and Politics in the New Guinea Highlands: Conflict Escalation Among the Jale." In L. Nader and H. F. Todd, Jr. (eds.), *The Disputing Process in Ten Societies.* New York: Columbia University Press, 1978.

Kuper, A. *Anthropologists and Anthropology: The British School 1922–1972.* New York: Pica Press, 1973.

Llewellyn, K. N., and Hoebel, E. A. "The Cheyenne Way: Conflict and Case Law in Primitive Jurisprudence." Norman: University of Oklahoma Press, 1941.

Lubman, S. "Mao and Mediation: Politics and Dispute Resolution in Communist China." *California Law Review,* 1967, *55,* 1284.

Meggit, M. *Blood Is Their Argument: Warfare Among the Mae Enga Tribesmen of the New Guinea Highlands.* Palo Alto, Calif.: Mayfield, 1977.

Rothenberger, J. E. "The Social Dynamics of Dispute Settlement in a Sunni Muslim Village in Lebanon." In L. Nader and H. F. Todd, Jr. (eds.), *The Disputing Process in Ten Societies.* New York: Columbia University Press, 1978.

Ruffini, J. L. "Disputing over Livestock in Sardinia." In L. Nader and H. F. Todd, Jr. (eds.), *The Disputing Process in Ten Societies.* New York: Columbia University Press, 1978.

Schwartz, R. D., and Miller, J. C. "Legal Evolution and Societal Complexity." *American Journal of Sociology*, 1964, *70*, 159.

Silbey, S. S., and Merry, S. E. "Mediator Settlement Strategies." *Law and Policy*, 1986, *8*, 7–32.

Silbey, S. S., and Merry, S. E. "The Problems Shape the Process: Interpretive Processes in Mediation and Court." Unpublished manuscript, 1987.

Spence, J. "Institutionalizing Neighborhood Courts: Two Chilean Experiences." In R. Abel (ed.), *The Politics of Informal Justice*, Vol. 2: *Comparative Studies*. Orlando, Fla.: Academic Press, 1982.

Witty, C. J. "Disputing Issues in Shehaam, a Multireligious Village in Lebanon." In L. Nader and H. F. Todd, Jr. (eds.), *The Disputing Process in Ten Societies*. New York: Columbia University Press, 1978.

Yang, M. C. *A Chinese Village: Taitou, Shantung Province*. New York: Columbia University Press, 1945.

Yngvesson, B. "Responses to Grievance Behavior: Extended Cases in a Fishing Community." *American Ethnologist*, 1976, *3*, 353.

FIVE

Labor Mediators, Managers, and Ombudsmen: Roles Mediators Play in Different Contexts

Deborah M. Kolb

Mediation is usually defined as a voluntary, nonbinding form of third-party assistance in resolving disputes. This broad definition is meant to capture a process that occurs in a wide variety of conflictual situations. Although there is general agreement about the broad outlines of mediation (as distinguished from other forms of conflict resolution), the specifics of the process and the ways it is enacted are highly variable. In particular, the way mediation is carried out will be shaped by the institutional

Note: I have been thinking about these issues for several years. Among the people who have helped me do this and who have commented extensively on earlier drafts of this chapter, I would like to thank Lotte Bailyn, Jeanne Brett, John Forester, Sally Merry, Blair Sheppard, Susan Silbey, and John Van Maanen.

91

context and culture in which it occurs and the ideology of its practitioners. My research on mediators who practice in different organizational settings has been concerned with understanding some of the forms mediation takes in three different contexts—formal labor-management negotiation, the work of ombudsmen, and the informal mediation practiced by managers—and the interpretive bases that underlie practice in each.

Background and Theoretical Framework

My interest in mediation began in 1974 with labor mediation and shifted, as I began teaching MBAs, to the two kinds of mediation that might occur in business firms. I began with mediators in formal roles—ombudsmen—but found that, unlike labor mediation, which has an institutionalized role in labor-management conflict, most conflict resolution activities in organizations take place outside formal channels. Thus, I expanded my purview to include more emergent forms of mediation that occur in managerial ranks. This required that I identify situations where mediation would be likely to occur and focus on people who take on mediatorlike roles on a short-term or more regular basis.

Several themes link these studies of labor, ombudsmen, and managerial mediation. One is the focus on those who do mediation. Obviously there are a variety of ways to study the process of mediation, many of them represented in this book; my particular interest is in what mediators actually do and how they perceive their work. In particular, I have focused on the roles that labor mediators, ombudsmen, and managers play in managing and resolving conflicts. (*Role*, a summary term, here refers to both cognitive and behavioral dimensions of the activity of mediation [Mead, 1934; Turner, 1966].)

The second theme, one that is related to the conception of role, is the interpretive theory that informs the work. Interpretive theory is not a unified model of human behavior, but rather a framework for understanding social activity. The theory emphasizes the meanings social actors give to their activities and considers that observed behavior is shaped by these meanings (Blumer, 1969; Rabinow and Sullivan, 1979). To understand what practitioners do, it is important for the researcher to learn to see behavior from their viewpoint. Ethnography is usually the method that accompanies this interpretive stance (Van Maanen and Kolb, 1985). It emphasizes rich description of routinely occurring activities, based on both observation of and interaction with those studied.

Why is interpretive theory, with its focus on meaningful action, particularly appropriate to the study of mediation? First, it is consistent with the way mediators think about their work. Labor mediators, in particular, describe their work as art, based on the ever-changing contours of disputes and the challenges they present (Meyer, 1960; Moore, 1986). Second, mediation is, at its core, interpretive work. What a case is about, what the parties want, what outcomes are sought — these are not matters of fact but issues with multiple interpretations that become the subject of negotiations between mediator and disputants. Capturing the mediators' understanding of these matters is central to explaining what mediators do.

The final theme that links these different studies of mediation is the relationship between context and practice. *Context* refers to the organizational setting in which mediators work, their status and position within the organization, the ideology that guides practice, the kinds of parties routinely encountered, the interplay between parties and their desires, and the issues brought and outcomes sought. The ways mediators mediate, how they interpret cases and structure their roles will be influenced, I believe, not only by the characteristics of the immediate case situation but also by the context in which they work. But mediators also shape the context through the actions they take over time (Berger and Luckman, 1966). Thus there is extensive interplay between reacting to case situations and enacting them.

In this chapter I describe three studies — involving labor mediators, ombudsmen, and managers who act as informal mediators in their organizations — focusing on roles mediators in different contexts play and the interplay between context and practice. There are some interesting contrasts. Labor mediators, ombudsmen, and managers who mediate share a set of activities aimed at resolving a particular conflict. The nature of the conflict and its clarity, however, differ among the three domains, and these differences have implications for how the mediators function (Kressel and Pruitt, 1985). As we move from institutionalized settings of mediation, where the process is structured into the role, to organizations where mediation is associated with certain roles (ombudsman) or with a more generic, emergent activity, the description of what constitutes mediation expands.

Labor Mediation

Labor mediation is an institutionalized part of a labor-management conflict. Labor mediators have well-defined roles in collective bargaining, but there are consistent contrasts in the way the role is understood and enacted. I have studied two government mediation agencies, one federal agency and one state (Kolb, 1981; 1983a, 1983b; 1985).

Labor mediators define their task as learning the issues in dispute, typically with reference to the last proposal made by each side, assessing which issues are of the highest priority, and then encouraging the parties to make moves in their positions. How different mediators accomplish these steps distinguishes one form of mediation—orchestration—from another—deal making.

The federal mediators in the study see their role as one of orchestrating a process that gives the parties themselves primary responsibility for developing their agreement. Thus, orchestrators structure meetings so that the parties directly confront their differences in joint meetings: they see concession making as a slow, incremental process managed by chief negotiators with help as needed from the mediators, and generally intervene on the substance of the conflict in the later phases of mediation. In contrast, the state mediators saw themselves more in the role of deal makers, attempting to shape the substantive development of the agreement. Deal makers tend to keep the parties apart and act as go-between; they build momentum by identifying key issues (with help from chief negotiators) and by pushing for moves early in the case.

These two approaches to mediation reflect the experience of mediators and the context and ideology of their practice (see Kolb, 1983a; pp. 150–173). Orchestration, the role favored by federal mediators, makes sense when parties have experience with collective bargaining and when their leaders, the chief negotiators, know how to make deals. But it also makes sense in a broader context where free collective bargaining, a value that holds the interests of the parties and prescribes a limited role for outsiders, is paramount. These values are apparent in the ways mediators are recruited and trained and in the kinds of collegial relationships they have with negotiators within and apart from particular cases.

Deal making, the approach of the state mediators, takes place in a different context. Working primarily in the public sector, where parties lack the experience and history of collective bargaining and where legal strikes are mostly proscribed, state mediators develop a style that they believe compensates for the missing dynamics.

There are consequences to each approach. Orchestrators, because they take their cues from chief negotiators, rarely find themselves in difficulty from overzealousness. However, because they are guided by pros they also reinforce the institutional interests these spokespeople represent. In other words, orchestrators preserve the status quo in a way that makes it difficult for innovators or other local interests to be heard. In contrast, deal makers, because they actively try to pressure both sides into a fair settlement, often make mistakes that jeopardize their standing with the parties. At the same time, these very efforts are often aimed at balancing the interests of the parties in a way that may yield to innovation and change.

Labor mediation, one of the most structured and institutionalized forms of practice, defines a type against which others may be compared. Labor mediators become involved in disputes over interests, usually when the parties have already negotiated with each other and reached an impasse. The task, as they define it, is to help the parties reach an agreement. Much of the empirical research on labor mediation concerns how to capture the nature of these resolution activities.

Ombudsmen

Ombudsmen have a formal mediation role within organizations. An ombudsman is a "neutral or impartial manager within a corporation who may provide confidential and informal assistance to managers and employees in resolving work related concerns" (Rowe, 1987, p. 127). In contrast to labor mediators, however, the disagreements that ombudsmen are called on to mediate are not well structured or defined. Thus, framing the situation into a concrete problem that can be mediated becomes as important as the actual steps they take to resolve it.

The broad guidelines of the ombudsman's job and the novelty of this corporate function mean that ombudsmen have considerable latitude to structure their job and the process they use. My study of ombudsmen was based on ethnographic interviews with seven ombudsmen in six organizations. Through repeated interviews over a six-month period, I followed fifty-six cases on an ongoing basis (Kolb, 1986; 1987a). In the earlier labor study, despite claims to confidentiality, the more or less public aspect of mediation conducted under government auspices meant that I could observe most mediation cases. In business organizations, issues of privacy and confidentiality, and the sometimes tenuous position of the ombudsmen, meant that I was not permitted to observe actual interactions. However, I worked with the ombudsmen to construct histories of a case, its initial presentation, the substantive discussions held with the complainant and others, and the ombudsmen's efforts to remedy or resolve the issues.

The findings suggest that diagnosis—interpreting the problem—is a major but often overlooked part of the ombudsman's activity. Clients who come to see the ombudsman are frequently upset about something. Their depiction of what occurred is usually complicated and open to multiple interpretations of several aspects: what the problem is, who the parties are, who is at fault, whether policy and practice have been violated, among others. What a case is about will get clarified as the ombudsman learns more. But ombudsmen actively contribute to defining the problem through the kinds of information they seek and the other parties they involve in the process. Further, the ways that ombudsmen define problems seem to be related to how they see their roles and the kinds of remedies that are available to them.

There were two basic patterns in the ways that the ombudsmen in the study defined their roles. Three believed their job was helping individuals out of situations that caused problems for them. As one of them said, "My natural proclivity is to be an advocate for people. In this role you have to take into account the impact of decisions on the system. But when people come and lay it on me, I listen, but I also know they want a response. People want some kind of assistance and I take on a lot of responsibility for assisting them rather than turning it back to them."

These "helping" ombudsmen handle a significant number of transfer and promotion cases, as well as cases that they classify as problems between managers and subordinates. In cases concerning harassment, receipt of obscene messages, and incomplete performance reviews, helping ombudsmen usually recommended a transfer for the affected employee.

The other four ombudsmen described their approach more as fact finding. As one reported, "I orchestrate due process in this company. I do not represent the employees but try to understand their point of view. My job is to do what is fair . . . I never arrange anything for anybody. I don't want to make a situation my problem. I don't want to get involved. I think of myself as an investigator to find the truth."

In the face of complaints, fact finders want to know whether proper procedures were followed and, if that cannot be directly ascertained, whether there is plausible explanation for the complainant's perception of unfair treatment. If fact finders can construct plausible explanations for a particular situation, then they try to persuade the claimant of that reasoning. If the fact finder believes policy, practice, or the law has been violated, a more extensive investigation will be undertaken. Fact finders have a somewhat higher proportion of cases that concern pay and benefits, discipline, and termination than helping ombudsmen do. Interestingly two quite similar cases — an employee receiving an anonymous obscene note — were approached very differently. A fact-finding ombudsman considered it a disciplinary case, and a helping ombudsman suggested transfer for the recipient.

Why are the kinds of cases that helping and fact-finding ombudsmen tend to get — and their approach to resolving them — so different? There are several possible reasons. It may be that different problems are more likely to arise in certain organizations, although there is no obvious empirical reason this should be so, given the sample of companies (see Kolb, 1987a). There is some evidence that ombudsmen develop localized reputations for what they do so that people seek them out for more of those kinds of problems than others. It is also possible that, faced with ambiguous case situations, they decide what the problem is and what to do about it within the range of remedies available. And the remedies that are available are related to the ombudsmen's history in their respective organizations. Those who tend to emphasize the helping role generally have long tenure in the organization, have held many jobs before becoming ombudsmen, and so have a rich social network on which to draw when arranging help. With the security of tenure and the reputations built over a long career, they can put the kind of pressure on an organization that helping implies. Fact-finding ombudsmen, in contrast, are relative newcomers to the organizations, and so it is not surprising that their approach is primarily one of inquiry and persuasion through formal channels.

The ombudsman function is a formal mediation role in organizations and one that is relatively new. It is a harmonizing role. Both helpers and fact finders try to keep conflicts quiet, and in their own way seek to avoid confrontation. The cases they encounter lack the clarity and predictability observed in labor mediation. To resolve particular conflicts, ombudsmen must frame them as problems that require help or the uncovering of facts (see Chapter Eight). These frames will be relatively consistent over a range of problems, and will be related to the kinds of remedies that are available; the remedies, in turn, are shaped by the context in which third parties work and their positions in it.

Emergent Managerial Mediation

The ombudsman is a mediator within an organization — but this is not the only way that mediation is accomplished in business organizations. It is not even the main way. The job of ombudsman is far from universal in corporations, and even where it does exist, it is not as widely used by either employees or managers as other complaint mechanisms (Lewin, 1986). Most mediation is of the emergent kind, that is, it is done by people who do not have a formal third-party role but who step in because they are forced to, or feel a need to, resolve a conflict between their associates. Such mediation is a common activity in organizations. At some point most managers, supervisors, secretaries, colleagues, and friends find themselves involved as third parties in some disagreement or conflict.

Emergent mediation must be understood in the context of an organization's tendency to avoid and deny conflict. Collaborative systems are a stated ideal in much managerial ideology, with the implication that conflict is undesirable when it occurs and best suppressed in the interests of harmony and integration (Boulding, 1964). The realities of task interdependence and the need for organizational members to work together keep disagreements quiet, so that ongoing relationships are not disturbed (Yngvesson, 1978). As a result, conflicts over a variety of issues and interests tend to be masked as rational discourse, misunderstandings, or personality problems, or controlled through rituals (Pettigrew, 1973; Kolb, 1986; 1987b; Kolb and Sheppard, 1985). In contrast to other mediation contexts, where conflicts of interest are legitimized and made public, conflict avoidance in organizations means that emergent mediators must make certain expressions of conflict legitimate if resolution is to occur.

My first impulse in this third study was to look at how managers handle conflicts between their subordinates. In preliminary case studies of managers I discovered that mediation was not a common role (Kolb, 1986; Kolb and Sheppard, 1985). It became clear that to study the emergence of managerial mediation, one needed to find the kinds of propitious situations where conflict was likely to exist, even if it was not openly expressed. Task forces, where representatives from different functional departments combine to work on a project or solve a problem, seemed likely candidates; the structural ingredients for conflict are present, and some modes of conflict resolution are usually required if the project is to be completed (Lawrence and Lorsch, 1967; Pettigrew, 1973). They are also a common feature of contemporary organizations.

I studied the activity of two task forces, one at Acton Investments and the other at Baker Laboratories. (The names of companies and individuals are disguised.) At Acton, the new-product division planned to introduce a new credit card in a joint venture with a bank, and formed a task force to develop the marketing, customer service, systems, and legal arrangements. The task force stayed in existence for four months, until the joint-venture contract was officially signed. I observed all formal task force meetings and met with the members on a weekly basis to track the progress of the project. To complete the project, the task force leader was *obligated* to take on a mediation role.

At Baker Laboratories, a high-technology firm, a task force of vice-presidents from research and development, sales, marketing, and administration was charged with developing a new marketing orientation for a set of products the company manufactures. I attended the weekly meetings, met informally with some of the members, participated in some training sessions with them, and consulted on a regular basis with a human resources manager who has responsibility for executive training programs and is married to one of the senior executives. As one task force disbanded and others formed in its stead, the human resources manager voluntarily took on a mediation role and continues to do so.

Acton Investments. The credit card task force was convened by Steven Richards, senior vice-president for new-product development. The group included another representative from the new-product group, two members from marketing, and representatives from customer service, information systems, and legal. The task force was to meet regularly to keep track of the work done by each member. Once the contract with the bank was signed and most of the development work completed, the product was to be turned over to marketing and the new-product group would move on to other projects. Richards described the purpose of the task force to its members: "We are not here to make decisions, but since this project is so different we want to use these meetings to know who's doing what to whom. The purpose is to see who has responsibility for what and to set tentative deadlines for completion of tasks."

The negotiation process proceeded on two levels. The attorneys and Richards met with representatives from the bank to formalize the language of the agreement. At the same time, members of the task force worked with counterparts in the bank to develop the systems and program for the credit card launch. There were spillovers from these negotiations into the formal contract discussions.

Disagreements arose between Acton and the bank partner about a host of contractual, procedural, and product issues. One issue, in particular, concerned the credit criteria Acton's customers would have to meet to receive the card. Acton wanted the criteria to be lenient, and the bank preferred them to be more stringent. The bank's position prompted the marketing task force members to enlist the support of their boss, the vice-president of marketing. Marketing wanted to back out of the deal over this issue and find a bank more compatible with its viewpoint, a bank that understood marketing better. Richards saw the situation differently.

"This issue could be a deal buster. I think that we made a mistake. By pushing for the April release date, we got the task force started too soon and operating issues became part of the package we were negotiating. Marketing assumes that if we don't sign that we can find another bank. But they don't realize that if we don't sign with them, the deal is off. It's my job to make sure that the contract gets signed by the end of the month."

To bring the bank and the marketing people to agreement, Richards engaged in a form of mediation. He orchestrated the negotiations between Acton and the bank. As the leader of the Acton team, he worked with the marketing members of the task force to gather data and prepare a presentation to the bank that would argue for more lenient credit criteria. At the same time, within Acton, Richards sowed some doubts about Acton's position on the lenient credit criteria. He presented and reinforced the bank's point of view. Finally, Richards made it clear that if the bank insisted on the stringent criteria and if marketing continued to press for abandoning the deal, he would have to involve the chairman of Acton.

"The chairman has given his approval to this product. I don't think he will be that worried about the smaller customer base, but he might be concerned about consumer debt. He will not be pleased about abandoning this product, but the decision will have to rest there."

Richards's efforts yielded a compromise agreement. The bank's position on credit criteria would prevail for the first round of customer solicitation. The bank conceded to Acton on the amount of additional financial information it would require, information Acton could easily get through a short application.

Richards's work as a mediator between Acton and the bank deserves comment. First, he was obligated to take on the role. As chairman of the task force, he had expected to oversee the marketing and operational implementation of the product. However, the implementation issues became intertwined with the formal negotiating process and thus became a subject of formal negotiations. As head of the task force, Richards was at the boundary between the bank and Acton, particularly the marketing department whose product it would eventually become, in a position where he had no formal authority over either. Further, as the new vice-president of new products, and this the first new product, he had interests to "do this deal." To save the project, he *had* to work out an agreement between part of his team and the bank. From this boundary role, in which he had responsibility for the product but not legitimate authority to compel compliance, he was forced to play a mediation role to save the project.

Richards used some recognizable mediation tactics. He orchestrated the meetings, tutored his team in their presentation, conveyed messages between the two parties, used objective criteria on both sides to persuade and influence, and threatened to escalate if no agreement was reached. These tactics are recognizable, in part, because his mediation occurred in the context of negotiation. But the fact that the attributes of the product became a subject of negotiations was his doing. In this way, a fight between the marketing and new-products department over the banking partner, which was understood as a battle over turf, was structured by him into a negotiated compromise.

One of the members of the task force described new products as political footballs. The implication is that people fight over their form and the right to make decisions about them. Often these disagreements are masked in decision-making terms. Leaders recognize that in order to reach an agreement, the bases of disagreement will have to be openly aired and negotiated and that part of the leadership function may be to assume a mediation role, at least temporarily. In Baker Laboratories, a person who emerged as a mediator was not obligated as Richards was, but rather volunteered.

Baker Laboratories. The mediation activity at Baker Laboratories took place in the context of significant changes in the company. A once profitable firm, Baker had suffered significant losses and, for the first time in its history, was forced to lay off employees. There were some strong differences of opinion about the kinds of actions Baker would need to take in order to turn the company around, but these differences were rarely discussed in public. Olivia Lane, a manager of executive training and development, took on a mediation role in which she created the conditions for some of these differences to be voiced and resolved.

Part of Lane's job is to develop training programs for vice-presidents. The first training seminar she organized was on corporate goal setting and planning. During the seminar, some of the vice-presidents expressed their frustration at the lack of serious planning at Baker and blamed senior management for failing to change its ways. An outcome of the seminar was a set of task forces to solve particular problems that the vice-presidents identified.

Lane was a frequent, but silent, attendee at these task force meetings. After the meetings, subgroups would often form to gossip about what had occurred, and she was part of these "off-line" sessions. Also, because of her access to senior management (from her marriage), some of the vice-presidents began to see her as a link to their superiors. Sometimes they would ask her to report to a senior vice-president about a particular issue or to arrange a meeting. They might complain to her about the actions of others. She became part of a gossip network among a core group of vice-presidents, where she described herself as a kind of "welcome pest." A few of them came to view her, or so it appeared, as their advocate with senior management around a range of issues. In this way she emerged as a mediator who passed on information, reactions, and interpretations among vice-presidents and between one level of the organization and another.

From these interactions, strategic planning came into focus as the issue around which some of the differences between vice-president and senior management coalesced. According to Lane, her role evolved in the following way. A group of four vice-presidents formed a strategic planning task force, met regularly, and began work on a formalized planning process. No senior managers were involved; indeed they were quite skeptical. The CEO showed no interest in the process of the planning but kept pushing the task force to set a date for its presentation. The vice-presidents claimed that it was all well and good to set a date, but the problem was not the plan, but its implementation. "At Baker, we are strategy rich and implementation poor." The vice-presidents felt that there was a black hole of planning between themselves and the senior managers that made implementation impossible.

At the same time, Lane, in her management development and training role, began discussions with two strategic planning consultants. The vice-presidents on the task force were glad to have the consultants but felt that without some senior vice-presidents involved, the discussions would fail. They asked Lane to go to Charles Ray, a senior vice-president of administration, to "get him on board." She arranged a meeting between the consultants and Ray, who listened to them and then announced that he was working on his own framework and had no use for either the consultants or the vice-presidents.

Lane consulted another senior vice-president, Adam Black of marketing, who she thought might help convince Ray. Next she arranged a meeting of the vice-presidents, Black, and the consultants. The vice-presidents used the occasion to talk about how the presence of the consultants would help them and legitimize planning at Baker. Again they asked her to talk to Ray about the consultants. Ray asked her to arrange a meeting so that he could present his planning framework. At the meeting, Ray made his presentation and then the vice-presidents asked him questions about "rolling it out" in the short and long term. She observed that the vice-presidents were not satisfied with his response and looked at her to do something. As the meeting was about to end, she asked, "Does this mean that I should cancel the consultants?" This led to a discussion by the vice-presidents of their belief that Baker was missing a key opportunity. This was the first time that the issue of strategic planning—who should participate in it and how much effort should be expended—had ever been publicly discussed. It was agreed that the consultants would be retained and that a task force of senior managers and vice-presidents would work with them.

Olivia Lane emerged as a mediator between various factions in the organization. Her role was emergent in the sense that it evolved as she experimented with a new job. By learning of the vice-presidents' concerns through the training program and then following up on the task forces that were formed in the context of her program, she established relationships with several of them. Her knowledge of the organization and her connections with senior management made her valuable.

Dimensions of Emergent Mediation. The role Lane played is multifaceted and seems considerably broader than that we usually associate with mediation. Unlike Richards, who had an immediate problem on his hands and was forced to deal with it, Lane was in a position to get involved in a diffuse conflict between different groups in the organization and chose to do so. Her primary contribution was not resolution of the disagreement. Rather, with some conscious intentions in mind, with much ad hoc extemporizing, and with the help of some serendipitous events, she and the network of vice-presidents created the conditions for an agreement. Resolution was possible because the general problem was narrowed into a dispute over strategic planning and because in her role as mediator she orchestrated a set of meetings where the dispute could be aired and discussed. Raising the conflict to the level of public discourse legitimated its expression.

Mediation is usually associated with resolution of disputes. A focus on these tactics, however, may mask the role emergent mediators play in shaping the dispute in such a way that it *can* be resolved. Such shaping often involves redefining the issues (Mather and Yngvesson, 1980–81). Lane through her intermediary role helped Ray, Black, and the other vice-presidents define the issues around strategic planning. Starting with whether the consultants would be engaged to work with the vice-presidents, the issues were expanded to include discussions of whether strategic planning would be done, who would do it, and what forms it would take. Similarly, Richards channeled an internal power struggle about what kind of bank should be a partner to Acton into a negotiation about some of the specific problems marketing had with the bank.

Emergent mediators also contribute to resolution of the redefined issues by orchestrating the process. Lane worked primarily through a series of one-on-one meetings with different people to get them to a joint meeting so that the issues could be aired. Richards also orchestrated the process. He tried to create better relationships between Acton and the bank by sending an experienced aide to meet socially with bank representatives the night before the negotiations were to start. He also tried to soften what many saw as a confrontational style of some of the younger managers (a problem that had surfaced during an earlier meeting) by rehearsing them in proper demeanor. Both Richards and Lane raised the disagreements to the level of public discourse so that they could be resolved. In these efforts, they used many of the common resolution tactics often associated with mediation: learning about the issues, identifying the relevant parties, aiding communication between the parties, and pressuring them to come to an agreement through threats or other forms of moral suasion.

Emergent managerial mediation occurs where conflict is an ongoing, but often hidden, part of the social fabric of organizations. The forms that mediation takes reflect this reality. Much emergent mediation is quiet and occurs out of sight in private offices, in one-on-one meetings. The examples given here provide only a glimpse of the forms this activity might take. Not included here, for instance, are the extremely sociable individuals others may seek out for help, or those who occupy formal administrative roles—the chiefs of staff, the assistants to the president—who probably spend a considerable amount of their time mediating (Auletta, 1986).

Those who find themselves mediating either out of necessity, like Richards, or voluntarily, like Lane, seem to occupy positions in organizations that are conducive to this activity. They operate at the boundaries between different parts of the organization. In these positions, they come to learn about the salient issues and concerns of different groups and are able to speak the language of each and so convey meaning to the others. Emergent mediators can identify and locate the interests and issues and channel them into forums where they can be discussed and perhaps resolved. This channeling may be the most important contribution of emergent mediation. For in this way, emergent mediators raise conflict to the level of public discourse and so legitimate its expression (Miller and Sarat, 1981).

Conclusion

Labor mediators, ombudsmen, and managerial mediators work in very different contexts, and the style of mediation they do reflects these differences. Labor mediators understand their role in the context of the contract negotiations that preceded their involvement. Labor mediation thus resembles, in structure, language, and activity, a form of assisted negotiation.

Individuals seek out ombudsmen with complaints about something that has gone awry in their work situations. The activities that ombudsmen engage in look more like a complaint-handling process, involving both diagnosis and remedy, than they do assisted negotiation. Managers who mediate do so in situations that require some form of coordinated action or joint decision making among organization members who are in conflict with each other but who rarely express this conflict directly in public forums. Emergent mediation activities take place, therefore, behind the scenes, or "off line," and are directed toward creating the conditions where differences can be expressed, clarified, and then resolved in a shared-task context.

These broad distinctions can be refined as we look more closely at particular situations. Ombudsmen and labor mediators develop individualized approaches reflecting their organizational location and their relationships with the parties involved in a given case. These approaches shape what happens in mediation. It is more difficult to discuss any consistent approach by emergent managerial mediators because their activity appears to be more ad hoc, responsive to immediate situations in which they find themselves and not formally attached to any regularly occurring role of conflict management. It may be that those managers who volunteer to mediate find themselves doing so more regularly and so develop a more clearly articulated approach.

Comparison of the three mediation roles suggests that the boundaries between the impartial third party and the primary parties blur as one moves away from institutionalized domains into organizational settings. Labor mediators are rarely impeccably neutral in their dealing with parties, even though some effort goes into maintaining this impression (Kolb, 1985). The kinds of cases they mediate and the relationships they have with some chief negotiators mean that they often have decided preferences for certain kinds of outcomes, ones that aid the institutional and professional interests of these chief negotiators (Kolb, 1983a). However, labor mediators, while they have their own interests, are still organizationally outside the dispute. The interests of the ombudsmen and the parties are not as easily separated. Ombudsmen are often caught between protecting the organization and helping a claimant. The balance between these sometimes conflicting requirements is not independent of the ombudsman's own managerial and career interests. In the two emergent mediation cases we examined, both managers (although Richards more than Lane) had specific preferences for particular outcomes. Their interests were intimately bound up with those of the other actors. In such a setting, it is difficult to separate the settlement role from a partisan one (Black and Baumgartner, 1983; Zartman and Touval, 1985).

These outsider-insider distinctions are also relevant to the issue of authority and the legitimate bases that are claimed and used by different mediators (Wrong, 1979; Merry, 1982). Labor mediators, as outsiders to the dispute, claim authority on the basis of professional expertise and, sometimes, a referendum from their membership in a shared community of players (Kolb, 1985). Ombudsmen have a formal claim in the sense of a bureaucratically sanctioned role that is endorsed by top management. There is some referential claim: at least helpers are part of a network that can be called upon. However, in organizations where there are norms against public expression of conflict, a formal conflict resolution role is likely to be marginal.

Emergent mediators derive their influence, it appears, from their position as interested insiders. It may be that others trust them because their interests are known. Their legitimacy seems to derive from their ability to produce agreements that reflect their interests. In this sense, when managers mediate, they are judged according to prevailing criteria — results.

There is an interesting paradox here. Compared to labor mediators, who frequently make lifelong careers of mediation, those in the organizations I studied were not enamored with the mediation role. Richards said the lesson he learned from the task force experience at Acton was to complete outside negotiations before other groups at Acton became involved. He did not want to have to mediate between an outside partner and his organization again. Olivia Lane describes what she does as "babysitting," and although she has volunteered to mediate in other situations, she wonders whether other members of the organization know what she does. Also, some of her other mediation efforts have not been as successful as the one described here. Of the seven ombudsmen studied, two have left their companies, two have moved into other jobs, and one minimizes the mediation part of this function. In organizations where status is officially related to one's track record and accomplishment, activities like mediation, which occur out of sight, may not be highly valued.

The roles played by mediators in different contexts have implications for the institutions of which they are a part. Labor mediators contribute to the settlement of industrial disputes, but in so doing, they also reinforce certain normative biases that exist in the system. When mediators share a professional community of interest with chief negotiators, they support these institutional interests through the actions they take. Substantive issues that are important to chief negotiators, which usually concern comparable wages and other economic benefits, are given more credence than local and often idiosyncratic work issues. This bias is evident in collective bargaining, but it is mobilized in mediation to the detriment of innovation and change.

Ombudsmen, too, are more likely to preserve the status quo of the organizations in which they work than to change it. While ombudsmen resolve localized problems in the organizations, the quiet ways in which they do it contribute the stability at the macro-organizational level. Ombudsmen who help employees, for example, do so on an individual basis and rarely keep any records of their cases or the disposition of them. Thus with no statistical patterns, it is unlikely that systemic problems would be uncovered or documented.

Emergent mediation may have important implications for the ways contemporary organizations are managed, particularly their ability to change the way they operate. To compete in complex and changing markets, to inspire product innovation, and to take advantage of advances in information technology, firms are experimenting with new organizational forms: multi-layered matrix structures, task forces, teams, networks, and joint ventures that span traditional organizational boundaries. These new forms challenge conventional functional structures and hierarchical modes of control. Organizations are beginning to resemble clusters of loosely connected nodes and networks more than ordered hierarchies, but the mechanisms for making decisions across these lateral structures are underdeveloped. This is particularly problematic where decisions are likely to lead to conflict and open airing of differences. The tendency to mask conflict and keep it out of sight in order to avoid direct confrontation often leads to delayed or inadequate decision making—to the detriment of innovation and change (Argyris, 1986).

If mediators who operate at the seams of organizational boundaries emerge to assist the kinds of decision making that might otherwise be avoided, they can fill an important function in contemporary organizations. As communicators across boundaries, they may clarify issues and interests in ways that cannot be discussed in face-to-face meetings. They may help to orchestrate the forums for discussion and then assist in the resolution of issues. It may be that these mediators constitute a shadow organization, one that is mostly out of sight and helps increasingly diffuse organizations work toward common aims.

It may be possible to bring this emergent mediation activity out of the shadows and make it a more formal dispute resolution function within organizations. However, there are problems with formalizing an activity of this kind. Where the overt expression of conflict and airing of disputes are discouraged, those who resolve conflicts perform a function that is not highly valued. Then we find that managers who mediate do so because they are already involved in the particular situation and have the independent managerial stature to legitimate the airing of issues and orchestrate resolution, and that their activities take place in the shadows. Were these activities to become formally recognized, it is conceivable that, like the ombudsman role, the function would be marginal to the resolution of ongoing conflict. To enhance the possibility that mediators will emerge to deal with conflicts in ways that are consistent with the values of a given institution, the skills of conflict management must be widely dispersed in an organization (Brett and others, 1985).

References

Argyris, C. "Skilled Incompetence." *Harvard Business Review*, Sept.–Oct., 1986, 74–79.

Auletta, K. *Greed and Glory on Wall Street*. New York: Random House, 1986.

Berger, P. L., and Luckman, T. *The Social Construction of Reality*. New York: Doubleday, 1966.

Black, D., and Baumgartner, M. P. "Toward a Theory of the Third Party." In W. O. Boyum and L. Mather (eds.), *Empirical Theories of Courts*. New York: Longman, 1983.

Blumer, H. *Symbolic Interaction*. Englewood Cliffs, N.J.: Prentice-Hall, 1969.

Boulding, K. "A Pure Theory of Conflict Applied to Organizations." In G. Fisk (ed.), *The Frontiers of Management*. New York: Harper & Row, 1964.

Brett, J., and others. *The Manager as Negotiator and Dispute Resolver*. Washington, D.C.: National Institute of Dispute Resolution, 1985.

Kolb, D. M. "Roles Mediators Play." *Industrial Relations*, 1981, *20*, 1–17.

Kolb, D. M. *The Mediators*. Cambridge, Mass.: MIT Press, 1983a.

Kolb, D. M. "Strategy and the Tactics of Mediation." *Human Relations*, 1983b, *36*, 247–268.

Kolb, D. M. "To Be a Mediator: Expressive Tactics in Mediation." *Journal of Social Issues*, 1985, *41*, 1–25.

Kolb, D. M. "Who Are Organizational Third Parties and What Do They Do?" In R. J. Lewicki, B. H. Sheppard, and M. H. Bazerman (eds.), *Research on Negotiations in Organizations*. Greenwich, Conn.: JAI Press, 1986.

Kolb, D. M. "Corporate Ombudsman and Organization Conflict." *Journal of Conflict Resolution*, 1987a, *31*, 673–692.

Kolb, D. M. "Repertoires of Avoiding Conflict." Paper presented at the 26th Annual Meeting of the Academy of Management, New Orleans, Aug. 1987b.

Kolb, D. M., and Sheppard, B. H. "Do Managers Mediate, or Even Arbitrate?" *Negotiation Journal*, 1985, *1*, 379–388.

Kressel, K., and Pruitt, D. G. "Themes in the Mediation of Social Conflict." *Journal of Social Issues*, 1985, *41*, 179–198.

Lawrence, P., and Lorsch, J. *Organization and Environment.* Cambridge, Mass.: Harvard University Press, 1967.

Lewin, D. "Conflict Resolution in Non-Union High Technology Firms." Paper presented at the 25th Annual Meeting of the Academy of Management, Chicago, Aug. 1986.

Mather, L., and Yngvesson, B. "Language, Audience and the Transformation of Disputes." *Law & Society Review*, 1980–81, *15*, 755.

Mead, G. H. *Mind, Self, and Society.* Chicago: University of Chicago Press, 1934.

Merry, S. E. "The Social Organization of Mediation in Non-Industrial Societies: Implications for Informal Community Justice in America." In R. Abel (ed.), *The Politics of Informal Justice: The American Experience.* Vol. 2. Orlando, Fla.: Academic Press, 1982.

Meyer, A. "Functions of the Mediator in Collective Bargaining." *Industrial and Labor Relations Review*, 1960, *13*, 159–165.

Miller, R., and Sarat, A. "Grievances, Claims and Disputes: Assessing the Adversary Culture." *Law & Society Review*, 1981, *15*, 525–566.

Moore, C. W. *The Mediation Process: Practical Strategies for Resolving Conflict.* San Francisco: Jossey-Bass, 1986.

Pettigrew, A. *The Politics of Organizational Decision-Making.* London: Tavistock, 1973.

Rabinow, P., and Sullivan, W. M. *Interpretive Social Science.* Berkeley and Los Angeles: University of California Press, 1979.

Rowe, M. "The Corporate Ombudsman." *Negotiation Journal*, 1987, *3*, 127–141.

Sheppard, B. H., Blumenfeld-Jones, K., and Minton, J. "To Control or Not to Control: Two Models of Conflict Intervention." Paper presented at the Faculty Seminar, Program on Negotiation, Harvard Law School, 1987.

Turner, R. "Role Taking, Role Standpoint and Reference Group

Behavior." In B. J. Biddle and E. J. Thomas (eds.), *Role Theory*. New York: Wiley, 1966.

Van Maanen, J., and Kolb, D. M. "The Professional Apprentice." In S. Bacharach (ed.), *New Perspectives in Organizational Sociology*. Vol. 3. Greenwich, Conn.: JAI Press, 1985.

Wrong, D. *Power: Its Forms, Bases and Uses*. New York: Harper & Row, 1979.

Yngvesson, B. "The Atlantic Fisherman." In L. Nader and H. Todd, Jr. (eds.), *The Disputing Process in Ten Societies*. New York: Columbia University Press, 1978.

Zartman, I. W., and Touval, S. "International Mediation: Conflict Resolution and Power Politics." *Journal of Social Issues*, 1985, *41*, 27–45.

SIX

Mediation in
International Conflicts

Saadia Touval
I. William Zartman

In today's nuclear world, most international conflicts tend to call
for efforts to mediate by representatives of states that are not
involved in the conflict. Yet while a considerable body of schol-
arship about conflicts has accumulated over the years, our understanding of mediation is much less advanced. The existing
literature on international mediation, contributed to more by
scholars than by practitioners (Berman and Johnson, 1977;
Campbell, 1976; cases by Davidow, 1983; Edmead, 1971; Fisher,
1978; parts of Gulliver, 1979; Ikle, 1964; Jackson, 1952; Pruitt,
1981; Raiffa, 1982; Raman, 1973; Touval, 1982; Young, 1967;
Zartman, 1984), has provided only the first step in understanding why and how parties try to mediate international conflict.

Note: The authors are grateful to the Center for International Affairs at
Harvard University for the support it extended while we were preparing this
chapter for publication.

Our discussion is concerned with conflicts over political or security issues. We believe that mediation in international economic or environmental disputes is somewhat different, mainly because the parties' orientation will not be as strongly competitive (see Winham, 1987). We assume that conflicts over political and security issues take place within a context of power politics, and that this context has a major effect on international mediation. This premise is the conceptual backdrop to our analysis of the motives of mediation participants, the conditions that affect the performance and roles of mediators, and the keys to their effectiveness.

The empirical base for our theoretical formulations is historical studies of successful mediation, particularly eight case studies, published in a project on international mediation of which we were cosponsors (Touval and Zartman, 1985; Zartman and Touval, 1985). Reference will be made to these cases, but specific sources will not be cited in the rest of this chapter. The eight cases are:

1. Soviet mediation between India and Pakistan at Tashkent, 1966, by Thomas P. Thornton.
2. Algerian mediation between Iran and Iraq, 1975, by Diana Lieb.
3. U.S. and British mediation of the conflict in Rhodesia and Zimbabwe, 1976–1979, by Stephen Low.
4. Western Five mediation of the conflict in Namibia, 1977–present, by Marianne Spiegal.
5. Algerian mediation for the release of the American hostages in Iran, 1980–1981, by Gary Sick.
6. Mediation by the Organization of African Unity (OAU), by Michael Wolfers.
7. Mediation by the Organization of American States (OAS), by L. Ronald Scheman and John W. Ford.
8. Mediation by the International Committee of the Red Cross (ICRC), by David P. Forsythe.

Additional cases in our data base are the mediation in the Arab-Israeli conflict (analyzed in Touval, 1982) and mediation

in four African cases: Sahara, Shaba, Horn, Namibia (analyzed
in Zartman, 1984).

Definitions

Mediation is a form of third-party intervention in a conflict, with the stated purpose of contributing to its abatement or
resolution through negotiation. Like other forms of peacemaking or conflict resolution, it is an intervention acceptable to the
adversaries, who cooperate diplomatically with the intervenor.
Mediation differs from other forms of third-party intervention
in two ways: it is not based on the direct use of force, and it is not
aimed at helping one of the participants to win. Like good
offices, mediation is concerned with helping the adversaries
communicate, and like conciliation, it emphasizes changing the
parties' images of and attitudes toward one another—but it also
performs additional functions. Mediators suggest ideas for a
compromise, and they negotiate and bargain directly with the
adversaries. Mediation is not arbitration; arbitration uses judicial procedure and issues a verdict that the parties have committed themselves to accept, whereas mediation is basically a political process without advance commitment of the parties to
accept the mediator's ideas.

Motives Behind Mediation

The intervention of mediators is legitimized by the goal of
conflict reduction, which they typically proclaim. Their desire
to mediate is, however, intertwined with other motives best
described within the context of power politics. For understanding these motives a rational-actor approach is most useful, one
that employs cost-benefit considerations, because mediators are
players in the plot of relations around the conflict, with some
interest in its outcome; otherwise they would not mediate. In
view of the considerable investment of political, moral, and
material resources that mediation requires, and the risks to
which mediators expose themselves, the motives for mediation
must be found in self-interest as well as in humanitarian im-

pulses. A parallel statement can be made about the parties' attitude toward mediation. It is unlikely that they invite or accept mediation because they are interested only in peace. Each party usually expects the mediator's intervention to work in favor of its own interests.

From the mediator's point of view as a player, two kinds of interests can be promoted through mediation. One is essentially defensive: the continued conflict between two actors threatens the mediator's own interests. In this case, solution of the conflict is important to the mediator because of the conflict's effects on its relations with the parties. For example, if two of the mediator's own allies or friends engage in a conflict, this can disrupt and weaken the alliance. A conflict between two states may be seen as upsetting a regional balance, or may provide opportunities for a rival power to increase its influence by intervening on one side of the conflict.

The second self-interested motive for mediation is the desire to extend and increase influence. Here the solution of the conflict has no direct importance to the mediator; it is only a vehicle for establishing closer relations with one or both parties. A third party may hope to win the gratitude of one or both parties in a conflict, either by getting them out of the conflict or by helping one achieve better terms. To be sure, the mediator cannot throw its full weight behind one party, but it can increase its own influence by rendering its involvement essential to the negotiations and by making each party dependent on the mediator. Mediators can also increase their influence by becoming guarantors of whatever agreement is reached.

It follows, then, that mediators are seldom indifferent to the terms being negotiated. Even when they seek peace in the abstract, they try to avoid terms not in accord with their own interests, although that usually allows for a wider range of acceptable outcomes than the immediate interests of the parties. They can also allow themselves greater flexibility in bargaining because they have incurred fewer commitments and have invested less in the conflict. Mediators are likely to seek terms that will increase the prospects of stability, deny their rivals opportunities for intervention, earn them the gratitude of one or both parties, or enable them to continue to have a say in the relations between the two adversaries.

These propositions can be illustrated by a number of historical examples. Both the U.S. mediation in the Rhodesia-Zimbabwe conflict and the Soviet mediation between India and Pakistan were inspired by a mix of defensive and expansionist motives. The United States feared the Rhodesian conflict would provide opportunities for the Soviet Union to gain influence by supporting the African nationalists. But since the African groups concerned were already close politically to the Soviet Union and China, one can also interpret the U.S. mediation as an attempt to win over, or at least to improve relations with, these groups and not to abandon them to the exclusive influence of its political rivals. Soviet mediation between India and Pakistan was partly inspired by the desire to improve its relations with Pakistan, which had previously been on far better terms with the United States and China. The Soviet Union also sought to build its prestige and establish a precedent that might help it justify future involvement in the affairs of the region. At the same time, there were important defensive motives for its intervention. The Indo-Pakistan conflict provided an opportunity for China to extend its influence in Pakistan, and thus to establish its presence close to the southern borders of the Soviet Union. The reduction of the conflict would make China's task more difficult.

Mediation by middle-sized powers may be motivated by a desire to enhance their influence and prestige. Egypt's and Algeria's mediation between Iran and Iraq resulted from their desire to prove their usefulness to both belligerents, as well as to reduce intra-Islamic conflict. Algerian mediation between the United States and Iran seems to have been inspired by the hope that it would generate goodwill toward Algeria among the U.S. public and thus help improve relations between Algeria and the United States. This hope was presumably related to U.S. support for Algeria's adversary, Morocco, in the Western Sahara war against the Algerian-supported Polisario movement.

Similar examples of other states seeking to enhance their international standing through mediation come to mind: India attempting to mediate between the United States and the Soviet Union and China in the 1950s; Nkrumah of Ghana trying to mediate in the Vietnam war in 1965–1966; Rumania playing an intermediary role in that same conflict in U.S.–Soviet relations, and in Arab-Israeli relations (notably in helping arrange President Anwar Sadat's visit to Jerusalem in 1977). There should be little wonder that small and medium states seek to enhance their international standing through mediation. They have few alternative instruments at their disposal, and such activity increases both their usefulness and their independence vis-à-vis stronger allies. Moreover, when pressed to take sides in a conflict, they may seek to escape their predicament by mediation.

While many states occasionally become mediators, the United States often finds itself "condemned" to play this role (Stephen Low's phrase, in Touval and Zartman, 1985). Since it fears that conflicts will provide the Soviet Union with opportunities to intervene and expand its influence, the United States often seeks to dampen conflict, and mediation is often a convenient instrument to that end. In addition, without reference to the Soviet Union, U.S. help is often solicited by smaller states engaged in conflict because of U.S. power and prestige. Pressed by its friends for support, and always fearful that support for one side in a local conflict will throw the other into the Soviet embrace, the United States apparently often finds that the least risky course is to mediate between the disputants. (Examples since 1946 abound: the United States has mediated between the Arab states and Israel since 1949; between Britain and Iran in 1950; between Holland and Indonesia; between the various Lebanese factions in 1958 and again since 1982; between Italy and Yugoslavia over Trieste; between Greeks and Turks in Cyprus; between whites and blacks in Rhodesia/Zimbabwe; between South Africa and the black Africans over Namibia; and between Britain and Argentina over the Falklands/Malvinas.)

International organizations are also frequently involved in mediation. But in their case, one could say they were "born to mediate," for that is a *raison d'être* enshrined in their charters. Mediation by regional organizations also has a defensive aspect, reducing the opportunities for external intervention and interference within their regions, a purpose seen clearly in the charter and actions of the OAS, OAU, and Arab League (with varying degrees of success).

Several motives lead the conflicting parties to seek or accept mediation. The most obvious is the expectation that mediation will help gain an outcome more favorable in the balance than continued conflict—a way out. Another motive is the hope that mediation will provide a more favorable settlement than could be achieved by direct negotiation. Although the adversary may still not have a similar assessment, it may accept and cooperate with the mediator, because a rejection might cause even greater harm—for example, damaging relations with the would-be mediator, decreasing the chances for an acceptable negotiated outcome, or prolonging a costly conflict. The parties may also accept mediation in the hope that the intermediary will help them reduce some of the risks entailed in concession making, protecting their image and reputation as they move toward a compromise. They may also believe a mediator's involvement implies a guarantee for the final agreement, thus reducing the risk of violation by the adversary.

An additional motive helps to explain the acceptance of mediation by international organizations. It appears to be premised more on the ability of these organizations to bestow normative approval than on their capacity to influence the adversary or arrange for a satisfactory compromise. This point is clearest in the case of the International Committee of the Red Cross (ICRC). This agency's ability to offer an improved image to a fighting or detaining authority can be a powerful incentive for the parties to accept its presence and services, and for acceding to its proposals.

Partiality and Acceptability

If acceptance of mediation is based on a cost-benefit calculation of obtainable outcomes, this has a profound effect on our understanding of the mediator's position and methods. The acceptability of a mediator to the adversaries in a conflict is not, as is sometimes believed, determined by their perceptions of the mediator's impartiality (Touval, 1975). What is important to the parties' decision is their consideration of the consequences of acceptance or rejection—for achieving a favorable outcome to the conflict above all, but also for their relations with the would-be mediator. Thus, meddling by third parties is tolerated because they are already part of the relationship, but third parties are accepted as mediators only to the extent that they are thought capable of bringing about acceptable outcomes. Although there is no necessary relation between past partiality and future usefulness, good relations between the mediator and one party may in fact aid in fostering communication, developing creative proposals, and bringing the two parties' positions into convergence. Closeness to one party implies the possibility of "delivering" that party and hence can stimulate the other party's cooperativeness. For example, the Africans' belief that British and U.S. sympathies were with the white Rhodesians rendered British and U.S. mediation promising for them, and stimulated their cooperation.

A mediator who is seen as motivated, and able to deliver the party to which it is closest, may turn its partiality into an asset. Thus, the Soviet Union was accepted as mediator by Pakistan despite its close relationship with India. Pakistan perceived the Soviets as concerned enough about its growing cooperation with China to want to improve their own relation with Pakistan, and as close enough to India to bring it into an agreement. Algeria was accepted by the United States as a mediator with Iran not because it was considered impartial but, on the contrary, because its ability to gain access to people close to Khomeini held promise that it might help to release the hostages.

The mediator may have two different partialities that balance each other only in the aggregate but that render it acceptable to both sides. Often a mediator motivated by its own concern for position in the area needs to use its intervention to maintain close ties with one side, while at the same time improving ties with the other. We are told that the Soviet Union was neutral in its mediation between India and Pakistan. But Russia and India had good relations neither wanted to jeopardize, and the Soviet motive of inhibiting the growth of Chinese-Pakistan relations meant that the Soviets desired an outcome that could induce Pakistan to lose interest in improving relations with China. If one of the Egyptian motives in mediating between Iran and Iraq was to improve its relations with the Shah, then clearly the fulfillment of its goals was dependent upon how much it supported the Iranian position.

Even in the case of the international organizations, acceptance is not automatic, but depends on the promise of attractive outcomes through mediation. When the OAU establishes a commission to mediate a dispute, consultation procedures give the parties an implicit say in the composition of the commission. The result will often be a balanced slate rather than an impartial commission, since members are likely to seek to protect the interests of their friends, not to form their views solely on the basis of objective criteria. The battle of the slate is separate from the actual practice of mediation, which comes to life only as long as the commission shows promise of providing an acceptable solution.

As an independent nonstate agency, the ICRC has problems neither of partiality nor of composition. Nevertheless, its acceptance as a mediator is not automatic. To quote Forsythe (in Touval and Zartman, 1985, p. 238): "While the ICRC is widely regarded as having a mediating role to play in wars, in any particular war the ICRC may be unwelcome." What concerns parties to a conflict is not whether the ICRC will perform its humanitarian functions objectively, but whether the legal framework of its involvement may affect their interests. Thus, states may contest that an armed conflict justifying an ICRC intervention actually exists, or that an international war has occurred. This framework is sometimes subject to negotiation, and the terms of involvement are influenced by their perceived effect on the interests of the parties rather than by the latter's perception of the ICRC's impartiality.

To say that it is not necessary for third parties to be perceived as impartial to be accepted as mediator is not to suggest that a mediator can espouse the cause of one side in a conflict while ignoring the interests of the other. Mediators must be perceived as having an interest in achieving an outcome acceptable to both sides, and not so partial to one side as to preclude that outcome. Again, the question for the parties is not whether the mediator is impartial, but whether it can provide an acceptable solution.

Although they cannot fully side with one party, there is some latitude in the degree of partiality that mediators can allow themselves. This latitude may go so far as to enable them to express their preference about the outcome of the negotiation. In the Zimbabwe and Namibia negotiations, the United States was not indifferent to the nature of the settlement to be reached. The outcome had to open the way for majority rule. Although this meant that the United States supported the essence of the African position and, by implication, sought to eliminate the white settlers as a sovereign political actor, its mediation was nevertheless accepted by the whites when it was seen as getting them out of a no-win situation and presenting certain lesser advantages for them.

An interest in specific outcomes is quite common in the mediations of the international organizations. The ICRC, OAU, and OAS all have some general criteria for solutions to disputes, beyond just agreement by the parties. They try to promote solutions that can be interpreted as compatible with the standards of the Geneva Conventions and of their charters, respectively, and that protect their image as a guardian of these standards. Indeed, they can use the weapon of condemnation for parties' deviation from these standards as a means of their enforcement.

Timing of Mediation

From our premise that mediators are motivated by self-interest, it follows that they will not intervene automatically but only when they think a conflict threatens their interests, or when they perceive an opportunity to advance them. But a threat or an opportunity is unlikely to be noticed when there is only a mild disagreement between the parties. It is usually only after the conflict grows serious and escalates that its implications are perceived. After the conflict has escalated, the parties are likely to become committed to their positions and to a confrontational policy, diminishing the likelihood that mediation will succeed.

For successful mediation it is necessary that the parties be disposed to reevaluate their policies. The cases suggest two situations especially conducive to such reevaluation: hurting stalemates, and crises bounded by a deadline; or, to use a metaphor, plateaus and precipices.

A plateau and its hurting stalemate begin when one side is unable to achieve its aims, to resolve the problem, or to win the conflict by itself; it is completed when the other side arrives at a similar perception. Each party must begin to feel uncomfortable in the costly dead end it has reached. Both must perceive a plateau not as a momentary resting ground but as a flat, unpleasant terrain stretching into the future, providing no later possibilities for decisive escalation or for graceful escape.

Mediation plays on perceptions of an intolerable situation: things "can't go on like this." Without this perception, the mediator must persuade the parties that escalation to break out of deadlock is impossible. Indeed, the mediator may even be required to *make* it impossible. Thus, deadlock cannot be seen merely as a temporary stalemate, to be easily resolved in one's favor by a little effort or even a big offensive or a gamble or foreign assistance. Rather, each party must recognize its opponent's strength and its own inability to overcome it.

For the mediator, this means emphasizing the dangers of stalemate as each party comes to recognize the other's strength. Each party's unilateral policy option (the action that it can take alone without negotiation) must be seen as a more expensive and less likely way of achieving a possible, acceptable outcome than the policy of negotiation. A plateau is thus as much a matter of perception as of reality for the parties and as much a subject of persuasion as of timing for the mediator. Successful exploitation of a plateau produces a shift from a winning mentality to a conciliating mentality on the part of both sides.

A precipice is, of course, the conceptual opposite of a plateau. It represents a realization that matters will swiftly get worse. A precipice can be an impending catastrophe, as the term implies, such as probable military defeat or economic collapse. It may be accompanied by a policy dilemma: to engage in a major escalation, the outcome of which is unpredictable, or to seek a compromise, with the first choice a matter of desperate uncertainty that threatens one side as much as the other. Or it may be a catastrophe that has already taken place, the stolen horse that drives both parties to lock the stable. Whatever its tense (since parties are bound to disagree about the inevitability of an impending event), it marks a time limit to the judgment that things "can't go on like this" (Zartman, 1987, pp. 285ff.).

For the mediator, the precipice merely reinforces the nature of the plateau, lest the parties become accustomed to their uncomfortable deadlock. Mediators can do two things with precipices: they can use them and they can make them. If there is a recognized danger impending, mediators can use it as a warning and an unpleasant contrast that can make the negotiated alternative appear more attractive. If there is no agreement on a precipice, mediators can work to improve a common perception of its existence, since it is useful to their work. In its most manipulative role, a mediator may have to bring some reality to the perception of—that is, create—a precipice, usually citing pressure by a fourth party. That is what the United States did in 1977 to get the Namibia negotiations started, citing irresistible pressure for sanctions if the sides did not start talking.

Mediators' Roles

Mediators operate in three principal roles to affect the positions of the parties in conflict, inducing them to agree to concessions necessary to reduce or resolve the conflict and also contributing to the advancement of the mediators' self-interested goals. The first—and least—is the *mediator as communicator*. Conflict often implies the breakdown of communications, with parties becoming locked in a situation they cannot escape simply because they dare not contact each other directly. Concessions may be required, which the parties cannot make unless they find a way of communicating them without losing face or appearing weak. In such cases, mediators may be required to start the initial contacts and to serve as a telephone wire. They may also carry word of the other's concession when conceding directly would be psychologically or procedurally impossible. And they may act as holders of concessions or agreements when direct communication of agreement between the parties is impossible. In this role, mediators are more or less a passive conduit and repository, although in human affairs no medium is completely passive. Tact, palatable wording, and sympathetic presentation are as important as, but must not impinge upon, accuracy and straightforwardness.

Mediators may also perform a more active role. The breakdown of communication may do more than impede the delivery of messages without the services of a messenger; it may also keep the parties from even thinking of solutions that meet the needs of both sides. In such a situation, the second role— *mediator as formulator*— is needed as well. Third parties must be capable of innovative thinking that is not possible for the parties to the conflict, constrained as they are by their commitments. Redefining the issues in a conflict, or finding a formula for its management or resolution, is the substantive key to its termination, and the parties frequently need help not only in finding a key hidden in the morass of bad relations but, more frequently, in inventing a key out of pieces of the conflict itself (Zartman and Berman, 1982). In this role, mediators need to add the qualities of creativeness and invention to the communicator's traits of tact and empathy, and must seek to discover the parties' real and basic interests, and their component ingredients.

Thus the roles of the mediator as communicator and formulator are facilitator roles, necessitated by a breakdown in physical and psychic aspects of communications that prevent the parties from working together to find a solution to their common problem. Mediators in these roles do nothing to change the nature of the problem or the circumstances of the conflict; at most, they work on perceptions. They are neutral hyphens in a dyadic relationship. This is "pure" mediation, in which they have no preference among solutions (except for a solution that satisfies the parties), exercise no power (except the power of persuasion to change people's minds), and have no weight (except the weight of the arguments required to get the parties' attention and confidence). As the exceptions show, nothing is pure in human relations; but mediators who carry messages and propose ideas for problem solving are engaged in about as pure an exercise in human relations as can be found.

In some situations, communication and innovation may not be enough to bring about the reduction of conflict or the promotion of self-interest. Mediators may have to take on a third, even more active role—that of *mediator as manipulator*, using their positions and other resources to move the parties into agreement, or perhaps into a particular agreement that appears most stable or favorable. This is a structural role, since it directly involves power and relations, and as such is a role of power politics. In this role, mediators transform the bargaining structure from a dyad into a triangle, and become actors with interests, or "full participants" (to use current diplomatic language), not just neutral intermediaries. American mediation between Egypt and Israel illustrates this role (Touval, 1982; Quandt, 1986). The parties may seek to reconvert the triadic relationship back into a dyad by forming a subtle coalition with the mediator, bringing that party in on one side or the other under the cover of its problem-solving guise, and thereby effecting a favorable solution preferable to continued conflict. It becomes the mediator's interest to counter such moves and keep the parties locked into a stalemate, ensuring that neither can prevail and therefore that both will look to the mediator for a way out of their deadlock. The triangular structure provides the mediator with bargaining power vis-à-vis the parties because of the constant possibility that it will join in a coalition with one against the other, or at least threaten to do so, if mediation fails. Parties too can use the triangular relations to discredit the mediator, labeling the mediator a tool or partner of the other party when they want to improve terms or withdraw their cooperation.

To achieve the goals of mediation, the country that mediates must use the triangular structure of relations to move both parties to agreement, rather than create a victory for one side. Yet, paradoxically, this may mean temporarily reinforcing one side to keep it in the conflict, to maintain the stalemate, and to preserve the triangular relationship. Mediation as power politics means maintaining the mediator's role, not simply allowing the parties to solve their own conflict by themselves; but it also means maintaining the parties' stalemate, not simply allowing one party to end the conflict by victory. This reinforcement can be physical, through tangible support for one party during the conflict, or it can be verbal, legitimizing one party's demands, but it must not be unconditional. Support should be used— implicitly or explicitly—to win the parties' commitment to join in a mediated agreement. The rationale is very sound within the dynamics of the conflict. A unilateral victory may not be stable because the defeated party may seek to overthrow it at the first occasion, and it may not be fair because the defeated party may have some important interests to be taken into account. But it may also not be desirable from the point of view of the mediator, who may have an interest in not seeing a party vanquished, or in seeing its own role maintained in the region. Stalemate is necessary to mediation, just as mediation is necessary to overcome stalemate.

Power in Mediation

The mediator can provide a way out of the stalemate in one of two ways: either by providing communications and ideas so attractive that they "naturally" lead the parties to agreement, or by adding arguments and inducements that make unattractive proposals look attractive. This distinction is useful conceptually, though it may be less so in practice. The mediator's power or ability to make the unpalatable palatable is often referred to as leverage (or power as an added value; see Zartman, 1974). Leverage is the ticket to mediation. Third parties are accepted as mediators only if they are likely to produce an agreement or help the parties out of a predicament, and for this they usually need leverage. This somewhat circular dilemma plagues every mediation exercise. Contrary to the common image, mediators are rarely "hired" by the parties; if they were, they would at least have a contract to perform the job of finding a solution. Instead, because they fear failure more than the parties do, they are more interested in ending the conflict, a position that actually weakens their leverage. In all eight cases studied, mediators staked their efforts and reputations on success at conflict resolution, while the parties clung to their conflict. Parties have a stake in winning. They criticize the mediator for meddling in their conflict and for not producing attractive outcomes. They welcome the mediator into the fray only to the extent that the mediator has leverage over the other party, and berate the mediator for trying to exert leverage over them.

There are only three sources of leverage, although each category may cover a number of different manifestations. Leverage comes first, from the parties' need for a solution that the mediator can provide; second, from the parties' susceptibility to shifting weight that the mediator can apply; and third, from the parties' interest in side payments that the mediator can either offer ("carrots") or withhold ("sticks"). It should be noted that in each case the source of the mediator's leverage lies with the parties, a characteristic that increases the difficulty of finding leverage (see Bell, 1971, p. 83, footnote 9).

The first source, the parties' perceived need for a solution, is extremely unstable, since it depends on a sometimes stubborn and sometimes flexible perception rather than an objective fact. As such, it responds above all to the mediator's persuasive skill in cutting through the noise of the situation, and changing the perceptions of the parties about the cost and benefits of alternative situations and outcomes. It is here that the mediator's role as communicator and formulator comes into play; the mediator must transmit and create information that will help change the parties' views about the ability of the proposals to fill their need for a way out of the conflict. The greater the parties' perceived need, the greater the mediator's leverage.

The second source, susceptibility to shifting weight, is even more delicate, since it involves both the mediator's ability to shift weight and the parties' sensitivity to that shift. The mediator must help maintain the balance between the parties in the conflict in a way that produces the painful stalemate that leads them to see a mediated solution as the best way out. The mediator must be able to tilt, threaten to tilt, or refrain from natural tilts toward one of the parties, but without being perceived as actually taking sides (Zartman, 1984). Shifting weight can be categorized in many ways: on a spectrum from tangible to intangible actions, such as arms supplies or U.N. votes; as negative or positive actions, such as statements or deliveries favorable or unfavorable to one side; or as present or future actions, such as condemnation of an attempt to change reality during the conflict, or condemnation of an incident or announced policy as an indication of a future attitude if the conflict were to continue. There does not seem to be any significant theoretical distinction to be made within these various typologies. Russia threatened to shift weight away from India in the Security Council debate on the Indo-Pakistani war, and Britain threatened to shift weight to the internal settlement in Rhodesia; the United States actually shifted some weight toward South Africa and avoided shifting weight against it in U.N. votes on the Namibian issue.

The third source, side payments, is perhaps less delicate, but it can be costly and can imply an ongoing commitment to a reform, which the mediator might want to avoid. Side payments, of course, should not have the appearance of buying adherence (which is what they do) but must be presented as a facilitating aspect of the general settlement. Secretary of State Henry Kissinger offered economic aid to the white Rhodesian settlers, Reagan offered economic aid to an Angola free of Cubans, and the OAS and Interamerican Development Bank (IDB) have told conflicting Latin American states that no development funds would be available until their conflict was settled.

Although this typology opens up possibilities for leverage, it also leaves some limitations common to all three types. Theoretically, the more ties mediators have with a party, and the more disposable goods they possess that the party values, the greater the potential they have for pressing the party by suspending ties and denying values. This insight is incontrovertible and forms the basis for the effective use of sticks—or, in reality, withheld carrots—in mediation. Unfortunately, it is only part of the story. Suspended ties also mean reduced influence, since certain elements of communication are thereby interrupted. Moreover, sticks of any kind cause resentment, and the party may decide it can just as well do without carrots in its diet rather than conceding to achieve their delivery. Finally, too intense a use of sticks can cause the party to withdraw its acceptance of the mediation, and turn the mediator into an intervenor or force the mediator out of a role altogether.

Leverage can also be seen as enhancing the mediator's ability to convey a future alternative preferable to the present conflict. Some of the inducements may be perceptional, produced indirectly by the mediator's ability to persuade the parties of a better outcome without conflict, and some may be tangible, produced directly by the mediator's ability to provide sweeteners of its own to add to the terms offered by the other side. But again there are limitations to the exercise of leverage. On the perceptional inducements, limits are imposed by the mediator's ability to convey convincingly or to produce a better outcome. Since the process of persuasion is gradual, the parties must be able to see each other's positions and concessions as initial steps, must be convinced that promises of concessions are deliverable, and must be able to feel that their own concessions will produce counterconcessions toward an acceptable midpoint of agreement by the other side (Bartos, in Zartman, 1978). Mediators dare not promise more than the other side can produce, and so their leverage on one party is limited by their leverage on the other. Limits are imposed on the sweeteners by the ability of the mediators themselves to pay, in a situation where the conflict is basically not their own, compounded by their limited ability to keep on paying (since sticks are put aside after they are successful, and carrots are expended when they are successful [Baldwin, 1971]). Our theory about the concept of leverage helps us understand more about its limitations than about how to increase it.

There are two major practical problems with leverage that these distinctions do not address: how to maximize it, and how to avoid counterproductive reactions. On these subjects the

Mediation in International Conflicts

cases give only limited insights. If anything, the cases reflect the anguish of mediators over the elusiveness of leverage and the unreasonable expectations of greater power under which they operate. Leverage, the cases indicate, comes above all from the first source—the parties' need for a solution that they cannot obtain without the mediator's help. The perception of this need can be enhanced by the mediator, but it cannot be created out of nothing. Side payments, the third source, can be useful when the mediation gets stuck, but they are not a major source of leverage throughout the process, and even at the end their use is limited—Kissinger in the disengagement negotiations between Israel and Egypt notwithstanding (see Zartman, in Rubin, 1981).

The first lesson, then, is that the mediator's challenge is primarily one of persuasion: to bring out the parties' sense of a need for help and enhance the first source of leverage. The second lesson is that the mediator's job is nonetheless dependent on the evolution of the conflict, on the particular conjuncture of forces that makes the undertaking appear as an opportunity for the parties to solve their problem at the least cost rather than as meddlesome distraction. Yet this lesson leads back to the first, for mediators cannot merely sit by until the parties feel the need with proper force. They must develop that need, arouse it, even anticipate it, so that as the moment ripens the parties will be ready to acknowledge and seize it. Parties come to agreement best when their own preferred solution is blocked but when they themselves are strong, so they can make a compromise decision and defend it against internal opposition. This condition, of course, makes mediation even more delicate, since strong opponents are difficult to deal with and are perhaps slower to see that their unilateral solutions are blocked.

Our discussion thus far is generally applicable to situations involving a single mediator and two antagonists. The process is considerably more complicated when several additional parties are involved, such as the mediation of the contact group over the Namibia question, in which five mediators and three principal antagonists took part (South Africa, SWAPO, and Angola). As in any multilateral negotiation, there are serious impediments that hinder effective mediation. A major problem is the need to accommodate so many interests, those of the several mediators and the several antagonists. The larger the number of participants, the more numerous the conflicting interests and the more complex the interrelations among them. While two antagonists may exchange concession, in a multi-lateral negotiation a concession offered to one participant may have variable effects on the rest, and may even be considered by some as detrimental to their interests. The need of the mediating group to coordinate its policies is another difficulty. Not only is the process cumbersome and time consuming, but the outcome is often a compromise that falls short of the coherence and consistency desirable in successful mediation.

Furthermore, in a multilateral setting, the mediator is likely to possess less leverage. Because of the participation of several parties, the mediator will have greater difficulty manipulating each participant and affecting its perceptions. The inducements that the mediator can provide, whether rewards or punishments, will also carry less weight. Unlike the single mediator who is the sole provider of inducements, in a multilateral setting there are likely to be several sources of rewards and punishment, neutralizing or at least diluting the mediator's influence.

Conclusion

This study of international mediation has assumed that mediators, as well as other actors, are motivated by self-interest. It has used an approach based on cost-benefit and power politics analysis of both mediators' and parties' interests as a key to motives, roles, and, above all, leverage. By taking mediation out of the realm of idealism and by bridging the artificial distinction between the disinterested facilitator and the interested manipulator, this analysis has sought to illuminate ways in which mediators have operated.

Most of the cases on which our analysis has been based were successful in reaching agreements, and many of them touched on core values. Yet, in the broadest sense, even where important issues were resolved, the mediation only provided conditions by which the parties could learn to live together; it did not effect any deep reconciliation of the parties or a restructuring of their perceptions of each other. One implication of this fact is that, left to their own devices, the parties may fall out of an agreement just as it is being made or implemented. For this reason, mediators should keep as firm a hand as possible on the procedures of settlement while helping the parties work out the substance of the solution. The physical presence of mediators in otherwise bilateral sessions between the conflicting parties, and their follow-through as observers and guarantors of any agreement's implementation, are important adjuncts to their role as communicators and builders of trust.

But mediators cannot chaperone forever, nor can they be expected to reorient all the perceptions underlying the conflict, perceptions that have often been years and even centuries in building. Successful though they were, the mediations did not change the basic distrust between Iran and Iraq, the United States and Iran, some blacks and whites in Zimbabwe, Indians and Pakistanis, Moroccans and Algerians, Somalis and Ethiopians. But to belittle their accomplishments on this account would be to measure them by superhuman standards. Mediators can be successful on three attainable levels. They can manage a conflict, by dampening or removing its violent means and manifestations. They can resolve a conflict, by arranging tradeoffs among its immediate causes and issues. They can provide mechanisms for handling future outbreaks of conflict among still suspicious and troubled parties. Any one of these is praiseworthy and shows skill; any combination is impressive.

References

Baldwin, D. "The Power of Positive Sanctions." *World Politics*, 1971, *24*, 19–38.

Bell, C. *Conventions of Crisis*. Oxford, England: Oxford University Press, 1971.

Berman, M. R., and Johnson, J. E. (eds.). *Unofficial Diplomats*. New York: Columbia University Press, 1977.

Campbell, J. C. *Successful Negotiation: Trieste 1954*. Princeton, N.J.: Princeton University Press, 1976.

Davidow, J. C. *A Peace in Southern Africa*. Boulder, Colo.: Westview, 1983.

Edmead, F. *Analysis and Prediction in International Mediation*. New York: UNITAR, 1971.

Fisher, R. *International Mediation: A Working Guide*. New York: International Peace Academy, 1978.

Gulliver, P. H. *Disputes and Negotiations: A Cross-Cultural Perspective*. Orlando, Fla.: Academic Press, 1979.

Ikle, F. C. *How Nations Negotiate*. New York: Harper & Row, 1964.

Jackson, E. *The Meeting of Minds: A Way to Peace Through Mediation*. New York: McGraw-Hill, 1952.

Pruitt, D. G. *Negotiation Behavior*. Orlando, Fla.: Academic Press, 1981.

Quandt, W. B. *Camp David*. Washington: The Brookings Institution, 1986.

Raiffa, H. *The Art and Science of Negotiation*. Cambridge, Mass.: Harvard University Press, 1982.

Raman, K. V. *The Ways of the Peacemaker*. New York: UNITAR, 1973.

Rubin, J. Z. (ed.). *Dynamics of Third Party Intervention: Kissinger in the Middle East*. New York: Praeger, 1981.

Touval, S. "Biased Intermediaries: Theoretical and Historical Considerations." *Jerusalem Journal of International Relations*, 1975, *1*, 51–69.

Touval, S. *The Peace Brokers: Mediators in the Arab-Israeli Conflict 1948–1979*. Princeton, N.J.: Princeton University Press, 1982.

Touval, S., and Zartman, I. W. (eds.). *International Mediation in Theory and Practice*. Boulder, Colo.: Westview, 1985.

Winham, G. "Multilateral Economic Negotiations." *Negotiation Journal*, 1987, *3*, 177.

Young, O. R. *The Intermediaries: Third Parties in International Crises*. Princeton, N.J.: Princeton University Press, 1967.

Zartman, I. W. "The Political Analysis of Negotiations." *World Politics*, 1974, *24*, 385–399.

Zartman, I. W. (ed.). *The Negotiation Process*. Beverly Hills, Calif.: Sage, 1978.

Zartman, I. W. *Ripe for Resolution: Conflict and Intervention in Africa.* New York: Oxford University Press, 1984.

Zartman, I. W. "The Middle East—The Ripe Moment?" In G. Ben-Dor and D. Dewitt (eds.), *Conflict Management in the Middle East.* Lexington, Mass.: Heath, 1987.

Zartman, I. W., and Berman, M. R. *The Practical Negotiator.* New Haven, Conn.: Yale University Press, 1982.

Zartman, I. W., and Touval, S. "International Mediation: Conflict Resolution and Power Politics." *Journal of Social Issues,* 1985, *41,* 27–45.

SEVEN

Can Negotiation Be Institutionalized or Mandated? Lessons from Public Policy and Regulatory Conflicts

Jonathan Brock
Gerald W. Cormick

Negotiation and mediation have been used with considerable success to resolve site-specific environmental and natural resource disputes (Bingham, 1986). Recently, these techniques have found growing interest and some application in regulatory disputes at the state and federal levels. Many of these disputes appear to be recurring; that is, the same or similar interests are joined in conflicts over similar issues under the purview of the same political or agency jurisdiction. So it is not surprising that there has been increasing interest in institutionalizing the use of mediation and related techniques (commonly designated alternate dispute resolution or ADR processes).

    This chapter reports on a study that examined the development and use of institutionalized ADR systems in various kinds of public policy conflicts. For purposes of the study, ADR systems were defined as those that use mediation or negotiation techniques to resolve disputes that would otherwise be resolved through adjudication in the courts, administrative bodies, or other forums. *Institutionalized systems* are statutory, regulatory, or other formal and continuing means of making negotiation and mediation available for settling disputes of a similar character.

Many ADR practitioners believe that complex issues of public policy presently addressed through administrative, regulatory, and judicial proceedings could better be solved by negotiation and mediation. They therefore have an interest in finding ways to institutionalize the process, to require everyone to enjoy its benefits. Our studies suggest that the perception of the need for such procedures is far higher among the ADR community than it is among potential user groups or political leaders. Even where there is a clear mandate for developing such procedures, providing the mechanisms within an institutionalized framework is complex and difficult. Often it is not even feasible. The case studies that follow set forth the bases for our skepticism.

Methods

This chapter draws primarily from four detailed case studies of attempts to institutionalize negotiation or mediation processes (Brock and Cormick, 1985). Our goal in these studies, completed in late 1984 and 1985, was to identify common factors in successful and unsuccessful attempts to institutionalize alternative dispute resolution systems.

Our research vehicle was the comparative case study. In selecting our cases we wanted variety in policy areas, geographical settings, and regulatory structure, but we also sought sufficient substantive similarity that the effects of different regulatory settings and traditions could be gauged. Two of the cases dealt with procedures to site hazardous-waste management facilities, one involved regulatory rate setting, and one resource allocation. We explicitly excluded from consideration alter-

native dispute resolution systems attached directly to the jurisdiction of a particular court.

The cases were prepared in the manner of Harvard Business School cases. They were written by different people to
ensure an independent look at the situations. Some were super-
vised jointly by Brock and Cormick, some were written by Brock.

Preliminary research on the subject germane to a case was
performed by the case writer or by someone working with the
case writer. This preliminary work served as a useful basis for
our case research and helped us to put our conclusions into
perspective. After the preliminary research was completed, the
case writer was selected and the work on the case itself was
begun. Access to case material and the important players in the
case was gained by contacting one or more key officials involved
in the situation. Through these contacts other potential infor-
mants were identified. Wherever possible, we sought to interview
people who held opposing points of view, to ensure a fair
description of what occurred.

Once drafted, copies of the cases were sent to most of
those we had interviewed, with a request to review the draft for
accuracy. These respondents did not have veto power, but in the
normal tradition of case writing, their permission was necessary
to gain access and to release the case. They also provided many
useful comments and criticisms that helped make the final case
report more accurate and complete. All final editorial judgments were made by the case writer in conjunction with the case
supervisor. Our conclusions also draw on other direct experiences — less thoroughly documented but no less relevant — and
from research and reports in the professional and academic
literature.

Resource Allocation

The Case. For decades, a bitter conflict over fishing rights
has raged between Pacific Northwest fish and game agencies,
non-Indian commercial fishermen, the sports fishing industry,
and nearly two dozen treaty tribes. During the past decade the
battle has been fought in the courts. Washington state was a

leading target and protagonist (United States v. Washington, 384 F. Supp. 312 W.D. Wash 1874; aff'd 520 F.2d 676 [9th Cir. 1975], Cert, denied, 423 U.S. 1086 [1976]). The litigation culminated in a Supreme Court ruling upholding a lower court decision that the treaties guaranteed the tribes the right to 59 percent of the catchable resource (popularly known as the Boldt decision after Judge Boldt). Unresolved even after the verdict were such issues as what portion of the resource was "catchable" (and, conversely, what portion needed to be permitted to escape to ensure propagation), how and where the catch would occur, and whether and how management of the resource would be shared. These issues led to some 250 court cases, virtually all of which were decided in favor of the tribes.

Several factors combined to complicate the issues and to provide broad scope for disagreement. First, all plans for catch limits are based on forecasts of the number of fish that would return from the open ocean, where they had gone three or more years earlier. The forecast was affected by such factors as the initial survival rate of juvenile fish, the impact of predators and other natural hazards, the prior catch of fishermen from Alaska and British Columbia in the open ocean during return migration, differences among species, and differences between hatchery and natural runs. To further complicate matters, tribes have traditional fishing grounds, which the fish would reach only after running the gauntlet of all the other fishing efforts, such as offshore trolling, river fisheries, and the like. Managers must ensure sufficient escapement that the last fishery has the opportunity to catch its share.

The disputes were complicated by racial overtones, and confrontations had grown sufficiently violent that the Coast Guard was required to separate the combatants. Congressional representatives were under constant pressure to introduce legislation to abrogate the treaties. The courts retained jurisdiction over the management of the fishery (the salmon fishing that took place in the areas affected by the treaty), appointing a master to oversee a joint state-tribal fisheries committee and make recommendations to the court in case of disagreement. In 1983, more than 75 disputes ended up before the court.

The disputes fall into two general categories: technical disputes, where state agencies and the tribes clash over opening and closing dates and catch limits for individual fisheries; and policy issues such as hatchery location, resource enhancement, and interjurisdictional rivalries. Because technical disputes concern immediate issues—a fish run was about to begin and would last for a short period—they were often referred to as emergency disputes requiring immediate adjudication. Policy disputes tended to fester and not be resolved.

There was general dissatisfaction with the existing dispute settlement procedures. They were expensive and embittering, decisions were seldom made in a timely manner, it was inappropriate and inefficient for the courts to be managing a complex resource, and there was a sense that the resource itself was suffering. However, the depth of the disenchantment with the existing procedures was difficult to gauge. The tribes seemed to be fairly well served by the courts, whose rulings had empowered them. And the state fisheries officials at times appeared to prefer that the courts order them to take measures that were unpopular with their non-Indian commercial and sports fishing constituencies, particularly since those constituencies were well represented in the legislature.

Meanwhile, Congress passed the Salmon and Steelhead Conservation and Enhancement Act of 1980, which established a Salmon and Steelhead Advisory Committee (SSAC) charged with developing and establishing a better dispute resolution system. There was evidence that the region's congressional delegation wanted to avoid being pressured into legislation or public positions that would further polarize the issues. Some two dozen tribes and government entities were affected, including the federal government and agencies in Oregon, Idaho, and Washington.

The SSAC drew its membership from the major interests in the dispute but had relatively low prestige. The lack of participation by key tribal leaders was particularly evident. Alternates, rather than actual members, usually attended the sessions. Dispute resolution, like other issues, was assigned to "task teams" for development at the staff level.

Other factors impeded the process. The tribes insisted that the courts be an integral part of any new dispute resolution process. The state agencies saw this as antithetical to their management responsibilities; they were also well aware of the more than 250 cases (on other than technical issues) that they had repeatedly lost. In some agencies it appeared impossible for staff members to reconcile themselves to cooperative efforts with tribal representatives—whatever the position of senior management.

The SSAC staff created a number of advisory committees to help develop recommendations for a dispute settlement process. There was relatively little tribal participation on the committees, as their membership was drawn largely from state and federal agencies. As a result there was neither effective representation of tribal concerns nor understanding or investment among tribal leaders in the recommendations that were developed.

Another complicating factor was the need to develop a system that could accommodate three different state resource management structures. Idaho, Oregon, and Washington have very different administrative structures in fisheries management. It was difficult to design a process that worked for all three: Hence, the boundaries of the dispute were not conducive to gaining agreement on a dispute resolution system.

The task teams worked well together and reached a consensus on the structure of a proposed system. However, they had difficulty getting the attention of the key leadership figures. At SSAC sessions, members were often not well prepared and the discussions tended toward generalities. The principals expressed little or no support for the recommendations, and they were unable to agree on a mechanism. Discussions centered on such broad issues as loss of autonomy and local authority. As a result, the final report of the SSAC contained little more than a description of general goals and principles that should be included in any dispute system.

Progress from Failure. The SSAC proceedings were not, however, entirely wasted. Constructive discussions were held between interests who had little previous experience in working together. The possibilities for creating dispute settlement systems were explored, and important dispute settlement concepts became familiar.

The situation changed in 1983, when El Niño (an abnormally warm ocean current arising in the South Pacific) combined with other factors to cause disaster for the Northwest salmon fishery. A Seattle newspaper editorial asked, "Will we still be fighting over the last fish?" There was now a crisis for all involved; there was now widespread dissatisfaction with the existing system.

The director of the Washington state Department of Fisheries asked James Waldo, an attorney with credibility in both state government and the Indian community, to convene a meeting of departmental and tribal leaders. A former U.S. Attorney who had represented the interests of the tribes in some of their court victories, Waldo was actively involved in state and national Republican politics and had served on the campaigns of Washington Governor John Spellman and U.S. Senator Daniel Evans.

Waldo conferred with major state and tribal leaders and, with their endorsement, called a "Salmon Summit." Only principals were invited to attend. Technical and legal advisers were left at home. Before the first session the parties also engaged the services of a mediator experienced in complex public issues. In presession discussions the representatives tentatively agreed to limit their geographic and substantive focus to issues arising from the fishery in Puget Sound, Washington. This narrowed geographic boundary enabled the participants to focus their efforts within the confines of a single state structure, involved only about a dozen tribes, most of whom had experience in working together on other issues, and represented a manageable number of fish species and runs.

A major breakthrough came when the fisheries director made a commitment to move beyond the question of who had the right to manage the fishery—a subject of recurring litigation—and instead work toward agreement on how best to manage the fishery. The first meeting focused on creating a framework for the continuing talks.

From this first meeting there emerged a self-selected

working group committed to resolving major policy issues and developing a process for settling disputes over technical issues. Key policy people, including the well-regarded director of the Department of Fisheries and respected tribal leaders, took personal responsibility for the effort. As the process continued, smaller working groups of technical people were created to provide information and generate options for implementing policy agreements.

To address polarized public perceptions, there was a conscious, extensive effort to involve the media. This resulted in broad issue-oriented coverage and editorial support for the effort.

And the results? The state and tribes successfully resolved a large number of policy issues, addressed concurrent technical disputes on an ad hoc basis, and agreed on the design of a dispute settlement system. (That system began operation in early 1986.) One measure of the success of this effort is the fact that the parties had no court determinations of technical issues during the year they worked together; in the previous year there had been eighty.

Discussion. This tandem set of fisheries cases provides an unusual opportunity to compare and contrast factors important to the development of dispute settlement procedures. The formal dispute resolution process developed as a result of the Salmon Summit began operation in 1986 as a result of the court-ordered Puget Sound Salmon Management Plan. The parties are following an agreed-upon schedule for its implementation. They have, for example, retained the services of a mediator, and the tribes recently held a joint training session for representatives expected to participate in the process.

Most of the failure of the SSAC effort can be traced to the lack of commitment of the tribes and the state, an inappropriate forum for addressing the matter, overly ambitious boundaries, and absence of some key actors. The need for a process and the mechanisms for developing it were the result of external decisions made by others, in this case key congressional representatives. They, in turn, saw the SSAC effort as a way of protecting themselves from the continuing importunities of the conflicting interests. Key tribal leaders appeared relatively satisfied with, although not enamored of, the existing court-dominated system. The state was less satisfied, but not sufficiently disenchanted or sanguine about the prospects of a new system to commit time and resources to the effort to replace it. In addition, years of battling tribal involvement in fishery management had hardened substantial opposition within departments to any joint efforts with the tribes. In a process organized along bureaucratic lines, such sentiment might be expected to be determinative.

The Waldo-initiated effort, on the other hand, arose from a crisis situation: the condition of the resource itself had begun to overshadow issues of politics and principle. The SSAC process was generated externally; the Salmon Summit was initiated by the parties at interest. The SSAC process lacked meaningful involvement of key leadership persons; the second effort involved them from the outset.

The SSAC effort also suffered from the lack of any influential leader whose primary interest was making the process work. The participants' major concerns continued to be adequately representing the interests of their own constituents. Waldo was committed to helping the parties agree on both substance and process. In the SSAC effort the chair limited his role largely to presiding over formal meetings. In the Salmon Summit, Waldo and the mediator had extensive involvement with the parties between sessions, testing alternatives, narrowing disagreements, and ensuring that acceptable background materials were developed. Frankness and informality characterized these talks.

The difference in roles played by staff was also important. In the SSAC process the staff defined the problems, generated the alternatives, and made reports to the policy people. In the Waldo process key policy makers defined the problems, addressed the differences, and wrestled with alternatives. Technical staff—biologists and lawyers—responded to requests, providing data, researching alternatives, and fleshing out agreements in principle readied by the parties themselves.

The differences in boundaries between the two efforts also played a major role. In the SSAC effort the need to craft a process that would meet the demands of the bureaucracies of three states, dozens of tribes, and widely varying fisheries made it difficult to develop a focus beyond the most general principles. The Waldo process focused on a narrower geographic definition and involved a smaller set of actors and issues. This led to working relationships among key leaders with a history and a continuing need to work together.

Finally, while the SSAC process focused on how to resolve issues of fact and equity, the essential problem of the tribes' right to participate in management and planning for the resource remained unresolved. While never on the table, it lurked behind the concerns and positions of the parties. In the Waldo effort, that issue was explicitly addressed and resolved. This not only clarified the situation but provided a basis of goodwill and sense of commitment upon which to build.

The clearest lesson to be learned from comparing these two situations may be that agreement on a dispute settlement process is not possible until the principals perceive that it is in their collective self-interest to develop the system for themselves.

Regulation and Rate Setting

The Case. When a new commissioner was appointed to the three-member Washington State Utilities and Transportation Commission, one of her first suggestions was that the commission experiment with using negotiation in rate setting and rule making. Under the existing process of contested hearings, the commission acted as judge and arbitrator in lengthy, ponderous, and backlogged hearings. The primary protagonists were the commission staff and the utility or transportation company, who argued their positions as relatively equal parties in a rate case, conducted much like a court proceeding. The public interest was represented by a public counsel appointed by the attorney general. While the process was conducted in a formal and legalistic manner, it was not unlike other rule-making procedures where informal bargaining settles points at issue and sometimes the case itself. For example, it was not unusual that a formal agreement, stipulating to facts and data, and often to a rate increase, was negotiated before the hearing.

The existing process had been developed for a regulatory milieu that no longer existed. Historically, utilities would seek rate increases every couple of years, and the facts in the case were relatively straightforward. Now, process and staff capacity were strained by frequent filings for rate increases brought about by wide fluctuations in energy prices, rapidly rising construction costs, technological advances, and deregulation of telephone utilities. Contested hearings were a satisfactory forum for settling narrow issues of cost assessment and rate calculations, but complex issues of public policy—equitable sharing of service, delivery costs between urban and rural customers, and special provisions for elderly or low-income groups—did not fit the process as well. The complexity and volume of cases engendered by these societal changes suggested the desirability of an alternative.

The commissioners concurred with the suggestion of their new colleague and formally authorized an experiment: a rate case would be handled using "principled negotiations" (see Fisher and Ury, 1983). The experimental negotiations were to be carried out within the existing regulatory structure.

Many of the commission staff members were uncomfortable with the idea. Some felt that entering into explicit negotiations and agreements would be constraining, denying them some of their power over the companies. They also feared that negotiating with "the enemy" might prove professionally damaging or place them in an ineffectual position. For example, under the existing system, whatever the outcome of their informal bargaining with the company, they maintained their special status before the commission, because they worked on other matters as staff and advisers to the commission. If formal agreements were reached they would be limited to what was agreed to. Other staff members were opposed for exactly the opposite reason: they felt that the special status of the staff would make negotiation as relative equals impossible.

The commission moved very quickly to begin the experiment. It selected a telephone rate case involving a small company with a good reputation for service whose president was a leader in the independent phone company community. For a facilitator the commission selected an assistant attorney general with expertise in telecommunications policy, technology, and law. He had significant credibility with both the utility and commission staff. He was informally detailed to the process by the deputy attorney general, with the understanding he would have no involvement in the case beyond the negotiations.

The commission asked the deputy attorney general to appoint a public counsel to participate in the negotiations. This request was refused, perhaps because of reluctance to grant further legitimacy to a process that was not yet clearly defined and where the risks to the agency appeared to outweigh any benefits. Further, legal training and experience until recently has considered only the more formal adversarial processes appropriate to such disputes.

Consumer groups and key elected officials in the service area were alerted that the negotiations were about to begin. State legislators and their staffs who had an interest or responsibility in telecommunications were also alerted.

The negotiations began with little prior experience or preparation, although the telephone company had been through a similar program in Oregon. Basic procedures were worked out at the outset. Small joint task forces were used extensively to collect and assess data and develop alternatives. The negotiating meetings were announced and open to the public. However, in only one session did anyone attend. On the other hand, public meetings were held in the service area and, unlike in formal commission hearings, there was a good deal of discussion of issues and concerns.

Reaching agreement took six months, compared to eleven months for the average contested case hearing. The joint agreement was presented as a normal filing by the utility, and the staff filing was an assent to the company's request. During a public hearing on the filing (which, since it was not contested, could be scheduled sooner and for a shorter period of time), only the public counsel, who was finally appointed after negotiations had been concluded, raised an objection.

When the agreement was assessed, there was general concurrence that the rate increase was less than might have been expected. Beyond the statement of tariffs and other formal and cryptic references, the filing contained an explanation of the process and issues, including matters not required by law. (These would not have been part of the formal hearings, but because they arose in connection with the hearings, the company wished to attend to them.) Time had been saved by all parties. The process had also required the commission and its staff to clarify requirements and objectives and educated a company somewhat unfamiliar with Washington's current requirements. The level of public participation was high, and no formal procedural steps were bypassed.

The commission was satisfied that the experiment, as a negotiated rate case, was a success. As a result, the commission invited leaders in the telecommunications industry, commission staff, and consumer interests to develop a standard process for selecting cases for negotiation and procedures for guaranteeing that the rights and responsibilities of all parties were defined and protected.

This attempt was blocked by strong opposition from several sources. A few consumer advocates, concerned with due process, open government, and consumer involvement, led the resistance. The public counsel raised concerns about whether it could become involved in a timely or constructive manner. A number of key legislators and staff expressed similar concerns. The opposition resulted in legislative action that attached a clause to the commission budget forbidding the use of any funds for negotiation of cases under its jurisdiction.

Discussion. This situation could be described as a successful experiment that failed to become a continuing process. A number of factors contributed to the failure.

First, the haste to begin the experiment contributed to a lack of internal and external support for the process. Its champion was the newest commission member, who may have lacked the contacts and credibility necessary to sell the concept to key statewide leaders. There was insufficient prior discussion with senior officials in the legislature, with consumer advocate groups, with agency staff, and with the state Department of Justice. The absence of the public counsel in the process confirmed the worst suspicions of consumer and other advocacy groups, who regarded the counsel as a protector of their interests. In short, some mitigating marketing was needed. Alternate dispute resolution processes are too often sold on the basis that existing legal processes are slow, expensive, and fail to deal with the real issues separating the parties. True or not, this approach tends to ensure the opposition of those who see their protection in existing procedures. This factor appeared to be operating in the limited cooperation of the Department of Justice, the agency staff, consumer groups, and others.

The case also highlights the difference between those primarily concerned with substantive outcomes (usually direct parties), and those concerned with principles and procedures (usually indirect parties). The consumers in the actual delivery area supported the process and the outcome. More broadly based groups, whose support was vital to the ultimate institutionalizing of the process, had no role in the experimental negotiations because they were not affected by the immediate service-delivery issues. This turned out to be a costly exclusion. Time invested at the outset, involving them in designing the procedures, monitoring the process, and assessing the outcome, might have won their support for translating the experiment into a continuing process.

A similar problem occurred with the legislature. Because key legislators and their staff were not carefully and consistently briefed, they were generally uninformed about the process — except by opponents. Thus, assertions of those opponents that the process would result in back-room deals shutting out legitimate public interests found fertile ground.

In sum, while the experiment was a success there was no meaningful constituency for translating the experiment into an ongoing process. It is clear that implementing an alternate dispute settlement process requires much more than demonstrating its value in a specific situation. There must be a strategy for capturing the interest, or at least the neutrality, of indirect actors whose support or acquiescence will be necessary, even though they are not particularly concerned about the outcome of a particular situation.

Siting

The Massachusetts Hazardous Waste Facility Siting Act of 1980.
There was general consensus within the Massachusetts industrial and environmental communities that the lack of facilities
for disposing of hazardous industrial wastes was a critical environmental problem. In 1979 State Senator Carol Amick, a
primary spokesperson for environmental issues and chair of the
Natural Resources and Agriculture Committee, introduced a
bill intended to govern the handling of such wastes. In addition
to provisions regulating the operation of facilities, the bill specified means by which new facilities would be sited. Among the
new siting tools was use of the state's power of eminent domain.
Amick, her staff, and the bill's cosponsors spent a good deal of
time and effort educating other legislators on the need for such
facilities and their proper regulation. Despite opposition from
some of the business interests that would be regulated, the bill
had broad support and its passage seemed assured.

Concurrently, the Department of Environmental Management had commissioned a study to identify sites in the state
appropriate for hazardous-waste management facilities. As the
hazardous-waste bill came up for consideration, the results of
the study, recommending three sites for consideration, were
leaked to the press. Legislators from the three towns immediately introduced, and got passed, bills forbidding the facilities
in their towns. Other legislators became concerned that the
Amick bill could lead to facilities in their districts, and chances
for its passage evaporated.

To save the regulatory and management aspects of her
bill, Amick severed the section specifying the siting process,
substituting a provision that established a special legislative
commission to develop siting procedures for submission to the
legislature. With this change, the Hazardous Waste Management
Act of 1979 was passed.

The commission established by the act was composed of
five members from the House, three (including Amick, although
she was not the chair) from the Senate, seven state environmental and health officials, and one representative each of local

health officers, boards of health, industry, and the general public. The commission hired a small staff and in February 1980 began working against its July 1 deadline.

The major issue was local control, with the controversy over sites on everyone's mind. Massachusetts's 351 cities and towns fiercely guard their rights to home rule. Town meetings to decide budgets and referenda on sensitive issues are common. Minutes of the commission meetings indicate that by April the commissioners had yet to find a means of balancing the issue of local control with the threat to public health and economic development posed by the lack of suitable waste-management facilities.

In early April the staff assumed leadership and presented a suggested approach. Two consultants, Professors Alan Weinstein from the University of Wisconsin and Lawrence Bacow from the Massachusetts Institute of Technology (MIT), presented a proposal for applying negotiations and compensation to conflicts over waste-facility siting. They argued that local communities could effectively block siting through legal and political avenues, but that with negotiated compensation packages (direct payments and other benefits) local communities might be willing to accept, perhaps even seek, such facilities.

The chair announced that all members would receive a copy of model legislation for facilities siting prepared by Bacow and a related paper coauthored by Michael O'Hare (representing the Department of Environmental Affairs on the commission) and one of Bacow's former colleagues at MIT. The O'Hare paper discussed the imbalance between the local costs of having an undesirable facility nearby and the broader benefits to the state of having the facility available. Compensation could help to redress this imbalance and, combined with education, reduce resistance.

On April 24, the staff presented a proposal that laid out a specific structure and process for siting facilities using negotiations and compensation. The commissioners at first resisted, fearing that such a specific proposal would "lock us in." The staff director convinced them that the proposal was only a draft and subject to change.

Several more meetings followed, during which the commission heard general testimony from environmental and industry representatives on the need for sites and debated whether to include siting criteria in its recommendations. Meanwhile, the staff were using members' written comments to refine the proposed process, and on June 25 the commission adopted the staff proposal as its report. After only one major amendment (changing the siting council from twelve to twenty-one members) and no debate, a bill specifying the new siting process was passed in the final hours of the legislative session.

The legislation established a twenty-one member siting council to oversee the negotiation and compensation elements of the process. The council has eight designated representatives of state departments, seven of specified interests or technical competencies, and six of the unspecified public. Two ad hoc members may be added to represent communities under consideration. Among the council's powers and responsibilities are (1) to determine which projects are "feasible and deserving of state assistance" (within fifteen days of notice of intent); (2) to appoint local assessment committees to represent the local community in negotiations if the local government fails to do so; (3) to declare an impasse in negotiations between a local assessment committee and the developer of a site; and (4) to appoint an arbitrator to resolve impasses.

The council started slowly. A staff director was not appointed until November 1981. Its elected chair was Dr. Norton Nickerson, a professor at Tufts University known for his work on environmental problems. Early in 1981 the council received its first three proposals for siting—long before the council had established its procedures or hired staff. The first was a proposal by SRS Company to build a facility in Haverhill. Under the pressure of the fifteen-day deadline to determine feasibility (and the fact that SRS had only a ten-day option on the land), the council voted seventeen to four in favor. Five minutes later, the mayor of Haverhill reportedly snapped, "Over my dead body!" The battle lines were drawn. (Local leaders had first been briefed by SRS forty-eight hours before submission of notice of intent to the council.)

Although a local assessment committee was established, the community was solidly opposed to the proposal. Council meetings were vitriolic. Negotiations were never begun. Revocation of the feasibility determination was sought on the basis of new information alleging that SRS had been sued by EPA for Superfund violations, that one of its plants had recently had a major explosion, and that still another was in violation of local sewer ordinances.

The other two proposals were also deemed feasible and deserving. In one, the establishment of a facility in the southeast, local leaders actually invited firms to propose a facility. However, even in this situation local opposition emerged. In the other, opposition grew when it was revealed that the proposed facility might become the largest in the nation, with the capacity to serve "the entire East Coast and as far west as Ohio" (Beem, 1985, p. 16).

The fifteen-day determination of feasibility, intended by the drafters of the procedures to screen out the most clearly undeserving proposals, had become a major new arena for conflict and source of delay, as lawsuits charged lack of due process and similar procedural allegations.

In response to the litigation, the council adopted very formal rules and procedures, producing verbatim transcripts of every meeting. The council was constantly moving between technical and political considerations. As Chair Nickerson observed, "They're not dealing with the substance. They're spending their time on politics." He also observed that running a twenty-one member body had its difficulties. Implementing his philosophy of making sure that all representatives had a chance to say their piece was very time consuming.

By late 1982 no negotiations had begun. The governor withdrew his support for siting the facility in Haverhill. No new proposals were generated, and in 1986 a new state administration ceased attempts to site facilities under the act.

The Wisconsin Solid and Hazardous Waste Siting Act of 1982. Since 1977, legislation had permitted Wisconsin's Department of Natural Resources (DNR) to waive local approvals if waste facility sites met all of DNR's licensing requirements. However, in

1980 the state Supreme Court ruled that DNR could not override local zoning ordinances. This made it virtually impossible to site a facility in the face of community opposition, since a zoning ordinance could be passed that explicitly excluded the facility. Meanwhile the DNR was under pressure to close a large number of old waste-disposal sites that threatened public health.

The private waste-management community, other industry groups, and citizen interests felt strongly that new legislation was required. Legislators concurred, and Representative Mary Lou Munts, the leading environmental legislator in the state and an acknowledged master at obtaining compromise in legislative negotiations, agreed to lead the effort. She had orchestrated the effort that resulted in the 1977 consensus legislation now undercut by the court ruling.

Wisconsin has a history of successfully addressing such problems through special committees established by the legislative leadership and representing both houses and public members. While it was too late to establish a formal legislative committee during the current session, Munts received the permission of the leadership to form an ad hoc committee (AHC) staffed by the legislative council. Munts and Senator Thomas Harnisch, chair of the Senate Natural Resources Committee and an environmental activist, were appointed to cochair the AHC. It was initially estimated that the effort would take six months, later extended to eighteen months.

Members of the AHC reflected the potential parties to a siting process. The waste-management industry was represented by its attorney and chief lobbyist; waste generators by the lobbyist for the Association of Manufacturers and Commerce and by representatives of the foundry and electric utilities. (All were veterans of the 1977 legislative effort.) Legislative members included Senator Strohl, urban Democrat, environmental advocate, and chair of the Senate Energy Committee; Senator Hanaway, rural Republican with strong ties to local government and industry; Representative Fischer, rural Democrat and former local government official who had several waste facilities proposed in his district; and Representative Knox, a Republican with strong ties to the manufacturing industry.

Local interests were represented on the committee by a well-known local planning director and director of public works. The public intervenor, a state official responsible to a citizen advisory board and with authority to intervene in proceedings relating to environmental and resource issues, was also a member. (The intervenor had intervened on behalf of local governments opposing waste facilities.) Citizen interests were represented by the League of Women Voters. Environmental groups chose not to participate, citing the need to focus scarce resources elsewhere; they felt their interests were well represented by Munts.

Statewide county and town organizations also chose not to participate. Having recently achieved the court victory upholding their zoning rights, it would have been difficult politically for them to participate in an effort designed to dilute their authority.

Munts made it clear that the purpose of the AHC was to reach a consensus on a legislative package. In her words, their charge was to "balance the state's need for hazardous-waste facilities and the local government's need to provide for orderly development." The AHC determined that it was necessary to differentiate among processes for determining the need for the facility, the technical adequacy of the site and facility design, and the socioeconomic impacts on the host community. They decided that on the basis of the overall situation and the cost of preparing a site proposal, need should be assumed. They also decided to separate technical and scientific issues from the social and political debate and to leave them to formal determinations through administrative hearings via DNR. The discussion of how to handle the questions of local impacts led the AHC to consider using negotiations.

To develop a viable negotiating process, Munts sought the assistance of Howard Bellman, an experienced labor mediator and arbitrator with experience in the fledgling field of environmental mediation. Bellman had recently completed a study of

Wisconsin's public-sector labor law for the legislature. He counseled that any structure had to provide clear incentives to negotiate and procedures that enabled the parties to define and address the issues. With his assistance the AHC developed procedures for selection and composition of the local negotiating committee, defined the range of negotiable topics, established a series of deadlines, provided for mediation assistance, established arbitration procedures, and included a default provision.

In another development that would prove important, the AHC began to recognize the close parallels between solid- and hazardous-waste facility-siting problems and decided to include both under the same siting process.

As the shape of the consensus became evident, the Towns Association lobbyist was invited to participate. The association now felt that the towns could no longer ignore the process. The majority of its members did not have local zoning authority (they were covered by county zoning) and therefore were not covered by the court action. For them the negotiations process was attractive. They joined the AHC.

As the end of 1981 neared, time to introduce the legislation in the current legislative session began to run short. Munts introduced a draft bill in her committee, representing her general sense of a consensus. She also had a series of individual meetings with key interests, seeking to forge the consensus. Her bill was amended in committee to represent some key accommodations and then forwarded to the legislature. The legislators on the AHC successfully countered amendments from the floor to protect the overall integrity of the bill, and on May 4, 1982, the governor signed it into law as recommended.

The act established a seven-member Waste Facility Siting Board (WFSB) to oversee the negotiation process. It is composed of two members nominated by the Towns Association, one by the Association of Counties, and four cabinet-level secretaries representing state agencies related to the waste-siting process. DNR is not on the board. The board determines questions such as whether issues are negotiable, can declare a party in default if there is not a good faith effort to negotiate, and ultimately serves as arbitrator. The WFSB has an executive secretary to administer the daily activities and provide staff services. The initial executive secretary was Cynthia Sampson, a former colleague of Bellman's with experience in negotiation and mediation procedures in environmental and public policy issues.

In 1983, as the board was beginning operation and the initial negotiations were under way, opponents to the act attached amendments to the fiscal 1984 budget designed to weaken the law by introducing a requirement to consider need for the facility as a first step in the process. While some opponents saw the amendment as a means of halting the siting process at the initial stage, others were troubled by an individual situation where a landowner apparently sought to increase the value of his property by getting a facility siting permit, even though a nearby landfill had more than fifteen years' capacity remaining. Political realities made the amendment difficult to oppose and it passed the legislature. However, with the encouragement of Munts and other supporters of the process, the governor vetoed the amendment and was not overridden.

By mid 1987 nearly one hundred siting proposals had been considered under the act. Several have been sited as a result of successful negotiations. In one case the parties reached agreement with the assistance of a mediator. No disputes have yet proceeded to arbitration. The first several dozen cases involved nonhazardous-waste facilities. However, as the process proved successful and withstood legal and political challenges, hazardous-waste facilities began to be proposed under the act. Twenty-eight such facilities have received substantial consideration. Of those, four had been settled and one actually licensed by the end of 1988 (Jane First, Wisconsin Facility Waste Siting Board, telephone conversation with the author, February 1989).

Discussion. The Massachusetts and Wisconsin cases provide an opportunity to compare contemporaneous efforts to develop a dispute settlement process. While there were important differences, such as Wisconsin's strong history of cooperative politics, there were also important similarities. In both states there was a general sense of crisis. In each state a respected legislative leader stepped forward to lead the effort. In both

states local government interests were opposed to any mechanism that threatened local independence. And, in both situations, negotiation was proposed as the basis of the siting
process.

There were, however, critical differences in three areas:
involvement of direct and indirect actors, the design characteristics of the process, and the initial implementation
experience.

In Massachusetts, legislation established a working committee with specified membership to design the process. The
membership was not particularly representative of the expected
users, key leadership figures, or other key indirect parties. Senator Amick, the initial champion of the process, was not asked to
chair the effort. In Wisconsin a flexible, familiar, and respected
procedure was used. Ad hoc committee members were selected
for their ability to represent important affected constituencies,
and a strong champion, Representative Munts, established and
managed the process. The AHC mandate permitted the addition of new members as necessary.

The two process-design bodies also operated differently.
Whereas the Massachusetts proposal was developed primarily
by consultants and staff, with members responding and com-
menting, the Wisconsin AHC itself clearly developed proposals
and directions and staff were used to flesh out and add particular expertise. Of particular importance was Munts's efforts to
forge a consensus outside the formal meetings.

While both efforts created siting authorities, the Wisconsin Waste Facility Siting Board was small enough to work effectively, provided for nomination of members directly from local
government, and had a clearly defined role that prevented it
from becoming mired in technical discussions. The twenty-one-
member Massachusetts siting council was never able to operate
efficiently and was constantly distracted by the confusion between political and technical considerations. The Wisconsin
board moved quickly to establish procedures and appointed a
staff director with relevant experience in negotiating siting and
other environmental disputes. The Massachusetts council did
not create procedures until after major problems arose in its

initial cases. The staff director, hired more than a year after the council was established, had no experience in the use of dispute settlement processes.

A number of design features differentiate the two processes. The Wisconsin design recognizes different types of issues (need, technical design, and local socioeconomic impacts) and provides differing procedures for each. The Massachusetts council was left to wrestle with all three and never succeeded in dealing with them. For example, technical issues were left in a political forum. The Wisconsin negotiation procedures created incentives to negotiate, set clear deadlines, specified issues for negotiation, and established a strong and threatening arbitration process. It also developed mediation procedures to assist the parties. In Massachusetts there was simply an assumption in design that, if there was provision of compensation, negotiations would naturally follow.

Finally, the initial implementation experience in the two states differed. The Wisconsin board had experience and involvement in waste-siting issues and a staff director with relevant experience. In Massachusetts the siting council was more political and staff was not appointed until after the first cases had been received. Massachusetts was further hindered by two initial siting proposals that were especially controversial because of the alleged poor prior performance of one company and the overwhelming size of the proposal facility in the second. In Wisconsin the first proposals were less overwhelming and controversial. Of particular interest is that the initial hazardous-waste proposals were introduced *after* the process had established credibility and a track record on nonhazardous issues.

Lessons from the Four Cases

As the cases demonstrate, it is difficult to institutionalize dispute settlement systems that make use of negotiation and mediation. However unsatisfactory existing administrative and legal systems may be, they are familiar and there are those who have a strong vested interest in maintaining and replicating them. To change to a negotiation-based process requires an unusual confluence of circumstances.

Drawing on the lessons from the cases described in this chapter and other experience, we determined a number of factors that seem to be critical in determining whether it will be possible to design and implement a system that uses negotiation for settling recurring disputes. (See Brock, 1982, for a formal framework for assessing viability of dispute resolution systems.)

First, there must be sufficient disenchantment with the status quo to force otherwise disparate interests to consider the need for new approaches. This was particularly clear in comparing the Salmon and Steelhead Advisory Committee with the subsequent Salmon Summit. The telephone rate case shows that a successful demonstration of the use of negotiation to settle one typical case will not be sufficient to convince the principals that a change is necessary.

Second, both the direct and indirect interests must concur in the design and development of the new process. The latter should also be informed or represented in the initial implementation. The telephone rate case lacked the acquiescence of these key interests.

Third, the interests must be represented by key leadership figures who can effectively and realistically represent their constituents and who can vouch for any system that is agreed upon. The interests or parties must be sufficiently organized and cohesive to permit such representation. The SSAC and Massachusetts attempts failed to meet this test. The Salmon Summit and Wisconsin met this criterion and implemented working systems.

Fourth, development takes time and requires flexibility. If the time allotted is too short and inflexible, it may not be possible to build the kind of informed consensus necessary to develop a functional process. Massachusetts was saddled by a short time frame and rigid structures imposed by legislation. In Wisconsin the initial estimate of six months for the process was expanded to more than a year and other interests were brought into the discussion as the situation dictated.

Fifth, there is a need for a strong champion, with the

stature to bring together the key actors and represent the effort to legislative and other affected interests. As we saw with Waldo in the Salmon Summit and Munts in the Wisconsin case, it is especially useful if that champion also has the ability to play a mediation role and has wide outside contacts. The SSAC and Massachusetts cases show that merely having a chairperson with a title who presides at official meetings is seldom sufficient. As in site-specific disputes, a strong and effective mediator can make a critical difference in negotiating a consensus.

Sixth, the process by which the dispute settlement system is developed should be dominated by principals. While useful ideas and concepts may be contributed by staff and experts, the system must be designed by those who will be using it if they are to have a commitment to making it successful. The Wisconsin and Salmon Summit cases are examples of a good balance of interaction and input by principals and staff.

Seventh, the boundaries of the range of issues and parties to be addressed by the system must be adequately and sufficiently defined to permit bringing together all the key principals and developing a mechanism that is appropriate to the various administrative and bureaucratic structures with which it must interact. The SSAC and Salmon Summit cases demonstrate how fitting the boundaries of the proposed system to parties and issues that can reasonably be handled enhances the ability to engage the major actors and construct a viable mechanism.

Eighth, the process that is designed must recognize what is required to foster and conduct negotiations. As the Wisconsin case illustrates, there is much to be learned from the labor-management context, where negotiation processes have a long and successful history of use.

Ninth, the initial experience in implementing a new system will be critical. It is important to have the implementation in the hands of those who understand negotiations and who can assist the parties in using the process. Oversight of the implementation should continue to involve representatives of the major users and other concerned interests to maintain support for the system. The Wisconsin successes and Massachusetts problems illustrate the importance of these factors.

Tenth, those considering the development systems should resist the temptation to import dispute settlement systems that have been successful elsewhere under similar circumstances or to use theory off the shelf. This may only ensure the system's failure. It is the joint efforts of principals to grapple with a crisis and reach consensus on a system that meets their substantive and political needs that is the essential ingredient in making the system work.

Finally, as we saw with the SSAC and Wisconsin experience, failed efforts can lay the substantive and relational groundwork for future success. It may even be useful to think in terms of pilot projects and demonstration efforts. As the Wisconsin experience indicates, building a record of success and legitimacy can provide the foundation for moving to more difficult issues and conflicts. And, as the telephone rate case demonstrates, key affected indirect interests need to be supportive or tolerant as well.

It is not surprising that these criteria are the same as those that characterize the successful use of the negotiation-mediation process in site-specific conditions (Cormick, 1982). However, establishing an institutionalized mechanism is likely to be far more hazardous and problematic than resolving a specific conflict.

To institutionalize a system, the intended user interests or direct parties must agree that such a mechanism is desirable. However, because the mechanism is intended to address a series of recurring disputes, the number of potentially affected interests or parties is likely to be larger than normally found in a single conflict situation. This complicates getting agreement on or acceptance of the institutionalized process. Further, since many parties to site-specific conflicts are mobilized by specific proposed actions, it may be difficult to find bona fide representatives who can speak for and to potential user interests.

In addition to these direct or user interests, there is a second set of interests in the political, administrative, and regulatory arenas whose acquiescence must also be forthcoming. These indirect parties may include key legislators, attorneys general, members of regulatory boards, and others who will assert their legitimate interest in process and possibly sub-stance. Many of their concerns — such as matters of turf and due process — may be divorced from the purposes of the dispute settlement mechanism. They may have little or no interest in the specific substantive issues being addressed. Our research sug-gests that it may be difficult to gain their agreement without imposing conditions on the mechanism that threaten its viability or its ability to handle well the substantive issues, or that make it unacceptable to representatives of the intended user interests.

In sum, although we have identified factors that contrib-ute to the institutionalization of negotiation and mediation, the confluence of such factors seems far less likely than many pro-ponents may have realized. The lesson of our cases is that the in-stitutionalized use of mediation and negotiation is a potentially beneficial public policy tool, but one not easily implemented.

References

Beem, Robert. "Siting Hazardous Waste Facilities in Massachu-setts." Unpublished manuscript, Seattle: Mediation Institute, 1985.

Bingham, G. *Resolving Environmental Disputes, A Decade of Experi-ence*. Washington, D.C.: Conservation Foundation, 1986.

Brock, J. *Bargaining Beyond Impasse: Joint Resolution of Public Sector Labor Disputes*. Boston: Auburn House, 1982.

Brock, J., and Cormick G. "Can Negotiation Be Mandated? Lessons from Recent Attempts. A Report to the National Institute for Dispute Resolution." Seattle: Mediation Institute, 1985.

Cormick, G. "Intervention and Self-Determination in Environ-mental Disputes: A Mediator's Perspective." *Resolve*, 1982 (Winter), pp. 1, 3–7.

Fisher, R. J., and Ury, W. *Getting to Yes*. New York: Penguin Books, 1983.

EIGHT

Informal Thirdpartyship: Studies of Everyday Conflict Intervention

Blair H. Sheppard
Kathryn Blumenfeld-Jones
Jonelle Roth

Most of the other chapters in this volume, like most research on mediation, concern conflict management efforts by third parties whose formal role is to act as a neutral intermediary. However, most mediation efforts are made in less formal, everyday settings by people who are called into the dispute or intrude of their own accord. Parents mediate disputes between siblings. Managers mediate disagreements at the workplace. Friends mediate arguments between other friends.

These interventions are different from more formal mediation or arbitration efforts in three ways (Kolb and Sheppard, 1985). First, the third party has a continuing relationship to the disputants (as parent, supervisor, colleague, or friend), rather than the transient relationship of a neutral party whose primary concern is resolution of the conflict. The various authority relationships, interdependencies, and social bonds that occur between parents and children, supervisors and employees, and among friends provide a context that can confuse, contradict, or define the third party's role as a conflict resolver. Second, the third party is frequently a part of the dispute in some form or another. For example, interpretation of a rule originally established by a parent may serve as the basis for an argument between siblings, or a supervisor may be asked to intervene in a problem between two subordinates, the outcome of which will affect the performance of her own job.

Finally, informal mediators seem to have a larger range of intervention options available to them. The procedures used by third parties with formal roles (mediators, judges, and arbitrators) are dictated in part by the description of the role and the training necessary to qualify for it. Thus mediators will mediate, not adjudicate, because that is what they are trained to do and that is what is expected of them in their role as mediator. Informal third parties are not generally as constrained by specialized training and disputant expectations. What options for intervention are employed by informal third parties and why they choose one of them over another are questions that have not yet been answered. Thus, we in the field are in the odd position of knowing the least about the most pervasive form of third-party intervention.

This chapter describes a program of research that we have conducted on the procedures used by such informal third parties and provides a preliminary model describing how and why parents, managers, neighbors, and friends come to intervene as they do.

Overview of Preliminary Research

Background Research. In essence, our research has evolved from an initial theory of dispute resolution procedure developed by John Thibaut and Laurens Walker (1975, 1978). They suggested that it is possible to differentiate conflict intervention procedures based on the degree of third-party control over two stages: a process stage, in which evidence is presented, and a decision stage, in which the solution is decided upon. Thus, a third party can exert either process control, much like a football referee who controls the flow of the game but has no direct influence on the outcome, or decision control, much like a diving judge who does not influence the dive in progress but simply decides on the dive's quality.

One of the most important insights from this work is that procedures matter. In particular, both third parties and dispu-tants are as concerned with the fairness of the way a dispute is handled as they are with the fairness of the outcome (see also Tyler, 1986). However, we know very little from their research about the procedures that third parties actually use, or the factors other than fairness that drive the choice of procedure.

Our research program has involved applying and extend-ing the Thibaut-Walker model to describe the sorts of pro-cedures informal third parties use and how they come to use the procedures they do. Because we were somewhat concerned about the relative simplicity of the legal-based Thibaut-Walker model when applied to more diverse informal third-party inter-vention, our first objective was to attempt to develop a more elaborate model.

A First Look at What Informal Third Parties Do. We started by asking sixty middle managers to describe, in their own words, a recent attempt to intervene in a dispute between two or more employees (Sheppard, 1983). We then content-analyzed their responses to determine the proportion that appeared to fall into five procedural types described by Thibaut and Walker. The forms of intervention most frequently used by these managers nicely matched two of Thibaut and Walker's types: arbitration and autocratic.

In the arbitration procedure, the third party controls the final decision on a solution, but the disputants control the evidence and information presented for consideration. Typ-ically the disputants are given an opportunity to present their side of the conflict and the third party then decides on a solu-tion, taking into consideration the disputants' evidence.

When using an autocratic procedure, the third party

controls both the final decision and the presentation of evidence. The disputants have little input into what the solution will be. In an autocratic intervention, often a manager does little investigation of what is really in dispute or what information may be relevant to solving the problem. In at least some of the interventions in the sample, this appears to have led to snap decisions based on past experience that did not really resolve the conflict or that created new conflict between the disputants, often involving additional actors.

The third most frequently used mode of intervention did not match any described by Thibaut and Walker. In this method the manager would initially contact the disputants to determine the nature of the conflict and then send them away with a strong incentive for reaching agreement. This could be called simply providing impetus, or the kick-in-the-pants procedure.

Interestingly, none of the third-party managers reported acting as mediators. It appeared, from this sample at least, that managers typically act more like adjudicators when intervening in disputes between their employees. Another clear conclusion from this study was that informal thirdpartyship does frequently occur, as our interview subjects had no trouble recounting an attempted intervention.

Adjudication Versus Mediation. To tease out why managers act more like adjudicators than mediators, we conducted a second study. One hundred managers were presented with a series of hypothetical dispute scenarios (adapted from disputes provided by subjects in Sheppard, 1983) and asked to indicate which of several procedures they would use to manage them (Lewicki and Sheppard, 1985). Across several sets of scenarios, we had three factors manipulated that we expected to influence the degree to which managers would mediate the dispute, rather than act like arbitrators or autocrats. These three factors came from interviews with managers in which we described the results of our earlier research and asked them to explain why managers do not mediate.

The first factor was the degree to which the manager might be held accountable for the consequences of the outcome. The second factor concerned the precedent value of the out-

come; that is, the number of people other than the direct disputants potentially affected by it. Based on these interviews, we
predicted that the manager would be more likely to adjudicate
as the degree of accountability and precedent value increased.
The third factor concerned the importance of the relationship
between the two parties. We predicted that managers would
more likely mediate when it was important to maintain a working relationship between the parties.

Results of the second study supported all three hypotheses. We also found that, in general, managers clearly prefer
mediation. This is quite inconsistent with our earlier research,
where managers did not report mediating disputes at all (Sheppard, 1983). Thus, if self-reported behavior can be trusted,
managers appear to act in a manner that is inconsistent with
their preferences. Lewicki and Sheppard (1985) suggested that
this inconsistency might be a result of the press of everyday
managerial activity, which leaves no time to mediate, or that
managers do not feel adequate to the task of mediation. Brett
(1986) has also suggested that discomfort with the task of mediation may be limiting managers' willingness to attempt it, in spite
of their preference for mediation in principle.

A Preliminary Look at Goals of Informal Third Parties. Based
on our second study, it appears that informal third parties are
worried about a range of criteria when deciding how to intervene. For example, managers who are responsible for a decision,
or are managing a precedent-setting dispute, are likely concerned about the effectiveness of the settlement.

A third study, by Lissak and Sheppard (1983), formally
introduced new criteria into our consideration of how dispute
resolution procedures are selected. Managers and police were
asked to describe a recent attempt to intervene in a dispute and
to indicate the factors they considered when deciding how to
proceed. The results of these and subsequent interviews indicate that informal third parties purport to take a large number
of factors into consideration when deciding how to intervene,
including most prominently fairness, effectiveness, efficiency,
and disputant satisfaction and commitment to the solution (see
Table 8.1).

Table 8.1. Procedural Effectiveness Criteria.

Qualities of Procedures Themselves	Qualities of Outcome Related to Procedure

Fairness
  Perceived fairness[a]
  Level of third-party neutrality
  Level of disputant control[a]
  Protection of individual rights[a]
 	
Participant satisfaction
  Level of privacy[a]
  Level of participant involvement and seriousness[a]
  Level of injury incurred by any party[a]
 	
Effectiveness
  Implementability of procedure[a]
  Quantity and quality of facts, ideas, or argument elicited[a]
  Degree to which dispute surfaces or gets into the open[a]
 	
Efficiency
  Cost[a]
  Timeliness and speed of resolution[a]
  Disruptiveness of other events and everyday affairs
	Fairness
	  As defined by equitability, consistency of results with similar conflicts, need, consistency with accepted rule or norm, and perceived fairness
	
	Participant satisfaction
	  Disputant commitment to solution
	  Benefit of outcome to participants
	  Level of disputant animosity[a]
	
	Effectiveness
	  Level of resolution achieved[a]
	  Permanence of solution[a]
	  Likelihood of future similar outcome[a]
	  Impact on indirectly involved parties[a]
	
	Efficiency

[a] Indicates criterion identified in Lissak and Sheppard, 1983.

It became clear from informal discussions during these interviews that third parties also consider aspects of the dispute when deciding what method of intervention to use. For example, managers indicated that they would do very different things when intervening between two co-workers who interact frequently, than when intervening between two relative strangers.

A fourth study provided preliminary evidence for a more extensive model of procedure. Sheppard (1984) suggested that there were really thirteen elements of dispute resolution, and that they differentiate types of third-party intervention. These steps (presented in Table 8.2) were defined by a thorough review

Table 8.2. Elements of Dispute Resolution.

Stage 1. Definition
        1. Select resolution procedure
        2. Feel out parties' emotional state
        3. Define what is in dispute
        4. Identify relevant information
        5. Identify possible alternatives for settlement

Stage 2. Discussion
        6. Present relevant information
        7. Present arguments for each alternative
        8. Clarify information and arguments

Stage 3. Alternative Selection
        9. Decide validity of information and arguments
       10. Select the solution

Stage 4. Reconciliation
       11. Reconcile parties with solution
       12. Enforce decision
       13. Hear appeals

of research across the many domains of formal conflict intervention, including labor mediation, community-based dispute resolution, marital and family therapy, international relations, organizational development, and the law (Sheppard, 1984). The thirteen elements are collected into four stages. We believe that these four stages occur in sequence, but within a given stage the elements do not need to occur in any order. The results of the study indicated that a complex procedure, involving piecing together elements of each stage, was considered fairer than simple arbitration or mediation.

A Comprehensive Study of Informal Intervention

The most detailed phase of our research to date involved field research, collecting information from a wide array of informal third parties describing how they managed others' disputes (Sheppard and others, 1986). Three hundred interviews have been conducted, sixty each from five samples: private-industry managers, city administrators, university administrators, parents, and students intervening in disputes among friends. The interviews were quite extensive and were based on the taxonomy developed in Sheppard (1984) and presented in Tables 8.1 and 8.2. The interview proceeded in four steps.

Subjects were first asked to describe in their own words a recent attempt to intervene in a dispute between two or more people. They were then asked a number of questions about the nature of the dispute and the dispute context. Based on a factor analysis, we classified their answers into four general themes: (1) the importance and complexity of the dispute, (2) the degree of interdependence between the parties, (3) the level of authority the third party had over the disputants, and (4) the degree to which the dispute involved an ongoing personality clash between the disputants.

Third, subjects were asked to rate the importance of the twenty-two criteria presented in Table 8.1 in determining the choice of method used. As expected, a factor analysis of these questions collapsed them into four general categories: concern for effectiveness, efficiency, fairness, and the satisfaction and commitment of the disputants.

Finally, subjects were asked to describe in detail the method of intervention they used. This part of the interview involved a series of structured questions based on the thirteen steps of dispute process presented in Table 8.2. For each step, subjects were asked whether they were involved at all in that element, and if so what specifically they did. Responses were content-analyzed to assess the degree of involvement exhibited by subjects in each phase and the range of specific things third parties did when intervening. The specific tactics used appeared to fit into two broad categories: attempts to direct the process (how things are done) and attempts to direct the content (specifically what is done or said). This study permitted us to consider for the first time in some detail what informal third parties do and why they do it.

What Informal Third Parties Do

From our earlier research it appeared that managers generally report acting like adjudicators when intervening in others' disputes. Because of the extensiveness of the sample in the present study it was possible to assess the degree to which this was true of a wide array of informal third parties. Also, because of the detailed nature of the interview format, it was possible to assess in far greater detail what third parties do.

The analysis of what informal third parties do during conflict intervention centered on the subjects' detailed descriptions of their involvement in each of the thirteen steps of Table 8.2. For each step, subjects were given a score of zero, 1, or 2 (zero = no involvement, 1 = either process or content involvement, 2 = both process and content involvement). We conducted a factor analysis on these two involvement scores within each step, to detect patterns that might exist. There appeared to be four general factors: diagnosing and clarifying, fact finding, identifying solutions, and implementing them. (The factor weights are reported in Table 8.3). These factors can be thought of as clusters of steps that third parties are likely to do together; they could represent either whole procedures or elements of procedures. Subsequent analyses indicate that it is best to think of these factors as procedural themes that can be combined together by the third party to form procedures, rather than discrete modes of intervention.

These four factors appear to have relatively straightforward interpretations. The first appears to reflect direct management of the interaction process between the parties. In this instance, third-party subjects focused on clarifying feelings, identifying problems, and eliciting information and arguments. Frequently used tactics included deciding who talks to whom, listening to the parties, facilitating communication, establishing rules for communication, asking questions, focusing the discussion, and interpreting and evaluating information. This factor appears to represent a focus on diagnosis and clarification and emphasizes many tactics common to mediational or therapeutic procedures.

The second factor involves gathering and presenting information about the problem. Subjects who emphasize this factor appear to be involved in asking questions, talking with other knowledgeable people, observing, relaying facts and in-

Table 8.3. Factor Weights and Eigenvalues from Factor Analysis on Third-Party Intervention Styles.

	Factor Loadings			
Steps of Dispute Resolution Process	Factor 1 Diagnosis and Clarification	Factor 2 Fact Finding	Factor 3 Solution Identification	Factor 4 Implementation
Select resolution procedure	.26	-.59	.23	.16
Feel out parties' emotional state	.60	.13	.04	-.12
Define what is in dispute	.53	-.04	.04	.12
Identify relevant information	.14	.67	.26	.10
Identify possible alternatives for settlement	.12	.06	.65	-.06
Present relevant information	.21	.63	.06	.10
Present arguments	.56	-.07	.14	.10
Clarify information and arguments	.67	.28	-.11	-.09
Evaluate information and arguments	.26	.36	.41	.07
Select the solution	-.08	-.06	.80	.08
Reconcile parties with solution	.37	.11	.13	.40
Enforce decision	-.07	-.44	.20	.55
Hear appeals	-.10	.15	-.13	.79
Eigenvalue	2.31	1.59	1.16	1.11

formation to the disputants, and presenting their own opinions. This factor represents a form of fact finding, in which the third party gathers information from various sources and presents it to the relevant parties. When acting as a fact finder, the third party tends not to get involved in selecting the procedure or in enforcing a solution. Thus, this seems a fairly circumscribed form of intervention.

The third factor entails identifying and evaluating alternative solutions and then selecting one. Identifying and choosing the solution to the problem involved introducing the third party's ideas and suggestions, encouraging the disputants to participate, and requiring the parties to solve it themselves. Another frequent tactic was to exclude the disputants totally from involvement with choosing the solution. Thus, this form of intervention appears to be quite intrusive and represents a focus on solution identification and selection. The existence of this factor is quite consistent with the earlier research in which informal third parties frequently acted as adjudicators.

The final factor involves reconciling parties to the solution, enforcing the decision, and hearing appeals, steps that occur after the solution has been chosen and deal with the implementation of the solution. The third parties were much less involved at this point. In those few instances when some intervention was required after a decision was made, the specific tactics used included providing explanations and facts, introducing threats or promises, monitoring agreements, smoothing feathers, and listening to appeals. Subjects were least likely to be involved in this implementation factor; the other three occurred quite frequently.

The themes represented by these four factors appear to be used in various combinations to create procedures that fulfill the general needs of the situation. In other words, they are the primary ingredients in ad hoc recipes created by third parties to suit the case at hand.

Why Informal Third Parties Do As They Do

A Rational Decision Perspective on Informal Intervention

From this study it was also possible to begin assessing the conditions under which informal third parties choose to em-

phasize one intervention theme over another. The basic logic of
the analysis was derived from a simple decision perspective in
which we assumed that third parties made a rational choice
about how to intervene after considering their goals and evaluating the nature of the dispute. For each of the four intervention
factors, we ran a regression predicting the use of that theme
from the four intervention goals (effectiveness, fairness, disputant satisfaction and commitment, and efficiency) and the four
dispute characteristics (dispute importance and complexity, disputant interdependence, personality clash, and third-party authority) identified in the study. A further set of analyses was
conducted predicting the four goals from the four dispute characteristics. For the sake of brevity and ease of interpretation the
results of these analyses are presented in Figure 8.1. Consider
the prediction of each intervention theme in turn.

Diagnosis and Clarification. Panel 1 of the figure presents
the variables that predicted the use of the diagnosis and clarification theme. It stands to reason that disputant satisfaction will
be maximized if the conflict is diagnosed and clarified; only
when the real issues and the disputants' feelings are well understood by all parties can they be responded to in a solution that
addresses everyone's concerns. Two aspects of the dispute also
directly affected the tendency to use this theme. Specifically,
subjects emphasized diagnosis and clarification when the dispute was perceived to involve an ongoing personality clash. It
makes some sense that subjects emphasized a mediational or
therapeutic procedure when the dynamic between parties was
poor. Also the more authority the third parties had over the
disputants, the less likely they were to emphasize this theme,
suggesting that third parties take the time to diagnose and
clarify issues surrounding the dispute only when they do not
have the authority to make and enforce a decision. This notion is
supported by our earlier work (Sheppard, 1983) in which managers did not report using mediation when intervening in disputes between their employees. Finally, the perceptions that the
dispute was complex and important and that the disputants
were interdependent led indirectly to an emphasis on diagnosis
and clarification, for both were strongly related to concern for
disputant satisfaction and commitment to the solution.

Figure 8.1. A Rational Decision Model of Procedural Choice.

Panel 1: Diagnosis and Clarification

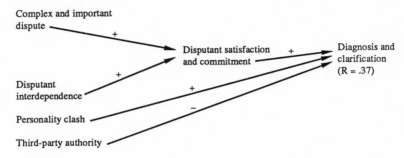

Panel 2: Fact Finding

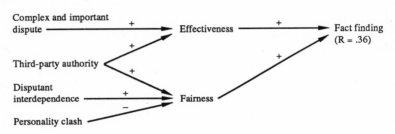

Panel 3: Solution Identification

Fact Finding. Panel 2 presents the variables that predicted an emphasis on fact finding. Unlike diagnosis and clarification, dispute characteristics did not directly affect an emphasis on fact finding, but instead their effect was mediated through concern for effectiveness and concern for fairness. Both higher concern for effectiveness and fairness were positively related to an emphasis on fact finding. In this study effectiveness included such concerns as maintaining privacy, minimizing injury, attending to the rights of uninvolved parties, and getting at the facts. Given this context, it is not surprising that informal third parties would emphasize data gathering. The complete and accurate gathering of information is critical to achieving a fair resolution and to making sure that the rights of all affected parties are considered. It also makes sense that the third party (rather than the disputants) should perform this task if maintaining privacy and preventing injury are concerns. The relationship between dispute characteristics and concern for fairness and effectiveness was quite straightforward. Third parties wished to be effective when the dispute was perceived as important and when they were in a position of authority. Subjects were concerned about fairness when they had authority and when the disputants were interdependent. It seems a good thing that third parties were concerned with being fair when they were most able to be unfair, when they have the authority to affect the ongoing relationship between others. Finally, third parties were less likely to be concerned about fairness when the dispute involved a personality clash.

Solution Identification. Again an emphasis on solution identification and selection (see panel 3) is only indirectly influenced by the perceived characteristics of the dispute. Third parties emphasized solution identification and selection when they were concerned about fairness and efficiency. Clearly, deciding on one's own is less time consuming and costly than involving others in the process, another finding consistent with our earlier work (Lewicki and Sheppard, 1985). Also, it appears that to ensure fairness, informal third parties feel the need for some control over the decision about what the solution should be. Finally, subjects concerned with disputant satisfaction and

commitment to the solution were less likely to emphasize control over decision making. It appears that subjects feel that
disputants are more satisfied with and committed to solutions
they choose for themselves even if those solutions may not be as
fair as those chosen by the third party. This potentially poses an
interesting dilemma for informal third parties when fairness
and disputant satisfaction are of equal concern.

Implementation. There is no panel describing the variables
that predicted implementation well, as none did. One explanation for the poor prediction is that such involvement depends
on how well the dispute resolution process proceeds, not on
anything that occurs before the intervention itself. In other
words, the need for implementation occurs only after a decision
has been made and a disputant is dissatisfied with it. A second
possibility is that important factors were not considered in the
study. For example, Carnevale's notion of the likelihood of a
mutually acceptable solution (1986) is not directly reflected in
the dispute factors identified in this study.

To summarize, the general multi-attribute decision perspective portrayed in Figure 8.1 accounts reasonably well for
third-party emphasis across three of the four intervention theme
factors. Moreover, these results make intuitive sense, and are
generally consistent with previous research.

Another Perspective: The Importance of Frames

To this point, informal third parties have been portrayed
as relatively unconstrained, rational decision makers choosing
the method that gives the best chance of achieving their objectives, given certain features of the dispute. However, from our
pilot interviews for this study and some recent research (see
Chapter Five) another perspective has emerged.

In this new view, third parties develop relatively simple
interpretations, or frames, of a given dispute, which suggest the
procedures they should use. These frames can be culturally
based views of the world (Goffman, 1959) or schemata that
individuals have evolved for interpreting and remembering past
events (Bartlett, 1932; Schank and Abelson, 1977). Frequently,

such frames are fictions created by a third party either for some ulterior motive or out of habit. For example, from an intensive examination of one manager's conflict intervention style, Kolb (1986) argued that managers frequently frame disputes so as to avoid dealing with interpersonal conflict and to maintain the myth that everyone in a given organization is working toward the same goal. Clearly, this point of view is based on a much less complex and less conscious process than the decision-making perspective that has driven our work to this point.

A particularly frequent dispute among siblings illustrates this perspective well. In the early stages of our study we inter- viewed several parents about a recent intervention in disputes between their children. Not surprisingly, the most frequent dis- agreements concerned which television show to watch. In de- scribing how they came to act as they did, parents would occa- sionally talk as an economist or decision theorist would expect, discussing tradeoffs between various objectives. However, more frequently parents seemed to make a quick interpretation about what was going on, and their choice of method was almost a foregone conclusion.

Some parents suggested that the dispute concerned the application of a family rule (such as a rule about who has priority). Once that interpretation was established, the problem was to decide who was right and who was wrong vis-à-vis this rule. Such parents tended to see themselves as fact finders or judges. Other parents would indicate that a night's television watching involved several time slots and that the real issue was to decide which time slots were most important to each child and to generate a solution that met all their needs — in other words, to reach a negotiated settlement. Frequently, such parents saw themselves as mediators or deal makers. A third set of parents indicated that this dispute was diagnostic of a much deeper conflict that had been going on for some time between the children and that their task was to help understand and resolve the underlying issues. These parents appeared to think of them- selves as counselors or diagnosticians. Finally, some parents did not care what the dispute entailed but simply wanted it to stop. Typically this occurred either when the children threatened to physically harm one another or when they were so noisy and contentious that the parent simply lost patience. Often these parents felt they had more important matters to attend to and, while they saw themselves as having no clear role in managing this dispute, they did describe several effective ways for making it disappear.

From this anecdotal evidence it appeared that parents would and do frequently interpret or frame apparently very similar sibling disputes in quite different ways and that these frames direct or constrain how these parents proceed to handle the dispute. We had similar anecdotal evidence on how deans or department chairs frame disputes over faculty recruiting, and how managers frame disagreements over a performance appraisal.

Four Kinds of Frames. However, such anecdotal evidence is of limited value. We had no evidence on their prevalence or their real relationship to method of intervention. To test these notions about framing more rigorously, we needed a way to code the frames. We developed the following four frames from several sources, including Kolb (1983), Sheppard (1984), and some preliminary interviews done before the present study.

1. *Right-wrong frame.* The problem requires identifying one party as right and one party as wrong, based on the rules or norms that apply to this particular dispute. In other words, a discrete choice is required.
2. *Negotiation frame.* Tradeoffs and compromises can be made so that a negotiated solution is possible.
3. *Underlying conflict frame.* This particular conflict is only symptomatic of a more important, ongoing problem between these two parties.
4. *Stop frame.* This dispute must be stopped. Resolving the issues is of secondary importance to making the conflict go away.

The first interview question—"Please describe the last conflict in which you intervened to help manage or resolve the conflict"—was used only for coding the frame and was independent of the questions that defined the variables used in the rational decision model. The subjects' descriptions of the dispute were coded by Blair Sheppard. As a reliability check, Kathryn Blumenfeld-Jones, who had not been involved in developing the coding scheme, independently coded forty randomly selected protocols. The percentage agreement on classifications was 84 percent. Three of the narratives appeared to fit none of the four classifications and were not included in later analyses of dispute frames.

Predictions from the Framing Perspective. As a test of the influence of third-party frame on procedure, a multivariate analysis of variance (MANOVA) was conducted with dispute frame as the independent variable and factor scores for the four intervention themes as the four dependent variables. This MANOVA was significant: $F(12,768) = 7.84$, $p < .0001$. Separate univariate analyses of variance (ANOVAs) were conducted on each intervention theme in order to help interpret this result. Table 8.4 presents the means for the four univariate ANOVAs. As can be seen, three of the four ANOVAs were significant. It appears that third parties with an underlying conflict frame were particularly eager to engage in diagnosis and clarification. Third parties with a stop frame were significantly less likely to engage in fact finding than third parties having other frames. Third parties with a right-wrong frame were particularly likely to identify and select a solution to the disagreement. Third parties with a negotiation frame were significantly less likely to identify the solution. This result indicates an alternative interpretation for the Sheppard (1983) finding that managers adjudicate rather than mediate. The two frames that are positively associated with choosing a solution (right-wrong and stop frames) were invoked by these subjects more than three times as often as the negotiation frame. This suggests that informal third parties may tend to make an initial interpretation of the dispute that is incompatible with a mediational intervention. Finally, the frames appeared not to significantly affect use of the implementation theme; this parallels the finding from the decision perspective.

The results of this study indicate that both the multi-

Table 8.4. Mean Intervention Theme Factor Scores for Four Dispute Frames.

Intervention Themes	Right-Wrong (n = 162)	Negotiation (n = 57)	Stop (n = 21)	Underlying Conflict (n = 57)	F	P
Diagnosis and clarification*	−.07[a]	−.10[a]	−.29[a]	.35[b]	3.60	.01
Fact finding	.11	−.03[a]	−.99[b]	.06[a]	8.27	.00001
Solution identification	.23[b]	−.74[a]	.50[b]	−.03[b]	17.76	.00001
Implementation	.01	−.10	.44	−.10	1.73	ns

* Mean intervention theme factor scores for each of the four frames.
[a, b] Means not sharing the same superscript are significantly different across rows (Newman-Keuls, $p < .05$).

attribute decision perspective and the notion of dispute frames are useful in predicting the intervention themes that third parties reported using in this study. (The only exception is the implementation theme, which was not well predicted by any variable.) However, these results raise as many questions as they answer.

Frames Versus Complex Decisions

Perhaps the most important unanswered question concerns how frame and decision processes function together to influence choice of intervention method. One possibility is that they operate separately; in other words, a simpler framing approach may compete with a more complex decision model.

A second possibility is that these two processes operate sequentially; a given frame suggests a preferred strategy, which is then reviewed for suitability in terms of the third party's objectives and identification of key aspects about the dispute. In other words, a process analogous to anchoring and adjustment (Tversky and Kahneman, 1974) may be operating, with a frame suggesting the initial anchor, which is adjusted through subsequent conscious review. From this perspective, it is also likely that the initial frame influences interpretation of the dispute and choice of intervention procedure. In other words, frames may be operating directly on third-party procedural choices and indirectly through objectives or interpretation of the dispute. In this sense a frame is an interpretive schema (Bartlett, 1932) directing how we process all other information. It is also possible that aspects of the situation and goals are primary and the frames represent rationalizations for what has to be done.

Clearly, the first sequential perspective begs the question as to where frames come from. One possibility is that frames are individual schemas acquired through personal experience and invoked whenever disputes arise (see Fiske and Taylor, 1984, for a discussion of recent research on schema). Another possibility is that frames are culturally determined vehicles for interpreting disputes, part of an organization's or family's institutional fabric (Berger and Luckman, 1966). Finally, frames may involve a preliminary abbreviated analysis of the dispute problem, used to simplify its complexity and provide a more tractable problem (Kahneman and Tversky, 1979). In other words, a frame is the result of a preliminary problem definition, which serves as the basis for a more elaborate decision analysis (see Payne, 1982).

Clearly, these interpretations are tentative and other possibilities exist. Further tests with explicit causal analysis of the role of frame and decision attributes are necessary.

Decision Perspective Revisited

The research described in this chapter suggests that the procedures used by informal third parties and the factors influencing their choice of procedure can be described reasonably well; that informal third parties seem to prefer mediation over adjudication, though in an actual dispute they often choose an adjudicatory intervention that is inconsistent with this preference; and that the choice of a particular procedure can be explained by both the objectives of the third party and the characteristics of the dispute (rational decision perspective), and a simple interpretation of the dispute (framing perspective).

A fundamental premise on which this research was initially based was that informal third parties act as rational decision makers with relatively unlimited capacity to intervene as they wish, except as dictated by the constraints of the dispute and its context. However, from our research on dispute frames, it is clear that the notion of an unconstrained, rational third party does not completely hold.

A reasonable amount of attention has been paid to some form of cognitive simplification structures such as frames in the psychology literature (see Fiske and Taylor, 1984). There appears to be some consensus that the world is very complex and people have limited processing capabilities. Therefore, people cognitively impose some structure on what they perceive to simplify and thereby make sense of it. This appears to be the case when individuals acting as third parties in disputes process information about the dispute. They simplify the information they receive and then respond to it based on their interpretation. However, this process has drawbacks also; it can constrain the way a third party interprets and responds to the conflict. This is true not just for informal third parties. For example, one thing that differentiates the sets of professionals who intervene in disputes (mediators, judges, police, or therapists) from one another is the sort of perspective or frame each brings to bear on disputes. Mediators generally think negotiation, judges generally think right-wrong, police frequently think stop, and therapists generally think underlying problem. This is all part of professional socialization.

One of the questions that naturally arises from this viewpoint is how these frames operate as a process over time. Most informal third-party interventions occur within the context of an ongoing relationship, in which the intervention is one of many instances. Siblings fight constantly, subordinates are subordinates for a while, friends argue more than once. In such instances it is quite likely that third-party intervention style will become "institutionalized" as a result of interaction with the disputants.

To illustrate this point, consider the following sequence. A manager becomes involved in a disagreement between two subordinates that could be interpreted as a long-term conflict with an underlying dynamic, a negotiation problem, or a problem of deciding who is right or wrong. This manager adopts one of these frames and proceeds to deal with the problem from the perspective of that frame. It is now more likely that the same frame will be adopted in the next disagreement between these same two disputants, for at least four reasons. First, the solution will have been influenced by the frame taken and thus will likely contain elements of that frame as the seeds of future problems. For example, if an underlying conflict frame were adopted it may uncover other problems in the relationship. Second, the disputants are learning something about how to deal with their boss in the future; if you are going to have a problem settled effectively you need to position it from a point of view that the boss will respond to. Third, the third party is teaching herself or himself to adopt the frame again, because of recency effects in memory, because the approach works, or simply because it is easier to be consistent than to think of a new approach. Finally, the third party is influencing how the disputants look at their own disputes, intentionally or unintentionally teaching disputants to adopt a frame.

The same cycle may be repeated over and over again, trapping the third party in one view of this dispute or all disputes and one mode of responding. In such cases, rational, conscious choice as portrayed in Figure 8.1 may have little to do with how the third party behaves. Therefore, assessing perceptions of the dispute and third-party goals may not describe the actual third-party choice process and it may be necessary to conceptualize and research the problem differently. To identify the approach or set of approaches that will help us tease out how social, schematic, and decisional factors influence third-party intervention is the aim of our next phase of research.

References

Bartlett, F. C. *Remembering*. Cambridge, Mass.: Cambridge University Press, 1932.

Berger, P. L., and Luckman, T. *The Social Construction of Reality*. New York: Doubleday, 1966.

Brett, J. M. "Commentary on Procedural Justice Papers." In R. J. Lewicki, B. H. Sheppard, and M. H. Bazerman (eds.), *Research on Negotiation in Organizations*. Vol. 1. Greenwich, Conn.: JAI Press, 1986.

Carnevale, P. J. "Strategic Choice in Mediation." *Negotiation Journal*, 1986, 2, 41–56.

Fiske, S. T., and Taylor, S. E. *Social Cognition*. Reading, Mass.: Addison-Wesley, 1984.

Goffman, E. *The Presentation of Self in Everyday Life*. New York: Doubleday, 1959.

Kahneman, D., and Tversky, A. "Prospect Theory: An Analysis of Decision Under Risk." *Econometrica*, 1979, 47, 263–291.

Kolb, D. M., *The Mediators*. Cambridge, Mass.: MIT Press, 1983.

Kolb, D. M. "Who Are Organizational Third Parties and What Do They Do?" In R. J. Lewicki, B. H. Sheppard, and M. H.

Bazerman (eds.), *Research on Negotiation in Organizations.* Vol. 1. Greenwich, Conn.: JAI Press, 1986.

Kolb, M., and Sheppard, B. H. "Do Managers Mediate or Even Arbitrate?" *Negotiation Journal*, 1985, *1*, 379–388.

Lewicki, R. J., and Sheppard, B. H. "Choosing How to Intervene: Factors Affecting the Use of Process and Outcome Central in Third Party Dispute Resolution." *Journal of Occupational Behavior*, 1985, *6*, 49–64.

Lissak, R. I., and Sheppard, B. H. "Beyond Fairness: The Criterion Problem in Research on Dispute Intervention." *Journal of Applied Social Psychology*, 1983, *13*, 45–65.

Payne, J. W. "Contingent Decision Behavior." *Psychological Bulletin*, 1982, *92*, 382–402.

Schank, R. C., and Abelson, R. P. *Scripts, Plans, Goals and Understanding.* New York: Wiley (Erlbaum), 1977.

Sheppard, B. H. "Managers as Inquisitors: Some Lessons from the Law." In M. H. Bazerman and R. J. Lewicki (eds.), *Negotiation in Organizations.* Beverly Hills, Calif.: Sage, 1983.

Sheppard, B. H. "Third Party Conflict Intervention: A Procedural Framework." In B. M. Staw and L. L. Cummings (eds.), *Research in Organizational Behavior.* Vol. 6. Greenwich, Conn.: JAI Press, 1984.

Sheppard, B. H., and others. "Informal Conflict Intervention: A Tale of Two Models." Unpublished working paper, Fuqua School of Business, Duke University, 1986.

Thibaut, J. W., and Walker, L. *Procedural Justice: A Psychological Analysis.* Hillsdale, N.J.: Erlbaum, 1975.

Thibaut, J. W., and Walker, L. "A Theory of Procedure." *California Law Review*, 1978, *66*, 541–566.

Tversky, A., and Kahneman, D. "Judgement Under Uncertainty: Heuristics and Biases." *Science*, 1974, *185*, 1124–1131.

Tyler, T. "When Does Procedural Justice Matter in Organizational Settings?" In R. J. Lewicki, B. H. Sheppard, and M. H. Bazerman (eds.), *Research on Negotiation in Organizations.* Vol. 1. Greenwich, Conn.: JAI Press, 1986.

NINE

Judicial Mediation of Settlement Negotiations

James A. Wall, Jr.
Dale E. Rude

The plea bargaining was going slowly—too slowly. Joyce Davenport wanted her client's charge reduced to voluntary manslaughter in exchange for his guilty plea and cooperation in the ongoing investigation. Second-degree murder (down from murder one) was all the prosecutor would offer. They bargained, salami style, as the clock ticked away, and I, Jim Wall, became more irritated. My favorite characters on "Hill Street Blues"— Washington, LaRue, and Belker—were out chasing crooks while we, the viewing audience, watched a slow, slow negotiation.

Finally an agreement was struck and presented to the judge, who asked a few questions. All parties responded politely and the minor conviction was recorded.

There was a commercial break.

"Hill Street" returned but I ignored the remaining segments, thinking, Why didn't the judge step in earlier? He could have listened to both sides, asked questions, perhaps made a suggestion, and expedited the process. In short, why did he not mediate?

To me it was an obvious question, because on that Thursday afternoon in 1980 I had been putting the final touches on an article reviewing mediation techniques (Wall, 1981). Early the following morning, I posed the question to Larry Schiller, a member of my department who taught business law. His response: "Judges don't mediate in criminal cases."

"Why not?"

"Because it's against the law." (Later we found it is illegal in forty-eight states.) "But," he quickly added, "they do mediate in civil cases, if they wish." He succinctly explained that attorneys negotiate in civil cases and usually settle out of court. Judges, in most cases, meet with the attorneys in a pretrial conference to prepare the case for trial. At this conference (or at *any* other time) the judge may take steps to facilitate settlement.

"What steps do judges take?" I asked.

"Anything they wish."

"Is there any literature on this?"

"Should be."

We spent the remainder of the day in the law library. The result—very little literature; there were some self-reports and thinkpieces by judges, but no empirical research. Immediately we laid plans to fill the void.

Settlement

Before describing the course of our research, it is perhaps useful to focus on settlement. It is a negotiation process in which the plaintiff and defendant, or their attorneys, attempt to reach an agreement about their civil dispute. Generally, it starts with the prospective plaintiff contacting an attorney about a dispute. After some discussion, they decide whether a complaint should be filed. If they decide to file, the plaintiff's attorney may negotiate directly with the defendant or with the defendant's attorney before filing the complaint. If no agreement is reached, the complaint is filed, but the plaintiff's and defendant's attorneys may still conduct negotiations in an attempt to settle out of court. When they fail to reach an agreement, the case is scheduled for a pretrial conference with the judge. Here, he or she reviews the case with the attorneys, facilitates simplification and stipulation of issues, discusses discovery, schedules the case for trial, and perhaps attempts to facilitate a settlement.

Settlement negotiations may continue in the intervening period before the case goes to trial and during the trial. Such efforts can continue even after the jury brings in a verdict. If the case is appealed, the attorneys may continue settlement negotiations. In many situations, a person appointed by the court will meet with the attorneys before the appeals trial and attempt to facilitate such a settlement.

Benefits of Settlement. The settlement process and agreement benefit the clients, the court, and society. Settlement saves money for both sides because the costs of trials and appeals are avoided.

Settlement gives the parties control of the case: they can settle before the case goes to trial, or before the verdict; they can settle inconsistently with the verdict that is returned; or they can appeal and settle before, during, or after the appellate process. Settlement yields certainty because it cannot be appealed. It offers confidentiality and expediency.

For the judicial system, settlement proffers many advantages. A settlement marks the final disposition of a case. It saves time for the judges because only unsettled cases come to trial. Determination by settlement also results in efficient calendar control and reduced time between filing and disposition. This last advantage, in addition to aiding the court, improves the public's evaluation of the judiciary's efficiency (Fox, 1972).

The Judge's Role in Settlement. Because out-of-court settlement yields many benefits to the disputing parties, to the judge, and to the judicial system, many judges mediate settlement negotiations. We wished to study judges' involvement, and our initial goal was modest: to determine which techniques judges were using to facilitate settlement. We interviewed fifty judges and lawyers, discussed the techniques they had used or observed, and unearthed approximately seventy-one techniques (forty of these are presented in column 1 of Table 9.1; Schiller and Wall, 1981).

Somewhat surprisingly, the interviews and subsequent correspondence with law-journal editors revealed strong differences of opinion about the frequency with which the various techniques were used and the appropriateness of each technique. An amusing example: three lawyers who practiced before the same judge noted that the judge quite often employed a certain technique. Two of the lawyers held that the technique was illegal and unethical. The third, who had experienced the technique, felt it was ethical and useful. Still other lawyers expressed disbelief that we had uncovered instances in which that particular technique was used at all.

On another technique, one editor of a leading law journal questioned our findings, stating that a judge would *never* use that because if he or she did, "the opposing party could obtain a writ against [the judge] so fast that the judge's head would spin." (Our later survey found that approximately 25 percent of all respondents had observed the use of this technique.)

Judges' Techniques: Use and Ethicalness

These differences in opinions and perceptions further enhanced our original interest in investigating judicial settlement techniques. In the next study (Wall and Schiller, 1982), we investigated the extent to which each technique was employed by judges and measured the perceived ethicalness of each technique. One thousand attorneys randomly selected from the current membership lists of the Association of Trial Lawyers of America and the Defense Research Institute were surveyed. Each was given a list of the seventy-one techniques and asked to indicate whether they had observed the techniques, and to evaluate each technique as either ethical or unethical.

Our study established that many judicial techniques were in use to facilitate settlement and most tacks were acceptable to the legal community (column 3, Table 9.1). The results, in addition, spawned a central query: "Which of these are effective in

Table 9.1. Use and Evaluations of the Judicial Techniques.

Techniques	Percent of Lawyers and Judges Observing and Using the Technique	Percent of Lawyers Judging This Technique as Unethical	Overall Effectiveness Rating from Attorneys and Judges[a]
1. Talks with both lawyers together about the settlement.	93	01	2.87
2. Asks both lawyers to compromise.	89	03	3.56
3. Meets with the lawyers in chambers for a settlement conference.	88	19	2.84
4. Sets a settlement conference upon request.	85	02	2.96
5. Calls a certain figure reasonable.	83	08	3.04
6. Channels discussion to areas that have highest probability of settlement.	82	03	2.93
7. Tells the attorney to concentrate on the relevant issues.	81	02	3.40
8. Notes, to the lawyer, the high risk of going to trial.	78	07	4.05
9. Argues logically for concessions.	78	04	3.10
10. Requires settlement talks.	77	03	3.42
11. Requires pretrial conference even though not mandated by court rules.	75	01	3.42
12. Has the lawyer immediately call the client to get response.	73	07	3.43
13. Evaluates one or both cases for the attorneys.	72	07	3.49
14. Suggests a settlement figure *after* asking for lawyers' inputs.	71	06	3.16
15. Notes, to the lawyer, the high cost of going to trial.	71	07	4.22
16. Offers alternative proposal not thought of by the lawyers.	71	03	3.42
17. Says split the difference.	69	13	4.41
18. Analyzes the case for a lawyer.	69	17	3.77
19. Informs the attorneys how similar cases have been settled.	68	04	3.47
20. Interprets the issues for the lawyers.	68	03	3.92

Item			
21. Subtly approves lawyers' concessions.	67	03	3.93
22. Continues to bring up settlement during trial recesses.	67	07	4.19
23. Requires settlement conference even though not mandated by court rules.	64	01	3.26
24. Informs an attorney that he or she has ignored important facts.	62	12	4.09
25. Brings client to the conference.	62	15	3.52
26. Comments on the credibility of some testimony.	60	25	4.09
27. Asks amount each would concede, going back and forth to break settlement into small steps.	59	06	3.41
28. Convinces a lawyer that he or she has a distorted view of the case.	59	08	3.89
29. Tells attorneys not to stall.	58	03	4.43
30. Notes, for the client, the rewards of a pretrial settlement.	57	16	3.95
31. Sets inexorable trial date to raise pressure to settle.	57	40	3.95
32. Emphasizes, for the client, the risks of a jury trial.	56	18	3.75
33. Argues one attorney's case to the other.	55	18	4.45
34. Talks to each lawyer separately about settlement.	51	25	3.89
35. Pressures the ill-prepared attorney.	50	18	4.04
36. Points out, to the client, the strengths and weaknesses of the case.	46	29	3.90
37. Shoulders responsibility for the settlement even though the figure was not suggested by him or her.	40	09	4.29
38. In talking with client, emphasizes the fairness of the figure.	39	22	4.15
39. Speaks personally with the client to persuade the client to accept.	35	43	4.01
40. Suggests a settlement figure to the client.	31	38	4.42

a 1 = Extremely effective; 7 = Not at all effective.

facilitating settlement?" Establishing which techniques were most useful, we felt, would be an important step, because judicial mediation seemed the most feasible immediate solution to crowded court dockets. (We had found the average case waits eighteen months before coming to trial.) Consequently we investigated the effectiveness of each technique, using a nationwide survey that tapped the opinions of judges and practicing attorneys.

Of interest to us also was the relationship between the reported effectiveness of each technique and the extent to which that technique is used. We hypothesized that the techniques most often observed would be rated higher in effectiveness than those observed less often. Likewise, we felt that judges would use techniques that they rate as effective and be less apt to use techniques they deem ineffective. Undergirding these assumptions was the rather general deduction that judges have, over the years, retained the techniques that have proved useful and abandoned those that were less effective.

To investigate our questions and propositions, we sent questionnaires to 500 attorneys, 500 state judges, and 500 federal judges. Each one was given a subset of the seventy-one judicial settlement techniques and asked to evaluate the effectiveness of each on a seven-point bipolar scale (extremely effective = 1; not at all effective = 7). In addition, each judge was asked to note, by checking "yes" or "no" spaces, whether he or she had ever used each technique, and the attorneys indicated whether they had observed the techniques.

The responses to our survey (columns 1 and 3, Table 9.1) allowed us to look at frequency of usage again and to establish which techniques are judged most effective (Wall, Schiller, and Ebert, 1984). In general the results were also internally consistent: the lawyers' reports of observed techniques corresponded roughly with the judges' reports of usage, $r = .86$, $p < .001$. And, as expected, the most highly used techniques were most highly rated as to effectiveness, $r = .92$, $p < .001$.

The survey also allowed an initial test of the hypothesis that the number of techniques used by judges would correlate positively with the percent of cases they reported settling. The

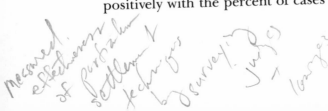

correlation we found ($r = .23$, $p < .001$), while not particularly strong, did indicate that the more techniques judges employed, the more settlements they would glean.

Mediation Strategies

As we were collecting and analyzing the data, Larry Schiller decided to work for a living—a higher-level one—and became a practicing attorney. Dale Rude, replacing him on the team, suggested that we analyze the combinations of techniques used by the judges.

To do so, we factor-analyzed the judges' ratings of the mediation techniques. State judges' reports were analyzed separately from those of the federal judges as a check on validity. From these analyses (Wall and Rude, 1985), three strategy combinations (factors) emerged from both the state and federal judges' ratings (first three groupings in Table 9.2). One set of techniques reflected a logical style; one reflected an aggressive style; and a third factor that emerged from both the state and federal judges was designated a paternalistic strategy.

Having established that both state and federal judges use mediation techniques in three approaches, we determined the effectiveness of these strategies. The lawyers' evaluations were employed in these tests because their assessments had not been used to identify the strategic clusters. Of the three strategies, the logical one was rated most effective. The paternalistic one was deemed somewhat less effective. And the aggressive approach received the lowest rating.

To replicate these results we asked selected attorneys nationwide to recall one recent civil case that had been filed in which the judge undertook one or more steps to facilitate settlement. Then each lawyer checked which techniques, out of a sample of forty, the judge had used. The lawyers' reports of techniques used in each case were then factor-analyzed. Three strategies emerged that were parallel to those found earlier—logical, aggressive, and paternalistic. In addition, a client-oriented strategy (final group, Table 9.2) surfaced rather clearly.

Table 9.2. Judicial Mediation Strategies.

Logical strategies
  Offer alternative proposal not thought of by lawyers.
  Argue logically for concessions.
  Analyze the case for a lawyer.
  Offer advice to a lawyer.
  Suggest a settlement figure after asking for lawyers' inputs.

Aggressive strategies
  Pressure the ill-prepared attorney.
  Require a settlement conference even though one is not mandated by
    court rules.
  Downgrade the merits of the stronger case or the demerits of the weaker.
  Talk to each lawyer separately about settlement.
  Set an inexorable trial date.

Paternalistic strategies
  Ask both lawyers to compromise.
  Call a certain figure reasonable.
  Channel discussions to areas that have the highest probability of
    settlement.
  Note to a lawyer the high risk of going to trial.
  Inform the attorneys about the way in which similar cases have been
    settled.

Client-oriented strategies
  Suggest a settlement figure to the client.
  Note, for the client, the rewards of pretrial settlement.
  Point out, to the client, the strengths and weaknesses of the case.
  Speak personally with the client to persuade him or her to accept.
  Bring the client to the conference.

Determinants of Judicial Mediation

By 1984 we had:

1. Identified the specific techniques (tactics) used by judges in
   their mediation endeavors
2. Determined which seemed to be most frequently used
3. Examined the perceived ethicalness of each technique
4. Determined the perceived effectiveness of each
5. Determined the patterns (strategies) of techniques employed by judges

We then chose to:

6. Ascertain the contingencies under which judges involve themselves in settlement mediation
7. Investigate the effectiveness of their involvement

As a first step toward goal 6, we interviewed fifty judges to learn which variables they thought determined and shaped their involvement in the mediation of settlement negotiations.

Some judges maintained that no situational variables altered the degree or manner of their involvement. Several judges became very involved in all cases; other judges played a moderate role in every negotiation; and others participated in none. Most judges, however, indicated that their mediation efforts were situation dependent, and we were able to identify about twenty variables that apparently influence judicial efforts (Wall and Rude, 1985).

In turn, we examined the effects of four of these variables—case size, trial length, trier of case (is the case to be bench tried or jury tried?), and trial judge (is the case to be tried before the current judge or another one?). Two additional variables—judges' attitude toward judicial involvement and geographical region were also studied (Wall and Rude, 1987).

Judges' responses to our earlier surveys spawned our interest in judicial attitudes. Judicial involvement in settlement, we found, is an emotional minefield for some judges. For example, one judge wrote that any judge not pushing settlement was simply lazy. The counterpoint was exemplified by a Missouri judge who maintained that judges should not become involved in settlement, and that our study of judicial mediation revealed a jaundiced view of the law. His scorching letters to us, to the business school dean, and to the dean of the law school clearly delineated his position. Unfortunately but amusingly, a second mailing to him by a forgetful research assistant raised the judge's ire a few notches. Again he voiced his opinion and further degraded our motives, this time in the news media.

Regional differences also seemed to surface in unsolicited responses from attorneys and judges. Yet the most salient evidence came in judges' responses to speeches. For instance, speeches to audiences in Missouri would typically be followed by questions as to why we were studying judicial mediation. California audiences, on the other hand, would ask which techniques were most effective and would query us about the contingencies under which different techniques should be employed.

In recent years there had been a rising interest in attorneys' preferences for judicial mediation of settlement negotiations (Brazil, 1985). Our survey and interviews had detected that, on occasion, attorneys want judges to involve themselves strongly in the settlement negotiations, and at other times they prefer judges to eschew mediation. However, there was no evidence as to which variables determined their preferences. To overcome this deficiency, our study investigated the effects that the aforementioned four variables have on lawyers' preferences for judicial mediation.

To test the effects of the situational factors, we mailed cases and questionnaires to 650 state judges and 1,100 practicing attorneys chosen randomly from nationwide listings provided by the National Judicial College and the Association of Trial Lawyers of America. Each judge or attorney was sent a product liability case that we developed with the help of several judges, incorporating the four variables: the plaintiffs were seeking $30,000, $500,000, or $30,000,000 (case size); the trial time was five, fifteen, or twenty-five days; the trier of the case was a judge (bench tried) or jury (jury tried); and the trial judge was to be the current one or a different judge.

To glean the judges' and attorneys' attitudes toward judicial involvement in settlement negotiations, at the end of the questionnaire they were asked to answer the question "In general, how strongly should judges facilitate the settlement of cases?" on a seven-point bipolar scale (1 = not at all; 7 = very strongly). To examine regional differences, the responses from the judges and attorneys in the fifty states were grouped into four sections: northeast, west, north-central, and south.

The judges' mediation efforts in the cases sent to them (and the attorneys' preference for that involvement) were scored in several ways. First, after reading the case the judges were asked to answer the question "In this case, how strongly would you facilitate settlement?" on a seven-point bipolar scale. Attorneys were asked, "In this case, how strong would you want the judge's settlement efforts to be?"

Next, the judges and attorneys were presented with twenty mediation techniques that could be used in the case. Judges checked the techniques they would use, and attorneys checked the ones they would want a judge to use. The number of techniques checked served as the second dependent variable. The number of aggressive and client-oriented techniques (the stronger techniques) chosen by the respondents were considered as the third and fourth measures of the judges' intervention in the case.

The assertiveness of the chosen techniques was also of interest. To develop this measure, 300 state judges were asked to score each technique on a seven-point scale (1 = not at all assertive; 7 = extremely assertive). Their responses provided an assertiveness rating for each technique. To calculate assertiveness of the subjects in this study, we averaged the assertiveness ratings for the techniques that each judge or attorney used and labeled this dependent measure "technique assertiveness."

An analysis of the judges' and attorneys' responses revealed that three factors—judges' and attorneys' attitudes toward judicial involvement in settlement, region of the country, and respondent (judge or attorney)—strongly affected the dependent variables. As the respondents' preferences for judicial intervention increased, so did the involvement in the case, the number of techniques used, their use of aggressive and client-oriented techniques, and the assertiveness of the respondents' techniques, multivariate $F (5,998) = 261.14$, $p < .001$. With regard to sectional differences, the respondents from the northeastern and western states, in general, favored stronger involvement in the case and were more assertive in their recommended actions, multivariate $F (15,2755) = 8.78$, $p < .001$. The analysis of the judges' versus attorneys' data reveals that, compared with judges, attorneys preferred stronger facilitation by judges, the use of more techniques, and the use of techniques that are more aggressive, multivariate $F (5,998) = 6.87, p < .001$.

For the elements of the case—size, length, trier, and judge—only size had a significant effect across all the dependent variables; the strength of the judges' mediation efforts (and the attorneys' preferences for judges' assistance) increased as the amount of money at issue decreased, multivariate $F (10,1996) = 2.35, p < .01$. Rather than having a strong main effect, trial length interacted with case size to affect judicial involvement, $F (4,1113) = 2.53, p < .04$. This interaction indicated that judges base their willingness to mediate (and that attorneys base their preferences) somewhat on the trial length of a case, but more on the consistency between the trial length and the case size. For a large case (say $30,000,000), extensive trial time (fifteen or twenty-five days) seemed to be acceptable; consequently, the judges did not express a strong disposition to mediate (nor did the attorneys wish them do to so). Yet for the smaller cases ($30,000 and $500,000) these times seemed excessive, and judicial involvement increased with the anticipated length of the case.

The trier of the case—judge, jury, current judge, or a different one—had no effect upon the judges' and attorneys' responses.

Effect of Judicial Involvement

In a nutshell, our 1985–1986 study (Wall and Rude, 1987) established that attitudes toward judicial involvement, region of the country, respondent (judge versus attorney), size of case, and trial length affect judicial involvement, specifically the number of techniques they use and the assertiveness of the techniques. Does this involvement aid the settlement process? Our last study sought an answer.

In general the war stories we had heard from judges over the years indicated that judicial involvement generates settlement: when judges participate in settlement negotiation, agreement is more likely to surface; and the more assertive judges are, the more likely cases are to settle. These responses are consistent with our earlier finding that the number of techniques used by judges correlates positively with the percentage of cases they reported settling.

Confidence in judicial mediation was strongly reflected in the judiciary's 1983 amendment of Federal Rule 16 (and the subsequent amending of the parallel state rules by most states). Federal Rule 16 is one of the procedural rules governing pretrial conferencs in the federal courts. The amendment encouraged judicial mediation at the pretrial stage. At the state level, some courts (California, for example) have introduced procedures such as weeks-long "trial holidays" in which all judges work at settling cases (Title, 1981). And many states have appointed settlement judges whose major responsibility is case mediation.

It is also worth noting that no studies have shown, nor has anyone suggested, that judicial involvement interferes with the settlement process or reduces the number of out-of-court settlements. Several studies (for example, Church, 1978) have found no relationship between the level of judicial involvement and the extent of settlement; yet these investigations relied on small sample sizes or did not control for the large variation in case and situational factors.

In sum, we felt the weight of evidence supports the hypothesis that judicial mediation—specifically the judge's involvement (versus no involvement), the number of techniques used, and the assertiveness of the techniques—increases out-of-court settlement. To test this idea, we again turned to a survey of the judiciary.

A product liability case similar to the one used in the Wall and Rude (1987) study was sent to 900 state judges chosen randomly from a nationwide listing supplied by the National Judicial College. The judges were informed that the plaintiffs in the case were seeking $3,000,000 ($600,000 each) and did not want to settle out of court. If the case went to trial it would be jury tried before a judge other than the one handling the pretrial hearings.

To test the perceived effects of judicial involvement, the case listed the techniques employed by the judge. Under one condition, the list included two techniques and in another, ten.

The techniques previously had been scored for assertiveness by state judges, and this scoring provided a basis for manipulating a second factor in the study. The judicial techniques in half of the cases were those that had been scored low on assertiveness; the other half contained techniques scored high on assertiveness. These manipulations gave us a two-factor design with two levels of judicial involvement (the use of two interventions versus ten) and two levels of judicial assertiveness (tough versus soft).

Since the judges' attitude toward judicial involvement in settlement had proved a powerful factor in the 1987 study, we also measured the attitude here. And we recorded the state for each respondent. As for dependent variables, we asked each judge:

1. How likely the case was to settle out of court if the pretrial judge did nothing to facilitate settlement
2. The likelihood that the case would settle if the judge took the steps listed in the case
3. How pleased the attorneys would be with the settlement if the judge took the listed steps and the case settled
4. How pleased the defendant would be with the settlement if the judge took the listed steps and the case settled
5. How pleased the plaintiffs would be with the settlement if the judge took the described steps and the case settled

Hypotheses. Our first hypothesis was that any judicial action — two or ten, tough or soft techniques — would enhance the chances of settlement. As for our manipulations in the case, we expected them to produce two main effects and an interaction. Specifically, the judges' use of ten techniques was expected to result in a higher likelihood of settlement than would two techniques. Likewise tough (versus soft) techniques were expected to give a high likelihood of settlement.

The interaction was expected to arise from a perceived overkill of ten tough techniques. This combination was predicted to produce a settlement likelihood only slightly larger than that generated by two tough techniques or by ten soft techniques.

Attitudes toward the propriety of judicial involvement had proved to have a very strong effect upon the judges' involvement in the settlement (Wall and Rude, 1987), but we were unsure of the effect they would have on the perceived effectiveness of judicial involvement. It was also predicted that number and type of techniques would affect the parties' satisfaction with any settlement. The attorneys, defendant, and plaintiffs, we felt, would be pleased with the settlement when the judge employed two (versus ten) or soft (versus tough) techniques. Note that an interesting contradiction was expected: judges' assertiveness — using ten or strong techniques — would more likely foster settlements. However, the parties would be more pleased with settlements that arise from mild judicial prodding, because they could feel responsible for the agreement.

Results. The response rate was 45 percent, with 405 of 900 judges responding, and our expectations of the effects of judicial involvement on settlement were generally supported. The likelihood of settlement was perceived as increasing when the judge facilitated settlement (two, ten, assertive techniques or unassertive) versus when he or she did nothing to assist settlement; repeated measures t (315) = 20.26, $p < .001$.

As for the main effects of technique number and assertiveness, the data supported our hypotheses. (See Table 9.3.) Ten techniques produced a higher likelihood of settlement than did two, F $(1,315)$ = 16.03, $p < .001$, and tough (versus soft) techniques spawned a higher settlement likelihood, F $(1,315)$ = 57.06, $p < .001$. As opposed to our expectation, the two factors did not interact to affect the likelihood of settlement. In addition, the attitude of the surveyed judges and the respondents' region had no effect on their evaluation of the effectiveness of the techniques employed in the case.

The effects of the independent variables on the parties' satisfaction were not as expected. The number and assertiveness of the techniques had no main effect on how pleased the attorneys, plaintiff, or defendant were perceived to be with the settlement of the case. Yet the factors interacted strongly to affect the

Table 9.3. Outcomes of Judicial Mediation.

Number of Techniques and Outcomes of Mediation	Assertiveness of Techniques	
	Tough	*Soft*
Two techniques		
Likelihood of settlement[a]	5.2	3.8
Reaction of attorneys[b]	4.2	3.9
Reaction of plaintiffs[b]	4.4	3.8
Reaction of defendant[b]	4.3	4.3
Ten techniques		
Likelihood of settlement	5.6	4.6
Reactions of attorneys	2.9	4.1
Reactions of plaintiffs	3.5	4.3
Reaction of defendant	4.2	4.7

[a] 1 = Not at all likely to settle; 7 = Extremely likely to settle.
[b] 1 = Not at all pleased; 7 = Very pleased.

judges' perceptions of attorneys' (F [1,315] = 13.42, $p < .001$) and plaintiffs' (F [1,315] = 14.22, $p < .001$) pleasure or displeasure with the settlement. As can be seen in Table 9.3, the use of ten techniques that were highly assertive significantly raised the judges' belief that the parties would be irritated by judicial intervention.

While the responding judges' attitudes toward judicial involvement did not affect their evaluation of the effectiveness of the techniques in the case, the respondents' attitudes toward judicial mediation did affect their opinions of the attorneys', plaintiffs', and defendants' pleasure or displeasure with the settlement. As might be expected, the relationship was strongly positive, with the judges' perceptions of the attorneys', plaintiffs', and defendants' evaluations being correlated with their own attitudes toward judicial involvement in settlement ($r = .34$, $p < .001$; $r = .21$, $p < .001$; $r = .21$, $p < .001$, respectively). Finally, the region of the country had no effect on the responding judges' evaluations.

Discussion. Comparisons among the above findings engender some material insights: judges nationwide, regardless of their attitude toward judicial involvement in settlement, conclude that judicial involvement facilitates settlement. In addition, they feel that the more techniques a judge employs, the more likely he or she is to glean an agreement. Likewise, the more assertive the applied techniques, the higher the probability of settlement.

Summary of Major Findings

We have outlined the history of our judicial mediation project, and traced the methodologies employed. Here it is perhaps useful to provide a short recap.

Initially we unearthed seventy-one techniques used by judges to facilitate settlement (Table 9.1). We then determined the frequency of use, perceived ethicalness, and perceived effectiveness of each. By performing factor analyses on responses from three independent samples — state judges, federal judges, and attorneys — we found that judges tend to use the techniques in groups of strategies (Table 9.2).

What situational factors have an impact on judicial mediation? We found four: judges' attitudes toward judicial involvement in settlement, section of the country, case size, and trial time for the case.

How effective is that mediation? We had found that the number of techniques used by the judge and the assertiveness of the techniques had a straightforward impact; both determine the perceived likelihood of settlement, without generating the attorneys' or disputing parties' displeasure. These individuals, however, are irked when they are targeted with a large number of assertive techniques.

Judicial Settlement Model. A combination of the 1987 results with those of the most recent study reported here provides an initial judicial settlement model (Figure 9.1). Four factors determine the level and type of judicial mediation. This mediation, in turn, partially determines the perceived likelihood that the case will be settled and the extent to which the disputing parties are pleased with the settlement.

While the model reflects our current findings, it concomitantly charts various paths for future research. One option is to

Figure 9.1. Judicial Mediation Model.

Situational Factors	Judges' Mediation	Mediation Outcomes
Judges' attitude toward judicial involvement	Number of techniques	Likelihood of settlement
Region of country →	Assertiveness of techniques	Disputing parties' reactions
Size of case		
Trial time of case		

test the effects of additional situational factors on judicial mediation. We suggest looking at the effects from these factors:

1. Judge's time constraints
2. Length of docket
3. Case complexity
4. Experience of attorneys
5. Number of parties requesting assistance
6. Cooperation of attorneys
7. Attorneys' absolute and relative competencies
8. Number of parties involved in the case
9. Expertise of judge
10. Extent of controversy
11. Disparity between parties' strength
12. Recalcitrance of clients

When studying the effects of the situational variables, researchers can also examine an expanded number of mediation approaches. To date two factors—the number of techniques and their assertiveness—have been treated as dependent and independent variables, but any of the seventy-one techniques can be investigated in the same manner. The various strategies—logical, aggressive, paternalistic, and client-oriented—provide mediation approaches for study. Also other groupings of the techniques (for example, a set designed to defuse high emotions) could be investigated.

Finally, the range of mediation outcomes needs to be expanded, beyond perceived likelihood of settlement and beliefs about the parties' reactions. The judicial literature is rife with suggestions (Brazil, 1985; Carter, 1962; Galanter, 1985). They include speed of settlement, quality of settlement, quality of trial when there is no settlement, number of appeals (again when there is no settlement), the parties' acceptance and implementation of the settlement, and their evaluations of the judge's mediations.

Methodological Reflection. The major research route implied by the model is also the most difficult. We need to conduct investigations in *actual* settings. Our research to date has been based on interviews or surveys that tap opinions of the judiciary and record their judgments about causal relationships.

Admittedly this approach possesses notable shortcomings, the major deficiency being that respondents' observations and evaluations may not be accurate reflections of reality. Like all of us, judges and attorneys see what they want to see, draw conclusions based on limited information, make attributions about causes, force consistency upon inconsistencies.

In addition, surveys have a response bias. In our studies we have been fortunate enough to glean response rates of about 50 percent overall; yet the respondents are probably ones who have strong opinions—pro or con—about judicial mediation. Practicing judges and attorneys who are ambivalent about judicial involvement, as well as overworked ones, are underrepresented in our sample.

Observations in actual settings overcome some of these problems—but such studies are Augean tasks. Most judges consider settlement negotiations as privileged conversation, and thus exclude observers. Since all settlement discussions are off the record, researchers cannot rely on court records. And if one is fortunate enough to observe or record settlement negotiations, the observer's presence may notably alter the parties' behaviors.

Time, though, is the major drawback to obtaining objective data. To rely solely on such data-collection techniques is to cripple progress. Consider an analogy with genetic studies. Geneticists preferred to study genetics via observations of humans, but doing so constrained their research. (Human beings, thankfully, reproduce very slowly.) Mendel compromised somewhat and used garden peas. Later, Castle and Morgan studied fruit flies. And today's geneticists probe the secrets of bacteria. Selecting these approaches involved compromises, but compromises were made because studying genetics in the perfect setting, with perfect techniques, would have predestined the genetics field to failure.

The same holds for the study of judicial mediation. If we had relied solely on observations, we would currently be at square one, identifying the techniques in use today. There is compromise in relying on judges' and attorneys' reports, but with the compromise comes progress—ideas and theories that can be tested by practitioners.

Relationship to Other Mediation Works. As you, the reader, reflect on judicial mediation—the actual process, the results presented here, and potential future work—bear in mind that this form of mediation is quite unique. It takes place *within* the judicial system, and the disputing parties as well as their attorneys have very little control over whether or not they will be parties to a mediation. If the judge wishes to mediate, she or he will do so. Since they have the constitutional right to a trial, the clients can reject the judge's overtures, but almost never do they ignore them.

As for the judges, they, unlike most mediators, are very powerful. Judges are accorded respect; people rise when the judge enters. Judges call attorneys by their first names; judges are called "Judge." Judges take off their coats; lawyers do not. Judges tell jokes; lawyers laugh.

Not only are judges powerful, they feel and use their power. Remember, these are individuals who normally exercise tremendous power on a day-to-day basis. They send people to prison for life. They fine corporations vast sums or order them to pay these amounts to plaintiffs. They set precedents on major cases. Frequently, they decide in whose home children will re-side. Some rule as to whether life-support systems will be switched off. Since judges have and are accustomed to using power, they are quite tempted to reign supreme in a settlement negotiation. A judge who has decided a multimillion-dollar toxic-shock case in the morning feels quite comfortable ordering the plaintiffs in an afternoon case to appear in chambers and explain why they will not accept a settlement.

Remember too that all settlement conversations are off the record, and no laws dictate what a judge can do. One judge refused to allow attorneys out of his chambers even though the courthouse was burning. Another told the attorneys he would be the judge if the case came to trial; he would give a ruling that was identical to his suggested settlement figure; result—the case settled.

In sum, judges are powerful mediators who are accustomed to exercising power. They are afforded the opportunity to use power in civil mediations, and they do so. Their power, used or not, enhances the effectiveness (the frequency of agreement) of any techniques they choose to employ. Therefore (it seems to us) any mediation approach that is effective in other settings—marriage, neighborhood, international, labor-management disputes—will, with some modifications, prove effective in the hands of judges.

On the other hand, extrapolations from judicial mediation to other mediation settings should be undertaken with caution. Many techniques (such as informing one party he has a poor case and should drop it) that are effective in the hands of a powerful judge can prove impotent when used by weak mediators.

Practical Implications. After years of observing judicial mediations, talking to attorneys, interviewing judges, and surveying both groups, our principal conclusion is that judicial mediation increases settlement. Judges who try to settle cases obtain more settlements than judges who eschew involvement. Also assertiveness in whatever form—number of techniques, repetition of techniques, extensive time with parties, assertive techniques—yields success.

This chapter delineates many of the techniques judges

can use and indicates the relative effectiveness of each. In addition, it reveals that effective mediation is based on many, rather than few, techniques. It would be fruitful for judges to build an inventory of techniques and to apply them, when they choose to do so, in sufficient numbers and in appropriate combinations to facilitate civil settlements.

References

Brazil, W. D. *Settling Civil Disputes*. Chicago: American Bar Association, 1985.

Carter, J. M. "Effective Calendar Control: Objectives and Methods." *Federal Rules Decisions*, 1962, *29*, 227–240.

Church, T. *Justice Delayed: The Pace of Litigation in Urban Trial Courts*. Williamsburg, Va.: National Center for State Courts, 1978.

Fox, T. "Settlement: Helping the Lawyers to Fulfill Their Responsibility." *Federal Rules Decisions*, 1972, *53*, 129–142.

Galanter, M. "A Settlement Judge, Not a Trial Judge: Judicial Mediation in the United States." *Journal of Law and Society*, 1985, *12*, 1–18.

Schiller, L. F., and Wall, J. A. "Judicial Settlement Techniques." *The American Journal of Trial Advocacy*, 1981, *5*, 39–61.

Title, S. "The Lawyer's Role in Settlement Conferences." *The American Bar Association Journal*, 1981, *67*, 592–597.

Wall, J. A., Jr. "Mediation: An Analysis, Review and Proposed Research." *Journal of Conflict Resolution*, 1981, *25*, 157–180.

Wall, J. A., and Rude, D. E. "Judicial Mediation: Techniques, Strategies, and Situational Effects." *Journal of Social Issues*, 1985, *41*, 47–63.

Wall, J. A., and Rude, D. E. "Judges' Mediation of Settlement Negotiations." *Journal of Applied Psychology*, 1987, *72*, 234–239.

Wall, J. A., and Schiller, L. F. "Judicial Involvement in Pretrial Settlement: A Judge Is Not a Bump on a Log." *The American Journal of Trial Advocacy*, 1982, *6*, 27–45.

Wall, J. A., Schiller, L. F., and Ebert, R. J. "Should Judges Grease the Slow Wheels of Justice? A Survey on the Effectiveness of Judicial Mediary Techniques." *The American Journal of Trial Advocacy*, 1984, *8*, 83–114.

TEN

Contingent Mediator Behavior and Its Effectiveness

Peter J. D. Carnevale
Rodney G. Lim
Mary E. McLaughlin

Success in mediation, much like success in other human endeavors, is achieved by applying the appropriate action, in this case the proper mediation tactic, to the problem at hand. The idea that successful mediators are adaptive—that they do different things in different situations—is central to the contingency approach to mediation.

On the surface, the contingency approach is simple and compelling. It suggests that some mediator behaviors that may succeed in one dispute may in another actually impede resolution, or at best be trivial. But it turns complicated quickly,

Note: The authors wish to thank Dean G. Pruitt and Kenneth Kressel for their very helpful comments on this chapter and are grateful to the Society of Professionals in Dispute Resolution for allowing this research. This work was supported by a University of Illinois Research Board grant to Peter Carnevale.

213

especially when we consider that such an approach requires a well-developed taxonomy of mediator behavior (what is it that mediators do?); a taxonomy of dispute features (what are the basic types of dispute?); a taxonomy of outcomes (what are the objectives of mediation?); and some assumptions about diagnosis, adaptation, and timing (which mediator behaviors go with which dispute features to produce which outcomes?). We can hardly say that such taxonomies exist, despite the fact that the contingency approach can be found in one form or another in just about every discussion of mediation.

The contingency approach to mediation is a useful analytical tool that can help researchers, practitioners, and just about anyone who is interested in learning about, doing, or teaching mediation. With it, researchers have a framework for collecting data and developing theories of mediation; practitioners have a systematic way to organize training and assessment; and teachers have a framework for presenting information. These advantages hold regardless of the dispute context. Indeed, the context—divorce, international, industrial, or judicial mediation—can be treated as one classification factor (a dispute feature) in a contingency model.

In this chapter we present two field studies of professional mediators; they were designed to assess the structure of mediator behavior and to test contingent mediator behavior and its effectiveness. Our data illustrate contingent effectiveness—the notion that some mediator tactics are more likely to produce success under some conditions than under others.

Empirical Background

The research that we describe was inspired by earlier studies by Hiltrop (1985) and Carnevale and Pegnetter (1985). Hiltrop's research (see Chapter Eleven) indicated that the same mediator tactics were associated with settlement in some circumstances but not in others. Carnevale and Pegnetter had thirty-two professional labor mediators rate the extent to which twenty-four sources of dispute were a problem for a recently mediated case (for example, "a key issue was at stake"), and also the extent to which thirty-seven mediation tactics were used in that case (for instance, "suggested a particular settlement"). A correlation analysis revealed that some tactics were tied to the problems that contributed to the dispute. When bargainers had unrealistic expectations, mediators attempted to change those expectations; when bargainers brought too many issues to the negotiation, mediators simplified the agenda or created priorities; when bargainers lacked expertise and experience, mediators attempted to educate them about dealing with impasses.

Our studies extend those earlier ones; we used a large sample of professional mediators and broad sets of dispute types and mediator tactics to examine basic dimensions and contingencies in mediator behavior.

Features of Mediator Behavior

Perhaps the best-known taxonomy of mediator behavior is Kressel's (1972), recently updated by Kressel and Pruitt (1985). They identify three basic types of tactics: reflexive, substantive, and contextual. Reflexive tactics are designed to orient mediators to the dispute and to create a foundation for their future activities; substantive tactics deal directly with the issues in the dispute, such as suggestions for settlement; and contextual tactics involve facilitating the dispute resolution process so that the parties themselves are able to discover an acceptable solution. But to date there is little empirical evidence on this or any other classification of mediator behavior (Kressel and Pruitt, 1985). We believe that the first step in understanding what leads mediators to use different tactics in different situations is to identify the key features of tactics.

Multidimensional Scaling of Mediator Tactics. One of our studies (McLaughlin, Carnevale, and Lim, 1988) was designed to identify mediators' perceptions of the major strategies of intervention. The method of the study was based on multidimensional scaling (MDS), a mathematical technique that can assess similarities in judges' ratings of a class of stimuli — in this case mediation tactics — by locating the ratings in a spatial configuration (Kruskal and Wish, 1978). The results of our effort are illustrated in Figure 10.1.

The respondents in the study were forty-nine members of the Society of Professionals in Dispute Resolution (SPIDR), an international organization of mediators who work in labor-management, environmental, judicial, and other kinds of disputes. They were asked to sort thirty-six mediation tactics into as many mutually exclusive categories as they wanted (up to thirty-five) on the basis of how strategically similar the tactics appeared to be. The thirty-six tactics, arbitrarily designed A to Z and 0 to 9, were taken from Carnevale and Pegnetter (1985). They are:

A.   Attempt to simplify the agenda by eliminating or combining factors.
B.   Clarify the needs of the other party.
C.   Discuss other settlements or patterns.
D.   Point out the costs of continued disagreement.
E.   Suggest a particular settlement.
F.   Control the expression of hostility.
G.   Express displeasure at the progress of negotiation.
H.   Express pleasure at the progress.
I.   Suggest proposals that help avoid the appearance of defeat on an issue.
J.   Help individuals save face.
K.   Suggest a review of needs with the parties' constituency.
L.   Try to change the parties' expectations.
M.   Teach the bargaining process.
N.   Try to gain the parties' trust and confidence.
O.   Call for frequent caucuses.
P.   Avoid taking sides on important issues in joint sessions.
Q.   Help develop a framework for negotiations.
R.   Keep negotiations focused on the issues.
S.   Help the parties deal with problems with their constituents or superiors.
T.   Make substantive suggestions for compromise.
U.   Press the parties hard to make compromise.
V.   Control the timing or pace of negotiations.
W.   Keep the parties at the table and negotiating.

X.   Tell the parties that their position is unrealistic.
Y.   Argue one side's case to the other side.
Z.   Use humor to lighten the atmosphere.
0.   Let everyone blow off steam.
1.   Have the parties prioritize the issues.
2.   Take responsibility for concessions.
3.   Suggest tradeoffs among the issues.
4.   Attempt to "speak their language."
5.   Assure each party that the other is being honest.
6.   Warn that the next impasse step is not better.
7.   Develop rapport.
8.   Use late hours or long mediation to facilitate compromise.
9.   Attempt to settle simple issues first.

The mediators' categorizations were scaled using KYST-2A, a multidimensional scaling program (Kruskal, Young, and Seery, 1977), and the results, keyed to the preceding list, are displayed in a three-dimensional spatial configuration in Figure 10.1. Incidentally, forty-nine is an ample sample for this analysis.

The first dimension of tactics reflects two of Kressel and Pruitt's categories: substantive and reflexive. The reflexive end of this dimension includes tactics such as (4) attempt to speak their language and (P) avoid taking sides on important issues in joint sessions. The substantive end of this dimension includes (E) suggest a particular settlement and (L) try to change expectations. In mediation this dimension may be related to time: reflexive tactics occur early in mediation and substantive tactics later (Kressel and Pruitt, 1985).

The second dimension in Figure 10.1 is affective-cognitive. At the affective end of this dimension are emotive tactics that reflect the mediator's consideration of the parties' feelings and psychological needs. These tactics include (F) control the expression of hostility, (G) express displeasure at the progress, (H) express pleasure at progress, (Z) use humor to lighten the atmosphere, and (0) let everyone blow off steam. Tactics at the cognitive end of the dimension reflect the mediator's control over the agenda of issues, and include (A) attempt to simplify the agenda by eliminating or combining issues,

Figure 10.1. Multidimensional Scaling Display of Mediation Tactics.

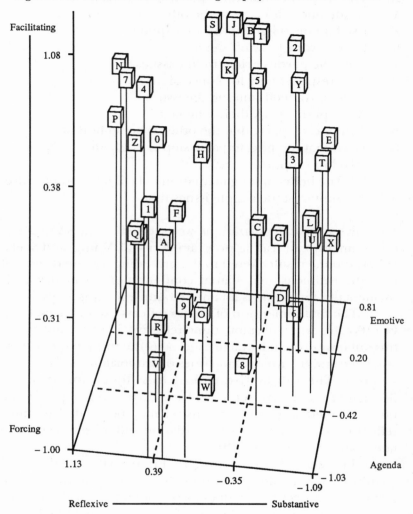

(Q) help develop a framework for negotiations, (R) keep negotiations focused on the issues, (1) have the parties prioritize the issues, (9) attempt to settle simple issues first. The distinction between emotive and agenda tactics is similar to the distinction between task-oriented and person-oriented aspects of leadership described by Likert (1967).

The third dimension of mediation tactics involves forcing and facilitating. At one end of this dimension are forceful, pressing tactics that reflect the mediator's desire to push the parties toward settlement. This includes tactics such as (6) tell them that the next impasse step is no better and (8) use late hours, long mediation, to facilitate compromise. At the other end of this dimension are mediator tactics designed to make it easier for the parties to make concessions, especially by managing their image with their constituents. These tactics include (I) suggest proposals that help avoid the appearance of defeat on an issue and (S) help the parties deal with problems with their constituents or superiors.

Factor Analysis of Mediator Tactics. Another of our studies (Lim and Carnevale, 1988) was designed to identify the key features of mediation tactics by assessing mediators' use of tactics. We expected a factor analysis of mediators' reported use of mediation tactics to yield a structure similar to Kressel and Pruitt's classification of tactics into substantive, contextual, and reflexive types. In addition, Carnevale (1986) presented a theoretical discussion of mediation that further divides substantive tactics into three types: those that move a party off a position, those that move a party onto a new position, and those involving outcome suggestions that specifically aid in face saving. To test this factor structure, factor analyses were conducted on mediators' ratings of their usage of tactics in their most recent case. This study differed from the multidimensional scaling (MDS) study reported earlier in that here we have data on the mediators' reports about the actual *use* of tactics, whereas the MDS study involved data on *perceptions* of mediation tactics. (See Lim and Carnevale, 1988, for more details on the factor analyses.)

The respondents in this study were 255 members of the Society of Professionals in Dispute Resolution (SPIDR). They were asked to recall their most recently completed mediation case, and then to rate the extent that twenty-four potential sources of dispute were a problem in that case, the extent to which they used forty-three different mediation tactics, and the extent to which nineteen outcomes were achieved. All ratings were made on five-point scales. The mediators also were asked to provide background information about themselves and the case. Many of the 255 cases were labor disputes (about 47 percent); the rest included marital (about 13 percent), community (about 11 percent), and judicial, family, environmental, marketplace, and landlord-tenant disputes (all less than 6 percent each). Table 10.1 presents ratings of the overall use of mediation tactics.

When the data in this table were factor analyzed, Kressel and Pruitt's classification of mediator activity into reflexive, substantive, and contextual tactics was confirmed; albeit with important modifications (Table 10.2). Thus, contextual tactics are subdivided into two types. One emphasizes activities important in building trust between the parties and the mediator, and includes tactics such as "formulated clear goals before and during mediation" and "develop trust between the parties"; the other involves tactics that control the agenda, including "help establish priorities among the issues" and "arrange agenda to cover general issues first, specific issues last." The final model also incorporates the three subdivided substantive factors: a coercive type designed to move a party off a position, a more positive type designed to move a party onto a new position through suggestions, and a face-saving type.

In the table, each factor appears under the factor we originally thought it belonged to. Most of the tactics that we expected to load on these factors did so. However, our expectations were not perfect. Two tactics crossloaded on a second factor in addition to their primary factors, and some tactics did not load on their hypothesized factors at all.

Goodness-of-fit indices for the final model can be found in Lim and Carnevale (1988); the values of these indices suggested a reasonable fit of the model to the data. A final note: the factor analysis and the multidimensional scaling analysis have features in common. Both point to reflexive tactics, substantive

Table 10.1. Overall Mean Use of Mediation Tactics.

Mediation Tactic	Mean Use Score*
1. Kept negotiations focused on the issues	3.88
2. Developed rapport	3.81
3. Avoided taking sides on important issues in joint sessions	3.79
4. Tried to gain trust and confidence	3.71
5. Clarified the needs of the other party	3.62
6. Let everyone blow off steam	3.41
7. Attempted to move one or both parties off a committed position	3.41
8. Helped devise a framework for negotiations	3.37
9. Helped establish priorities among the issues	3.33
10. Discussed the interests of all parties affected by the dispute	3.22
11. Attempted to develop trust between the disputants	3.18
12. Made substantive suggestions for compromise	3.14
13. Helped one or more parties save face	3.08
14. Suggested proposals that helped avoid the appearance of defeat on an issue	3.08
15. Discussed the costs of continued disagreement	3.03
16. Formulated clear goals before or during mediation	3.03
17. Used humor to lighten the atmosphere	3.02
18. Controlled the timing or pace of negotiations	3.02
19. Attempted to settle simple issues first	2.95
20. Attempted to simplify agenda by eliminating or combining issues	2.94
21. Kept the parties at the table and negotiating	2.91
22. Tried to change expectations	2.89
23. Attempted to "speak their language"	2.84
24. Expressed pleasure at the progress in negotiations	2.80
25. Pressed the parties hard to make compromise	2.80
26. Controlled the expression of hostility	2.76
27. Suggested a particular settlement	2.75
28. Kept the caucus focused on the impasse issues	2.70
29. Allowed the parties themselves to initiate and maintain momentum	2.67
30. Suggested tradeoffs among the issues	2.65
31. Argued one party's case to the other party	2.64
32. Discussed other settlements or patterns	2.60
33. Called for frequent caucuses	2.59
34. Assured each party that the other was being honest	2.41
35. Helped the parties deal with problems with their constituents or superiors	2.37
36. Teach the bargaining or impasse process	2.31
37. Told the parties their position was unrealistic	2.29
38. Arranged agenda to cover general issues first, specific issues last	2.15
39. Warned that the next impasse step was not better	2.11
40. Suggested that the parties review their needs with their constituency	2.09
41. Used late hours, long mediation, to facilitate compromise	1.93
42. Took responsibility for concessions	1.86
43. Expressed displeasure at the progress in negotiations	1.63

* On a five-point scale, 5 being highest.

Table 10.2. Confirmatory Factor Analysis of Mediation Tactics: Final Model.

	Factor					
Tactic	1	2	3	4	5	6
Factor 1: Substantive 1 (Press)						
Press parties hard	77(06)					
Move them off position	68(07)					
Say they are unrealistic	65(07)					
Change their expectations	60(07)					
Say next step is bad	51(07)					
Factor 2: Reflexive						
Develop rapport with parties		71(07)				
Speak their language		63(07)				
Let them blow off steam		62(07)				
Use humor		57(07)				
Avoid taking sides on issues		44(07)				
Keep caucus focused on issues	60(07)					
Call for frequent caucuses	58(07)					
Keep them at the table	32(09)	33(09)				
Factor 3: Contextual 1 (Trust)						
Form clear goals for mediation			74(07)			
Develop trust between parties			73(07)			
Discuss interests of others			61(07)			
Gain parties' trust			56(07)			
Express pleasure at progress			48(07)			
Clarify needs of other party			45(08)			
Factor 4: Contextual 2 (Agenda)						
Help prioritize the issues				70(07)		
Cover general issues first				64(07)		
Devise framework for negotiations				62(07)		
Settle simple issues first				58(07)		
Focus negotiations on issues				58(07)		
Simplify agenda				41(08)		
Factor 5: Substantive 2 (Face-Saving)						
Suggest face-saving proposals					90(07)	
Help save face					76(07)	
Deal with constituent problems	41(08)				27(08)	
Take responsibility for concessions						50(07)
Factor 6: Substantive 3 (Suggestions)						
Suggest compromises						83(07)
Suggest tradeoffs among issues						64(07)
Suggest a settlement						59(07)

Note: $N = 191$. Blank entries indicate model parameters fixed at zero. Standard errors of parameter estimates in parentheses. Decimal points are omitted.

tactics (general pressure, face saving, suggestions), and contextual tactics (trust, agenda) as meaningful features of mediator behavior.

Features of Disputes and Dispute Outcomes

Our data also allowed us to examine basic dimensions of the disputes reported by the SPIDR mediators as well as their outcomes. Because no a priori factors were hypothesized for dispute sources or mediation outcomes, exploratory factor analyses were performed separately on these two data sets. Five such analyses were performed, all of which yielded highly similar results. We report only the principal axes solution. Table 10.3 shows loadings of each source of dispute on the five-factor solution that appeared to be most appropriate. The table shows loadings of each source of dispute on the five factors, eigenvalues for each factor, item communalities, proportion of variance accounted for by each factor, item-total correlations, and Cronbach's coefficient alpha for each factor. The coefficient alphas ranged from .51 to .83, which given the exploratory nature of our study was acceptable.

The first factor, hostility, involved such items as interparty hostility, no interest in settling, no trust in the other party, and unreceptiveness to mediation (the last source also loaded on factor 4). The second factor, internal party problems, included items such as a lack of leadership, the chief negotiator's lack of authority or experience, or the parties not being prepared for negotiations. The third factor, comparison problems, included two items: holding to a comparison position and breaking from a comparison pattern. This refers to an agreement reached in a comparable negotiation that has attained the status of prominence and thus influences subsequent negotiations (see Pruitt's discussion of prominence and pattern bargaining [1981, pp. 57–70]). The fourth factor, resistance to mediation, involved items such as no trust in the mediator, desire for control over the proceedings, and bringing too many issues to mediation. The fifth factor, single important issue, involved two items: a key issue at stake and a major principle.

Table 10.3. Principal Axes Factor Analysis of Sources of Dispute.

Source of Dispute	Factor					h^2	Item Total Correlation	Mean Rating
	1	2	3	4	5			
Factor 1: Hostility								
Interparty hostility	.64	.07	-.11	.01	.34	.55	.57	2.81
No interest in settling	.63	.05	.06	.13	-.07	.42	.53	1.87
No trust in other party	.58	.22	-.12	.08	.35	.52	.57	3.00
Unreceptive to mediation	.56	.13	.03	.46	-.11	.56	.50	1.65
Intransigent person present	.43	.19	.21	.30	.20	.39	.45	2.57
Factor 2: Internal Party Problems								
Lacked leadership	.23	.64	.04	.08	-.16	.49	.51	1.74
Chief negotiator lacked authority	-.06	.57	.21	.09	.01	.38	.47	1.52
Backed off initial proposal	.00	.51	.05	.08	.22	.32	.32	1.83
Not prepared for negotiations	.43	.46	.04	.17	-.05	.43	.46	1.76
Chief negotiator lacked experience	.23	.42	.18	.13	.05	.28	.44	1.74
Factor 3: Comparison Problems								
Hold to comparison position	-.02	.16	.79	-.01	.07	.65	.70	1.96
Break from comparison pattern	-.01	.15	.74	-.06	.17	.60	.70	1.91
Factor 4: Resistance to Mediation								
No trust in mediator	.19	.04	-.07	.58	-.01	.38	.45	1.27
Wanted control over proceedings	.38	.25	-.03	.45	.10	.42	.36	1.80
Too many issues brought to table	.00	.12	.12	.45	.21	.28	.29	1.88

Factor 5: Single Important Issue							
Key settlement issues involved	−.02	.02	.14	.05	.59	.37	.43	3.32
Major principle at stake	.23	.05	.09	.09	.53	.35	.43	3.39
Sources Not Included								
No bargaining before mediation	.22	.18	−.14	.31	.01	.20		1.74
Unrealistic expectations	.30	.07	.33	.26	.17	.30		2.72
Commitment to a position	.31	.00	.24	.25	.28	.30		2.92
Internal disagreements on issues	.14	.38	−.01	.04	.16	.19		2.26
Bargaining team too large	−.05	.24	.10	.23	.20	.17		1.36
Eigenvalues	2.44	1.86	1.57	1.44	1.26			
Proportion variance accounted for	.11	.08	.07	.07	.06			
Coefficient alpha	.75	.68	.83	.51	.60			

Note: N = 134.

Table 10.3 also presents ratings of the overall occurrence of the dispute sources. The mediators reported these five most common dispute problems:

1. Major principle involved
2. Key issue at stake
3. Lack of trust between the parties
4. A commitment to a position
5. Interpersonal hostility

Factor Analysis of Outcomes. As with dispute sources, a variety of exploratory factor analyses were performed for the mediation outcome data. All these analyses produced highly similar results. Again, the results for the principal axes are reported. The criteria used to evaluate different factor solutions suggested that a three-factor solution was the most reasonable. Table 10.4 presents loadings of each outcome on the three factors, eigenvalues for each factor, item communalities, proportion of variance accounted for by each factor, item-total correlations, and coefficient alpha for each factor. The coefficient alphas for these factors were high, ranging from .76 to .94.

The first factor, general settlement, represented general aspects such as reaching settlement, especially one that was mutually beneficial, lasting, and unambiguous. The second factor, mediator outcomes, reflected outcomes relevant to the mediator, such as feelings of trust toward the mediator, satisfaction of the mediator's needs, and the parties' satisfaction with mediation. The third factor, improved relationship, involved an improved relationship and better communication between the parties.

Table 10.4 also presents ratings of the overall occurrence of the dispute outcomes. The mediators reported the five most likely outcomes:

1. The parties were satisfied with mediation.
2. The number of issues was reduced.
3. Settlement was achieved.

Table 10.4. Principal Axes Factor Analysis of Mediation Outcomes.

Outcome	Factor			h^2	Item Total Correlation	Mean Rating
	1	*2*	*3*			
Factor 1: General Settlement						
Dispute settled	.85	.30	.21	.86	.87	4.01
Nothing ambiguously stated	.72	.37	.20	.69	.80	3.52
Mutually beneficial settlement	.71	.43	.41	.77	.84	3.56
Lasting agreement reached	.70	.35	.25	.67	.80	3.48
No adverse political ramifications	.63	.32	.31	.60	.76	3.51
Agreement felt to be their own	.62	.33	.26	.56	.72	3.44
Overall success	.62	.60	.17	.78	.79	3.89
Underlying core conflict resolved	.59	.19	.44	.57	.70	3.11
Number of issues reduced	.56	.46	.24	.58	.70	3.99
Settled in reasonable time	.46	.38	.37	.50	.66	3.39
No future problems expected	.41	.09	.32	.28	.48	2.54
Factor 2: Mediator Outcomes						
Feelings of trust toward mediator	.19	.72	.28	.64	.72	3.81
Parties satisfied with mediation	.29	.63	.26	.55	.65	4.15
Mediator's needs, goals satisfied	.37	.61	.23	.56	.65	3.59
Distance in positions narrowed	.53	.56	.20	.64	.63	3.85
Factor 3: Improved Relationship						
Interparty relations improved	.19	.34	.69	.63	.63	2.80
Parties learned to communicate	.24	.20	.68	.56	.64	2.70
Resources gained or recovered	.41	.25	.46	.44	.53	2.99
Eigenvalues	5.25	3.25	2.39			
Proportion variance accounted for	.29	.18	.13			
Coefficient alpha	.94	.83	.76			

Note: $N = 150$.

4. The distance was narrowed between the parties.
5. Interparty relations were improved.

Sources of Dispute, Mediation Tactics, and Outcomes

What are the relationships between the different sources of dispute, the mediation tactics, and the outcomes of dispute? Are some sources of dispute more likely to be associated with success? Are some mediation tactics more successful? To answer these questions, we created factor-based scales using the results of the factor analyses of the tactics, sources, and outcomes described above. These scales represented each of the five sources, six tactics, and three outcomes that were indicated by the factor analyses (see Lim and Carnevale, 1988, for details).

Sources of Dispute and Outcome. The correlations among the factor-based scales produced several interesting statistically significant patterns. Two dispute scales — hostility and resistance to mediation — were negatively associated with the three outcome scales — general settlement, mediator outcomes, and improvement of the parties' relationship. Two other dispute scales, internal problems and single issue at stake, were unrelated to the outcome scales. The remaining source scale, comparison problems, was positively associated with general settlement and mediator outcomes, but was unrelated to improvement in the parties' relationship. In other words, the mediators reported that hostility and unreceptiveness to mediation are especially unlikely to result in success.

Mediation Tactics and Outcome. The correlations between the factor-based scales revealed that four of the tactic scales — reflexive, contextual 1 (trust), contextual 2 (agenda), and substantive 2 (face-saving) tactics — were positively associated with all three outcome scales — general settlement, mediator outcomes, and improvement of the parties' relationship. The two remaining tactic scales, substantive 1 (press) and substantive 3 (make suggestions), were unrelated to general settlement and improvement in the parties' relationship, but were positively associated with mediator outcomes. Taken together, these correlations suggest that mediators in general believe that their activities produce positive outcomes. They also indicate that forceful tactics have a positive bearing on mediator outcomes more than on settlement or improvement in the parties' relationship.

Characteristics of the Mediator. We also examined the relationships between various demographic characteristics of the mediators, the use of mediation tactics, and dispute outcomes. Age and gender were not related to any of the outcome scales, but were associated with the use of different tactics. Male mediators were more likely to use substantive/press and substantive/suggestions than female mediators. Older mediators also used general pressure more, and also made more suggestions, which was not surprising since older mediators also tended to be male.

The only mediator characteristics that related to dispute outcomes were the mediators' self-reported general knowledge about the issues in the dispute, which was positively associated with achieving general settlement and mediator outcomes, and the number of cases that the mediator handled in a typical year, which was significantly associated with general settlement. This latter finding is consistent with results of Kochan and Jick (1978), who reported that mediator experience was positively associated with the probability of settlement.

Taken together, our results suggest several interesting observations about the relationships between the different sources of dispute, the use of mediation tactics, and dispute outcomes. One is that certain mediator behaviors are associated with different kinds of outcomes. The use of either reflexive, contextual/trust, contextual/agenda, or substantive/face-saving tactics was positively associated with settlement, mediator outcomes, and improvement of the parties' relationship; but the mediators' reported use of either substantive/press or substantive/suggestion tactics, although positively associated with mediator outcomes, was unrelated to settlement and improvement in the parties' relationship. A second noteworthy finding was the difference between male and female mediators: male mediators were more likely to use substantive/press and substantive/suggestion tactics than female mediators. This finding supports the idea that gender differences in mediator behavior reported in Chapter Sixteen, involving college students in a laboratory simulation, generalize to professional mediators.

Contingent Use of Mediation Tactics

Are mediation tactics used contingently; that is, are some disputes likely to elicit some mediation tactics and not others? To answer this question, we did a correlational analysis involving dispute sources and dispute tactics (Lim and Carnevale, 1988).

Several correlations were consistent with the correlations reported in Carnevale and Pegnetter (1985). For example, when hostility was a problem, the mediators reported attempting to control the parties' expression of hostility. When the parties had unrealistic expectations, the mediators reported trying to change the parties' expectations, telling them that their position was unrealistic, and pressing them hard to make a compromise. When the parties were committed to a position, the mediators reported attempting to move them off the committed position, and keeping them at the table and negotiating. When there was a single intransigent person, the mediators reported letting that person blow off steam. When the parties were not interested in settling, the mediators reported mentioning the costs of continued disagreement. And when there was a lack of authority and leadership on a bargaining team, the mediators reported attempting to speak the parties' language.

The correlations between the factor-based scales indicated that the presence of hostility was positively associated with three mediation tactic scales—substantive/press, contextual/agenda tactics, and substantive/face saving. The presence of internal team problems and resistance to mediation were both positively associated only with the use of contextual/agenda tactics. The presence of comparison problems was positively associated with the use of the three types of substantive tactics and contextual/agenda tactics. The presence of a single issue was positively associated with all tactic scales except the use of reflexive and contextual/agenda tactics.

Contingent Effectiveness of Mediation Tactics

The data reported above indicate that mediators to some extent select tactics in a contingent manner; but that does not tell us whether mediators who select tactics in a contingent manner are *more effective*. Contingent effectiveness can be assessed by using mediation tactics as predictors, dispute outcomes as criteria, and dispute situations as moderator variables. To address the contingent effectiveness of mediation tactics, we (Lim and Carnevale, 1988) performed canonical discriminant analyses (see Tatsuoka, 1970) that were patterned after Hiltrop (see Chapter Eleven).

Each of the source-of-dispute factor-based scales was di-chotomized into two levels via a median split; one level repre-sented cases where the type of dispute was less of a problem, and the other level represented cases where the type of dispute was more of a problem. Each outcome scale was also dichotomized via a median split; one level represented cases where the type of outcome was more likely to arise, and the other level represented cases where the type of outcome was less likely to arise. For each outcome type, ten separate canonical discriminant analyses were performed: each analysis involved the six tactic scales as predictors and an outcome scale as criterion. These analyses were conducted for high and low levels of each of the five types of dispute.

Table 10.5 reports the standardized discriminant coeffi-cients that indicated significant relationships between the medi-ators' reported use of tactics and success, as a function of the five different types of dispute. That is, the numbers in the table indicate the degree of association between the use of six types of mediation tactics with outcome, as a function of low and high levels of each of the five types of dispute. For predicting general settlement, seven of the ten canonical discriminant analyses produced statistically significant canonical structures at $p < .05$. For predicting an improvement in the parties' relationship, nine of the ten canonical discriminant analyses produced statistically significant canonical structures. However, we had little success in predicting mediator outcomes: in this case, just two of the ten structures were significant at $p < .05$ (the tests under high levels of hostility and high levels of resistance). Thus, we limit our discussion of the discriminant analyses to just two criterion variables: general settlement in mediation and improved rela-tionship between the parties; Table 10.5 does not report results for mediator outcomes.

Substantive 1 (Press). We expected that the use of substan-tive pressing tactics would be positively associated with settle-ment under high levels of dispute problems, but negatively associated under low levels of dispute problems. As can be seen in the first row of Table 10.5, Section I, our expectation was strongly supported for comparison problems. Some support

Table 10.5. **Standardized Canonical Discriminant Coefficients That Indicate Relationships Between Mediation Tactics and Dispute Outcomes Under Low and High Levels of Five Types of Dispute.**

I. Outcome Type: General Settlement in Mediation

Dispute Type	Hostility		Internal Problems		Comparison Problems		Resist Mediation		Single Issue	
Dispute Level	Low[a] N=103	High[a] N=88	Low N=122	High[b] N=69	Low[b] N=116	High[a] N=75	Low[a] N=98	High[a] N=93	Low N=106	High N=85
Tactic										
Substantive/press	-.048	-.332		.092	-.807	.649	-.612	.036		
Reflexive	-.404	.406		.334	.101	-.332	-.049	.312		
Contextual/trust	.990	.378		.428	.641	.603	.731	.331		
Contextual/agenda	.260	.463		.446	.048	.502	.124	.549		
Substantive/face	.218	.180		.306	.497	-.089	.234	.350		
Substantive/sugg.	.213	.240		-.173	.324	-.062	.717	-.467		

II. Outcome Type: Improved Relationship Between the Disputants

Dispute Type	Hostility		Internal Problems		Comparison Problems		Resist Mediation		Single Issue	
Dispute Level	Low[c] N=103	High[b] N=88	Low[c] N=122	High[b] N=69	Low[c] N=116	High N=75	Low[c] N=98	High[c] N=93	Low[c] N=106	High[c] N=85
Tactic										
Substantive/press	-.373	-.057	-.354	-.203	-.547		-.172	-.400	-.699	.317
Reflexive	.033	-.213	-.252	.305	-.117		-.380	.293	-.060	.139
Contextual/trust	.983	1.075	1.175	.731	1.075		1.346	.499	.680	1.176
Contextual/agenda	.121	.007	-.086	.358	.036		-.213	.530	.214	-.017
Substantive/face	.153	.519	.226	.330	.397		.176	.456	.395	-.238
Substantive/sugg.	-.118	-.381	-.044	-.357	-.232		-.024	-.434	-.273	-.299

Note: A blank column indicates that the canonical structure was nonsignificant at $p < .05$.

[a] $p < .05$.
[b] $p < .01$.
[c] $p < .001$.

was also found for resistance to mediation, though the positive coefficient under high levels of resistance was weak.

The use of substantive pressure was in almost every case negatively associated with an improvement in the parties' relationship (see Section II); in most cases, it was less negatively associated when there were high levels of dispute types than low levels, the one exception occurring when resistance to mediation was high. When a single important issue was a problem, the use of substantive pressure was positively associated with an improvement in the parties' relationship, and negatively associated when a single issue was not a problem.

Reflexive. The second rows of the table, Sections I and II, show that most of the discriminant coefficients are small, indicating that the use of reflexive tactics generally was weakly related to outcome. This is not surprising when we consider that reflexive tactics tend to be used early in mediation and thus are less likely to be directly related to mediation outcomes. There was, however, a general tendency for reflexive tactics to be negatively related to outcome under low levels of dispute types, but positively related to outcome under high levels. This pattern is consistent with the view that difficult disputes require intense mediator behavior. It suggests that the use of reflexive tactics, such as developing rapport and speaking the parties' language, is associated with settlement when dispute problems are severe, but it is regarded as intrusive under low levels of dispute problems (Rubin, 1980).

Contextual 1 (Trust). The third row of Section I of the table shows that the reported use of contextual/trust tactics was positively associated with settlement across the board. The same row of Section II indicates a similar pattern but with much larger coefficients in most cases. This suggests that contextual/ trust tactics were more strongly positively associated with an improvement in the parties' relationship than with settlement. This finding is consistent with the results of Thoennes and Pearson (1985), that mediators who facilitated communication and provided clarification and insights were most likely to achieve settlement.

Contextual 2 (Agenda). The fourth row of Table 10.5, Section I, shows that the reported use of contextual/agenda tactics was positively associated with general settlement in every case. The use of these tactics was more positively associated with general settlement when the presence of hostility, internal party problems, comparison problems, and resistance to mediation were high than when they were low. Comparing outcome types indicates that agenda tactics related less positively to improvement in the parties' relationship (see the fourth row of Section II). The relationship between the use of agenda tactics and improved relationship outcomes was positive under high levels of internal party problems and resistance to mediation, and negative under low levels of these dispute types.

Substantive 2 (Face Saving). The fifth row of Section I shows that the reported use of substantive/face-saving tactics was in most cases positively associated with general settlement. Face saving was positively associated with settlement regardless of the level of hostility or resistance to mediation, and was positive when there were internal team problems. It was also positive when there was a low level of comparison problems, but weak and negative when there were high levels. As shown in the fifth row of Section II, a consistent pattern of positive coefficients was also found for improved interparty relations, with the additional finding that face saving was negatively associated with improvement when a single issue was the problem.

Substantive 3 (Make Suggestions). The last row in both sections of the table indicate that the reported use of substantive/ suggestions was in general negatively associated with settlement and improvement in the parties' relationship—especially the latter—and especially when dispute problems were high (hostility being an exception). Perhaps the most interesting finding is that making suggestions was positively and strongly associated with settlement (and weakly associated with improved relations) when resistance to mediation was low; but when this resistance was high, making suggestions was negatively associated with settlement and improved relations.

How Mediators Organize Their Strategic Thinking

How mediators make decisions about what to do in mediation is one of the least understood but most important issues in the study of mediation. There are many possible methods. One is trial and error: the mediator tries something and if it appears unsuccessful drops it and tries something else. A second method is the use of rules learned in formal training. For example, mediators who work in the public sector in Iowa are trained to hold a sidebar (a private meeting with the chief negotiator of both sides) as an extension of a caucus (a private meeting with the negotiating team of one side) and never directly from a joint session (a meeting with both negotiating teams). A third method that may guide mediator decisions is the use of rules or heuristics derived from personal experience or from another's experience. Carnevale (1986; and Chapter Sixteen, this volume) presents a model that represents a possible set of social rules that mediators hold about the causes and consequences of their strategic behavior.

Concluding Observations About Mediator Behavior

This chapter began with the assumption that successful mediators are adaptive—that mediators do different things in different situations to achieve success. Our analyses of the SPIDR mediators' reports about their behavior in different disputes and outcomes of the dispute supported this assumption. The data suggest that in some circumstances, the successful mediator attends to the features of the dispute and selects tactics in reaction to those features. In other words, the contingent application of mediation tactics can be the ticket to success.

Our analyses of the contingent effectiveness of mediation tactics (Lim and Carnevale, 1988) prompt several basic observations about mediator behavior. First, some mediator behaviors may be used in a noncontingent manner and be effective; this was the case with the use of contextual/trust tactics. Second, all the dispute types involved mediator behaviors that predicted success in a contingent manner. As can be seen in Table 10.5, each dispute type had at least one mediation tactic that sometimes was positively associated with success, sometimes negatively associated with success, and sometimes unrelated to success. Third, the concept of contingent effectiveness requires that not only the type of tactic used in a given type of dispute be specified, but also the type of outcome. The data in Table 10.5 suggest that in some circumstances a mediation tactic can affect the likelihood of settlement differently than it affects an improvement in the parties' relationship. Two examples of this are the data in the third row of the table, indicating that contextual/ trust tactics are more positively tied to improving the relationship between disputants than to achieving settlement, and the data in the fourth row, indicating that contextual/agenda tactics are more positively tied to achieving settlement than to improving the parties' relationship.

Perhaps the most noteworthy aspect of the present study is the evidence that some tactics are *contingently effective*; they are more likely to be associated with success under some conditions than under others. This is seen dramatically in Section I of Table 10.5, with the data on mediator suggestions. When resistance to mediation was high, mediator recommendations were negatively associated with settlement; but when resistance to mediation was not a problem, mediator recommendations were positively associated with settlement.

The data also support Rubin's point (1980) that mediator forcefulness may in the long run be detrimental. Making suggestions may be positively associated with immediate settlement, but in the long run it is the contextual/trust tactics that improve the parties' relationship. In every circumstance, the use of mediator suggestions was negatively associated with an improvement in the parties' relationship. This suggests that mediator recommendations may not be sensitive to the parties' long-term mutual welfare. It also suggests that measures of success in mediation should not be restricted to the occurrence or nonoccurrence of agreement.

Another noteworthy observation is that mediators are apparently impressed with the need to help parties deal with *internal* issues as much as with the *external* dispute. The second factor that was obtained for dispute problems (internal party problems; see Table 10.5) reinforces our finding that face saving (which often is used within one side to preserve the chief negotiator's image in front of constituents) is a central mediation activity (see Table 10.2). This is an important point, since most people think of mediation as addressing primarily the external issues.

It also should be noted that the use of mediation tactics was not predictive of *mediator outcomes* under any combination of dispute type and level except two (high levels of hostility and high levels of resistance to mediation). An implication of this is that mediator outcomes are not achieved in the same contingent manner that general settlement and an improvement in the parties' relationship are achieved.

As a final observation, there appear to be several interesting inconsistencies between the contingent *use* of mediation tactics and the contingent *effectiveness* of these tactics. One case was the mediators' use of substantive/press tactics. The correlation analysis indicated a positive relationship between the use of pressure tactics and the presence of hostility. But the contingent effectiveness analysis (the first row of Table 10.5, Section I) indicated that the use of substantive/press tactics — under high levels of hostility — was negatively associated with settlement. Is it possible that mediators in some cases do not always use the tactics that actually pay off?

Implications for Training and Assessment

The notion of contingent effectiveness of mediator behavior has important implications for mediator training and performance evaluation. Our data (Lim and Carnevale, 1988) suggest that mediators should be trained to recognize that regardless of the circumstances, some tactics are positively associated with favorable outcomes (such as developing trust between the parties), whereas others are often negatively associated with favorable outcomes, especially if the goal is to improve the parties' relationship (such as the use of non–face-saving suggestions). Equally important, our data suggest that some tactics are most likely to be associated with success if they are exercised contingently (such as the use of substantive/pressure tactics). It seems reasonable to suppose that greater effort will be required to train mediators to use tactics that are contingently effective (such as the substantive/pressure tactics) than tactics that are uniformly effective (such as contextual/trust tactics). It may be that expert mediators are especially skilled at dispute diagnosis and are adroit with contingently effective tactics.

Our results suggest that assessments of mediator performance in different dispute situations should be based more on mediators' use of contingently effective tactics than on the use of tactics that are uniformly effective. This should provide a better estimate of the mediators' ability to identify and diagnose dispute problems, and adjust their behavior accordingly. The data suggest that performance evaluations of mediators should consider the type of dispute; in some circumstances mediation is unlikely to succeed regardless of what the mediator does, and lack of agreement in these cases should not imply poor mediator performance. In addition, our results suggest that feedback to mediators concerning their performance should be designed to strengthen their abilities to diagnose disputes and effectively adjust their behavior.

One final note: the data of the present study are exclusively about mediator *perceptions* of what happened and are not objective measures of actual behavior. As with all studies that use retrospective reports, our inferences about behavior are only as strong as the correspondence between the mediators' reports of what happened in mediation and the reality of what actually happened.

References

Carnevale, P. J. "Strategic Choice in Mediation." *Negotiation Journal*, 1986, *2*, 41–56.

Carnevale, P. J., and Pegnetter, R. "The Selection of Mediation Tactics in Public-Sector Disputes: A Contingency Analysis." *Journal of Social Issues*, 1985, *41*, 65–81.

Hiltrop, J. M. "Mediator Behavior and the Settlement of Collective Bargaining Disputes in Britain." *Journal of Social Issues*, 1985, *41*, 83–99.

Jöreskog, K. G., and Sörbom, D. *LISREL VI: Analysis of Linear*

Structural Relationships by the Method of Maximum Likelihood. Chicago: National Educational Resources, 1984.

Kim, J., and Meuller, C. *Factor Analysis: Statistical Methods and Practical Issues.* Sage University Paper series on Quantitative Applications in the Social Sciences, 07-001. Beverly Hills, Calif.: Sage, 1978.

Kochan, T. A., and Jick, T. A. "The Public Sector Mediation Process: A Theory and Empirical Examination." *Journal of Conflict Resolution,* 1978, *22,* 209–240.

Kressel, K. *Labor Mediation: An Exploratory Survey.* Albany, N.Y.: Association of Labor Mediation Agencies, 1972.

Kressel, K., and Pruitt, D. G. "Themes in the Mediation of Social Conflict." *Journal of Social Issues,* 1985, *41,* 179–198.

Kruskal, J. B., and Wish, M. *Multidimensional Scaling.* Sage University Paper series on Quantitative Applications in the Social Sciences, 07-011. Beverly Hills, Calif.: Sage, 1978.

Kruskal, J. B., Young, F. W., and Seery, J. B. *How to Use KYST-2A, a Very Flexible Program to Do Multidimensional Scaling and Unfolding.* Murray Hill, N.J.: Bell Telephone Labs, 1977.

Likert, R. *The Human Organization.* New York: McGraw-Hill, 1967.

Lim, R., and Carnevale, P. J. "Contingencies in the Mediation of Disputes." Unpublished manuscript, Department of Psychology, University of Illinois, Urbana-Champaign, 1988.

McLaughlin, M., Carnevale, P. J., and Lim, R. "Professional Mediators' Perceptions of Tactics: A Multidimensional Scaling and Clustering Analysis." Unpublished manuscript, Department of Psychology, University of Illinois, Urbana-Champaign, 1988.

Pruitt, D. G. *Negotiation Behavior.* Orlando, Fla.: Academic Press, 1981.

Rubin, J. Z. "Experimental Research on Third-Party Intervention in Conflict: Toward Some Generalizations." *Psychological Bulletin,* 1980, *87,* 379–391.

Tatsuoka, M. M. *Discriminant Analysis: The Study of Group Differences.* Champaign, Ill.: Institute for Personality and Ability Testing, 1970.

Thoennes, N. A., and Pearson, J. "Predicting Outcomes in Divorce Mediation: The Influence of People and Process." *Journal of Social Issues,* 1985, *41,* 115–126.

ELEVEN

Factors Associated with Successful Labor Mediation

Jean Marie Hiltrop

The last several years have been marked by a surge of interest in the process of mediation. Labor mediation in particular has been the focus of an increasing number of books and articles in the field of industrial relations (for example, Kolb, 1983; Moore, 1986). Despite this welcome proliferation of interest, however, no adequate understanding of the mediation process has been developed.

    This chapter reports on two field studies of labor mediation (or "collective" conciliation) conducted under the auspices of the British Advisory, Conciliation, and Arbitration Service (ACAS). The first study was based on data collected from 260 mediation cases completed by the ACAS in 1981 and 1982. Via questionnaires and semistructured interviews with the mediators involved in these 260 cases, this research examined how certain mediation techniques and some aspects of the dispute situation, including the nature of the issues involved, influence the outcome of a mediation intervention. The second study was based on data collected from the chief management and union representatives involved in 213 mediations conducted by the ACAS in 1985. Using the first study as a guide, this later research sought to improve our understanding of the various strategies that professional mediators use to resolve industrial disputes and the conditions under which different strategies and tactics are most effective.

Research Setting

In Britain, two decades of free collective bargaining have been complemented for nearly a century by voluntary mediation (or conciliation) services provided by the state (Lowry, 1983). As long ago as 1896, a public conciliation agency was established in a government ministry, and this institutional arrangement did not alter until September 1974 when, as a result of changes in public opinion, the full-time practice of labor mediation was transferred from the Department of Employment to the Advisory, Conciliation, and Arbitration Service (ACAS).

Briefly, the ACAS is an independent statutory organization established under the Employment Protection Act of 1975. Its task is to help workers, employers, and union representatives in both the public and private sectors resolve trade disputes and improve the conduct of their industrial relations. The autonomy of the ACAS is protected by a statutory provision explicitly exempting it from direction by any government ministry. Controls rests with a full-time chairperson and a tripartite council consisting of nine part-time members: three representatives of employers, three representatives of trade unions, and three independent academic members with expertise in industrial relations or related matters. The ACAS approach is impartial and confidential. It provides conciliation, legal advice, mediation, arbitration, and inquiry into any questions relating to industrial relations. These services are voluntary and free of charge.

Requests for ACAS assistance come from either trade unions or employers, or they are made by the parties jointly

(Hiltrop, 1985). In addition, the ACAS itself may suggest concil-iation (for example, where there are overriding public interests at stake), and a small proportion of its cases arise out of such initiative. Under the Employment Protection Act of 1975, any such intervention calls for the most scrupulous adherence to the principle of not undermining agreed procedures for negotia-tion or the settlement of disputes; normally the ACAS will not seek or agree to intervene unless such procedures have been exhausted, or until a bargaining impasse has occurred.

During 1985, a reasonably typical year, the ACAS sought or agreed to mediate in 1,337 collective bargaining disputes. Most of this work was carried out quietly and unobtrusively by its 700 staff members through a network of nine regional offices, from which they are able to develop close and ongoing working relationships with employers and trade unions in the area. The staff of the ACAS head office in London conciliated in only 128 disputes in 1985; the main ones were industrywide disputes and disputes of considerable national economic significance and public concern (for example, in the mining industry).

According to the annual reports of the ACAS, settlement or progress toward a settlement (including reference to arbitra-tion) was achieved in 1,104 (83 percent) of the 1985 cases. In the remaining 233 disputes, the parties either settled by negotiation (7 cases), proceeded to arbitration (162 cases), or went on strike (64 cases). This is a small total, however, when compared to the 813 officially recorded stoppages in Britain during 1985.

Method

1981–1982 Study. The first major objective of this study was to build a picture of the mediation (or "collective" concilia-tion) process from the views of those who conducted it. To this end, we interviewed the ACAS officials involved in 260 concilia-tion cases, randomly sampled from the 3,350 collective bargain-ing disputes in which the ACAS conciliated during 1981 and 1982. Over three-quarters (84 percent) of the establishments involved in the 260 disputes were engaged in manufacturing industries, 12 percent were in the service sector, and the remainder in the construction/extraction industries (Hiltrop, 1985). The sample represents a wide range of occupational groups (from professional staff to unskilled labor). In just under three-quarters of the cases, the employees involved were members of a manual-trade union; the others belonged to a white-collar union. The majority of cases (148 out of 260) were resolved by mediation. Of the 112 disputes that continued beyond mediation, 63 were resolved by negotiation and 14 resulted in strike action. The study did not reveal any significant differences between manual and nonmanual groups in terms of mediation outcomes.

To measure what the mediation process consisted of, a questionnaire was sent to the ACAS official identified as the chief conciliator in each case. The data collected in this questionnaire contained two sets of measures on determinants of mediation outcomes as independent variables. First, to assess the climate and conditions prevailing between the parties, respondents were asked a series of fixed-choice questions about the parties and issues involved in each case. (For example: Who requested ACAS assistance? What was the cause of this dispute? Was strike action threatened or taken during the intervention?) Second, to assess what the mediation process consisted of, respondents were asked to indicate their use of thirteen mediation strategies during the intervention. (For example: Did you suggest solutions? Did you make procedural arrangements? Did you act as a communication link between the parties?) These thirteen activities were chosen in preliminary discussions with two senior conciliation officers of the ACAS. The selection was based on the classification of mediator strategies proposed by Kressel (1972). Although this typology has subsequently been modified, following Kressel's initial formulations, I shall refer to directive, nondirective, and reflexive interventions.

All questionnaires were completed and discussed by the ACAS officers involved within six months of their meetings with the union and management negotiators. This was followed by a further discussion of the data with the senior conciliation officers of the ACAS and the administrative staff in each of nine ACAS regions. The questionnaire results and the data from the discussions were then used to examine the types of disputes that mediators were best able and least able to resolve, and to assess the impact of mediator tactics on the outcome of labor mediation.

1985 Study. This project was carried out from November 1984 to December 1985. Originally, it was proposed to observe the activities of the ACAS officials working on 213 conciliation cases. However, although the ACAS was prepared to cooperate to some extent with this effort, its governing council would not allow us to observe the conciliation process in action. Consequently, we decided to build up a picture of the mediation process from the views of the disputing parties. To this end, two weeks after the resolution of the dispute (which could require bargaining, mediation, fact finding, and arbitration), the chief union and management negotiators involved in each case were mailed a questionnaire that collected data on the nature of the dispute, the characteristics of the disputants, when and how mediation was started, what the mediator was doing to help resolve the dispute, and what outcomes were achieved during the intervention. In addition, respondents were given an opportunity to make their own comments about the mediation process and the quality of the agreements reached in the process. (A copy of the complete questionnaire is available from the author on request.)

Completed questionnaires were received from 161 management and 171 union negotiators, giving an overall response rate of 78 percent. Approximately one-third (28 percent) of the management responses came from establishments with fewer than 100 employees; 43 percent came from medium-sized establishments (between 100 and 500 employees); and 29 percent from establishments with more than 500 employees. The sample represents a wide range of industries (including the service industries, mechanical engineering, and the food, drink, and tobacco industry). In 74 percent of the cases, the employees belonged to a manual-trade union; in the remainder, to a white-collar union. According to the ACAS records, 130 of the 213 disputes in our sample were resolved by conciliation, giving a settlement rate of 61 percent. Of the 83 disputes that continued beyond intervention, 54 were resolved by negotiation and 29 resulted in strike action. The longest strikes were in coalmining (where a return to work took place in March 1975, twelve months after industrial action had started), and in schoolteaching (where industrial action continued throughout 1985).

Situational Determinants of Successful Mediation

Type of Issue. While it is generally acknowledged that the nature of the issue in dispute affects the outcome of a mediation intervention (Gerhart and Drotning, 1980; Roehl and Cook, 1985), there is no consensus and little evidence on what type of disputes mediation is best able and least able to resolve. For example, two major field studies on the effectiveness of mediation reach opposite conclusions about mediator capacity for dealing with issues of principle. Kochan and Jick (1978) found that impasses arising out of such issues were especially likely to be resolved by mediation. Yet Kressel (1972) found that mediators viewed such issues as among their biggest problems.

To assess the nature of the issue in dispute, we asked mediators in our two samples to indicate the cause of dispute in each case. Answers were given on a six-point checklist, using the typology of industrial disputes developed by the ACAS to assess the nature and frequency of impasses in which conciliation takes place. Not surprisingly, the types of issues most frequently mentioned were "pay and other terms" and "conditions of employment." On the average, some 57 percent of interventions carried out by the service each year concern these issues. Union claims to negotiate on behalf of their members—recognition disputes—accounted for about one-third the cases, and 21 percent concerned discipline and dismissal.

Having identified the cause of dispute in each case, we examined the percentage of disputes that were resolved by mediation. As expected, this percentage varied considerably by the nature of the issue involved. For example, of the 104 disputes in our 1981–1982 sample where the issues were pay and other terms and conditions of employment, 73 percent were resolved by mediation. By comparison, the settlement rate for disputes concerning recognition or other nonsalary matters was only 46 percent. Similarly, of the 66 pay disputes in the 1985 sample, the majority (71 percent) were resolved by mediation, compared with only 47 percent of the nonpay cases. Thus, it is evident that there is a strong association between the type of issue in dispute and the probability of achieving a settlement by mediation $(\chi^2 = 29.4; df = 5; p < .001)$.

These findings are not surprising; issues involving pay and related matters more readily lend themselves to compromise solutions than issues that do not involve a continuous scale, such as recognition. Also, in disputes concerning recognition or matters of hiring and firing, positional commitments and dedication to principles often do interfere with the exchange of concessions. For example, the union may insist on its right to represent its members and negotiate on their behalf with the employer. Clearly, this makes the mediator's task of helping the disputants reach agreement extremely difficult, especially if the employer strongly believes that it is the fundamental right of management to run the business as it likes without interference on the part of other people, including members of a trade union.

Source of Request. According to the annual reports of the ACAS, the action that brings the ACAS into a dispute is most commonly a request by one or both parties. This may come, without any prompting, when all agreed procedures for negotiating and settling disputes have been exhausted, or when the negotiations appear to have reached a deadlock. On the other hand, there are also disputes in which the ACAS takes an initiative by reminding the parties that they might find it helpful to consider mediation. Where both parties are reluctant to ask for mediation but the circumstances suggest it might be useful, such an initiative can sometimes set intervention in motion without either side appearing to make any concession.

To assess the impact of each type of request on the outcome of mediation, we examined the proportion of settlements reached in our two samples of mediation cases. Our analysis of the 1981–1982 data showed that of the 97 disputes in which the mediator intervened at the request of the two parties, 71 percent were resolved by mediation. By comparison, the settlement rate for unilateral requests was 50 percent, and for ACAS initiatives only 33 percent. Similarly, of the 97 joint requests in our 1985 sample, 77 percent were resolved by mediation, compared with 55 percent of the unilateral requests and 44 percent of the ACAS initiatives.Thus, our two sets of findings indicate that, apart from being more effective in pay disputes, mediation also is more likely to be successful when there is a joint request for assistance than when there is a request from only one of the parties, or when intervention is the result of the mediator's own initiative ($\chi^2 = 30.12$; $df = 2$; $p < .001$).

There are several possible reasons for this finding. First, as Jones and Dickens (1983) point out, in cases where a joint request is made it may be assumed that both sides are prepared to deal with the mediator. In contrast, when mediation is undertaken at the request of only one of the parties, or when the ACAS has taken the initiative itself, the mediator's first task may be to persuade one or both disputants to discuss the issues with a third party. In addition, when both parties request mediation it can often be assumed that at least one side is prepared to move its position somewhat, but there can be no such assumption when the mediator decides to intervene (Stevens, 1963). Finally, the very act of seeking ACAS assistance may create a psychological commitment to cooperating with the mediator, making the mediator's task easier and the achievement of a settlement more likely (Moore, 1986).

Timing of Entry. If the ACAS decides to intervene, when should this occur? The optimal timing of entry into a dispute is one of the most intensely debated topics in the conciliation literature (see for instance Rubin, 1981; Moore, 1986). Some practitioners favor early intervention because, they argue, delaying intervention too long may encourage unproductive negotiation behavior, making negotiation more difficult and successful intervention less likely (Kerr, 1954; Carpenter and Kennedy, 1979). Proponents of late intervention, on the other hand, argue that for mediation to prove maximally effective, the disputants need to have experienced sufficient tension to mobilize their powers, to establish their bargaining range, and to modify their positions — a process that may be delayed or otherwise hindered through early intervention (Wall, 1981; Rubin, 1981).

According to Jones and Dickens (1983), the limited amount of ACAS initiatives to intervene means that in Britain the timing of entry into a dispute is influenced largely by the parties themselves; as a result, in about one-third of the disputes dealt with by the service annually, the parties are already taking some form of industrial action when mediation occurs. Thus, in 31 percent of the cases in the 1981–1982 sample (80 out of 260), the ACAS intervened when the disputants were already threatening or imposing industrial action. Most often it was strike action (in 56 of the 80 cases), but other sanctions such as an overtime ban, work slowdown, or "working by the book" had also sometimes been threatened or imposed (in 24 cases). Overall, only 180 out of the 260 mediations were free of any form of prior industrial action.

Not surprisingly, the results of our 1981–1982 study showed that the number of disputes resolved by mediation varies considerably by the type of industrial action taken during the process. For instance, of the disputes in which a strike or lockout was imposed during the intervention, 80 percent were resolved by mediation. Yet the resolution rate when a strike was threatened was 67 percent and, when no industrial action was either taken or threatened, only 53 percent. Similar percentages were obtained in our 1985 sample. The results of this second investigation also showed higher settlement rates when mediation occurred under strike conditions than when there was no strike ($\chi^2 = 15.54$; $df = 3$; $p < .002$).

Presumably, as Kressel and Pruitt (1985) suggest, a strike produces a specially strong commitment to resolve the issues that produced the impasse. If so, then it stands to reason that the ACAS should wait before intervening until the disputants are well into the final stages of their negotiations, or until a bargaining impasse has occurred and the pressure to settle is mounting. On the other hand, by intervening rather early in the conflict, the mediator may be able to help the disputants identify the issues and understand the size and scope of their conflict. Thus,

early intervention may have benefits other than dispute resolution, although the nature of these benefits has not been studied.

Characteristics of the Disputants. In addition to preexisting
characteristics of disputes, certain personal characteristics of
the disputants have also been found to be associated with the
success or failure of mediation. For instance, Kochan and Jick
(1978) found three disputant characteristics that predicted nonsettlement: the parties lacking motivation to settle, the employer
being unable to pay, and the bargainers having unrealistic expectations. Similarly, Carnevale and Pegnetter (1985) found a
significant negative relationship between the employer not
being able to pay and the probability of a mediated settlement.
On the other hand, there are many gaps in our understanding of
the disputant characteristics associated with successful labor
mediation; and although there is evidence that the personal
qualities of the disputants can, and frequently do, affect the
outcome of a mediation intervention, the nature of this influence is often unclear. For example, the deeply entrenched belief
that mediation is more difficult when inexperienced negotiators are involved is supported by Kressel's 1972 study. But
Kochan and Jick (1978) found just the opposite, and negotiator
experience was unrelated to settlement in Carnevale and Pegnetter's sample (1985) of mediation cases.

To assess the impact of disputant characteristics on the
outcome of mediation, the union and management representatives identified as the chief negotiators in our 1985 sample
were asked a series of fixed-choice questions about the characteristics of the disputants in each case. (For example: Did you
trust the mediator? How experienced were the negotiators?
What was the general level of hostility between you and the other
party?) Consistent with Kochan and Jick (1978), the following
three disputant characteristics were associated with nonsettlement in mediation: (1) the bargainers having unrealistic expectations; ($r = -.26$, $p < .01$); (2) the parties being hostile to each
other; ($r = -.21$, $p < .05$); and (3) a low motivation to settle on the
part of the union or management negotiators. ($r = -.24$,
$p < .05$). In addition, settlement was less likely when the parties
were inexperienced ($r = -.17$, $p < .05$), were unenthusiastic

about mediation ($r = -.17$, $p < .05$), and were distrustful of the mediator ($r = -.48$, $p < .001$). Thus, it is evident that, in labor negotiation and mediation, certain kinds of conflicts are much harder to resolve than others.

Effective Mediator Tactics

Given that labor mediators are usually low-power individuals with no authority to impose a settlement, what strategies and tactics can they employ to move the disputing parties in the direction of settling their differences? More generally, is it reasonable to envision an optimal style of intervention? If so, what is this style?

To answer these questions, the data from our two surveys were transformed into dummy variables (coded as 1 if a specific tactic was used by the mediator, and as 0 if it was not used), and then subjected to discriminant analysis. The dependent variable in this analysis was settlement (versus nonsettlement) by mediation. Independent variables were examined in a stepwise procedure in which the selection criterion (Wilk's lambda) sought to maximize the overall F-ratio for the test of differences among the group centroids.

First, let us look at the results of the 1981–1982 study. As noted earlier, the data were collected from the ACAS officers involved in 260 conciliations. Of the thirteen mediation tactics examined in this study, only seven were identified in the analysis as significantly associated with successful and unsuccessful mediation. Together these seven tactics explained 45 percent of the variance. The two tactics that contributed most (in terms of discriminating power) to settlement were arranging preliminary separate meetings with the parties to explore the issues, and assisting the negotiators in their relationships with constituents. These two tactics accounted for over half (54 percent) of the explained variance. Positive coefficients (indicating positive association with settlement) also appeared for three other tactics: threatening to quit if no progress was made in the negotiations, separating the parties, and acting as a communication link. In contrast, mediator attempts to make procedural arrangements and reduce emotional tensions were associated with nonsettle-ment. Among the six remaining tactics that did not significantly contribute to settlement were suggesting solutions, synchroniz-ing concessions, and discussing the parties' bargaining posi-tions in closed meetings.

Thus, the most effective strategy appeared to be predomi-nantly serving as go-between and prod (Hiltrop, 1985). That is, successful mediators worked with the parties separately, acted as a communication link between them, intervened with their constituents, and occasionally threatened to stop these actions when the parties failed to make satisfactory progress. Mediators appeared to encounter the greatest difficulty, on the other hand, when they tried to regulate the interactions between the dispu-tants (making procedural arrangements), and when they tried to reduce emotional tensions between them.

Next, consider the results of the 1985 study, which em-ployed data collected from the chief union and management representatives involved in 213 conciliations. The three tactics that contributed most to settlement in these cases were meeting the two parties both separately and together in closed meetings, acting as a communication link between the parties, and asking the negotiators to recommend a possible agreement to their constituents. Thus, three of the five mediator tactics that con-tributed to settlement in the 1981–1982 study (namely, holding separate meetings, acting as a communication link, and assist-ing with constituents) were also positively associated with settle-ment in the second analysis. In addition, positive relationships with settlement appeared for two other tactics: suggesting to separate multiple issues to reach a partial agreement, and em-phasizing the need to make concessions. Negative relationships with settlement appeared for three: suggesting to deal with the most difficult issues first, grouping multiple issues to reach a package agreement, and asking the parties to identify their bottom-line positions.

Contingent Mediator Strategies

Up to now we have focused for the most part on *non-contingent* mediator strategies—relatively systematic activities that mediators perform in any dispute regardless of the cause of dispute, the number and variety of issues, or the characteristics of the parties. I now turn to *contingent* mediator strategies, primarily the interventions labor mediators employ to respond to specific problems posed by the characteristics of the disputing parties. First, I summarize the results of our 1981–1982 investigation.

As noted earlier, this research was largely exploratory in nature, but it did show some rather surprising differences in the effectiveness of mediation techniques under various circumstances (Hiltrop, 1985). Briefly, on the basis of observations and the associated explanations the mediators provided for their activities, mediator pressure tactics, such as threatening to quit and invoking arbitration, were positively associated with settlement in nonpay disputes but negatively associated with settlement in pay disputes. In a similar vein, mediator pressure was associated with settlement when mediation occurred under strike conditions, but was unrelated to settlement when mediation took place in the absence of a strike. Analysis of the disputants' attitudes in each type of dispute suggested that differences in the parties' willingness to make concessions may provide the most compelling explanation for the effectiveness of mediator pressure tactics in different of types of conflict. Essentially, however, these findings must be seen as a first approximation of how the mediator's choice of tactics affects the outcome of labor mediation.

To improve our understanding of the virtually limitless array of interventions that labor mediators employ in facilitating negotiations, the data from the 1985 survey were subjected to a discriminant analysis designed to assess the impact of mediator tactics on outcomes in six types of mediation cases:

1. Disputes in which the parties' motivation to settle was especially low
2. Disputes in which the parties were under strong pressure to resolve their differences
3. Disputes in which the relationship between the disputants was very hostile

4. Disputes in which there was a low level of hostility between the disputants
5. Disputes in which the parties' bottom-line positions were far apart
6. Disputes in which the parties were close to agreement

These six groups were based on the chief union and management responses to a series of fixed-choice questions about the dispute situation. (For example: Was the relationship between the parties very hostile? Were important matters of principle involved? Were the parties enthusiastic about the mediation process? To what extent were they motivated to settle by means of mediation?) Thus, in accomplishing the present division of disputes, we relied on the chief negotiators' perceptions of the parties' motivation to settle, the level of hostility, and whether the parties were close to agreement.

Table 11.1 shows the mediator tactics that were associated with settlement in each type of dispute. As expected, no single tactic was ideally suited for dealing with all types of cases. The coefficients in row 5 show, for example, that introducing additional issues for discussion was associated with settlement when perceived hostility was low (column 4) but not when it was high (column 3). Similarly, the data in row 6 show that suggesting possible solutions increased the chances of settlement when perceived hostility was low, but had the opposite effect when hostility was judged high by the chief negotiators.

These findings can be interpreted as supporting the proposition that substantive interventions (exploring the potential areas of compromise, suggesting possible agreements) have their greatest utility in disputes of relatively modest intensity. This proposition is also supported by the finding that suggesting possible solutions was associated with settlement when the parties were close to agreement (column 6). In contrast, mediator efforts to narrow the gap by putting forward proposals of their own was associated with nonsettlement when the parties' motivation to settle was low (column 2), and when there was a big gap between their bottom-line positions (column 5). Thus, it would appear that the timing of mediator proposals is critical to the effectiveness of mediation. Indeed, some mediators believe that a proposal should never be made unless the parties' bottom-line positions are close enough to press for a modification that would produce an agreement (Kochan, 1980).

Our findings also suggest that mediators, to be effective, must engage in a variety of diagnostic activities. The discriminant coefficients in column 3 show, for example, that when hostility was high, there was a significant connection between the achievement of a mediated settlement and reports by the chief negotiators that the mediator had helped them understand the position of the other party, discuss the strengths and weaknesses of both parties' case, and identify specific points of agreement and disagreement. In addition, there is evidence that mediators were more likely to be effective under conditions of high hostility when they met the disputants both separately and together, and acted as a communication link between the parties. A similar pattern was found when there was a big gap between the bottom-line positions of the parties. Thus it would appear that activities of this kind are positively related to settlement in the more difficult cases.

This is not to say that contextual interventions (meeting the parties for separate exploratory discussions, meeting the parties both separately and together, acting as a communication link) were ineffectual in the less difficult disputes. The coefficients in the bottom part of the table show that these activities were also associated with settlement when mediation occurred under more auspicious conditions of conflict (columns 1, 4 and 6).

Finally, the findings provide some guidance on the use of mediator pressure tactics. As the coefficients in rows 11 and 12 show, strong-arm tactics such as threatening to quit and emphasizing the need to make concessions were positively related to settlement when perceived hostility was high and when the parties' bottom-line positions were far apart. In contrast, these activities were unrelated to settlement when hostility was low; and threatening to quit was associated with nonsettlement when the parties were close to agreement. Thus, it would appear that mediator pressure tactics work best in disputes of high intensity.

Table 11.1. Discriminant Function Coefficients:
The Impact of Mediator Strategies on Outcomes as a Function of Case Characteristics.

Mediator Strategies	Motivation to Settle		Perceived Hostility		Positional Differences	
	High (N = 89)	Low (N = 128)	High (N = 72)	Low (N = 129)	Large (N = 142)	Small (N = 59)
Directive Strategies						
1. Suggest dealing with the most difficult issue first	−0.850	−0.265	−0.362		−0.370	
2. Suggest tackling the least difficult issue first						
3. Suggest grouping separate issues	−0.819	—				
4. Suggest separating multiple issues				−0.231		
5. Introduce additional issues for discussion			−0.254	0.450		
6. Suggest solutions for resolving issues	0.412	−0.302	−0.652	0.367	−0.363	0.712
7. Suggest the use of "phasing" (or step-by-step implementation) of an agreement			0.457		0.236	
8. Suggest altering or reviewing the proposed agreement		0.250			0.188	−0.264
9. Suggest the use of arbitration			−0.445			
10. Suggest the use of joint consultation		0.544	0.310		0.343	
11. Threaten to quit			0.323			−0.400
12. Emphasize the need to make concessions			0.403		0.344	
13. Ask the parties to identify their "final" positions				−0.431	−0.398	
14. Ask the negotiators to recommend a possible agreement to their constituents		0.481	0.151	0.443	0.145	0.421

Nondirective Strategies

Strategy						
1. Meet each party for separate exploratory discussions						0.524
2. Help the parties understand the other side's position		0.558	0.800		0.526	
3. Act as a communication link between the parties			0.534		0.393	
4. Meet the parties separately throughout the negotiations	0.369					0.456
5. Meet the parties together throughout the negotiations		0.670				
6. Meet the parties both separately and together	0.559		0.252		0.282	
7. Identify specific points of agreement and disagreement			0.553	0.550	0.635	
8. Discuss the costs and benefits of a possible agreement		0.282	0.487			
9. Point out the implications of continued disagreement					0.277	0.420
10. Help the parties to abandon their bargaining positions	0.928	0.390				0.680

Notes: + Indicates positive association with settlement.
 − Indicates negative association with settlement.
 Only significant coefficients ($p < .05$) are reported.

This finding echoes a point made by Kressel and Pruitt (1985) in their review of recent field studies of mediation: mediator pressure tactics have been found to be especially common when there is a high level of tension or hostility between the parties.

Summary and Conclusion

Without systematic empirical analysis of the strategies and tactics employed by mediators, it has frequently been assumed that mediation is an art, highly idiosyncratic and resistant to generalizations. Our evidence shows, however, that certain generalizations can indeed be made:

1. Pay disputes are more amenable to mediation than disputes in which a matter of principle (such as union recognition) is involved.
2. It is important that both parties, rather than only one of them, seek the services of the mediator before assistance is offered.
3. Mediation works best when operating under a real and immediate strike threat, namely at the final stages of a negotiation process or at the point during a dispute where the parties are taking strike action.

Furthermore, our analysis of the types of disputes that the ACAS was best able and least able to resolve also shows that:

4. Mediation has a better chance of working when the parties are willing to settle and their enthusiasm about the mediation process is high.
5. Bargainer hostility is negatively related to the success of mediation.
6. Inexperienced negotiators are more difficult to help than experienced parties.
7. Obtaining the trust and confidence of the disputants is a necessary condition for success.

In addition, our findings provide some guidance on the conditions under which different mediator tactics are likely to be effective. Overall, the three most positive tactics were: meeting the parties separately to explore the issues and the attitudes of the bargainers; serving as a communication link between the parties; and helping the disputants in their relationship with their constituents. Mediator pressure tactics such as threatening to quit and emphasizing the need to make concessions were positively related to settlement in high-hostility cases and when the parties' bottom-line positions were far apart. In contrast, suggesting possible agreements proved highly effective when the parties were under strong pressure to resolve their differences, and when the number and magnitude of the obstacles to a settlement were relatively small.

When we supplement these findings with the results of our 1981–1982 investigation, it is evident that to be effective, a mediator must do more than act as a facilitator for the parties. Especially when conflict intensity is high, mediators must also act in ways that enhance the disputants' motivation to reach agreement. On the other hand, several things are needed before we can make definitive statements about the factors associated with successful mediation.

To begin with, more research is needed to determine the long-term effects of mediator tactics. Our findings suggest that, in certain instances, directive mediator tactics are positively associated with settlement. Yet, as Rubin (1981) points out, in the long run it may well be the nondirective tactics that yield greater durability in any agreements reached. Hence, it is particularly important that the long-term effects of directive mediator tactics be examined, so that the effectiveness of different styles of behavior is not measured by their ability to produce settlements alone.

Second, we need to know more about the situational determinants of successful mediation. For instance, the effects, if any, of power imbalances between the parties are unknown. Also, as Kressel and Pruitt (1985) point out, only a small percentage of outcome variance has as yet been accounted for by situational factors; and while there have been new and important contributions to the subject (Thoennes and Pearson, 1985; Carnevale and Pegnetter, 1985), it is impossible to say whether the findings on factors that facilitate settlement apply specifically to mediated agreements or relate to successful negotiations in general. Consequently, there is, at present, a good deal of confusion and misapprehension conceptually and analytically about the characteristics of disputes and disputants that lead to successful or unsuccessful labor mediation.

Third, more research is needed to determine how the strategies and tactics employed by mediators vary with differences in the number of parties to a dispute. Obviously, many disputes involve three or more parties. Yet there is almost no theory or research about the mediation of multilateral conflicts. Indeed, the gap is so wide that the first step of describing how mediators intervene in such conflicts has scarcely been taken.

Finally, theory development and research are also needed to close a big gap in our understanding of how the strategies employed by mediators change from the early stages of intervention to the achievement of settlement. This gap is largely a result of the heavy use of the self-report, large-sample, quantitative type of methods employed in the present analysis. For all the virtues associated with these methods, they have the liability of telling us little about the more dynamic aspects of mediation. In addition, research employing more direct observation methods is needed to improve our understanding of how professional mediators identify sources of impasse and select appropriate mediation tactics. Although the naturalness of mediator behavior is inevitably compromised to some degree by the presence of observers, perhaps it is time to apply observational methods to supplement the empirical findings of investigations like this one.

References

Carnevale, P., and Pegnetter, R. "The Selection of Mediation Tactics in Public Sector Disputes: A Contingency Analysis." *Journal of Social Issues*, 1985, *41*, 65–81.
Carpenter, S., and Kennedy, J. "Conflict Anticipation: A Site

Specific Approach for Managing Environmental Conflict."
Paper presented at fall meeting of the Society of Mining
Engineers of AIME, Tucson, Arizona, Oct. 1979.

Gerhart, P. F., and Drotning, J. E. "Dispute Settlement and the
Intensity of Mediation." *Industrial Relations*, 1980, *19*,
352–359.

Hiltrop, J. M. "Mediator Behavior and the Settlement of Collective Bargaining Disputes in Britain." *Journal of Social Issues*,
1985, *41*, 83–99.

Jones, M., and Dickens, L. "Resolving Industrial Disputes: The
Role of ACAS Conciliation." *Industrial Relations Journal*, 1983,
14, 6–17.

Kerr, C. "Industrial Conflict and Its Mediation." *American Journal
of Sociology*, 1954, *60*, 230–245.

Kochan, T. A. *Collective Bargaining and Industrial Relations: From
Theory to Policy and Practice*. Homewood, Ill.: Irwin, 1980.

Kochan, T. A., and Jick, T. "The Public Sector Mediation Process:
A Theory and Empirical Examination." *Journal of Conflict Resolution*, 1978, *22*, 209–240.

Kolb, D. M. *The Mediators*. Cambridge, Mass.: MIT Press, 1983.

Kressel, K. *Labor Mediation: An Exploratory Survey*. Albany, N.Y.:
Association of Labor Mediation Agencies, 1972.

Kressel, K., and Pruitt, D. G. "Themes in the Mediation of Social
Conflict." *Journal of Social Issues*, 1985, *41*, 179–198.

Lowry, P. J. "Conciliation Services in Great Britain." In *Conciliation Services: Structures, Functions and Techniques*. Geneva: International Labour Organisation, 1983.

Moore, C. W. *The Mediation Process: Practical Strategies for Resolving
Conflict*. San Francisco: Jossey-Bass, 1986.

Roehl, J. A., and Cook, R. F. "Issues in Mediation: Rhetoric and
Reality Revisited." *Journal of Social Issues*, 1985, *41*, 161–178.

Rubin, J. Z. "Introduction." In J. Z. Rubin (ed.), *Dynamics of Third
Party Intervention: Kissinger in the Middle East*. New York:
Praeger, 1981.

Rubin, J. Z. "Editor's Introduction." *Negotiation Journal*, 1985, *1*,
5–8.

Stevens, C. M. *Strategy and Collective Bargaining Negotiation*. New
York: McGraw-Hill, 1963.

Thoennes, N. A., and Pearson, J. "Predicting Outcomes in Divorce Mediation: The Influence of People and Process." *Journal of Social Issues*, 1985, *41*, 115–126.

Wall, J. A., Jr. "Mediation: An Analysis, Review and Proposed Research." *Journal of Conflict Resolution*, 1981, *25*, 157–180.

TWELVE

Divorce Mediation:
Characteristics
of Clients and Outcomes

Joan B. Kelly
Lynn L. Gigy

The Divorce and Mediation Project (DMP) was developed to assess the effectiveness of a comprehensive divorce mediation intervention as contrasted to the traditional two-attorney adversarial approach. Begun in 1983, this study of divorcing families sought to explore the enthusiastic claims made on behalf of mediation and to expand the body of knowledge about divorce.

Initial results from two interrelated studies of parents contesting custody or visitation matters in the court context were available at the beginning of the project (see Chapter One). While this work suggested strongly that mediation was a viable alternative to traditional legal approaches, it was not possible to

Note: The Divorce and Mediation Project was supported by grants to Joan B. Kelly from the San Francisco Foundation, the Marin Community Foundation, and the Hewlett Foundation.

establish whether the differences reported were a result of the type of intervention or basic initial differences between the mediation and control groups. In addition, the studies focused on court-connected custody disputes. The findings could not, therefore, be confidently generalized to voluntary, private-sector mediation involving economic as well as co-parenting issues. The DMP was concerned with this latter form of divorce mediation.

Study Design and Methods

The DMP is designed to compare two samples of divorcing people—one that uses mediation and one that takes the traditional adversarial route—at five points in time. The first point for the mediation sample is entry into mediation; for the adversarial sample, six weeks after filing a divorce petition. Time 2 is at the completion (or termination) of mediation for mediation respondents, and six months after time 1 for the adversarial sample (a comparable average period). For both groups, the third point is immediately after the divorce is final, and times 4 and 5 are one and two years later. Data collection for times 3, 4, and 5 is still in progress; we shall focus in this chapter on the data collected in the first two periods.

The mediation sample consisted of 212 individuals (106 couples) who came to the Northern California Mediation Center (NCMC) for mediation of all the issues pertaining to their divorces. Thirty-eight percent of them were referred by legal (21 percent) or mental health (17 percent) professionals, 35 percent came at their own or their spouse's initiative, 16 percent learned of the center from friends or prior clients, and 11 percent had other or overlapping referral sources. The 225 individuals (including 47 couples) in the adversarial sample were contacted from court records of the divorce petitions filed in Marin County, California, between February 1984 and May 1986. We excluded individuals who had been married less than one year or who filed *in pro per* (on their own behalf without attorney assistance).

Sampling procedures, participation rates, and data collection methods have been described in more detail elsewhere (Kelly, 1987; Kelly, Gigy, and Hausman, 1988). With the exception of the SCL-90, a ninety-item standardized inventory of psychological symptoms (Derogatis, 1977), the Impact Message Inventory (Perkins and others, 1979), several questions from the Denver Custody Mediation Project (Pearson, Thoennes, and Vanderkooi, 1982), four scales measuring the postdivorce co-parenting relationship (Ahrons, 1981), and the Child Behavior Checklist (Hodges and Bloom, 1984), all other objective measures and questionnaires were developed in the course of the project.

The Mediation Intervention

The divorce mediation intervention provided at NCMC was a voluntary, comprehensive dispute resolution and problem-solving process. The explicit goal of the mediation was to enable divorcing couples to reach agreement on all relevant issues. The intervention was different in several important regards from that described in other studies of the efficacy of divorce mediation (Emery and Wyer, 1987; Emery, Shaw, and Jackson, 1987; Pearson and Thoennes, Chapter One this volume): the mediation was not court connected or mandated; it addressed property and spousal and child support, as well as custody and parenting issues, and it was not procedurally rule bound (compare Coogler's structured mediation model considered by Kressel, 1985). The exact process and mediator responsibilities have been described in detail elsewhere (Kelly, 1983; Kelly, Zlatchin, and Shawn, 1985).

Responsibility for decision making rested with the couple, rather than the mediator, and in the event of irresolvable impasse, mediation terminated. Shared mediation training and ongoing team consultation, as well as familiarity with California family law and psychosocial aspects of the divorce process, enabled the three mediators to provide a procedurally and philosophically consistent mediation intervention, either separately or in teams.

Sessions were generally one and a half hours long. Clients

paid hourly sliding-scale fees at the time of each session, based on the combined gross income of the couple. Reduced rates were available for low-income clients who qualified.

The typical mediation took five to six months from initial consultation to signed memorandum of understanding. The number of sessions required to complete a comprehensive mediated settlement varied in relation to the complexity of the issues and the parties' level of conflict and motivation to resolve their differences; the average was ten. The complexity of California family law and the precision required in valuing and dividing community property also influenced the length of the process.

Fifty-eight percent of mediations were conducted by individual mediators, and 42 percent by coed or two-male mediation teams. There was no significant difference in completion rates of the coed versus all-male teams, and although a higher percentage of those who were unable to reach a mediated settlement had solo rather than team mediators, the difference was not statistically significant.

Who Chooses to Mediate?

To investigate the question of whether couples choosing to mediate their divorce were significantly different from those using the traditional adversary process, time 1 data analysis focused on demographics, marital history, spousal interaction and perception, separation and divorce, and individual psychological variables. Reported in greater detail elsewhere (Kelly, Gigy, and Hausman, 1988), the major results are summarized below.

The major demographic differences between the mediation and adversarial groups were age, education, and the presence of minor children. Mediation men (mean age, forty-one) and mediation women (mean age, thirty-eight) were on average three years younger than adversarial men and women, and had attained significantly higher levels of education. These differences may mean that mediation respondents were more aware of available alternative services and perhaps more willing to try a new community service. Pearson and Thoennes (see Chapter One) also report higher levels of education among those who accepted a custody mediation offer. However, in the current study, the adversarial comparison group included those who did not know about mediation as well as those who chose not to mediate.

Eighty-six percent of the mediation respondents, compared to 66 percent of the adversarial group, had children under eighteen. While the difference in age may account for some of this difference, it may also be that mediation disproportionately draws couples with children because of the recognition of their continuing co-parental relationship.

The two groups did not differ in their combined median household income ($59,000), or in the number of women working full- or part-time at entry into the study (75 percent). As expected, the men's income was significantly higher than the women's. The average length of marriage was thirteen years for both groups. Because the adversarial group were located through filed divorce petitions, they were more likely to be separated at time 1 than mediation couples (92 percent versus 69 percent), but among those separated in both groups, the length of time between separation and time 1 was eight months.

One of the surprising findings reported earlier (Kelly, Gigy, and Hausman, 1988) was the absence of significant differences in the amount of marital conflict in the two years preceding the separation. More than half of the men and women in both groups reported that conflict occurred "often" or "always." Also, there were no group differences in the amount of child-specific conflict reported by those with minor children. On six different measures of marital communication, both groups reported equally poor communication.

Thus, the data did not support the common view that mediation couples are the "easier" divorce cases, or that they enjoyed more "civilized," friendlier, or more communicative marriages than those in the traditional adversarial process. While Pearson and Thoennes report that a higher percentage of respondents rejecting mediation reported no communication at all with their spouse, compared to those accepting mediation, the current finding of no group differences in marital conflict and communication may be attributed to the fact that Pearson and Thoennes studied a sample of couples who had come to the court with an identified and ongoing custody or visitation dispute. The NCMC couples had just initiated their divorce process, and the sample included those with no specific identified dispute as well as those for whom some court hearings had occurred (such as temporary custody or restraining orders).

No overall group differences or sex differences within groups emerged with regard to whether the decision to divorce was mutual or more unilateral, nor were there group differences in positive or negative feelings about the divorce. Women in both groups were significantly more likely than men to have decided to end the marriage, except for women over forty-five. Men not only had less control over the decision to divorce, but expressed greater interest in reconciliation.

Women indicated a more wide-ranging and greater dissatisfaction with their marriages than men on a checklist of twenty-seven reasons for divorce. Factor analysis of the checklist responses yielded eight meaningful factors, and group differences emerged on two of these. Adversarial respondents were likely to have sought divorce when a spouse was perceived as emotionally unstable and abusing drugs or alcohol, and they also more often said conflicts about employment and financial matters led to divorce. Mediation and adversarial respondents did not differ on these reasons: angry, demeaning, or violent spouse; loss of closeness and love; own substance abuse and affairs; seriously divergent lifestyles and values; role and career conflicts; spouse's jealousy.

The level of reported cooperation between spouses in the mediation and adversarial groups did not differ significantly at the beginning of the study. While twenty-six percent reported "very poor" or "no cooperation," forty-five percent reported "some" or "good" cooperation. There were no group differences between ratings of how powerful a spouse was perceived to be, their perceived ability to argue with their spouse in the marriage, or how often they reported that they won arguments during their marriage: both men and women believed that they won less than half. Men and women had similar degrees of confidence in being able to reach a fair settlement in the two divorce processes.

Thus, some of the central marital and relationship variables expected to discriminate between the mediation and adversarial respondents did not do so. Marital conflict and poor communication, nonmutuality in the divorce decision, and strained cooperation apparently did not act as barriers to selecting mediation in this sample.

Another surprising finding was the absence of significant differences in self-ratings of divorce-specific anger at the spouse, and on SCL-90 hostility scale scores. (Regardless of group, women reported significantly higher levels of anger at their mates.) The differences between the two groups are focused instead on the spouses' views of each other's integrity, and their own psychological responses to the divorce. Mediation clients believed their spouses were significantly more honest and rated their spouses higher on a fairmindedness scale. Mediation parents also expressed more confidence in their ability to cooperate about their children after divorce. Thus, despite equally dissatisfying marriages and equal anger at spouses, the mediation respondents seemed more able to acknowledge certain positive qualities of the spouse, indicating perhaps an ability to reject the marriage but not the total person. Respondents' views of their spouse's integrity was not related to age or educational attainment.

Mediation respondents also reported significantly higher levels of divorce-related depression, guilt, and stress. SCL-90 anxiety scale scores also distinguished between the two groups, with mediation respondents scoring significantly higher. The mediation group appeared to be dealing with their psychological reactions to marital failure and divorce in a different way, even though anger and resolve to divorce were the same as in the adversarial sample. The more intense sadness, stress, and guilt experienced by the mediation group may reflect an acknowledgment that they shared some responsibility for the marital failure. If so, the tendency would not be to completely and angrily reject the "bad" spouse, but rather to accept and retain a more mixed view of the spouse's character.

The mediation respondents' more favorable view of the spouse's integrity, and their greater internalized psychological distress, may enhance motivation to seek out mediation as a more humane, constructive, and psychologically safe environment in which to end a relationship. Sillars' (1981) finding that students who felt they shared blame were more likely to take a problem-solving approach to resolving conflict with a roommate supports this observation. Mediation may present an option that allows divorcing people to retain some respect for each other as well as safeguard their own self-esteem. If there are minor children, this may be particularly beneficial.

Motivation for Entering Mediation

We now turn to the mediation sample exclusively. What reasons did they give for choosing divorce mediation? What marital, spousal, and psychological variables were related to these reasons and to positive or negative attitudes about mediation?

Reasons for Entering Mediation. Mediation respondents were asked to indicate all their reasons for entering divorce mediation, including the first and second most important reasons, from a checklist giving fourteen reasons for entering mediation. The following reasons were most frequently checked by both men and women:

- Reach an overall agreement satisfactory to both me and my spouse (91 percent)
- Reduce or avoid hostility between me and my spouse (83 percent)
- Reduce the cost of obtaining the divorce (82 percent)
- Reduce contact with lawyers and court proceedings (81 percent)
- Want a fair property division agreement (70 percent)
- Retain a friendly relationship with my spouse (65 percent)

There was little consensus about the most important reasons. Forty percent indicated that reaching a mutually satisfactory agreement was first or second in importance, and reducing the cost of divorce and working out good custody and visiting arrangements were checked by more than 20 percent of men and women. Significant sex differences emerged on two of the fourteen items: women more often indicated they entered mediation to reach a good support agreement (73 pecent, versus 53 percent of the men), and men more often indicated a desire for reconciliation as a motivation for beginning mediation (19 percent; 5 percent of the women).

A principal components factor analysis suggested two major groups of clients who come to divorce mediation with substantially different motivations. Factor 1 (practical or financial reasons) described individuals who wanted a divorce process that is cost efficient, amenable to more personal input and control, avoidant of lawyers and legal procedures, and personally advantageous in terms of support and property agreements. Factor 2 (retain friendly relationship) described those who wanted to end the marriage with minimal hostility, obtain an agreement that *both* would consider satisfactory, and improve communication and remain friendly in the future. There were no sex differences for either of these factors.

Analysis of the correlations between factor-based scores derived from the reason-for-mediation checklist and marital, spousal, and psychological variables enhanced our understanding of the differences in these groups of mediation clients. Clients who sought mediation primarily for practical or financial reasons (factor 1) more often were divorcing because they had an angry or demeaning spouse [$r(183) = .21, p < .05$], or an emotionally unstable or substance-abusing spouse [$r(183) = .24, p < .01$]. Men seeking mediation for practical or financial reasons were likely to report poor marriages (frequent conflict or poor communication) [$r(88) = .27, p < .01$], and to have initiated the decision to divorce [$r(90) = .24, p = .01$]. There were no such associations among the women who indicated their motivation for entering was primarily practical or financial.

Men and women who entered mediation primarily because of a desire to retain a friendly relationship with their spouse (factor 2) reported different reasons for seeking divorce than the first group. They were more likely to have decided to divorce because of a loss of love and caring [$r(183) = .27$, $p < .001$], or diverging life-styles and values [$r(183) = .20, p < .01$]. Both of these reasons for divorcing imply a more gradual diminution over time in intimacy and love, or changes in life-style or values. The likelihood of mutual participation in the decision to divorce is greater in these kinds of marriages, as is some recognition that while the relationship has withered, the spouse is not necessarily abhorrent and may continue to be a friend. Beyond these reasons for divorce, women who placed importance on retaining a friendly relationship with their spouse were those who were less angry at their spouse [$r(94) = -.31, p < .001$]. They viewed their spouses as being more honest and fairminded [$r(93) = .29$, $p < .01$] and reported high levels of cooperation [$r(93) = .29$, $p < .05$]. There were no such associations for men.

Attitude Toward Mediation. Men were significantly more positive about beginning the mediation process than women (Mann-Whitney U, $z = 2.61, p < .01$). On a five-point scale indicating positive or negative attitude about entering mediation, 82 percent of the men and 67 percent of the women were "very positive" or "positive" about entering mediation; twice as many women as men had a "neutral" attitude.

For both sexes, a more positive attitude toward beginning mediation was found when the reason for divorce was loss of love and caring [$r(182) = .19$, $p < .01$], when there was more participation in initiating the decision to divorce [$r(183).19$, $p < .01$], when anger was low [$r(183) = -.25$, $p < .001$], and when the spouse was viewed as reasonably honest [$r(184) = .16$, $p < .01$]. The relationship between having some control over the decision to divorce and a positive attitude toward mediation was particularly strong for men [$r(89) = .38, p < .001$], while a belief in spousal integrity was more strongly correlated to willingness to mediate for women [$r(93) = .37, p < .001$]. Women were also likely to be very positive about mediation if they felt cooperation was good [$r(96) = .24, p < .01$]. In contrast, cooperation and spousal integrity were not critical in determining men's willingness to mediate, but the acknowledgment of a troubled (high conflict or poor communication) marriage [$r(88) = .36, p < .001$] was associated with a positive attitude toward mediation.

Thus, while participating in the decision to divorce enhances willingness to mediate for both men and women, women's attitudes additionally are shaped by the divorce-related anger they hold toward their spouse, their view of spousal integrity, and perceived level of cooperation, whereas men's willingness to mediate is related to their recognition of a poor marriage.

Mediation Outcomes

The earliest outcome that can and should be considered is whether the couple is able to reach agreement or settlement in mediation. Kressel (1985) reported that, across studies, settlement rates ranged from 22 to 97 percent, with most falling between 40 and 70 percent. In the Divorce and Mediation Project sample, a successful or completed mediation was defined as one in which the couple reached agreement on all relevant and final divorce issues, resulting in a written memorandum that could then be incorporated into the marital settlement agreement by their reviewing attorney. This arbitrary definition excluded clients who mediated initial separation issues or who reached interim but unwritten agreements on custody, parenting, and temporary support but did not return to complete the final divorce negotiations. Although such mediations served a worthwhile purpose, they were classified as terminated mediations either because of the lack of a written agreement or because they did not represent the type of final agreements necessary to complete a divorce action. Using these criteria, 57 percent of the NCMC couples completed the mediation process and 43 percent terminated mediation before reaching final and written agreements. It is important to understand what factors distinguish couples who complete mediation from those who terminate without reaching full agreement.

Reasons for Terminating Mediation. Couples who terminated mediation at NCMC were asked to fill out a twenty-one-item checklist of reasons for not completing the mediation process. "Mediation is too expensive" was the most frequently checked reason. (There was no evidence that it was cited more often by respondents from low-income brackets than by those better able to pay.) "Stopping mediation was my spouse's decision" was the second most frequently checked item. Most of the remaining items fell into two distinct correlational clusters: feeling overwhelmed or lacking empowerment within the process, and feeling that the spouse was unreasonable, untrustworthy, angry, and intolerable (Kelly, Gigy, and Hausman, 1988).

Although we attempted to construct an exhaustive list of reasons for early termination of mediation, 42 percent of the respondents gave at least one reason other than those listed. For example, items about difficulties between the parties were included in the checklist but there were couples who terminated for exactly the opposite reason: "We decided that we really wanted to redirect our energies into rebuilding our marriage instead of terminating it. Your organization certainly played a role in helping us reach that decision." "I rate your service very highly and credit the process with saving our marriage." These certainly cannot be classified as "failures" even though the purpose of the divorce mediation was not realized.

Along similar lines, there were couples who reported that after a few sessions they were able to work out an agreement between themselves without the aid of a third party, or that mediation had redirected them along a more productive path. "Although we didn't continue, I do feel the mediator helped my spouse to be more open to more equitable and realistic solutions. We then managed to come to an agreement through our attorneys without needing to go to court. Also, the process helped me to avoid capitulating to his initial perspective and in the end to stand firm for a fair agreement." "I'm satisfied with my mediation experience. It definitely opened the way for my husband and me to communicate more effectively."

Timing was also mentioned as a factor: "I was thunderstruck and in a state of shock at being served with divorce papers after over thirty years of marriage. I wasn't ready to 'mediate.' I felt I was being forced to enter a situation I wasn't prepared to enter. I really feel [the mediator] might have been very successful if the timing hadn't been (for me) so bad." "We attempted to mediate within the month after separating and, in my opinion, that was too soon. . . . I feel the mediation process is extremely effective and although we did not continue, I would still recommend it over the traditional court system."

There were also a number of idiosyncratic reasons for terminating, including job loss, deaths in the family, bankruptcy, and, in one case, legal charges of fraud. Clearly, beyond our original expectations, termination can occur for reasons other than dissatisfaction with the process or the parties involved. Confirming these observations is the finding that although the couples completing mediation are significantly more satisfied with the process than terminators, over half of the terminators reported they were either neutral or satisfied with mediation (Kelly, Gigy, and Hausman, 1988).

Distinguishing Outcome Groups. Clients who terminate the mediation process before reaching agreement on all divorce issues are not easily distinguished from those who complete mediation with an agreement. For example, there was considerable overlap in the number of sessions the "terminators" and the "completors" participated in. The completors ranged from three to twenty-seven sessions with an average and median of ten; the terminators ranged from one to eleven sessions with an average of four and a half and a median of four. And some terminators had successfully negotiated difficult and important issues while a few completors did not accomplish their original stated goal of comprehensive mediation.

Further analysis of the two groups led us to redefine the overly broad groups into four subgroups:

1. Comprehensive completors (50 percent; $N = 102$), those who reached final and written agreement on *all* issues involved in their divorce
2. Partial completors (8 percent; $N = 18$), those who came to mediation intending to negotiate all issues, but instead reached the final, written-agreement stage in only a circum-

       scribed area, such as custody and parenting or property
       division
3.   Productive terminators (15 percent; $N = 32$), those who ne-
       gotiated and resolved one or more critical issues related to
       their separation but did not negotiate final divorce issues or
       reach the written-agreement stage
4.   True terminators (26 percent; $N = 54$), those for whom me-
       diation was apparently totally unproductive, who were un-
       able to resolve or negotiate anything

       The comprehensive completors were primarily distin-
guished by a similarity between the husband's and wife's self-
reported financial knowledge. On a 10-point scale (with 10
representing a high level of financial knowledge), the
comprehensive-completor males had the lowest average self-
rating of financial knowledge among the males (7.31), while the
comprehensive-completor females had the highest average rating among the females (6.02). Of particular interest was the
finding that these couples were able to reach comprehensive
agreement even though they were not any more cooperative or
committed to maintaining friendly relationships than the other
subgroups.
       The partial completors were unique in being the furthest
along in the divorce process at the beginning of mediation.
They were more likely to be separated, to have filed for divorce,
and to have had attorneys active on their behalf when they came
to mediation. They were also more likely to have children under
the age of ten. While the intent to mediate comprehensive
settlement was expressed, the majority of the partial completors
reached final custody and parenting agreements but were not
able to successfully negotiate final support or property-division
agreements. Several findings may have contributed to this. The
partial completors had the largest discrepancy between the husbands' and wives' self-ratings of financial knowledge. The
partial-completor males had the highest average ratings (8.17) of
financial knowledge while the partial-completor females had
the lowest (4.25) of all the subgroups. They gave low ratings of
their spouse's honesty, fairmindedness, and level of cooperation.

Further, on two scales derived from the Impact Message Inventory (Perkins and others, 1979), the partial completors rated their spouses as significantly more competitive and significantly less nurturant than did the other three groups. These characteristics of the partial completors did not prevent them from mediating parenting agreements, but appeared to interfere with the more detailed and complex property and support negotiations. Their more extensive prior contact with attorneys may have also contributed to greater intransigence on support and property matters.

The productive terminators entered mediation with strong desires to preserve or build a friendly relationship with their spouse (factor 2). This interest in improving communication and reducing hostility was combined with an unusually high interest in reconciliation. Thus it would appear that many spouses in the productive-terminator group were not fully committed to proceeding with their divorces. Many couples in this group reached informal agreement on critical separation issues necessitated by one spouse's stated desire to divorce but did not continue on to negotiate final agreements. Some productive terminators used the mediation process to guide them toward agreements reached later on their own. Others terminated because the process of working actively on final agreements conflicted with their desire for reconciliation.

The true terminators more than the other three groups indicated that the primary factor leading to divorce was an angry, demeaning spouse or an emotionally unstable, substance-abusing spouse. Despite these differences, they did not report more anger at their spouse, nor were their ratings of the spouse's honesty and fairmindedness lower than the other groups. The couples in this group failed to reach agreement on anything, staying in mediation only long enough for us to begin the data-collection process. Just as mediators could not reliably predict whether couples would terminate mediation before the third session (Kelly, Gigy, and Hausman, 1988), it may be that the true terminators needed that time as well to determine if the basis for good-faith negotiations existed.

Satisfaction with Mediation. Respondents' overall satisfaction with the mediation process and results was measured on a seven-point scale ranging from "very dissatisfied" to "very satisfied." At the completion of the mediation process (time 2), 78 percent of the men and 72 percent of the women indicated they were "somewhat" to "very satisfied." Fourteen percent of the men and 26 percent of the women expressed some dissatisfaction, and the remainder were neither satisfied nor dissatisfied. Partial completors did not differ significantly from comprehensive completors on satisfaction levels. As might be expected, those who terminated mediation before reaching agreement were significantly less satisfied with the process [$F(1,103) = 9.17$, $p < .01$]. However, 42 percent of those terminating expressed moderate to high levels of satisfaction, 20 percent were neutral, and 39 percent were dissatisfied. Differences between men and women were not significant.

Among those completing mediation, 74 percent of both men and women would generally or enthusiastically recommend mediation to a friend, 13 percent thought they "probably" would, and 18 percent indicated they would do so reluctantly or not at all. Among those who terminated mediation before reaching final agreement, 76 percent of the women and 41 percent of the men said they would recommend mediation to a friend, 12 percent of the women and 29 percent of the men thought they probably would, and 12 percent of the women and 29 percent of the men would do so reluctantly or not at all. The women in the terminator group seemed more forgiving of the failed mediation than the men. They were more likely to say, "Even though it didn't work for us, I would still recommend it to others . . . it's a good thing." These findings are comparable with those of Pearson and Thoennes on user satisfaction in court-connected custody mediations (see Chapter One), in both the high levels of satisfaction among those who reach agreement and substantial satisfaction among those who try but are unable to reach agreements.

Clients' reactions to more specific aspects of the mediation process and outcomes were obtained on a fifty-four-item questionnaire, the Client Assessment of Mediation Services (CAMS). Described in detail elsewhere (Kelly, 1987; Kelly and

Gigy, 1988), this questionnaire explored such process issues as mediator behavior, skill and impartiality, efficiency, instrumental effectiveness, power and balance, self-efficacy, and assessed satisfaction with property, support, and custody outcomes.

Considering specifically those who completed mediation, in many important ways men and women did not differ in their responses on the questionnaire at the completion of mediation (time 2). Approximately three-quarters of both the men and women agreed that the mediators were skillful, showed concern for their feelings, helped identify important issues, provided enough information to protect their interests, did not impose their viewpoint, and were impartial. Eighty-two percent of the women and 71 percent of the men felt that the mediator helped them stand up for their rights. There were no statistically significant sex differences on any of these process items.

With regard to outcomes, two-thirds of the men and the women agreed that the spousal support was fair, and more than two-thirds were satisfied with the division of property. Three-quarters felt the custody and visitation agreements they reached were best for everyone. The only sex difference was with regard to child support agreements; 37 percent of the women agreed that child support was not adequate, in contrast to 3 percent of the men. (In a preliminary analysis of the final divorce [time 3] data, significantly more adversarial women than men also believed that child support was not adequate.)

Women reported that the mediation process had helped them assume more responsibility in managing their personal affairs than did men, and women had greater confidence in their ability to stand up for themselves as a result of the process. Women were also more likely than men to believe that mediation had helped them better understand their spouse's point of view. The data did not support the notion, advanced by critics of mediation, that women are disadvantaged in the mediation process or are forced into agreements that are unfair. As indicated earlier and discussed in more detail elsewhere (Kelly, Gigy, and Hausman, 1988), women appear to terminate mediation for essentially the "right" reasons—feeling unempowered or overwhelmed by the data or the process, or perceiving their spouses

as obstructive in negotiating fair agreements. Women who complete mediation affirm the process and results in multiple ways.
Preliminary time 3 (final divorce) comparisons between adversarial and successful mediation respondents further confirm
this: mediation women were more satisfied with their property,
custody, and spousal support agreements than were the adversarial women. Further, men and women in mediation were significantly more satisfied with both the process and the various
outcomes than adversarial men and women at final divorce
[$F(1,195) = 8.96, p < .01$] (Kelly, 1987).

Implications of the Research

In considering the implications of this research, it is
important to note that the mediation sample was voluntary, self-
selected, predominantly white, middle to upper-middle class,
and well educated. The mediation intervention itself was offered
in the private sector and addressed all the issues and disputes
involved in the divorce. The mediators were highly experienced,
well trained in mediation, and knowledgeable about relevant
psychological and family-law matters.

This research highlighted the diversity among clients
seeking mediation and the complexities in the various outcomes
of mediation. The findings led us to reject many stereotypes and
oversimplified notions about mediation. People came to mediation with varied motivations, psychological states, and marital
histories. Compared to those using the traditional adversarial
divorce process, their divorces were not "easier" or friendlier.
Mediators were confronted with some individuals who expressed great anger at their spouses, and some who did not; they
mediated with men and women who had no desire to have any
future interaction with a spouse, and those who sought through
the process to maintain a friendly relationship; and within the
couple dyad there was almost always an imbalance in the extent
to which each spouse wanted the divorce.

Regardless of their motivations, their marriages, spousal
interactions, or personalities, the men and women who came to
mediation seemed quite capable of determining what they

needed from the process and taking appropriate action if their needs or goals were not being met. While voices opposed to mediation have expressed great concern that women, in particular, are less powerful than men and therefore automatically disadvantaged by mediation, our findings are more encouraging. Consistent with the underlying principle of self-determination and decision making, men and women apparently did not feel locked into the mediation process. Instead, they readily terminated if they perceived the process or pending agreements to be unsatisfactory or contradictory to their stated or unstated goals.

Four different outcome groups were identified that increased our understanding of the diverse and sometimes unanticipated results of the divorce mediation process. Thus, for example, contrary to the usual standard for judging the success of a mediation intervention, termination was revealed to be something other than a failure or bad outcome in some cases. While some men and women terminated mediation because they perceived that the process could not overcome the obstructive behaviors of a demeaning, recalcitrant spouse, others terminated because they were sufficiently encouraged by the process to attempt a reconciliation, or because the process was moving them too quickly toward a goal they had not embraced, that of final divorce.

Finally, the variables found to be predictive of the outcome profiles should not be used to screen for suitability for, or exclusion from, mediation. As always with statistical analyses, these variables are linked to group profiles rather than specific individuals or couples. Such factors as a high imbalance in financial acumen within a couple, a couple's actual commitment to the decision to divorce, and the emotional instability of one or both parties found to be associated with differing outcomes within this research sample were not necessarily observable in the initial consultation or the first working session. Both clients and mediators need time to determine whether the process is suitable and productive (Kelly, Gigy, and Hausman, 1988). These predictor variables may serve instead to heighten mediator sensitivity to particular issues that may need to be addressed and openly discussed early in the mediation process.

References

Ahrons, C. R. "Continuing Coparental Relationship Between Divorced Spouses." *American Journal of Orthopsychiatry*, 1981, *51*, 415–428.

Derogatis, L. "SCL-90 Administration, Scoring and Procedures Manual — Revised Version." Unpublished, 1977.

Emery, R. E., Shaw, D. S., and Jackson, J. A. "A Clinical Description of a Model of Child Custody Mediation." In J. P. Vincent (ed.), *Advances in Family Intervention, Assessment, and Theory.* Vol. 4. Greenwich, Conn.: JAI Press, 1987.

Emery, R. E., and Wyer, M. M. "Child Custody Mediation and Litigation: An Experimental Evaluation of the Experience of Parents." *Journal of Consulting and Clinical Psychology*, 1987, *55*, 179–186.

Hodges, W., and Bloom, B. "Parents' Report of Children's Adjustment to Marital Separation: A Longitudinal Study." *Journal of Divorce*, 1984, *8*, 33–50.

Kelly, J. B. "Mediation and Psychotherapy: Distinguishing the Differences." *Mediation Quarterly*, 1983, *1*, 33–44.

Kelly, J. B. "Mediated and Adversarial Divorce: Respondents' Perceptions of Their Processes and Outcomes." *Mediation Quarterly*, in press, *24*.

Kelly, J. B., and Gigy, L. "Client Assessment of Mediation Services (CAMS): A Scale Measuring Client Perceptions and Satisfaction," *Mediation Quarterly*, 1988, *19*, 43–52.

Kelly, J. B., Gigy, L., and Hausman, S. "Mediated and Adversarial Divorce: Initial Findings from a Longitudinal Study." In J. Folberg and A. Milne (eds.), *Divorce Mediation: Theory and Practice*. New York: Guilford Press, 1988.

Kelly, J. B., Zlatchin, C., and Shawn, J. "Divorce Mediation: An Emerging Field." In C. Ewing (ed.), *Psychology, Psychiatry, and the Law: A Clinical and Forensic Handbook*. Sarasota, Fla.: Professional Resource Exchange, 1985.

Kressel, K. *The Process of Divorce: How Professionals and Couples Negotiate Settlements*. New York: Basic Books, 1985.

Pearson, J., Thoennes, N., and Vanderkooi, L. "The Decision to Mediate: Profiles of Individuals Who Accept and Reject the

Opportunity to Mediate Contested Custody and Visitation Issues." *Journal of Divorce,* 1982, *6,* 17–35.

Perkins, M., and others. "The Impact Message Inventory: A New Measure of Relationship in Counseling/Psychotherapy and Other Dyads." *Journal of Counseling Psychology,* 1979, *26,* 363–367.

Sillars, A. L. "Attributions and Interpersonal Conflict Resolution." In J. H. Harvey, W. J. Ickes, and R. F. Kidd (eds.), *New Directions in Attribution Research.* Vol. 3. Hillsdale, N.J.: Erlbaum, 1981.

THIRTEEN

International
Dispute Mediation:
A Comparative
Empirical Analysis

Jacob Bercovitch

In all social systems, however simple or complex, there are three
basic methods of conflict management: violence and coercion
(both physical and psychological), various forms of negotiation
(bargaining), and the involvement of a third party. A review of
the relations between nations suggests that these methods are as
common in international politics as they are in any other sphere
of human activity.

Note: I wish to thank Mark Laffey for his help with the collection and
tabulation of the data, and Paul Hare, Jean Hiltrop, and Jeffrey Rubin for
their insightful comments. Special thanks are due to Dean G. Pruitt and
Kenneth Kressel for their many helpful suggestions. An earlier, different
version of this paper was delivered at the Ninth Scientific Meeting of the
International Society of Political Psychology in Amsterdam, 1986, and published in *Cooperation and Conflict 21* (3) (1986). It is reprinted here with the
permission of the editor and the Norwegian University Press.

Of the available methods for managing international conflicts, negotiation has attracted the most attention. Scholarly concern with this method is now well established, and a substantial body of work exists to account for structure, tactics, approaches, and effectiveness (see for instance Bercovitch, 1984b; Druckman, 1977; Pruitt, 1981; Rubin and Brown, 1975). In contrast, the practice of conflict management by third parties, although as old as conflict itself and steadily growing in importance, remains much less understood. Today, just as more than two decades ago, "there is relatively little theoretical analysis of the mediation process and even fewer results and conclusions in consequence of such analysis" (Stevens, 1963, p. 123). It is against such a background that this study is undertaken.

Third-Party Involvement in Conflict Situations

Third parties, be they individuals, representatives of states, or representatives of international institutions, may find themselves involved in an international dispute as a result of their own initiative or in response to a call from one or both of the adversaries. As a peaceful form of conflict management, mediation usually occurs when these four conditions exist: (1) an international dispute is long, drawn out, and complex; (2) the adversaries' own conflict management efforts have reached an impasse; (3) neither side is prepared to countenance further escalation of the dispute; and (4) the adversaries are sufficiently cooperative and prepared to break the stalemate by having some contact and communication (Bercovitch, 1984a).

When intervening in an international dispute, a third party may undertake a range of activities designed to separate hostile factions, create the conditions for a settlement, or maintain and monitor a ceasefire agreement. These third-party activities, ranging from a passive to a more active involvement, are traditionally described as *fact finding* or inquiry (providing an impartial determination of the facts in dispute), *good offices* (acting as a go-between, transmitting messages and information between the protagonists), and *mediation* (aiding or influencing the adversaries to find a solution). This chapter is mostly concerned with mediation.

As a method of peaceful settlement, mediation is particularly important in international relations. Even a cursory survey of recent international disputes reveals the extent, and heterogeneity, of third-party involvement. In the last decade we have seen the involvement of such parties as the United Nations (in the Vietnam-Kampuchea dispute), the Organization of African Unity (in the Tanzania-Uganda dispute), the Organization of American States (in the Nicaragua dispute), the United Kingdom (in the Rhodesia-Zimbabwe dispute), and the United States (through various special representatives in the Middle East). Less formal, publicized, or institutionalized cases occur on a daily basis. Mediation, though it may be little understood, is certainly not unpopular.

Why, one must ask, would parties to a dispute accept, or even seek, the involvement of a third party? There are several reasons. Mediation by a third party can prevent a dispute from escalating. It imposes few losses on any of the parties and it offers instead some distinct advantages (providing ideas for possible solutions, defusing the intensity of conflicts, and so on). Parties may accept or seek mediation in the hope of securing a more favorable settlement, but more commonly they accept mediation because it is a cheap, flexible, adaptable, and effective method of conflict management.

Why, then, would individuals, organizations, or states agree to serve as mediators? There are a number of possible reasons. Mediators may be genuinely motivated by humanitarian or altruistic reasons. They may be approached by one or both of the disputing parties. They may have a constitutional mandate to intervene in certain disputes (the Arab League, for example, is committed under Article 5 of its charter to mediate disputes between Arab states), or they may do so to protect or promote their own interests. One way or another, both the disputing parties and the potential mediator usually have good reasons for engaging in international mediation.

Studying International Mediation Systematically

Two different traditions have dominated the study of mediation in international disputes: the legal and the historical. The legal tradition places a strong emphasis on terminology and the appropriateness of various third-party procedures; the historical tradition stresses the uniqueness of each case and offers findings that treat this form of conflict management as art. A more recent and systematic tradition undertakes to examine the relationship between types of mediation and dispute outcomes. It is with this tradition that I am particularly concerned.

Several studies, characteristic of this tradition, show the importance of mediation as a form of international conflict management. Northedge and Donelan (1971) find that third parties were involved in 31 out of 50 major international disputes between 1945 and 1970. Holsti (1983) notes that third parties were involved in 42 out of 94 international disputes between 1919 and 1980. Levine (1971) finds that throughout a 150-year period (from 1816) international mediation was attempted, on the average, every four months. Zacher (1979) finds that regional organizations were involved in 110 out of 116 international disputes between 1945 and 1977. Butterworth (1976) finds that some form of peaceful third-party intervention took place in 255 of 310 international disputes between 1945 and 1974.

What these studies do not offer is a case list of international disputes based on explicit coding criteria, propositions about the conditions associated with successful mediation, or an articulated theory of international mediation. This chapter reports an effort to remedy this situation.

The data set used covered the four decades following 1945. The geographical focus of the study was global, and the sovereign, independent state was used as the basic unit of analysis. Political actors that did not satisfy the Singer-Small international system membership (Small and Singer, 1982) criteria of independent statehood (for instance, western Sahara), were excluded. In our definition, an international dispute has three criteria: (1) two or more states were directly involved; (2) the states were pursuing mutually incompatible objectives or values and were engaged in mutually opposed actions and reactions by organized groups; and (3) at least 100 military or civilian deaths could be attributed to such actions and reactions. Using, for the most part, information gathered from *Keesings Archives, The Times (London) Index,* and the *New York Times Index,* these criteria yielded a total of seventy-two international disputes in the 1945–1984 period. (The list of disputes may be obtained from the author.)

International Disputes: Incidence and Characteristics

Looking at the frequency of disputes over time, we note thirteen international disputes in the 1945–1954 period, twenty-three in the next decade, seventeen in the next, and nineteen in the 1975–1984 period. If we take into account the tremendous increase in the number of actors in the international system after 1964, some satisfaction may be had by noting that more states did not necessarily mean more disputes.

If we examine the regional distribution of international disputes, by dividing the globe into six subsystems, we note that the Middle East with twenty-two international disputes was the most conflict-prone region, and the western hemisphere (six disputes) and Europe (two disputes) the least conflict-prone.

An important characteristic of international disputes concerns the nature of the issues that give rise to mutually incompatible goals and behaviors. Issues define the basic structure of a dispute. A number of ways of distinguishing between issues have been suggested (Aubert, 1963; Deutsch, 1973; Hirsch, 1977; Mitchell, 1981). In this study disputes were divided into five types: those over sovereignty (here defined as claims by one state to territory controlled by another); ideology (disputes over values, beliefs, and preferences); security (disutes over limited territorial possessions); independence (disputes over the creation of new states); and a residual category. Most international disputes fell into those involving sovereignty issues (40 percent of cases), followed by ideology (25 percent), independence (18 percent), security (11 percent), and other (6 percent).

The next stage involved identifying disputes that were officially mediated. Of the seventy-two international disputes, forty-four were mediated. Some disputes, however, experienced more than one mediation effort. The range of mediation efforts per dispute varied from one to sixteen (with a mean of 2.92 and a median of 1.50), giving us a total of 210 official mediation efforts between 1945 and 1984.

Conditions of Successful Mediation in International Disputes

What variables or conditions influence the usefulness and effectiveness of this form of conflict management? This question will be answered by examining how mediation outcomes are affected by three clusters of structural variables: the identity and characteristics of the disputing parties, the nature of the dispute, and the identity and characteristics of the mediator.

The Identity and Characteristics of the Parties. Conflict management by mediators has a better chance of success when the adversaries have a well-defined identity (Modelski, 1964) and can deal with each other through representatives who are recognized as the legitimate spokesmen for their parties. Disunity or lack of cohesion within either state makes it hard for a mediator to resolve an international controversy (Frei, 1976). A mediator's job is especially difficult if the incumbent government of one of the adversaries is experiencing an insurgency, rebellion, or other serious internal threat. The successive failures of recent mediation attempts in Lebanon and Latin America illustrate these points only too well.

Mediation may also have a greater likelihood of success when cultural or ideological differences between the adversaries are low (Glenn and others, 1976; Druckman and Zechmeister, 1970). Statistical research similar to ours by Frei (1976) demonstrates that states that receive or depend on external help are considerably more inclined to accept mediation than states that do not. Mediation, it seems, is more likely to be effective in managing international disputes between small or medium powers. In the present bipolar international system, it can be safely argued that disputes involving the superpowers would not be particularly amenable to mediation. Such states are well able to resist any form of external pressure or influence a mediator may bring to bear.

Another condition that may influence the effectiveness of international mediation concerns the degree of power disparity between the adversaries. Numerous qualitative studies, including those by Ott (1972), Young (1967), Curle (1971), and Randolph (1973), suggest that the smaller the power differences between the adversaries, the greater the effectiveness of international mediation. Logically this seems quite obvious, for in cases of clear power disparity the stronger adversary would not be prepared to offer concessions or entertain proposals that call for it to make compromises. The idea that mediation is most effective in disputes involving parties of relatively equal power receives strong empirical support from a reinterpretation of Butterworth's data (1976). In a study examining power resources and the impact of international mediation (Bercovitch, 1985a), a clear pattern emerged showing a high mediation impact (that is, abatement or settlement of a dispute) when power capabilities were evenly matched and a low impact when power disparity was high.

Deutsch (1973) has suggested that the previous relationship between the parties is one of the main variables affecting the course and outcome of a dispute. An examination of our data reveals that the parties' previous relationship can influence the *course* of a dispute but has only a slight impact on its *outcome*. Mediation was accepted in 75 percent of the cases involving parties who had been engaged in a previous dispute, compared to 38 percent for those who had not. On the other hand, mediation between parties who had been engaged in a previous dispute was less likely to succeed: 33 percent, compared to 48 percent between parties who had not experienced a previous conflict.

The Nature of the Dispute. To be effective, mediation must take place at a propitious or ripe moment. There is, however, little agreement about what constitutes such a moment or how to recognize it. Edmead (1971) claims that mediation is more likely to succeed if it is attempted at an early stage and certainly before the adversaries cross a threshold of violence and begin to inflict heavy losses on each other. Others, like Northedge and Donelan (1971) argue that mediation can be effective only with the passage of time, after each side has suffered some costs and has shown a willingness to moderate its intransigence and revise its expectations. Assessing the best time to initiate mediation is both ambiguous and difficult, but interviews with experienced intermediaries (Bercovitch, 1984a) lend considerable support to later rather than earlier initiation of mediation moves.

Mediation, it seems, is more effective when it follows, rather than precedes, some of the disputants' own efforts at de-escalation. The passage of time, a stalemate, or a painful impasse would seem to provide the necessary conditions and constitute the ideal phase in the dispute to initiate mediation. International mediation must not be an instantaneous or automatic response to any dispute. It should be activated only when the moment is ripe; that means after the parties' activities and perceptions have shifted and both have come to realize that neither party can prevail in the dispute.

Closely related to this factor is dispute intensity (Kriesberg, 1987). Here again the literature on mediation offers two contradictory notions. Jackson (1952), Ott (1972), and Latour and others (1976) suggest that the greater the intensity or salience of a dispute, the higher the likelihood that mediation will be accepted and be successful (as a way of cutting losses, if nothing else). An opposite view (Burton, 1969; Fisher, 1964) contends that the greater the intensity and the higher the losses, the more polarized the parties' positions will become and the more determined each party will be to reject any mediation effort and attempt to "win" at all costs. In our study dispute intensity was measured in terms of the number of fatalities experienced by each party with the results seen in Table 13.1.

These data show that mediation is more likely to be successful in low-intensity disputes. Only 15 percent of media-

Table 13.1. Mediation Outcomes and the Intensity of Disputes.

	Fatalities							
	100–500		501–1,000		1,001–10,000		>10,000	
	N	%	N	%	N	%	N	%
No success	5	21.7	11	64.7	40	60.6	33	84.6
Ceasefire	6	26.1	2	11.8	11	16.7	3	5.1
Partial success	6	26.1	3	17.6	11	16.7	2	5.1
Settlement	6	26.1	1	5.9	4	6.1	1	2.6
Total	23	15.9	17	11.7	66	45.5	39	26.9

Note: Eta = 0.41312 $\chi^2(3) = 24.06$ $p < .001$.
χ^2 was calculated lumping all three forms of success.
Entries are the number of mediation attempts of each type.

tion attempts had *any* degree of success in disputes of more than 10,000 fatalities, compared with 78 percent in disputes of 100–500 fatalities. Protracted and intense international disputes are not particularly amenable to mediation or other forms of third-party intervention.

The literature on mediation abounds with notions linking its effectiveness to the nature of the issues in dispute. The key findings, grouped into the five issue subgroups noted earlier, are summarized in Table 13.2. We can see that mediation is more successful in security disputes (60 percent of which show some success) and sovereignty disputes (some success in 52 percent of the cases) than in ideology disputes and independence disputes. The success of mediation in security cases flies in the face of conventional wisdom (Ott, 1972; Randle, 1973).

Using Frei's data (1976), we can see much the same pattern. There is a strong association between successful mediation and security disputes. When, on the other hand, the issues involve honor or ideology, the chances of successful mediation are substantially reduced. The latter point gains added support from a reanalysis of Butterworth's data (Bercovitch, 1985b). Mediation was found to have little success in Cold War disputes (only one out of ten disputes in this category resulted in some

Table 13.2. Issues in Dispute and Mediation Outcomes.

	Sovereignty		Ideology		Security		Independence		Other	
	N	%	N	%	N	%	N	%	N	%
No success	30	47.6	32	69.6	4	40.0	10	83.3	15	71.4
Ceasefire	9	14.3	8	17.4	2	20.0	1	8.3	3	14.3
Partial success	15	23.8	4	8.7	3	30.0	0	0	2	9.5
Settlement	9	14.3	2	4.3	1	10.0	1	8.3	1	4.8
Total	63	41.4	46	30.3	10	6.6	12	7.9	21	13.8

Note: Eta = 0.29334 $\chi^2(4) = 11.28$ $p < .05$.
χ^2 was calculated lumping all three forms of success.
Entries are the number of mediation attempts of each type.

success), but was relatively successful in nonideological disputes (thirteen out of thirty-one disputes).

There can be no doubt that successful mediation is related to the nature of the issues at stake. Ideological disputes, or disputes about values and desirable future contexts, do not lend themselves to a compromise solution, and are thus more difficult to mediate. When values, beliefs, or ideologies are not involved, the parties may come to share the same conceptualization of the situation and mediation may make a significant contribution to the settlement of their dispute. We hope that future research will enable us to specify issues in dispute more accurately and order them in terms of their amenability to mediation.

The Identity and Characteristics of the Mediator. It is possible to argue that the effectiveness of international mediation depends on the mediator's personal characteristics (Young, 1967), or alternatively that personal characteristics are essentially irrelevant (Ott, 1972). Unfortunately there is no systematic evidence on this issue.

International mediation is a voluntary process. This means that mediators cannot function without securing the trust and cooperation of the disputing parties. Elmore Jackson, himself an experienced international mediator, makes this quite clear: "It would be difficult, if not impossible, for a single mediator, who was distrusted by one of the parties, to carry out any useful function" (1952, p. 129). To be accepted by the adversaries, and to secure their positive attitudes and disposition, a mediator must be perceived as independent and credible. The adversaries' motivation to engage in conflict management and their confidence in a mediator will be enhanced if the mediator is seen by both sides as a knowledgeable and skilled participant in the process.

Successful mediation depends not only on the mediator's knowledge and skill about conflict and conflict management, but also on his prestige and authority, originality of ideas, access to resources, and ability to act unobtrusively. Wehr, in a theoretical discussion (1979), lists these required attributes for successful mediation: (1) knowledge about conflict situations;

(2) an ability to understand the positions of the antagonists; (3) active listening; (4) a sense of timing; (5) communication skills; (6) procedural skills (for example, chairing meetings); and (7) crisis management. A mediator is not expected to be a modern version of a Renaissance man, but to be effective he (I use the pronoun advisedly; international mediation is still very much the exclusive domain of males) must possess most of these characteristics.

Another important mediator characteristic is leverage — the capacity to exercise influence. Leverage, derived from the mediator's status or control over valued resources, enhances a mediator's chances of achieving a successful outcome (see Chapter Six). This notion is borne out by Frei's analysis (1976), which shows that mediation efforts by superpowers are more likely to be accepted than mediation efforts by medium or small powers.

Mediator Strategies

The relationship between mediation strategies and case outcomes merits investigation. Mediators may follow several strategies (Bercovitch, 1984a; Carnevale, 1985; Kressel and Pruitt, 1985). Here I propose to use the typology developed by Touval and Zartman (see Chapter Six), which reduces the vast array of mediation strategies to three basic types: communication strategies, formulation strategies, and manipulation strategies.

In our data, mediators were coded as using communication strategies when they acted as go-betweens, clarifying and supplying information. Formulation strategies were defined as identifying issues and suggesting concessions. Manipulation strategies involved promising rewards or threatening sanctions. The relationship between these strategies and mediation outcome was not quite statistically significant but showed interesting trends. As can be seen in Table 13.3, communication strategies were used in 44 percent of all mediation efforts but had any degree of success in only 34 percent of the attempts. The most successful strategy was manipulation, with over 52 percent of the attempts having some success. In short, the more active the

Table 13.3. **Mediation Strategies and Mediation Outcomes.**

	Mediation Strategies					
	Communication		Formulation		Manipulation	
	N	%	N	%	N	%
No success	40	65.6	24	61.5	19	47.5
Ceasefire	10	16.4	7	17.9	5	12.5
Partial success	6	9.8	7	17.9	9	22.5
Settlement	5	8.2	1	2.6	7	17.5
Total	61	43.6	39	27.9	40	28.5

Note: Eta = 0.21514 $\chi^2(2) = 3.35$ $p < .25$.
χ^2 was calculated lumping all three types of success.
Entries are the number of mediation attempts of each type.

mediator's strategy, the more effective he was in moving the disputants toward a settlement. Leverage, resources, power, and influence are at the heart of successful mediation in international relations (see Kochan and Jick, 1978).

Conclusion

In an era when international disputes cannot, indeed must not, continue unabated, mediation is becoming an increasingly important method of international conflict management. Left alone to their own devices, disputing parties may engage in unacceptable or unconstructive behavior. Bringing in a mediator may well change that course of action. Notwithstanding the importance and effectiveness of mediation in international relations, it has only recently begun to attract the serious attention it so richly deserves.

This chapter has been predicated on the assumption that real-life mediation is susceptible to systematic analysis and that the study of mediation should be oriented toward explanation rather than prescription. International mediation should, in my view, be taken out of the realm of idealized prescriptions and normative approaches (see Burton, 1972, 1979) and placed within an empirical context.

With this in mind, this chapter has shown just how widespread the practice of international mediation really is. The results of the study, though not conclusive, indicate that international mediation works best when the disputing parties are small or medium-sized states, experiencing no serious internal threat and having roughly equal power resources. Timing is a crucial factor: successful mediation follows, rather than precedes, the parties' own conflict management efforts. A strong pattern emerged between the nature of the dispute and the effectiveness of mediation: disputes over tangible issues (rather than values and principles) are particularly amenable to mediation. We have also seen that much depends on the strategies employed by the mediator.

The analysis presented in this chapter provides us with a pretheoretical framework that can foster a better understanding and a more thorough investigation of the mediation process. Naturally, much still remains to be done.

References

Aubert, V. "Competition and Dissensus: Two Styles of Conflict and Conflict Resolution." *Journal of Conflict Resolution*, 1963, 7, 26–42.

Bercovitch, J. *Social Conflicts and Third Parties: Strategies of Conflict Resolution*. Boulder, Colo.: Westview, 1984a.

Bercovitch, J. "Problems and Approaches in the Study of Bargaining and Negotiation." *Political Science*, 1984b, 36, 125–144.

Bercovitch, J. "International Mediation: Incidence and Outcomes." Department of Political Science, University of Canterbury, 1985a.

Bercovitch, J. "Third Parties in Conflict Management." *International Journal*, 1985b, 40, 736–752.

Burton, J. W. *Conflict and Communication: The Use of Controlled Communication in International Relations*. London: Macmillan, 1969.

Burton, J. W. "The Resolution of Conflict." *International Studies Quarterly*, 1972, *16*, 5–29.

Burton, J. W. *Deviance, Terrorism and War*. Oxford, England: Martin Robertson, 1979.

Butterworth, R. *Managing Interstate Conflicts, 1945–1974*. Pittsburgh, Pa.: University of Pittsburgh Press, 1976.

Carnevale, P. "Mediation of International Disputes." In S. Oskamp (ed.), *International Conflict and National Public Policy Issues*. Beverly Hills, Calif.: Sage, 1985.

Curle, A. *Making Peace*. London: Tavistock, 1971.

Deutsch, M. *The Resolution of Conflict*. New Haven, Conn.: Yale University Press, 1973.

Druckman, D. (ed.). *Negotiations: Social Psychological Perspectives*. Beverly Hills, Calif.: Sage, 1977.

Druckman, D., and Zechmeister, K. "Conflict of Interest and Value Dissensus." *Human Relations*, 1970, *23*, 431–438.

Edmead, F. *Analysis and Prediction in International Mediation*. New York: UNITAR, 1971.

Fisher, R. "Fractionating Conflict." In R. Fisher (ed.), *International Conflict and the Behavioral Sciences*. New York: Basic Books, 1964.

Frei, D. "Conditions Affecting the Effectiveness of International Mediation." *Peace Science Society Papers*, 1976, *26*, 67–84.

Glenn, E., and others. "A Cognitive Interaction Model to Analyze Culture Conflict in International Relations." *Journal of Conflict Resolution*, 1970, *14*, 35–48.

Hirsch, F. *Social Limits to Growth*. London: Routledge & Kegan Paul, 1977.

Holsti, K. *International Politics: A Framework of Analysis*. (4th ed.) Englewood Cliffs, N.J.: Prentice-Hall, 1983.

Jackson, E. *The Meeting of Minds: A Way to Peace Through Mediation*. New York: McGraw-Hill, 1952.

Kochan, T. A., and Jick, T. "The Public Sector Mediation Process: A Theory and Empirical Examination." *Journal of Conflict Resolution*, 1978, *22*, 209–240.

Kressel, K., and Pruitt, D. G. "Themes in the Mediation of Social Conflict." *Journal of Social Issues*, 1985, *41*, 179–198.

Kriesberg, L. "Timing and the Initiation of De-escalation Moves." *Negotiation Journal*, 1987, *3*, 375–384.

Latour, S., and others. "Some Determinants of Preference for Modes of Conflict Resolution." *Journal of Conflict Resolution*, 1976, *20*, 319–356.

Levine, E. "Mediation in International Politics: A Universe and Some Observations." *Peace Science Society Papers*, 1971, *13*, 23–43.

Mitchell, C. R. *The Structure of International Conflict.* London: Macmillan, 1981.

Modelski, G. "International Settlement of Internal Wars." In J. Rosenau (ed.), *International Aspects of Civil Strife.* Princeton, N.J.: Princeton University Press, 1964.

Northedge, F., and Donelan, M. *International Disputes: The Political Aspects.* London: Europa Publications, 1971.

Ott, M. C. "Mediation as a Method of Conflict Resolution." *International Organization*, 1972, *26*, 595–618.

Pruitt, D. G. *Negotiation Behavior.* Orlando, Fla.: Academic Press, 1981.

Randle, R. *The Origins of Peace.* New York: Free Press, 1973.

Randolph, L. *Third Party Settlement of Disputes in Theory and Practice.* New York: Oceana, 1973.

Rubin, J. Z., and Brown, B. R. *The Social Psychology of Bargaining and Negotiation.* Orlando, Fla.: Academic Press, 1975.

Small, M., and Singer, J. D. *Resort to Arms.* Beverly Hills, Calif.: Sage, 1982.

Stevens, C. M. *Strategy and Collective Bargaining Negotiation.* New York: McGraw-Hill, 1963.

Wehr, P. *Conflict Regulation.* Boulder, Colo.: Westview, 1979.

Young, O. R. *The Intermediaries: Third Parties in International Crises.* Princeton, N.J.: Princeton University Press, 1967.

Zacher, M. *International Conflicts and Collective Security.* New York: Praeger, 1979.

FOURTEEN

What People Want
from Mediation

Dean E. Peachey

He leaned forward, his face reflecting the ambivalence that played in his mind. "But how can I expect my boy to ever believe in justice, if he sees a man get away with something like this?"

Mr. Brilhart's query came toward the end of a mediation session with his neighbor, who had been charged with assaulting Brilhart's ten-year-old son after the boy threw gravel at the man's pickup truck. It had been a volatile session with the two men and their wives, but now the tension in the room had diminished and Brilhart was trying to decide if the other man's explanation and apologies were sufficient, or whether he really wanted to see the neighbor prosecuted. Brilhart seemed largely satisfied with the tentative outcome that had been drafted, but a doubt lingered in his mind: was this really "justice"?

This man's question also lingered with me in the days following the meeting, and it served to redirect my research interests in mediation. What *does* constitute justice when someone has suffered injury or violation, and can mediation provide

300

that justice? It is a question that forms the core of many mediation efforts, and it is a question that has been largely ignored,
both in the mediation literature and in the broader social
sciences.

This inattention is not for lack of rhetoric about justice in
the alternative dispute resolution movement. The rising interest
in mediation in the past decade has often been expressed as part
of the elusive search for justice. Mediation has been presented as
making justice accessible (Cappelletti and Garth, 1978), or
providing a low-cost and expeditious forum for achieving it
(McGillis, 1980; McIsaac, 1981). Some mediation services are
even called neighborhood *justice* centers or community *justice*
centers. But despite the frequently expressed hope for a better
form of justice, the swelling literature on mediation contains
scant examination of what constitutes justice in the eyes of the
disputing parties.

What Do We Mean by "Justice"?

When will an incensed neighbor insist that the man next
door be punished for chasing and tackling his son, and when
will he be prepared to accept an apology for the behavior? What
prompts disputants to sometimes quietly accept compensation
for an inconvenience, and other times to seek public vindica-
tion for their position? The difficulty in answering these questions arises from the fact that "justice" is a highly complex
concept (Reis, 1984). This concept has frequently been represented in the social sciences as possessing two primary components: procedural fairness and distributive fairness (for example, Austin, 1986; Leventhal, 1976).

Procedural justice refers to the individual's perception of
the fairness of the rules or procedures that regulate a process or
give rise to a decision (Austin and Tobiasen, 1984; Deutsch,
1975; Leventhal, 1976). Within the legal system, this approach
produces the common understanding of justice as the right
application of the right rules.

The notion of *distributive justice* can be applied to conflicts
related to resource allocation, ranging from wage disputes to

sharing household income to international fishing treaties. Whenever resources are being allocated, there can be different criteria (in addition to fair procedures) for determining what is a just distribution. These criteria form the basis of the various approaches to distributive justice. There can be a justice of *equality*, where all parties receive an equal share of goods (Sampson, 1975), or justice can be based on some principle of proportionality. One such approach, *equity* theory, defines a fair distribution as one where each person's outcomes are proportional to his or her inputs (Homans, 1961; Walster, Walster, and Berscheid, 1978).

Another proportional approach defines justice as a distribution based primarily on *need*, with little regard for other factors. Although justice according to need often seems to play only a minor role in capitalist societies, several writers (Lerner, 1977; Berg and Clark, 1985) have pointed out that it is, in fact, a common expression of fairness in established social relations, particularly among friends, relatives, and family members.

These concepts of justice as correct procedure or fair distribution of resources find ready application in courtrooms and mediation sessions where the parties are attempting to develop a fair division of family assets, allocate municipal water supplies from a river basin, or determine a wage scale and benefit package. But they did not help me deal with Mr. Brilhart's question. To address his concern required looking at an added dimension of fairness that might be termed "restorative" justice. I use the term in an attempt to develop a nomenclature for describing a variety of approaches to "make right the wrong," ranging from retribution to forgiveness. This term is problematic if it is understood as providing a superficial patchup or returning to a status quo that was never just in the first place. Nevertheless, I have used the term *restorative justice* throughout this chapter because it captures better than any other term available to me the full range and purposes of seeking justice in the aftermath of injury. When people are injured and relationships are broken, the pieces of their lives cannot readily be put back together, at least not without cracks and scars. We may never "make right again," but hopefully, we can "make right" in the sense of doing the best we can to achieve justice in difficult and painful situations.

Restorative justice, then, is concerned with righting wrongs—restoring a situation or relationship as best one can following damage, injury, or other wrongdoing. Whereas distributive justice hinges on people's concern with getting resources or positive benefits they and others are entitled to, restorative justice deals with the negative side of the ledger, seeking redress for injury and suffering. In effect, distributive justice is directed at preventing injury or injustice, *while restorative justice comes into play after a transgression has been committed*. It is a response not just to a conflict of interest, but to a grievance or claim against a particular entity (Felstiner, Abel, and Sarat, 1980 –81).

The psychological experience of having a resource damaged or stolen is quite distinct from a conflict over possession of the resource. A dispute among siblings over how to divide a houseful of heirlooms and antiques following a parent's death changes dramatically when several of the parties learn that the most valued and beloved items have already been transported to one sibling's home halfway across the country. Before this revelation, the discussions may have centered on equity inputs such as birth order, who has helped to refinish the antiques, who bore the burden of caring for mother during her protracted illness, and so forth. Or they may have focused on developing a procedural scheme that would be viewed as fair to everyone, such as taking turns choosing items, with a lottery to determine who got the first turn. But now the concern is much more likely to be how to exact retribution or get back at the offending sibling.

Mediators frequently encounter such reactions when one party has acted unilaterally outside of established rules or norms. People often come to mediation (or the courts) looking for retribution. In addition, the desire to "get back" can play a significant role in the further development or escalation of the conflict (Pruitt and Rubin, 1986). In the above example we see, in addition to the more concrete loss of the antiques, the element of symbolic or psychological violation that often exists.

Some of the siblings now define themselves as victims at the hands of an unscrupulous other. The basic trust among family members—which could have formed the basis for productive bargaining—has been shattered, with repercussions for many other issues and future interactions (Pruitt, 1981).

What Is Restorative Justice?

If distributive and procedural fairness considerations are not adequate in such a scenario, what does constitute justice when a wrong has been committed? Austin (1986) refers to Aristotle's corrective or "rectificatory" justice, but limits his discussion to remedying unjust distributions and rules, and does not deal with redress for injury. Hogan and Emler (1981) argue for the importance of retribution in everyday situations, but their approach casts justice in a narrow and somewhat negative light. They present a retribution theory that "defines justice as provided by that situation [social circumstances] wherein everyone suffers alike" (p. 134).

In addition to retribution, however, there are other significant approaches to remedying wrongs: restitution, compensation, and forgiveness (Peachey, 1986). Hence, I am using the broader term *restoration* rather than *retribution*. The various approaches to restoration share a common goal: restoring justice to a situation where an injustice has already occurred. However, they represent quite different processes:

1. *Retribution.* The injured party requires that the person responsible for creating the injustice suffer in a way that is commensurate with the way the victim has suffered. Retribution can be either limited ("an eye for an eye") or unlimited ("death for an insult"). The crucial element is that justice has been served when the perpetrator has been punished. Retribution need not be administered by the actual victim. Indeed, retribution is very often carried out by a powerful third party, such as a parent, teacher, or the state.

2. *Restitution.* Another way to "make things right" is to replace or renew whatever has been damaged. The smashed fender is taken to the body shop and repaired, with the offend-

ing driver paying the bill. The damaged fence is rebuilt, or the injured person receives payment for lost wages resulting from a fight. Whereas retribution is frequently executed by the third party, restitution is more likely to directly involve the second party (the victim or recipient of the injustice). The victim receives some material good or service to repair or replace that which was damaged, while with retribution the satisfaction realized by the victim is primarily psychological or emotional.

3. *Compensation.* Like restitution, compensation focuses on the needs of the victim. However, it may not always be possible to restore that which was lost or damaged. Grandma's broken china cannot be replaced, nor can a severed arm or a dead relative. In such a situation it is still possible, nevertheless, for the perpetrator to attempt to address directly the needs of the victim through some form of compensation, such as money, material aid, or performing a service for the victim. For example, people frequently claim financial compensation for "pain and suffering." Compensation is also frequently administered by third parties such as insurance companies or criminal injuries compensation programs.

4. *Forgiveness.* A fourth way to restore justice is through forgiveness. Although rarely discussed in the social sciences literature, this approach nevertheless is important, particularly in established relationships. Justice is restored when the debt is cancelled, usually following an admission of wrongdoing or demonstration of remorse. However, forgiveness can also be a unilateral act that is not contingent on any particular response by the culprit.

Retribution, restitution, compensation, and forgiveness are distinct ways to restore justice, but they are not mutually exclusive. For example, someone who has been injured in a car accident may desire restitution for lost wages as well as a retributive sanction in the hope that it would deter the offending driver from future drinking and driving.

Can Mediation Provide Restorative Justice?

My purpose in this chapter is to describe the forms of restorative justice in their basic terms and identify areas where restorative justice may pose problems for mediators. A central question is the extent to which these various forms of restorative justice can be achieved through mediation. This issue is focused most sharply when an individual is pursuing the conflict in hopes of achieving retribution. Retribution entails pain of one type or another, and suffering is rarely undertaken voluntarily. Thus, because mediated settlements are agreed to by the participants rather than imposed upon them, such agreements rarely include provisions for retributive sanctions.

This is the crux of a fundamental confusion in the mediation literature on the relationship between process and outcome. Mediation is described by many as a value-free process through which the parties can arrive at whatever outcome they wish (Shonholtz, 1984; Moore, 1986). Yet this obviously is not the case. The prerequisite of mutual agreement for a mediated settlement clearly biases this forum away from certain types of outcomes. In most cases, the requirement of mutual "satisfaction" effectively precludes any agreement where one party will suffer significant physical or financial punishment or social stigma.

Thus the movement to take cases out of the courts goes beyond the usually stated goals of giving participants greater control over their disputes and fostering win/win rather than win/lose outcomes. Inherent in this movement is a shift away from a common conception of justice, namely retribution. Whether one welcomes this shift or not, it is essential to recognize it and to realize its implications.

The inherent connection between the mediation process and potential outcomes is a critical factor in two problems that have consistently proved most difficult for community mediation or neighborhood justice centers: receiving adequate referrals from the "gatekeepers," and convincing disputants to engage in mediation when a referral is made. Consider first the experience of disputants deciding whether to try mediation. Unless there are strong external incentives, only in 20 to 40 percent of the cases referred to mediation do both parties agree to mediate (Cook, Roehl, and Sheppard, 1980; Garofalo and Connelly, 1980). This phemonemon is often explained in terms of conflict avoidance, and the general reluctance of people to face somebody with whom they are in conflict. No doubt this is an important factor. But the fact remains that in many situations, mediation simply cannot deliver the kind of outcome desired by one of the parties. Disputants sometimes desire revenge or they want their position to be vindicated by a third party (preferably someone in authority). It does not take long for these individuals to realize that mediation cannot deliver the kind of justice they desire.

A similar process operates with lawyers, judges, city officials, and others who refer disputes to mediation. Numerous mediation projects have languished in the uncomfortable position of not receiving the referrals they want, or receiving those they did not want (Cook, Roehl, and Sheppard, 1980; Roehl and Cook, 1985; Wahrhaftig, 1982). Despite clearly worded referral criteria, this condition continues.

My strong hunch is that the principal factor influencing referral agents is not whether the case fits the *process* of mediation, but whether mediation offers an *outcome* that is congruent with that person's sense of justice in the case at hand. For example, a prosecutor may refer a case to mediation not because the case fits certain referral criteria, but because the prosecutor does not think anyone should be punished in this situation and he or she intuitively knows that mediation outcomes are nonpunitive. Thus mediation programs get the "garbage" or trivial cases.

On the other hand, cases that clearly fit the mediation criteria are not referred to the program. Again, I suspect that this is because the person in a position to make the referral has an understanding of justice in this matter that would call for retribution. Thus "more serious" cases are often not referred, not because it is seen as impossible for the people involved to sit and talk, but because a mediated outcome simply would not meet the referral agent's requirements for "justice."

There are three approaches that mediators can use in situations where either the disputants or other interested parties are seeking retribution. The first is to accurately identify variables that give rise to a strong orientation toward retribution.

The mediator can then appropriately refer selected cases to the courts or other forums that can rule on the legitimacy of the retributive claim. A second approach is to work with the disputants to persuade them to accept compensation or restitution as justice in full. A third alternative is to engage in public education aimed at fostering a broader understanding of restorative justice, and reducing society's reliance upon retribution.

A mediator's choice among these options will be aided if we can identify the variables that influence a disputant's orientation toward retribution rather than other approaches. I will therefore present hypotheses on several such variables, and describe initial data relevant to them.

What Determines Whether Retributive Justice Is Sought?

Relationship Between Disputing Parties. Lerner's formulation of justice motive theory posits interpersonal relationships as the key to determining distributive justice (1977; Lerner and Whitehead, 1980). In the area of restorative justice, such relationships are also likely to be important, but their effect is potentially very complex. For example, one could predict that intimate relationships would give rise to a perception of justice based on forgiveness or reconciliation. But close relationships can also yield some of the most intense and violent conflicts (Nettler, 1982; President's Commission on Crime, 1966). Thus, transgressions in close relationships may be most likely to involve a demand for retribution.

However, at the same time love or other forms of emotional attachments can also create dramatic ambivalences. As the severity of the violation is heightened by the intensity of the relationship, the interpersonal costs of redefining or dissolving the relationship are also enhanced. In addition, genuine concern for the perpetrator may lead the victim to forgive the transgression or to try in some way to reform the offending behavior.

In casual relationships or interactions among strangers, the preferred form of justice can also vary. Strangers may be strongly oriented toward retribution because of reduced personal inhibition and interpersonal consequences, or alternatively, the lack of emotional conflict may yield less desire for retribution than would similar events between associates and intimates.

As I first reflected on these variables, I wanted to gather data to inductively refine some hypotheses. At the time, I was engaged in an evaluation of a program offering services to victims of crime (Brown and Peachey, 1984). The evaluation included in-depth personal interviews with an extensive sample of crime victims, and the interview readily lent itself to adding questions that explored restorative justice issues.

The data reported here are drawn from 140 interviews conducted in the victims' home or other location of their choosing. The interviews generally occurred two to six weeks after the victimization. The offenses represented in the sample were drawn from three general categories: break and enter into residential premises (20 percent), domestic and neighborhood assault or harassment (54 percent), and assorted serious offenses involving weapons, serious bodily injury, and so on (26 percent).

One of the questions was an open-ended item that asked victims what they thought would be the fairest thing to happen in this situation. Their responses could readily be coded into the categories of retribution (29 percent) and compensation/restitution (21 percent). Victims did not volunteer forgiveness at this point, but there were a large number of responses aimed at rehabilitating the offender (41 percent). (The relation of forgiveness to rehabilitation will be discussed below.) An additional group of responses could best be classified as a concern for the safety and protection of the victim or society at large (9 percent).

As expected, the victims' views on what would be fairest were significantly affected by the relationship between victim and offender, $\chi^2(12, N = 139) = 38.99$, $p < .0001$. A contingency table analysis is, of course, limited in that it can only indicate whether the overall pattern of results is significant; one cannot reliably claim that a particular cell or group of cells is responsible for the effect. Thus, I will simply describe these results as an aid to further reflection on the hypotheses.

For those in intimate relationships, such as spouses and

lovers ($n = 75$), 51 percent were primarily oriented toward rehabilitation. However, the next highest category was punishment (24 percent), reflecting something of the swing between the extremes of retribution and forgiveness that was discussed above. The remainder of this group were divided between concerns for compensation or restitution (13 percent) and protection (9 percent). When the relationship was that of a relative (other than spouse) or friend ($n = 18$), the majority (66 percent) were oriented toward rehabilitation, with the remaining responses distributed fairly evenly among the other options (punishment, 11 percent; compensation, 17 percent; protection, 6 percent). When the relationship was casual, such as neighborhood or commercial contacts ($n = 17$), the largest number of responses favored punishment (59 percent). Again, the remaining responses were uniformly distributed. When the offender was a stranger or of unknown identity ($n = 29$), 48 percent of the victims were oriented toward compensation, while 34 percent favored a punitive response.

The results of the survey confirm the difficulty in predicting simple relations in this area. In the most intense interpersonal relationships (spouses and lovers), the most frequent desire was for rehabilitation, but these relationships also produced a considerable proportion of punishment responses. Relatives, however, opted more heavily for rehabilitation, while casual relationships produced primarily punishment choices. In fact, this was the only category in which a majority of the respondents favored punishment.

Thus a casual relationship, which is the basis for many complaints that mediation programs attempt to service, appears to be more likely to invoke a desire for punishment than either no relationship or a very intense relationship. The casual relationship perhaps allows the victim to focus on a real person, to have some sense of having been personally targeted as the victim. Such a victimization strikes close to home, and in addition to the actual crime, the event violates the expectations we have for how neighbors, acquaintances, or business associates will treat us. But this type of relationship does not hold the emotional closeness to evoke the ambivalence about punishment versus rehabilitation that might typically be present in a spousal or love relationship.

Reason for Behavior. An additional variable that will likely affect justice orientations is the psychological meaning that one party imputes to the other's behavior. More specifically, what will be seen as the cause or motive for the other's behavior? A critical perception here is the intentionality of the behavior. Did the person intend the injury or was it caused by accident or negligence? If the injury or damage was intended, was it an act of deliberate malice toward me, or did I just happen to be the victim of the offense? A desire for retribution would likely be stronger when the offense is personalized, that is, when victims perceive the offenders as trying to harm them in particular.

Another critical perception is the likelihood of the behavior being repeated. Did the other's behavior originate from an enduring trait, or was it caused by external conditions or temporary internal states? The preponderance of attributional evidence would suggest that victims (as observers of another's actions) will routinely make internal, dispositional attributions and will tend to see a particular action as part of a more general pattern of behavior (Jones and Nisbett, 1972; Nisbett and Ross, 1980). In turn, we might expect the desire for retribution to predominate when it appears that the behavior is likely to recur. This may be linked to a belief in the deterrent value of punishment, but there are additional factors involved. If the offender is seen as "just plain bad," and indicates no remorse for his or her action, then punishment can also serve to reassert moral and social values (Vidmar and Miller, 1980).

When the offending behavior is attributed to external factors in the environment, or to a momentary weakness on the part of an otherwise upstanding citizen, repayment or compensation will be preferred. These forms meet the victim's losses, and because the offender is not likely to continue to engage in such behavior, there is little need for deterrence or reasserting society's values.

Moreover, if the offender is remorseful, the victim may come to believe that such incidents are not likely to be repeated and conclude that justice can best be restored through forgiveness (or restitution or compensation). On the other hand, the absence of such remorse can intensify demands for punishment. To have one's perceived rights violated can produce anger; but to have the culprit refuse to acknowledge them is nothing less than infuriating.

Thus, we can derive several hypotheses:

- People who attribute the behavior to stable, internal causes will prefer retribution over other forms of justice.
- People who attribute the offending behavior to external or temporary internal causes will prefer restitution or compensation.
- When the offending behavior is attributed to external or temporary internal causes, and the offender demonstrates remorse, forgiveness is more likely to be exercised.

These hypotheses assume that the victim is able to come up with a reasonable attribution, or otherwise make sense of the experience. But what happens when this is not the case? When an event cannot be understood, it is more difficult to "make it right," or take steps to prevent a recurrence. In the absence of such options, the only possibility that the victim may see for restoring justice is to be retributive; "at least then the perpetrator will suffer as I have suffered."

Lerner's justice motive theory also offers some insight into this process. He suggests that an individual who is viewed as "not my kind of person" will be seen as deserving different outcomes from someone who is like me. In this case, an action that is totally inexplicable or is performed without any apparent rationale could only be done by someone who deviates from my standards of socially and morally acceptable behavior. Therefore the person may merit harsher treatment. This leads to a further hypothesis:

- Victims will be more likely to favor retribution when they cannot understand why the event happened, or if they cannot understand why the perpetrator acted as he or she did.

A number of victims in the survey (44 percent) were unable to offer an explanation or possible reason for the offender's behavior. Of those who could, the perceived cause of the offending behavior was strongly related to views of fairness, $\chi^2(9, N = 78) = 23.66$, $p < .005$. Victims did not opt for punishment when they attributed the action to emotional upset or environmental stress. On the other hand, the highest number of punitive responses (58 percent) came when the victims saw the offending behavior as being specifically targeted at them, whether out of revenge or some other interpersonal motive. In such cases, a victim may interpret the act as a sort of symbolic challenge: the offender has won the first round and the victim now wants to even the score (or reverse it) to restore face or control future interactions.

In considering these results, we must keep in mind the clear confounds that exist in survey data. Type of damage is not independent of the victim's relationship to the offender. Assaults are most likely to happen between people who know each other, while a large proportion of property offenses involve strangers or unknown parties. How well the victim knows the offender (if at all) will also affect the amount and type of information that is available to the victim in making attributions about the cause of the behavior.

In a follow-up laboratory investigation (Peachey, 1986), I examined the interaction between the victim-offender relationship and perceived cause. Subjects were presented with videotaped and written descriptions of a burglary where the offender and the victim lived in the same apartment building. The offender was portrayed as either a stranger, a casual acquaintance of the victim, or a casual acquaintance for whom the victim expressed some positive regard. The availability of an external attribution for the offender's behavior was also manipulated. In some conditions, subjects received information implying that the offender would need the money to buy cocaine; in other conditions, no information was given for the behavior on the premise that subjects would make an internal attribution (Jones and Nisbett, 1972; Nisbett and Ross, 1980). Note that the type of external attribution that was available (needing money to buy cocaine) was one that would not readily be seen as excusing or justifying the behavior.

The results clearly revealed an interaction between the victim-offender relationship and the availability of an external attribution. Subjects were oriented toward retribution with the strangers when an external attribution was available for the behavior, but for the acquaintance, the orientation toward retribution came when an external attribution was not readily available to the subjects and they drew an internal attribution. This pattern was even stronger in the positive-acquaintance condition. Thus, people may be vindictive toward a drug-using stranger, but with an acquaintance they are more likely to favor retribution when no external explanation is available for the behavior.

Nature of Offense. An obvious variable to consider is the type of harm that has been suffered. As I am discussing it here, injustice refers to damage or injury that is seen to be unwarranted or illegitimate to oneself or one's resources. Physical injury and property damage are obvious categories, and are frequently the focus of criminal proceedings. But the current definition also allows for other types of damages. For example, Vidmar (1981) describes violations of one's perceived "rights" or a failure to honor contractual or implied obligations as events that also give rise to a sense of injustice.

The survey respondents' views of what would be the fairest outcome were strongly related to the nature of the offense, $\chi^2(9, N = 140) = 24.58$, $p < .005$. Compensation was the most popular option with victims of property offenses, with 40 percent preferring this over retribution (28 percent) or rehabilitation (23 percent). (In the follow-up experiment [Peachey, 1986], where the reported crime involved the theft of money, subjects universally rated repayment as the fairest option, regardless of other factors.) Material goods are likely much easier to quantify or appraise of a monetary value. A simple and oft-cited formula for justice is "an eye for an eye." While this prescription is often used in relation to retribution, the principle of an exchange in kind likely has implications for other forms of justice as well. Thus a "dollar for a dollar" may be just as apt in a compensatory fashion. Coupled with the greater ease of translating material goods into economic terms, this could also account for the finding.

Rehabilitation. An unpredicted finding in the victim survey was the frequent mention of rehabilitating the offender when victims were asked what would be the fairest thing to happen. These comments generally took the form of suggesting counseling, treatment for alcohol abuse, or other forms of supervision or guidance. Although they were not predicted, such findings are not without precedent. Cohn and Rabinowitz (1980) found that victims generally did not favor imprisonment over rehabilitation. Similarly, in a study of victim-offender reconciliation programs (Coates, 1985), victims were asked to rank-order their reasons for having participated in the program. These victims rated "help the offender" second only to "recover restitution for loss."

Is rehabilitation a form of restorative justice, or is it a consideration apart from justice? Is rehabilitation another way of expressing the approach previously defined as forgiveness — a cancellation of a debt, usually following an admission of wrongdoing or demonstration of remorse? Indeed, rehabilitation resembles a form of forgiveness. In this case the forgiveness or subsequent reconciliation is *contingent on change by the offender.* It may be a way of saying that the victim wants reconciliation with the offender, but that such forgiveness is impossible so long as the offender persists in the present state. Thus, acceptance of the offender is conditional upon the person proving or producing indications that he or she will not repeat the offending behavior.

The studies I report here offer important findings for determining which cases are most amenable to the nonpunitive outcomes typical of mediation. They indicate that repayment and compensation are in fact widely accepted as "justice in full" when the primary complaint involves loss or damage of replaceable material goods. They also reveal that the casual relationship, which is the focus of many neighborhood dispute centers, is precisely the type of relationship where people may be most vindictive if one or both parties perceives that an injustice has already occurred. The effect of the casual rela-

tionship is magnified if the offending behavior is attributed to
the internal character of the culprit, or no apparent purpose or
motivation is known.

How Can Mediators Change Disputant Orientations?

Having identified these variables, it is worth considering
the conditions under which a person may shift from one orientation to another. For example, to what extent can a mediator
encourage someone oriented toward retribution to accept compensation instead? The improved communication between disputants that mediators often attempt to foster can have such an
effect. The significance of the mediator's ability to help the
parties understand the reasons for each other's behavior cannot
be overemphasized. Even a poor excuse (such as wanting to buy
drugs) can be better than no reason at all. To the extent that such
dialogue provides a plausible external attribution for the other's
behavior, we might expect to see a decreasing concern for
retribution. In addition, people are often prepared to dismiss
their claim for repayment or retribution if it appears that the
other party will acknowledge responsibility for the wrongdoing
and take steps to ensure that it will not happen again.

My comments here imply that it is ethically acceptable for
a mediator to encourage disputants to seek and accept a certain
range of outcomes (especially settlements other than retribution). Some might argue, however, that to do so is outside the
bounds of acceptable mediator behavior because the mediator
is departing from the role of manager of the process and is
beginning to shape the outcome to which the parties will agree.
I would reply that there can never be a dichotomy between ends
and means. By my choice to enter a conflict situation as a
mediator (rather than other roles such as advocate, judge, or
vigilante) I am necessarily presenting a bias for a certain range
of outcomes.

Regardless of one's position on this issue, the mediator's
recognition of and sensitivity to justice concerns is of paramount importance. In the course of intake or of assessing
whether a dispute is appropriate for mediation, the mediator

may well need to discuss with the parties whether mediation can satisfy their sense of justice. When a mediation is in process, mediators need to continually listen for indications of concerns about justice. Mediation sessions often hinge on symbolic issues, where the parties become committed to certain matters of principle. To mediators, or other observers, the parties often appear to be posturing or attempting to save face. In contrast, the disputants are likely to view their own behavior as critical efforts to bring justice to the situation. Similarly, disputants can appear to be stuck on events that sometimes seem like ancient history. A mediator or other third-party observer may be frustrated by disputes that are entrenched in past grievances. But such a situation does not necessarily imply pettiness on the part of the disputants. Instead, mediators must maintain an awareness of the significance of justice when people have been wronged and explore with them ways that their sense of justice can be fulfilled.

This discussion assumes that the disputants have agreed to enter mediation. However, a major challenge mediators face is getting the disputants to agree to meet for mediation. The solution to this problem is not likely to be easy. Those who advocate a greater role for mediation in our society must be fully cognizant of the challenge that lies before them. If the public is ever to embrace mediation, it is not sufficient to educate people on the *process* of mediation. It is also necessary to foster a climate where the types of justice that result from mediation become generally desired. The need for public education and attitude change is not only about mediation, but also about justice. Until people are willing to acknowledge and examine their basic attitudes on justice, they are not likely to significantly alter their conflict resolution behavior.

Summary

From the anecdotal experience of disputants who raised questions about justice in mediation, I developed the concept of restorative justice that includes retribution, restitution, compensation, and forgiveness. Restorative justice is significant for mediators whenever they are dealing with situations where damage has already been done and one or more parties see themselves as victims of an injustice.

Because mediated settlements must be mutually agreeable to the disputants, mediation does not lend itself to situations where someone desires retribution. The incompatibility between mediation and retribution may be a major reason why mediation services are underutilized by disputants and court personnel or others in a position to refer cases to mediation. To deal with this problem we need to understand the variables that give rise to an orientation toward restorative justice in a given situation.

An initial survey suggests that justice orientations of people who have been victimized are shaped by their relationship to the offending party, the perceived reason for the behavior, and the nature of the offense. In the survey, repayment and compensation were preferred over retribution in situations involving property damage. Retribution is a more frequent response in casual relationships or when the offending behavior is attributed to the character of the other party.

There are three possible ways mediators can deal with disputants who seek retribution. One is to recognize the inappropriateness of mediation to their purpose and to refer them to court. A second is to shift their orientation away from retribution by helping them understand the reasons for each other's behavior. A third, which may be necessary if mediation is to achieve widespread acceptance as a process for restoring justice, is to establish the legitimacy of alternatives to retribution.

References

Austin, W. G. "Justice in Intergroup Conflict." In S. Worchel and W. G. Austin, *Psychology of Intergroup Relations*. Chicago: Nelson-Hall, 1986.

Austin, W. G., and Tobiasen, J. M. "Legal Justice and the Psychology of Conflict Resolution." In R. Folger (ed.), *The Sense of Injustice: Social Psychological Perspectives*. New York: Plenum, 1984.

Berg, J. H., and Clark, M. S. "Differences in Social Exchange Between Intimate and Other Relationships: Gradually Evolving or Quickly Apparent?" In W. Ickes (ed.), *Compatible and Incompatible Relationships.* New York: Springer-Verlag, 1985.

Brown, S. D., and Peachey, D. *Evaluation of the Victim Services Program in the Region of Waterloo, Ontario.* Ottawa: Solicitor General of Canada, 1984.

Cappelletti, M., and Garth, B. "Access to Justice: The Newest Wave in the Worldwide Movement to Make Rights Effective." *Buffalo Law Review,* 1978, *27,* 181–291.

Coates, R. B. *Victim Meets Offender: An Evaluation of Victim-Offender Reconciliation Programs.* Michigan City, Ind.: PACT Institute of Justice, 1985.

Cohn, E. S., and Rabinowitz, V. C. "Restitution: The Egalitarian Sentence." Paper presented at the Annual Meeting of the International Political Psychology Society, Boston, June 1980.

Cook, R. F., Roehl, J. A., and Sheppard, D. *Neighborhood Justice Centers Field Test: Final Evaluation Report.* Washington, D.C.: Government Printing Office, 1980.

Deutsch, M. "Equity, Equality, and Need: What Determines Which Value Will Be Used as the Basis of Distributive Justice?" *Journal of Social Issues,* 1975, *31,* 137–150.

Felstiner, W. L. F., Abel, R. L., and Sarat, A. "The Emergence and Transformation of Disputes: Naming, Blaming, Claiming. . ." *Law & Society Review,* 1980–81, *15,* 631–654.

Garofalo, J., and Connelly, K. J. "Dispute Resolution Centers Part I: Major Features and Processes." *Criminal Justice Abstracts,* 1980, *12,* 416–439.

Hogan, R., and Emler, N. P. "Retributive Justice." In M. J. Lerner and S. C. Lerner (eds.), *The Justice Motive in Social Behavior: Adapting to Times of Scarcity and Change.* New York: Plenum, 1981.

Homans, G. C. *Social Behavior: Its Elementary Forms.* San Diego: Calif.: Harcourt Brace Jovanovich, 1961.

Jones, E. E., and Nisbett, R. E. "The Actor and the Observer: Divergent Perceptions of the Causes of Behavior." In E. E. Jones and others (eds.), *Attribution: Perceiving the Causes of Behavior.* Morristown, N.J.: General Learning Press, 1972.

Lerner, M. J. "The Justice Motive in Social Behavior: Some Hypotheses as to its Origins and Forms." *Journal of Personality*, 1977, *45*, 1–52.

Lerner, M. J., and Whitehead, L. A. "Procedural Justice Viewed in the Context of Justice Motive Theory." In G. Mikula (ed.), *Justice and Social Interaction*. New York: Springer-Verlag, 1980.

Leventhal, G. S. "Fairness in Social Relationships." In J. W. Thibaut and others (eds.), *Contemporary Topics in Social Psychology*. Morristown, N.J.: General Learning Press, 1976.

McGillis, D. "The Quiet (R)evolution in American Dispute Settlement." *Harvard Law School Bulletin*, 1980, 20–25.

McIsaac, H. "Mandatory Conclusion of Custody/Visitation Matters: California's Bold Stroke." *Conciliation Courts Review*, 1981, *19*, 73–81.

Moore, C. W. *The Mediation Process: Practical Strategies for Resolving Conflict*. San Francisco: Jossey-Bass, 1986.

Nettler, G. *Criminal Careers*. Vol. 2: *Killing One Another*. Cincinnati: Anderson Publishing, 1982.

Nisbett, R. E., and Ross, L. *Human Inference: Strategies and Shortcomings of Social Judgement*. Englewood Cliffs, N.J.: Prentice-Hall, 1980.

Peachey, D. E. "Restorative Justice in Criminal Conflict: Victims' and Observers' Perspectives." Unpublished doctoral dissertation, Department of Psychology, University of Waterloo, 1986.

President's Commission on Crime in the District of Columbia. *Report of the President's Commission on Crime in the District of Columbia*. Washington, D.C.: U.S. Government Printing Office, 1966.

Pruitt, D. G. *Negotiation Behavior*. Orlando, Fla.: Academic Press, 1981.

Pruitt, D. G., and Rubin, J. Z. *Social Conflict: Escalation, Stalemate, and Settlement*. New York: Random House, 1986.

Reis, H. T. "The Multidimensionality of Justice." In R. Folger, *The Sense of Injustice: Social Psychological Perspectives*. New York: Plenum, 1984.

Roehl, J. A., and Cook, R. F. "Issues in Mediation: Rhetoric and Reality Revisited." *Journal of Social Issues*, 1985, *41*, 161–178.

Sampson, E. E. "On Justice as Equality." *Journal of Social Issues,* 1975, *31,* 45–64.

Shonholtz, R. "Neighborhood Justice Systems: Work, Structure, and Guiding Principles." *Mediation Quarterly,* 1984, *5,* 3–30.

Vidmar, N. "Justice Motives and Other Psychological Factors in the Development and Resolution of Disputes." In M. J. Lerner and S. C. Lerner (eds.), *The Justice Motive in Social Behavior: Adapting to Times of Scarcity and Change.* New York: Plenum, 1981.

Vidmar, N., and Miller, D. T. "Social Psychological Processes Underlying Attitudes Toward Legal Punishment." *Law & Society Review,* 1980, *14,* 565–602.

Wahrhaftig, P. "An Overview of Community-Oriented Citizen Dispute Resolution Programs in the United States." In R. Abel (ed.), *The Politics of Informal Justice: The American Experience.* Vol. 1. Orlando, Fla.: Academic Press, 1982.

Walster, E., Walster, G. W., and Berscheid, E. *Equity: Theory and Research.* Boston: Allyn & Bacon, 1978.

FIFTEEN

Communicative Competence
in Mediators

William A. Donohue

While I was serving as a visiting professor of speech communication at the University of Georgia in 1983, one of my colleagues,
Deborah Weider-Hatfield, told me about a conference being
held there dealing with peacemaking and dispute resolution.
Since my research up to that time had focused on the communication strategies negotiators use to facilitate agreement making, I decided to attend. From the opening plenary session I
continued to hear about mediation and its creative applications
in managing disputes involving divorce, the environment,
schools, community problems, and criminal courts.

More impressive than the scope of mediation's use was the
nearly evangelical fervor that mediators expressed in describing
the potential of this process. Nearly all the conference partici-

Note: Thanks to Jessica Pearson for her assistance in acquiring the tapes for
this analysis, and Deborah Weider-Hatfield for preparing the transcripts.
This research was supported by a grant from the Michigan State University
Foundation.

pants chided the legal system for its inflexibility in dealing with disputes that simply do not belong in the courts. Mediation offered a way for disputants to bypass this formality and work through their own problems with the assistance of a neutral third party. Some of the most enthusiastic supporters were those interested in divorce problems. They argued, quite cogently, that the traditional legal system perpetuates parental fighting, which in turn tends to victimize the children.

Impressed by their enthusiasm, I decided to focus my attention on divorce mediation, for three reasons. First, I recognized an opportunity to get involved in an important social problem and possibly offer some assistance to divorce mediators trying to help distressed couples and their children. Second, mediators depend very heavily on communication to facilitate agreements between couples. Unfortunately, the quantity of research directed toward this topic appeared very limited and in need of expansion if mediators were to be helped in their efforts. Third, divorce mediation is among the most intense and emotional of dispute contexts. Its intensity places great stress on the communication process. As a result, the capabilities and limitations of this process are quickly revealed and available for study.

I began to search the communication literature for a theoretical perspective that was both skills oriented and conceptually sound. I selected communication competence (see Bostrom, 1984) because it allowed me to ask the question: Which mediator communication strategies and tactics, in response to which disputant negotiation strategies and tactics, would create a collaborative dispute resolution context?

To test the viability of the model we had begun to develop, my colleagues and I searched for tape recordings of actual divorce mediation sessions. We learned that Jessica Pearson had collected eighty audio tapes in her three-state study of divorce mediation programs (Pearson and Thoennes, 1984), and she graciously agreed to send us these tapes for our research. We transcribed twenty of the most audible tapes—ten in which agreement was reached and ten in which couples deadlocked. We reasoned that establishing two agreement conditions would allow us to compare mediator and disputant communication patterns along some meaningful dimension. To date, we have conducted seven separate analyses of these tapes, the three most critical of which are reported in this chapter.

Mediator Communicative Competence

Understanding the role of communication in mediation remains a longstanding interest for professional mediators. For example, Haynes (1981) focuses on communication strategies mediators can use to remove barriers to progress: setting goals, articulating hidden agendas, and managing floor time. Kolb (1983) suggests that communication can be facilitated by clarifying positions, serving as a conduit for information, or raising questions to promote interaction. Similarly, Folberg and Taylor (1984) and Moore (1986) emphasize the need to facilitate communication through a variety of tactics intended to provide insight to the couple about their dispute.

While such suggestions are useful, they provide few insights about how people *actually* communicate during mediation. Unfortunately, few studies focus on communication in mediation. Recent empirical works by Slaikeu, Culler, Pearson, and Thoennes (1985) found that mediators who expose relevant issues, manage floor time equally, and identify solution options are more favorably evaluated by disputing parties. Apparently, such mediator communication strategies help parties understand their own feelings and those of others. Still, mediators need more systematic observations about how communication processes structure the flow of information during the dispute. Can mediators control these processes to facilitate agreements? The studies described in this chapter work toward creating a systematic understanding of communication in divorce mediation so mediators can feel more in control of their actions.

The model of communicative competence in divorce mediation begins with the assumption that the divorce mediator must *actively intervene* in the dispute to direct couples toward positions and issues that can help them work equitably together (Bernard, Folger, Weingarten, and Zumeta, 1984; Folger and

Bernard, 1985). Active intervention is necessary for two reasons. First, divorce produces tremendous stress on parents and children (see Wallerstein and Kelly, 1980), and that stress confounds rational discussion of issues. Second, most disputants approach mediation as a distributive activity, looking to dominate the other person to accomplish specific goals. Allowing such domination severely hinders the equitable exchange of information. Mediators must assume an interventionist role to reduce emotional intensity and to teach disputants integrative dispute resolution tactics (Haynes, 1981).

To effectively implement this interventionist role, the mediator must establish control and foster a climate of trust and mutuality. The research reported here assumes that some mediators are better at these tasks than others. Timing is vital. Timing refers to the mediator's ability to discriminate between disputants' constructive and destructive communication patterns. The failure to either interrupt destructive conflict cycles or to reinforce productive patterns deprives disputants of the guidance they need to develop trust and mutuality.

The competent mediator must also learn not only when to intervene, but how. Mediators must be able to determine what interventions will work most effectively to facilitate communication. Without access to a full range of intervention strategies and tactics, they run the risk of losing control of the interaction. Disputants will sense they are not being helped and they will turn once again to the destructive communication patterns that originally brought them to mediation. However, there is as yet little empirical evidence on the kinds of interventions that seem to work most effectively in reducing conflict and moving couples closer to agreement. This chapter presents findings addressed to both the timing of mediator interventions and their quality.

Methodological Overview

The Research Strategy. Our basic approach was to closely study mediations that had resulted in a settlement and those that deadlocked. Our goal was to identify patterns of mediator communication that regularly distinguished the two. Clearly, we cannot claim that any such observed differences are the "cause" of settlement or nonsettlement. It could well be, for example, that the couples' behaviors or characteristics "caused" the mediators' behaviors. More likely, there is some reciprocal and interactive pattern of causality. To argue that certain mediator communication patterns *caused* the disputants to settle or not settle would require independent manipulations of mediator communication in addition to controlling for several potentially intervening variables such as conflict intensity. Divorce mediation programs are reluctant to allow researchers such high levels of experimental control when the futures of families are at stake. Moreover, at this early stage, researchers are poorly equipped to say which mediator communication patterns are promising candidates for study, even if ethical and practical obstacles to such research could be overcome.

If causal claims cannot be forwarded, of what value is the research? Clearly, the lack of descriptive work in this area mandates that we look for communication patterns that may discriminate between outcome conditions. Building this descriptive base lays the foundation for developing a theory of mediator communicative competence and the potential effects of certain communication behaviors.

Research Methods: Transcript Features. Tape recordings of twenty predivorce and postdivorce custody and visitation disputes (ten in which agreement was reached and ten in which couples deadlocked) were transcribed following the rules for transcription presented by Schenkein (1978). The audio tapes were part of the approximately eighty collected by the Divorce Mediation Research Project (1981–1984), funded by the Children's Bureau of the U.S. Department of Health and Human Services and administered by Jessica Pearson, director of the research unit of the Association of Family and Conciliation Courts, Denver. The twenty sessions came from various branches of the Los Angeles County Family Mediation and Conciliation Court. They were conducted by nine mediators, eight men and one woman. When these tapes were gathered, all had at least three years of mediation experience.

Research Methods: Reliability Information. Reliability estimates for each of the coding schemes presented in this chapter were computed using Guetzkow's (1950) procedure. The procedure calls for two individuals to code independently the same number of utterances (we settled on about 300) and determine the percentage of agreement between the coders.

Results

Study One: Frequency of Mediator Intervention
and Its Relationship to Conflict Intensity

Timing is a central and complex issue in the practitioner literature, but the subject has not been systematically studied. Should the mediator establish a policy of interrupting when the couple gets caught up in a very heated, emotional exchange? Should the mediator wait until they calm down? Or does it really make any difference when the mediator interrupts? As a preliminary foray we studied timing in terms of the simple frequency with which the mediator interrupts the parties and the relationship of these interruptions to the level of conflict characterizing the disputants' exchanges. These results are reported in this first study.

One of the rare discussions of timing in mediation appears in Rubin (1981), who argues that early intervention may prevent the parties from experiencing sufficient tension to motivate them to work on their problem. He contends that disputants need to have achieved a state of readiness that can be hindered by premature intervention. On the other hand, waiting too long to intervene may intensify the conflict to the point that the opinions are polarized and positions are frozen in intransigence. Rubin argues (p. 38) that the mediator must decide precisely where to intervene along the "slippery slope of an escalating conflict."

Coding Procedure. My colleagues and I identified and numbered each speaking turn in each of the twenty transcripts. Speaking turn became the unit of analysis in the study. Coders were then trained to judge whether each nonmediator utterance was an attacking, bolstering, or integrative disputant strategy. Based on the Donohue, Diez and Hamilton coding scheme (1984), *attacking* was any utterance that made a personal accusation of the other disputant's character, proposed a negative evaluation of the other's past behavior, or made a negative evaluation of the other's proposal, position, or personal views. *Bolstering* was coded as any utterance that presented a proposal, provided information or opinion not related to the other person, requested information or clarification, or provided a rationale for the speaker's position. Finally, an *integrative* move was any utterance that agreed with the prior utterance, demonstrated qualified support for the proposal, or provided unqualified support for the position or proposal on the floor at that time. The following values were given to each of these codes: attacks = 3, bolsters = 2, and integrations = 1. Reliability for the coding scheme was computed using Guetzkow's (1950) formula. The reliability estimate for the attack-defend-integrate scheme was .98.

   Results. To answer the question of intervention frequency, the average number of talking turns within a disputant sequence was calculated. A sequence was defined as an exchange by disputants of two or more talking turns between mediator utterances. The results indicated that 37 percent of the disputants' turns in the agreement group and 39 percent of the disputants' turns in the deadlock group were sequential in nature. A comparison was also made between the means of the number of turns within a sequence between the agreement (4.70) and deadlock (4.87) mediation conditions. No significant difference was observed between these conditions.

   However, while the overall mean turn levels were about the same for each group, the standard deviations were quite different (agreement Sd = .96; deadlock Sd = 2.72), indicating that the mediators in the deadlock condition were more extreme in allowing couples very extensive or very limited freedom in exchanging information. To assess these differences more systematically, a mean turn exchange rate was calculated for each of the twenty transcripts. Using these means the transcripts in each of the two conditions were ordered from high to low mean turn exchange rate and divided into four equal groups and assigned codes. The five deadlock-low transcripts were all coded as 1, the five agreement-low group received a 2, the agreement-high group received a 3, and the deadlock-high group received a 4. The respective means of these groups were 3.51, 4.05, 5.36, and 6.24. A correlation was then computed between the mean of each transcript and its group code ($r = .74$, 19 df, $p < .05$). This finding confirmed our sense that the deadlock mediators allowed disputants either extensive or very restricted freedom to exchange information, while the agreement mediators adhered to more moderate intervention timing in allowing couples to communicate among themselves.

This result supports Rubin's (1981) argument that agreement mediators are more moderate in their intervention frequencies. They allow couples to talk with each other long enough to exchange information, yet they do not let them continue on to the point of polarizing their positions. These patterns suggest that the agreement mediators are more sensitive to some of the qualitative features of the interaction.

To answer the question of the mediator's response to conflict intensity, it was necessary to calculate the mean change from one turn to the next in a sequence. Only sequences of two, three, and four turns were used in the analysis because there was not a sufficient number of longer sequences to warrant extending the analysis to five or more turns. For example, a husband-wife sequence of four turns might have been coded as bolster/attack/integrate/attack. Assigning the numbers indicated above to these codes would yield the value 2, 3, 1, 3. The average relative change for this sequence is $-.33$ ($2 - 3 = -1$, $3 - 1 = 2$, $1 - 3 = -2$; $-1 + 2 - 2 = -1$; $-1 \div 3$ turns $= -.33$). A positive number indicates a general net integrative or cooperativeness for the exchange, while a negative change score indicates a more attacking or competitive interchange. Thus, as conflict intensity increases, the scores become more negative.

The average relative change in the agreement condition was $-.03$, compared to $-.05$ in the deadlock condition. These values are not statistically different. The result indicates that the total amount of change in conflict intensity between mediator

Table 15.1. Mean Changes in Disputant Conflict Intensity
Prior to Mediator Interventions.

Number of Turns	Mean Turn Changes			N
Agreement Condition	2	3	4	
2	−.14 (.59)			153
3	.04 (.53)	−.09 (.55)		81
4	.02 (.68)	.14 (.66)	−.10 (.67)	49
Deadlock Condition	1–2	2–3	3–4	
2	.02 (.68)			99
3	−.17 (.70)	.04 (.71)		48
4	−.27 (.81)	.05 (.66)	.03 (.72)	21

Note: Standard deviations in parentheses.

interventions is the same for both conditions. However, of greater interest is whether agreement and deadlock mediators differ in the kinds of sequences that trigger their interventions. In other words, are mediators choosing to intervene after more integrative, neutral, or attacking sequences? Table 15.1 provides the mean levels of relative change in conflict intensity for both conditions.

The scores on the diagonal indicate the average change in conflict intensity that triggered the mediators' interventions. The scores on the off diagonal indicate the level of conflict intensity during the interchanges when the mediator chose not to intervene. For example, when the agreement mediators chose to intervene after two turns (one husband-wife exchange), the average level of conflict intensity was − .14. When the agreement mediators intervened after three turns (two exchanges), the two-turn level of conflict intensity was .04. When they intervened after the third turn, the level of conflict intensity was − .09. The average change at the trigger point is − .11 for the agreement mediators, and .03 for the deadlock mediators. The difference between these two means is statistically significant [$t = 8.58$, $df = 4$ (6 trigger points), $p < .05$], and the trigger-point change score for the agreement mediators is also statistically significant from zero (t = − 3.14, $df = 282$, $p < .05$). These differences are particularly impressive given the attenuated nature of the intensity scale. If the range of values for conflict intensity had been calculated on a scale ranging from, for example, 1 to 7, these observed differences would have been even more significant.

These results indicate that agreement mediators choose to intervene more frequently during periods of increased conflict intensity, and less frequently during periods of decreased conflict intensity. On the other hand, the deadlock mediators intervene randomly since their trigger-point values are nearly zero. However, they are clearly choosing not to intervene when conflict intensity increases, as evidenced by the highly negative relative mean change from turns one to two in the sequences of length 3 and 4. The deadlock mediators may be experiencing some difficulty implementing any consistent intervention plan that decreases conflict intensity. They intervene either too frequently or too infrequently, and their interventions do not appear to be timed to move the interaction in a more productive direction.

Study Two: Issue Types in Mediation

To determine why the deadlock mediators had significantly more difficulty controlling the interaction, we decided to explore the substantive features of disputant-mediator interaction. Perhaps the deadlock mediators were forced to contend with significantly more complex and difficult issues than the agreement mediators.

One attempt to classify the substantive features of issues is found in Wehr's (1979) conflict map. This map consists of a set of conflict features intended to help users analyze their interpersonal conflict. In this map, Wehr identifies four types of issues: (1) fact based: disagreement about the truth or falsity of some perception or judgment, or the existence or nonexistence of some phenomena or event; (2) value based: disagreement about prescriptions related to policies, relationships, or some other source of conflict; (3) interest based: disagreements over wants and the distribution of resources, such as power, privilege, or rewards; (4) nonsubstantive disagreements originating else-where, including interaction style, quality of communication, relationship issues, or aspects of the immediate physical setting, such as discomfort.

The Wehr categories appear capable of capturing the substantive essence of mediation interaction; most custody and visitation disputes center on such problems as desired visitation arrangements (interests), the suitability of the other parent (values), the extent to which the parent has complied with past arrangements (facts), and deep-seated emotional issues about prior relational problems, feelings about the other, or past failures that have little or nothing to do with the substantive nature of the dispute (nonsubstantive).

For mediators, managing disputant issues is a timing problem and a performance problem. The timing difficulty relates to interpreting how disputants are communicating about the issues. Are they exposing issues in some sequence that facilitates their resolution, or are they following up on each other's issues to develop a coherent discussion of their dispute? The performance part of the problem is to decide what issues to direct couples to discuss. Recently, McIsaac (1986) and Staffeld (1987) found that mediations dominated by nonrealistic, relationally oriented issues are most difficult to settle. They suggest exploring emotional issues in the context of the substantive issues as a means of helping families focus more rationally on their specific bargaining task. Thus, we might suspect that mediations dominated by nonsubstantive or emotional and relational issues might prove more difficult to settle.

Coding Procedures. The unit of analysis used in this study was the uninterrupted talking turn. To begin the coding the authors identified and numbered each utterance in each of the twenty transcripts. Each utterance was coded using the same four issue categories — fact based, value based, interest based, or nonsubstantive — plus a fifth category — "other" — used when no issue was apparent in an utterance. For example, when a speaker simply agreed with the prior utterance, asked the other to repeat a statement, or used some other conversational organizing device, the coders were instructed to code it as "other."

Coders were instructed to follow a specific set of procedures in applying these issue codes. First, they were trained to code both the mediator's and the disputants' utterances. For the mediator, the coders were instructed to identify the type of issue the mediator directed the disputants to discuss. For example, the mediator might interrupt and comment on a relational issue that disputants brought up and attempt to refocus their attention on some interests associated with that relational issue. In that case, the mediator's comment would be coded as an interest-directed issue. If the mediator did not direct the conversation toward a particular type of issue, then the utterance was coded as "other."

Second, the coders were instructed to select the dominant issue code in each utterance. The dominant code, based on the issue hierarchy described above, was the one that reflected those issues most difficult to manage by mediators. As we have seen, emotional and relational issues represent the most difficult challenges for mediators since these issues often access problems that caused the dissolution of the marriage. The next most difficult issues were individual values that access disputants' perceptions of right and wrong, and therefore access individual core beliefs and values about the world. Interest issues were considered third most dominant or difficult for mediators to manage, since articulated positions can be negotiated when they are not based on deep-seated emotional or relational problems or value concerns. Finally, factual issues were judged least difficult to manage by the mediators since most of the factual issues, such as how much money each parent makes, can be easily resolved by examining the case record. While coders were instructed to use this procedure of dominance when multiple issues were discussed, the problem arose very infrequently, probably because most comments in mediation are relatively brief. Only when the mediator specifically asks for complex information does a disputant begin to bring up complex, interrelated issues.

Using Guetzkow's reliability formula, the categorizing reliability for this coding procedure using two coders over five

Table 15.2. Chi-Square Analyses of Issue Type Frequencies.

		Fact Issue	Interest Issue	Value Issue	Relational Issue
Agree[a]	Husband	549 (.37)*	526 (.36)	21 (.01)	388 (.26)
	Wife	574 (.38)	539 (.36)	50 (.03)	355 (.23)
	Mediator	398 (.32)	778 (.62)	5 (.003)	80 (.06)
No Agreement[b]	Husband	372 (.36)	177 (.17)	39 (.04)	433 (.42)
	Wife	294 (.34)	171 (.20)	21 (.02)	388 (.44)
	Mediator	297 (.43)	291 (.43)	24 (.04)	72 (.10)

* Row percentages in parentheses.
[a] $\chi^2 = 342.6$, 6 df, $p < .05$
[b] $\chi^2 = 290.5$, 6 df, $p < .05$

categories was .91. This reliability estimate was considered sufficiently high to proceed with data analysis.

Results. The twenty transcripts revealed 2,486 issue comments by the husband, 2,377 by the wife, and 1,927 issue directives by the mediator. Approximately 3,800 utterances were coded in the "other" category since no issues were disclosed.

Table 15.2 provides the frequency distributions for issue statements by husbands, wives, and mediators in both the agreement group and the no-agreement group. Regarding husbands and wives, the table indicates that in the agreement condition, facts and interests are discussed most, with relational issues third and value issues last. In the no-agreement condition, relational issues dominate, with factual issues second, interest issues third, and value issues again last.

The data pertaining to mediators reveal other interesting patterns. In the agreement condition the mediators focus twice as much on interests as on facts, with very little discussion of values or relational issues. In the no-agreement condition, the mediator splits evenly between fact and interest directives, with little time spent on values or relational issues. Reading any of the deadlock transcripts reveals that couples often use factual disputes to disguise relational disputes. For example, couples often fought about trivial logistical issues such as what time the husband returned the child last week after visitation: several exchanges might be used to determine whether it was 6:00 or 6:30. The no-agreement mediators often chose to get involved in these disputes at the factual level without digging deeper into the relational problems underlying them.

These issue data suggest that the one important factor inhibiting the deadlock mediators from controlling their interaction relates to the issues couples were willing to discuss. The dominance of relational issues, combined with the mediator's unwillingness to intervene after these attacks, suggests that the mediations simply spun out of control. Neither the agreement nor the deadlock mediators chose to help process these relational issues, probably because of the lack of time afforded them by the court's constraints. This problem suggests that couples entering mediation in such distressed states may need some other therapy before beginning the negotiation process.

Study Three: Phase Use in Mediation

In the third study we examined a more complex aspect of the timing problem: the point at which the mediator moves from orientation and gathering data to identifying areas of difference and generating proposals. Nearly every professional guide to mediation advocates using phases as a means of moving disputants through some kind of controlled decision-making process. As a result, in this third study, we set out to learn the relationship between agreement condition and systematic phase use, and to identify cycles of conflict associated with given phases (Donohue, Allen, and Burrell, 1986). This task seemed particularly appropriate since little empirical validation of phase structures was apparent in the literature.

To begin this study we reviewed the seven major works in divorce mediation that make explicit attempts to prescribe mediation phases (Kessler, 1978; Black and Joffee, 1978; Haynes,

1981, Bienenfeld, 1983; Saposnek, 1983; Moore, 1986). While these authors expressed some key differences about prescribing phases, a general consensus emerged on a model of four phases: (1) orientation, or providing disputants with an understanding of mediation rules and procedures and the role of the mediator; (2) gathering background information as a means of developing the information foundation of the dispute; (3) identifying key issues, including those issues that can serve as roadblocks to cooperative interaction; and (4) developing proposals including creating options, gaining accommodations, or providing some educational debriefing about the implications of disputant agreements.

While these authors remain reasonably consistent in their phase prescriptions, some subtle differences appeared in the timing they advocate. Perhaps the most distinct timing differences emerged in the second phase. While Black and Joffee advocate using the second phase primarily as a means of gathering background information about the dispute, Kessler and Haynes advocate identifying issues during this period. The ostensible purpose of pursuing issues sooner than later is to move as quickly as possible to expose the elements that might undermine building a cooperative negotiation context.

A second timing difference relates to when it is appropriate to disclose positions, goals, or general proposals for settlement. Haynes (1981) and Folberg and Taylor (1984) advocate using either the first or second phase of mediation to identify goals of a settlement. Their logic for discussing goals sooner is that it exposes hidden agenda that can undermine cooperative interaction later in the mediation.

Coding Procedures. The unit of analysis used in this study was the uninterrupted talking turn. To begin the coding my colleagues and I identified and numbered each mediator intervention in each of the twenty transcripts. Each speaking turn attempted by the mediator was defined as an intervention. Coders were instructed to determine whether the intervention topic related to orienting disputants to mediation, gathering background information, identifying the disputed issues or problems, or developing the proposals to resolve the current dispute. If multiple topics were identified, coders were instructed to identify the first topic used. Multiple coding was rarely a problem since nearly all interventions were very terse.

Using these procedures, the twenty transcripts revealed 2,779 mediator interventions: 339 related to orientation about the process of mediation, 597 related to the background or history of the dispute, 763 related to issue processing, and 1,080 related to proposal development. A total of 1,647 interventions were observed in the agreement sessions and 1,132 in the deadlock sessions.

The intercoder reliabilities for each of the four main strategies using Guetzkow's (1950) procedure were .81, .83, .84, and .83, respectively. These reliabilities provide some confidence that the categories were being accurately applied to the data.

Results. A chi-square analysis was used to test the extent to which the mediations proceeded through a set of phases. To conduct this analysis the total interventions in each transcript were divided into thirds. This procedure does not have any relation to real time since any number of disputant utterances could be observed between each intervention. Dividing the transcripts into thirds appeared preferable to other means of determining phases simply because there were no conceptual guideposts to use in making divisions. None of the mediators announced when they were proceeding into a new phase, and since some of each intervention types were used throughout the mediations, no specific numerical divisions could be selected to indicate phase transitions.

Table 15.3 provides the chi-square analyses associated with each mediation phase across both agreement conditions. A nonsignificant chi-square analysis indicated that mediators allocate their orientation interventions fairly equally throughout the interaction. However, the first section ("Interventions Involving Background or History Topics") reveals significant differences concerning directives aimed at developing background information about the disputes. Specifically, this section indicates that mediators in both conditions allocated most of their

Table 15.3. Mediator Interventions.

	Period 1	Period 2	Period 3	Totals
Interventions Involving Background or History Topics[a]				
Agreement	230 (73%)*	57 (18%)	30 (9%)	317 (53%)**
Deadlock	196 (70%)	69 (25%)	15 (5%)	280 (47%)
Totals	426 (71%)	126 (21%)	45 (8%)	597
Interventions Involving Issues or Problems[b]				
Agreement	168 (42%)*	131 (33%)	103 (25%)	402 (53%)**
Deadlock	102 (28%)	161 (45%)	98 (27%)	361 (47%)
Totals	270 (36%)	292 (38%)	201 (26%)	763
Interventions Involving Proposals to Resolve the Dispute[c]				
Agreement	210 (28%)*	305 (41%)	238 (31%)	753 (70%)**
Deadlock	59 (18%)	108 (33%)	160 (49%)	327 (30%)
Totals	269 (25%)	413 (38%)	398 (37%)	1,080

[a] $\chi = 6.54$, 2 df, $p < .05$
[b] $\chi^2 = 17.48$, 2 df, $p < .01$
[c] $\chi^2 = 29.93$, 2 df, $p < .001$
* Row percentages in parentheses.
** Column percentages.

attempts to gather background information about the dispute toward the beginning of the interaction.

However, the second and third sections of Table 15.3 demonstrate that agreement and deadlock mediators differed significantly in their allocation of issue-processing and proposal-making interventions across periods. With respect to issue processing, the second section ("Interventions Involving Issues or

Problems") indicates that the agreement mediators concentrated on identifying key issues much earlier in the dispute than the deadlock mediators. This result contradicted our expectations. We expected that the agreement mediators would wait till later portions of the mediation to expose and process issues, based on the logic that such exposure must be founded on a thorough development of background information. Our other analyses revealed that the agreement mediators are pursuing both courses at the same time. Perhaps the mediators are using the discussion about background information to stimulate discussion of critical issues.

The results in the third section of Table 15.3 ("Interventions Involving Proposals to Resolve the Dispute") indicate that the agreement mediators are soliciting and processing proposals toward the beginning and middle periods of the mediation while the deadlock mediators are waiting for later periods in the interaction. Again, this observation remains inconsistent with our expectations. We expected that mediators would experience difficulty in subsequent phases by exposing proposals early in the interaction, based on Fisher and Ury's view (1981) that establishing specific positions early in a dispute makes it difficult to offer concessions later without losing face.

Regarding the models of mediation proposed by the professional mediation texts cited above, the issue-exposure and proposal-development patterns associated with agreement mediators tended to support the timing priorities advocated by Haynes (1981) and Folberg and Taylor (1984). Exposing issues earlier, rather than later, and identifying goals and proposals earlier, rather than later, were more associated with agreement mediators in this study. This pattern suggests that the agreement mediators sought a more flexible course in dealing with disputants. That is, they seem to go with disputants' needs as they arise instead of walking disputants through a rigid set of prescribed phases.

Discussion

Collectively, the results of these three studies provide some useful insights about both mediator and disputant interaction patterns. Regarding mediators, we identified some important differences in intervention timing. Our conceptualization of timing focused on an ability to discriminate between productive and unproductive patterns of disputant communication. Study 1 revealed that the two groups of mediators differed significantly in their timing patterns. Specifically, the agreement mediators appeared very responsive to conflict intensity by choosing to intervene after significant increases in intensity levels. The deadlock mediators, on the other hand, seemed less responsive to conflict intensity by choosing not to intervene after either escalations or de-escalations in intensity. Study 2 revealed that the deadlock mediators more frequently directed couples to discuss their factually related disputes than agreement mediators. Since couples may use factual disputes to disguise more fundamental, complex concerns, the deadlock mediators may have, in effect, encouraged couples to use mediation to play out their time-worn conflict cycles. The preponderance of relational issues in the deadlock sessions would certainly support this interpretation.

These two studies suggest that the deadlocked couples may have simply overpowered their mediators and, in the process, severely attenuated the mediators' ability to interpret disputants' behavior. In a study not reported here we found further support for this observation. By coding interruption patterns we found that husbands interrupted wives more frequently in the deadlock interactions; in the agreement interactions, interruptions were less frequent and equally distributed. In addition, the husbands and the mediators interrupted one another much more frequently in the deadlock interaction. Thus, deadlock mediators may have found themselves in a control struggle with the disputants, which in turn could have escalated their own emotional involvement in the dispute. Such involvement can distract mediators from formulating refined interpretations of disputant communication patterns, particularly when mediators work under the time pressures imposed by the court. If the mediators had had more time to work through some of the relational issues, they might have gained more control over the interaction and exerted more influence on the disputants.

Mediators also demonstrated different intervention strategy decisions, as Study 3 indicated. Perhaps in response to their loss of control, the deadlock mediators appeared to force disputants through phases of mediation they were ill prepared to adopt. The deadlocked couples wanted to talk about their relational problems while the mediators wanted them to talk about other topics. The agreement mediators seemed more sensitive to disputant needs, while not allowing disputants to escalate conflict intensity and to discuss topics that recycle old disputes.

In addition to learning about mediators, our research reveals a great deal about the interaction of distressed marital couples. Prior research by Gottman (1979) indicates that distressed couples are more likely to reciprocate negative affect, they are less skilled in negotiation, and they are more likely to be dominated by husbands. Other researchers have found that distressed couples react more intensely to negative behavior (Fitzpatrick, 1987), tend to dwell on each other's personality defects, form rigid attributions about the other's motives, and use more personal accusations.

Our research supports these patterns. In a more comprehensive analysis of disputants' attacking behaviors in another study, we found that the deadlock couples are twice as likely to attack each other as the agreement couples. Specifically, 24 percent of the deadlocked partners' interchanges are verbal attacks, versus only 12 percent of the agreement couples'. Also, our deadlock husbands seek to dominate both their wives and the mediators, and the couples' focus on relational problems prevents them from making progress in negotiating key interest issues. Clearly, mediators who allow couples to exhibit these patterns will have greater difficulty encouraging any kind of cooperative dispute resolution.

My colleagues and I began this research program with the intention of gaining a better understanding of mediation communication patterns, and through this understanding, developing concepts that make sense to practitioners. The overall thrust of our findings is that increased mediator communicative competence means developing a sophisticated sense of control. Struggling with disputants to control the interaction, forcing them to discuss topics they are not ready to discuss, or getting lost in the disputants' prior conflicts seem dysfunctional in promoting long-term agreements. I hope further research reveals other insights capable of refining ways in which mediators can manage control of this very difficult process.

References

Bernard, S., Folger, J., Weingarten, H., and Zumeta, Z. "The Neutral Mediator: Value Dilemmas in Divorce Mediation." *Mediation Quarterly*, 1984. *4*, 61–74.

Bienenfeld, F. *Child Custody Mediation.* Los Angeles: Science and Behavior Books, 1983.

Black, M., and Joffee, W. "A Lawyer/Therapist Team Approach to Divorce." *Conciliation Courts Review*, 1978, *16*, 1–5.

Bostrom, R. *Competence in Communication.* Beverly Hills, Calif.: Sage, 1984.

Donohue, W., Allen, M., and Burrell, N. "A Lag Sequential Analysis of Mediator Intervention Strategies." Paper presented to the Speech Communication Association, Chicago, 1986.

Donohue, W., Diez, M., and Hamilton, M. "Coding Naturalistic Negotiation Interaction." *Human Communication Research*, 1984, *10*, 403–425.

Fisher, R. J., and Ury, W. *Getting to Yes.* New York: Penguin Books, 1981.

Fitzpatrick, M. "Marital Interaction." In. C. Berger and S. Chaffee (eds.), *The Handbook of Communication Science*, Beverly Hills, Calif.: Sage, 1987.

Folberg, J., and Taylor, A. *Mediation: A Comprehensive Guide to Resolving Conflicts Without Litigation.* San Francisco: Jossey-Bass, 1984.

Folger, J., and Bernard, S. "Divorce Mediation: When Mediators Challenge the Divorcing Parties." *Mediation Quarterly*, 1985, *10*, 5–24.

Gottman, J. *Marital Interaction.* Orlando, Fla.: Academic Press, 1979.

Guetzkow, H. "Unitizing and Categorizing Problems in Coding Qualitative Data." *Journal of Clinical Psychology*, 1950, *6*, 47–58.

Haynes, J. M., *Divorce Mediation: A Practical Guide for Therapists and Counselors.* New York: Springer-Verlag, 1981.

Kessler, S. "Counselor as Mediator." *Personnel and Guidance Journal*, 1978, *58*, 94–106.

Kolb, D. M., "Strategy and the Tactics of Mediation." *Human Relations*, 1983, *36*, 247–268.

McIsaac, H. "Toward a Classification of Child Custody Disputes: An Application of Family Systems Theory." *Mediation Quarterly*, 1986, *14–15*, 39–50.

Moore, C. W., *The Mediation Process: Practical Strategies for Resolving Conflict.* San Francisco: Jossey-Bass, 1986.

Pearson, J., and Thoennes, N. "A Preliminary Portrait of Client Reactions to Three Court Mediation Programs." *Mediation Quarterly*, 1984, *3*, 21–40.

Rubin, J. Z. (ed.). *Dynamics of Third Party Intervention: Kissinger in the Middle East.* New York: Praeger, 1981.

Saposnek, D. "Strategies in Child Custody Mediation: A Family Systems Approach." *Mediation Quarterly*, 1983, *2*, 29–54.

Schenkein, J. *Studies in the Organization of Conversational Interaction.* Orlando, Fla.: Academic Press, 1978.

Slaikeu, K., Culler, R., Pearson, J., and Thoennes, N. "Process and Outcome in Divorce Mediation." *Mediation Quarterly*, 1985, *10*, 55–74.

Staffeld, W. "Mediation vs. Conciliation: A Model for Michigan's Circuit Courts." Unpublished manuscript, 1987.

Wallerstein, J., and Kelly, J. B. *Surviving the Breakup: How Children and Parents Cope with Divorce.* New York: Basic Books, 1980.

Wehr, P. *Conflict Regulation.* Boulder, Colo.: Westview, 1979.

SIXTEEN

Experimental Research on the Strategic-Choice Model of Mediation

Peter J. D. Carnevale
Donald E. Conlon
Kathy A. Hanisch
Karen L. Harris

The strategic-choice model of mediation predicts the strategies that mediators select in different circumstances and the way the negotiating parties react to different forms of mediation. First proposed by Carnevale (1986), this model is general enough to apply in a wide variety of mediation contexts. In this chapter, we describe the results of a series of laboratory experiments that test and extend the model, and discuss their implications for the study and practice of mediation.

Note: We are grateful to Dean G. Pruitt and Kenneth Kressel for their very helpful comments, and to numerous others for their advice and assistance at all stages of this research program. The research reported here was supported by a University of Illinois Research Board grant to Peter Carnevale.

The strategic-choice model was inspired by firsthand observations of professional labor mediators, case analyses of international and organizational mediation, and by two models of negotiation: the dual-concern and perceived-feasibility models developed by Pruitt (1981) and Pruitt and Rubin (1986).

Four Basic Mediator Strategies

Our reading of the mediation literature suggests that there are four basic mediation strategies. The four strategies can be viewed as manifestations of different forms of social power (Raven and Kruglanski, 1970). In most cases, the strategies are designed to produce agreement; the difference between them is the manner in which agreement is sought. The four strategies, defined and illustrated with examples, are:

1. *Integrate*, a form of informational power, involves efforts to find a solution that satisfies both parties' limits or major aspirations. This is what Ralph Bunche did in the Syria-Israel negotiations of 1949. As the U.N. acting mediator in the Middle East, Bunche proposed that Syrian troops withdraw and that certain areas along the border be demilitarized—a proposal that eventually led to an armistice agreement (Touval, 1982).

2. *Press*, a form of coercive power, involves efforts to reduce one or both parties' limits or aspirations. This is what a labor mediator did when he told a teachers' association that its position was unreasonable, and threatened to convey this opinion to the news media unless a softer position was adopted (Carnevale and Pegnetter, 1985); this mediator also scheduled negotiations to begin late in the evening, believing that concessions would more likely come at four in the morning than at four in the afternoon.

3. *Compensate*, a form of reward power, involves mediator provision of rewards or positive benefits in exchange for agreement or compromise. Follett (1940) observed this when two groups of workers fought over access to a loading dock; the dispute was resolved when the company agreed to enlarge the dock so that both groups could be accommodated at the same

Figure 16.1. The Strategic Choice Model.

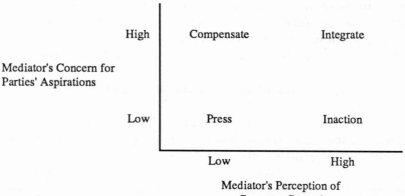

time. This was also seen in 1954 when Italy and Yugoslavia quarreled over territory at the northern end of the Adriatic Sea. One concern of Yugoslavia was giving up the port city of Trieste; in its mediation effort, the United States promised economic aid in developing a new port city for Yugoslavia (Campbell, 1976).

4. *Inaction,* involves letting the disputants handle the controversy by themselves. This is what a labor mediator did when she excused herself from a joint negotiation session involving a city council and police officers' association, and stayed away for an hour, because she wanted them to try and work things out on their own.

The Strategic-Choice Model

The choice of pressing, compensating, integrating, or inaction in mediation is a strategic problem that can be cast within the framework of strategic analysis (Schelling, 1965). The choice of one particular strategy is determined by the mediator's assessment of its costs and benefits, its perceived feasibility, and the mediator's incentives. The strategic-choice model (see Figure 16.1) proposes that a mediator's choice of strategy is determined by the relative strength of two factors:

1. The value that mediators place on the disputants' achieving their aspirations. Mediators value these aspirations when they want to see the disputants achieve a satisfactory outcome from the dispute. This may result from a mediator's genuine concern for the disputants' welfare and general happiness, or from a more strategic concern such as when the mediator is dependent on the disputants. This type of mediator incentive can affect the costs that the mediator is willing to incur in mediation (Carnevale, 1986).

2. The mediator's assessment of the probability that a mutually acceptable solution will be found, or "perceived common ground" (Pruitt and Rubin, 1986). Perceived common ground implies that the parties have low aspirations, or that they are being cooperative with one another.

Predictions for Mediator Behavior

Mediators will *integrate* when it is important to them that the parties achieve their aspirations and it appears that there is common ground. In this case an integrating strategy is worth the time and effort, and it is feasible because there is a good chance of finding a mutually acceptable solution. Also in this case, pressing, compensating, and inaction can be ruled out. Compensating is not necessary since it appears that there is a good chance of finding an integrative agreement; pressing is not feasible since it reduces the parties' aspirations; inaction is not feasible because the parties might not discover an integrative outcome on their own.

Mediators will *press* when it is unimportant to them that the parties achieve their aspirations and when it appears that there is little common ground. In this case, pressing is feasible because the mediator is not afraid to alienate parties he does not care about. Also in this case, integrating, compensating, and inaction can be ruled out. Integrating is not feasible because of the low probability of finding an integrative agreement; compensating is not worth the costs because of the low concern for the parties' aspirations; inaction can be ruled out because of doubt that the parties will agree on their own since they are so far apart.

Mediators will *compensate* when it is important to them that the parties achieve their aspirations and it appears that there is little common ground. In this case, compensating is worth the costs. And integrating, pressing, and inaction can be ruled out. Pressing and inaction are ruled out because the mediator values the parties' aspirations and these strategies are not likely to satisfy those aspirations; integrating is ruled out because of the low probability of a mutually acceptable agreement.

Mediators will be *inactive* when it is unimportant to them that the parties achieve their aspirations and when it appears that there is much common ground. In this case, inaction is feasible: there is a good chance that the parties will reach agreement on their own. And in this case, integrating, compensating, and pressing can be ruled out. Compensating and pressing are not necessary since it appears that there is a good chance that agreement will be reached, and compensating and integrating are ruled out because the parties' aspirations are unimportant to the mediator and thus these strategies are not worth the cost and effort.

In this chapter, we report the results of four laboratory experiments that were designd to test one or another aspect of the strategic-choice model, and to extend it.

Experiments and Major Findings

Experiment 1: Test of the Model

The first study in the series was designed to directly test the predictions of the strategic choice model for mediator behavior. Mediator concern for the parties' aspirations and the mediator's perception of common ground varied from low to high. The effect on efforts at mediator compensation, integration, pressing, and inaction were evaluated (see Carnevale and Henry, 1989). The subjects for this study were fifty-eight male undergraduate psychology students who participated in part to fulfill a course requirement. The laboratory procedure used in this study was essentially the same for all our studies, so it will be described in some detail.

Procedure. IBM personal computers presented the instructions, the task, and a questionnaire to each subject, and also stored the data. The instructions stated that each subject would interact with two other subjects, via the computer, in a simulated organizational dispute. They were told that one person would be the "product manager" and that the product manager's task was to settle a dispute between the two other subjects, the "Boston manager" and "New York manager." The computers were actually not connected. All the subjects were told that the computer had randomly assigned them to the product manager position; the Boston and New York positions were computer programs.

The scenario was based on veridical case materials of a dispute in a large securities firm. The subjects were told that a dispute had arisen between the New York manager and the Boston manager over three issues: how large an account should be before transferring it from Boston to New York; how long employees had to work in Boston before they would become eligible for promotion to New York; the criteria that would be used in making promotions.

The three issues were displayed on the computer screen, as in integrative bargaining studies (Pruitt, 1981). For each issue there were nine proposal levels, designated "A" through "I" (see Table 16.1). The subjects were told that to reach an agreement, the managers would need to agree on one proposal level, or letter, for each issue. Points were displayed next to each proposal level, representing the value of each proposal level to each manager. The subjects (mediators) were told that while they, as product managers, would be able to see these point values, the two branch managers would not know each other's point values. The pattern of point values on the three issues was such that tradeoffs were possible; the high-priority issue for one manager was the low-priority issue for the other, and vice versa (to see this, compare the AEI outcome to the EEE outcome).

The subjects were told that the New York and Boston managers would negotiate through the computer network for a

Table 16.1. Issue Schedules of the New York and Boston Managers.

Cut-Off Money		Number of Years		Promotion	
Proposal	Points	Proposal	Points	Proposal	Points
New York Issue Schedule					
A	120	A	80	A	40
B	105	B	70	B	35
C	90	C	60	C	30
D	75	D	50	D	25
E	60	E	40	E	20
F	45	F	30	F	15
G	30	G	20	G	10
H	15	H	10	H	5
I	0	I	0	I	0
Boston Issue Schedule					
A	0	A	0	A	0
B	5	B	10	B	15
C	10	C	20	C	30
D	15	D	30	D	45
E	20	E	40	E	60
F	25	F	50	F	75
G	30	G	60	G	90
H	35	H	70	H	105
I	40	I	80	I	120

number of rounds, and that each round would consist of the New York manager making a proposal followed by a counterproposal from the Boston manager. On each round, the subjects were first shown the New York manager's issue chart and three-letter proposal, and then the Boston manager's issue chart and counterproposal. (The managers' issue charts were not shown simultaneously.) Then the subjects were given an opportunity to make an outcome recommendation and also to send one of twenty messages to the managers. Their main task was to facilitate an agreement between the two managers.

Independent Variables. Concern for the managers' aspirations was manipulated in three ways simultaneously, in line with the sources of concern identified by Carnevale (1986). In the high-concern conditions, the subjects were told the following:

1. Both managers had been outstanding performers for the company; both had made excellent decisions that saved the company money; and both managers had a positive impact on the product manager's own ability to get work done.
2. At the end of the experiment, both managers would rate the subject's mediation performance on ten-point scales and if the sum of these two ratings equaled fifteen or higher, the subject would receive $1 as a reward.
3. At the end of the experiment, they would meet with and get to know both subjects who were the New York and Boston managers.

In the low-concern conditions, the subjects were told:

1. Both managers were scheduled for termination from the company at the end of the year; both managers had made poor decisions that cost the company money; both managers had a negative impact on the product manager's own ability to get work done.
2. At the end of the experiment, they would evaluate the New York and Boston managers' negotiation performance on ten-point scales.
3. They would not meet or get to know either subject who was a manager at the end of the experiment.

The subject's perception of common ground was manipulated in two ways, in line with our belief that mediators perceive common ground when disputants have low aspirations and show low competitiveness. In the high perception of common-ground conditions, the disputants were presented as having relatively low aspirations: each was trying to achieve at least 80 points. In addition, the disputants (the computer program) made substantial concessions (New York offered BBC, BDD, BEE, BEG, and AEH, and Boston responded with GHH, FFH, EEH, CEH, BEI on the five rounds). In the low perception of common-ground conditions, the disputants were presented as having relatively high aspirations: each was trying to achieve at least 165 points. In addition, the disputants made few concessions (New York offered AAA, AAA, AAB, ABA, and ABA, and Boston responded with III, III, HII, IHI, IHI).

Dependent Variables. After two practice rounds, the negotiation began. On each round, the subject was free to choose one of twenty messages to send to the two managers; these messages are shown in Table 16.2. Each of the twenty mediator messages was designed to represent one of the four strategies identified by Carnevale (1986). The messages, most of which had been taken from transcripts of live mediation sessions, were classified on the basis of the authors' judgment that each message reflected a particular strategy. The validity of this classification was evaluated by having additional subjects rate each tactic for the extent to which each reflected a mediator's desire to integrate, press, compensate, or be inactive. These validity data are reported in Carnevale and Conlon (1988).

All the subjects were told that the negotiation rounds between the parties would continue until agreement was reached or eighteen exchanges of proposals had occurred. The computer kept a record of the proposals and messages that the subject sent, as well as how long the subject took to select and send messages. In all conditions, after five rounds of actual negotiating, the mediation was interrupted and the subjects were given a questionnaire that measured mediator perceptions of their situations, goals, and the relationship between the disputants. At the end of the experiment, the subjects were debriefed and were paid for participating.

Results. Analyses of variance of the subjects' responses to questionnaire items indicated that the experimental manipulations were successful (see Carnevale and Henry, 1989).

On each of the five rounds, a subject could choose to send one of the messages shown in Table 16.2, or could choose not to send a message. Table 16.3 shows the mean frequency with which each type of message was sent as a function of the manipulations of concern and perception of common ground.

As the strategic-choice model would lead us to expect, the highest level of pressing occurred with low concern and low perception of common ground, and the highest level of compensating occurred with high concern and low perception of

Table 16.2. Mediator Messages.

The list of messages actually given to the subjects was randomly ordered.
(C = Compensating, I = Integrating, N = Inaction, P = Pressing)

01	If you agree, I'll transfer some new accounts to your region.	C
02	Agree to the other's proposal, and I will see to it that you get promoted.	C
03	Agree, and I will arrange for that new office furniture that you want.	C
04	Agree, and I will see to it that you get a raise.	C
05	Agree, and you can attend that "business convention" in Hawaii.	C
06	You should try to see the other's point of view.	I
07	Let's try to come up with something mutually acceptable.	I
08	You should be direct and honest with one another.	I
09	I am trying to consider both of your needs in my recommendation.	I
10	Let's find a creative solution that makes everyone happy.	I
11	I really don't know what to say or suggest to you.	N
12	Maybe I'll have a recommendation for you later.	N
13	I'm keeping out of this for now.	N
14	I think you can work this out yourselves.	N
15	You seem to know what you are doing, so I will keep quiet for now.	N
16	You are greedy little suckers; give something up.	P
17	You are too stubborn—you better make more concessions.	P
18	You better reach an agreement or you will get fired.	P
19	There is hardly any time left to negotiate.	P
20	The more time we spend, the costlier it's going to be.	P

common ground. The inaction messages were hardly used at all, and no significant effects were obtained for them. But the number of times the subjects decided not to send a message, which we interpret as a decision to be inactive, showed the predicted patterns; the highest level of inaction (defined this way) occurred with low concern and high perception of common ground. Partial support was found for the model in the use of integrative tactics. Although there was greater integrating in the high-concern conditions than the low-concern conditions, the level of integrating was the same in high concern and low perceived common ground as in high concern and high perceived common ground. This suggests that, at least in the pres-

**Table 16.3. Evidence for the Strategic-Choice Model:
Mean Use of Each Type of Message as a Function of Concern
and Perception of Common Ground (PCG).**

	High Concern		Low Concern	
	Low PCG	High PCG	Low PCG	High PCG
1. Pressing	.79$_a$	.14$_a$	1.27$_b$	.67$_a$
2. Compensating	1.07$_a$	.14$_b$	.40$_b$	.47$_b$
3. Inaction	.21$_a$	.57$_a$	.33$_a$	.20$_a$
4. No message	.64$_a$	1.86$_b$	1.20$_{a, b}$	2.66$_c$
5. Integrating	2.29$_a$	2.29$_a$	1.80$_b$	1.00$_c$

Note: Common subscripts indicate no significant difference between
means in the same row.

ent study, highly concerned mediators will try integrating tactics
regardless of the amount of perceived common ground.

In general, the two dimensions of the strategic-choice
model predicted mediators' choices of strategy well. This first
study had male psychology majors as subjects. Our next step was
to generalize the model to female business administration students, and more important, to extend the model to the effects of
time pressure on mediation.

Experiment 2: Extending the Model to Time Pressure

Mediators experience time pressure to the extent that
they want to end a dispute quickly. Many factors contribute to
time pressure, including the mediator's nearness to a deadline
or the total amount of time available to mediate. To some extent,
because it is costly, all mediation involves time pressure; as
disputes proceed, mediators often become fatigued or frustrated. While little is known about time pressure in mediation,
there is anecdotal evidence that time pressure causes mediators
to increase their use of pressing (Kressel, 1972). We (Carnevale
and Conlon, 1988) designed a study to explain why mediators
press over time, and also to assess possible changes in other
mediator behaviors over time. From the strategic-choice model

we derived two hypotheses about time pressure and increased mediator pressing over time:

1. Over time, mediators' perception of common ground diminishes. According to the model, pressing occurs when mediators believe that there is little common ground. If mediator pressing increases as time passes, one possibility is that, over time, mediators lower their estimate of the likelihood of a mutually acceptable agreement. This seems plausible, for two reasons. First, mediators often enter disputes with an overly optimistic assessment of the likelihood of success (Carnevale and Pegnetter, 1985); as the dispute continues, this optimism may diminish. Second, over time, and in conditions of high time pressure, disputants are more vigorous in defending their positions. Many studies show that bargainer concession rate is fast at the early stages of bargaining and then slows over time (Pruitt, 1981); and there is evidence that time pressure can heighten bargainer competitiveness (Carnevale and Lawler, 1986). These changes in bargainer behavior over time may lower mediators' perception of common ground.

2. Over time, mediators place less value on the parties' aspirations. Over time, or in conditions of high time pressure, mediators may become fatigued or frustrated as the disputants refuse to reach agreement; this may lead them to care less that the disputants' aspirations are satisfied. According to the model, pressing occurs when mediators do not value the parties' aspirations. Thus, if mediator pressing increases as time passes, one explanation is that, over time, mediators reduce their value of the parties' aspirations.

We tested these predictions about the effect of time pressure on mediation by examining changes in mediator behavior over time, and also by manipulating the amount of time available to mediate. The logic of the strategic-choice model allowed testing three very specific alternative predictions:

1. If the increase in pressing was caused by a reduction in perceived common ground and not a reduction in concern for the disputants' aspirations, then over time there should be an increase in pressing and compensating, and a de-

crease in integrating and inaction (the two strategies in the left half of the model in Figure 16.1 should increase).

2. If the increase in pressing was caused by a reduction of the concern that mediators have for the parties' aspirations, and not a reduction in perceived common ground, then over time there should be an increase in pressing and inaction, and a decrease in integrating and compensating (the two strategies in the lower half of the model in Figure 16.1 should increase).

3. If the increase in pressing was caused by a reduction in concern for the disputants' aspirations *and* a reduction in perceived common ground, there should be an increase only in pressing and a decrease in integrating, compensating, and inaction (only the lower-left strategy of the model in Figure 16.1 should increase over time).

We manipulated time available for negotiation, mediator concern for the disputants' aspirations, and perceived probability of a mutually acceptable agreement in a two-by-two factorial design (the latter two manipulations in the same manner as in experiment 1). Time pressure was implemented by the number of rounds available to mediate: six when time pressure was high, eighteen when it was low. One hundred thirty-eight female business administration students served as subjects, and the procedure was identical to that described above.

The data supported the notion that time pressure increases mediator pressing, and that this is because of a reduction of perceived probability of a mutually acceptable agreement—not to a reduction in mediator concern for the parties' aspirations. Five pieces of evidence supported this conclusion:

1. The time-pressure manipulation affected the measure of perceived common ground; when there was high time pressure, mediators reported that the disputants were less likely to reach agreement and that the disputants were more competitive than when there was low time pressure.

2. The time-pressure manipulation had no effect on measures of the mediator's concern for the parties' aspirations.

3. Pressing and compensating increased over time, whereas integrating and inaction decreased over time, consistent with our first alternative prediction mentioned earlier.
4. An interaction was observed between the manipulations of time pressure and perceived common ground; by the last round, when they were under high time pressure, mediators with high perceived common ground were pressing as much as those with low perceived common ground; this interaction suggests that time pressure transformed the condition of high perceived common ground into one that resembled low perceived common ground.
5. There were no interactions between the manipulations of time pressure and concern for the parties' aspirations.

Taken together, our results on the effects of time pressure in mediation are consistent with derivations from the strategic-choice model, and suggest that the model may be useful for understanding other variables as well. The next study that we present was designed to test hypotheses about the influence of mediation on negotiation.

Experiment 3: Negotiation in the Context of Mediation

To be useful, models of mediation should not only make predictions about mediator behavior, but should also say something about negotiator behavior in the context of mediation. We (Harris and Carnevale, 1988) derived predictions from the strategic-choice model about how negotiators react to two different mediator strategies—compensation and pressure. The assumption underlying these predictions was that negotiators sometimes act in a manner designed to influence mediator behavior, especially when they know about the mediator's incentives—an assumption not inconsistent with case analyses of international mediation (Chapter Six; Young, 1972, p. 63).

Our first prediction was that negotiators would make the fewest concessions when dealing with a mediator who could compensate and who had high concern for their aspirations. According to the strategic-choice model (see Figure 16.1), mediators are most likely to offer compensation when they have high concern for the negotiators' aspirations. Negotiators who want compensation from a mediator, and know that the mediator has it and supports their aspirations, can elicit compensation by convincing the mediator that there is little common ground; otherwise the mediator might engage in integrating, which may not have the tangible, material benefits of compensation. Negotiators can convince mediators that there is little common ground by taking a rigid, competitive stance. Some have argued that such an effect occurred in the Middle East during the late 1970s when the United States offered both sides economic and military aid in return for concessions and agreements (Pruitt, 1981; Rubin, 1981).

Our second prediction was that negotiators would make the greatest concessions when dealing with a mediator who could press and who had low concern for their aspirations. According to the strategic-choice model, mediators are most likely to press when they have low concern for the negotiators' aspirations. A negotiator who wants to avoid pressure from a mediator, and knows that the mediator has that capacity, can avoid it by convincing the mediator that there is much common ground; this way, the negotiator receives inaction instead of pressure. Negotiators can convince mediators that there is much common ground by taking a flexible, cooperative stance.

We manipulated the mediator's ability to compensate (compensation versus no compensation), the mediator's ability to press (pressing versus no pressing), and the subjects' belief about the mediator's level of concern for their aspirations (concern versus no concern) in a two-by-two-by-two factorial design. The procedure was identical to that described for experiment 1, except that the subjects were negotiators and computer programs played the role of opposing negotiator (from New York) and mediator (the product manager). One hundred twenty-nine undergraduate male students participated to fulfill a requirement for an introductory psychology class.

In the compensation conditions, subjects were told that, for the final round of the negotiations, the mediator had the option to increase the potential points available for all proposal levels in the payoff schedule. In the pressing conditions, subjects were told that, for the final round of the negotiation, the mediator had the option to decrease the potential points available for all proposal levels; they were told that the mediator could decrease any point value to zero if he saw fit. In conditions of high mediator concern, subjects were told that the mediator could make money from the negotiation, but "only if you and the New York manager reach agreement." In the low-concern conditions, the subjects were told that the mediator had nothing at stake in the negotiation.

The results strongly supported the hypotheses. Tests indicated that negotiators facing a mediator who could compensate made fewer concessions, sent more contentious messages, and reported on a questionnaire that they were less cooperative than those in the control (no compensation) conditions; and this effect was stronger when the mediator had high concern for their aspirations than when the mediator had low concern. In addition, negotiators faced with a mediator who could press made greater concessions, sent more cooperative messages to the other negotiator, and reported being more cooperative on a questionnaire; and this effect was stronger when the mediator had low concern for their aspirations than when the mediator had high concern.

Several questionnaire items produced interesting effects regarding mediator compensation and pressing. The availability of compensation may cause negotiators to downgrade the mediator, and the availability of pressure may cause negotiators to upgrade their evaluation of the mediator. Relative to those who expected no compensation, subjects in the compensation condition reported that the mediator was less acceptable, that they were less satisfied with the mediator's efforts, and that the mediator's suggestions were having less influence on them. Compared to those in the no-press condition, subjects told that the mediator was able to press reported that the mediator was more acceptable, that they were more satisfied with the mediator's efforts, and that the mediator was more qualified to help them reach agreement. It should be noted that these effects are not simply the negotiators' reaction to a mediator who did not compensate or did not press, because the pressure of compensation could occur only on a later round of negotiation.

One major conclusion from this study is that a mediator's ability to compensate can sometimes undermine the effectiveness of mediation, especially if the mediator has an overt high concern for the negotiators' welfare. Negotiators view a mediator who can compensate and who has high concern as a soft touch, as weak and ineffective. A second conclusion is that a mediator's ability to press can enhance his or her effectiveness. The prospect of a punitive mediator can facilitate concession making, especially if the negotiators believe that the mediator has low concern for their welfare. This may be driven by the negotiators' desire to avoid the mediator's punishment.

We believe that in many situations, mediator compensation is a necessary tool in forming agreements. But our data suggest that mediators who can compensate should not act too concerned for the parties' welfare, lest they become a player in the negotiators' strategic game; if they appear too concerned, disputants may make fewer concessions and view the mediator as weak and a target for easy rewards. The ability to press may be a more effective strategy in securing negotiators' cooperation and respect than the ability to compensate.

In sum, the strategic-choice model did well at predicting negotiator behavior in the context of mediation. Moreover, our results suggest that mediator power has at least two components: rewards (compensation) and punishment (pressure) (see Raven and Kruglanski, 1970, Rubin, 1986). We have shown that these components have distinct consequences for the effectiveness of mediation in a manner predicted by the strategic-choice model.

Experiment 4: Extending the Model to Gender

The strategic-choice model may also help us understand gender differences in mediator behavior. The literature on gender differences notes that males tend to be task oriented and instrumental, and females tend to be communal and socioemotional (Eagly and Crowley, 1986). This suggests that female mediators should be more concerned that negotiators achieve their aspirations than male mediators. If so, and given the logic of the strategic-choice model, then female mediators should integrate and compensate more than male mediators, and male mediators should press and be inactive more than female mediators. Alternatively, if female mediators more than male mediators have high perceived common ground (more strongly believe that a mutually acceptable agreement will be found), then female mediators should integrate and be inactive more than male mediators, and male mediators should press and compensate more than female mediators.

We (Hanisch and Carnevale, 1988) conducted a laboratory experiment to examine mediator gender and behavior. The subjects were ninty-four male and ninety-four female undergraduates. The procedure and task were identical to that used in experiment 1.

The subjects' responses to questionnaires indicated that, as expected, and as shown in rows 1 and 2 of Table 16.4, it was more important to female than male mediators that the negotiators approve of their recommendations and that the negotiators achieve an outcome that they felt was good (both items on a six-point scale with 1 = very unimportant to 6 = very important). These data are consistent with the findings of others: females exhibit more concern for approval and interpersonal relationships than males (Eagly and Crowley, 1986). There was a marginal difference between males and females on a measure of perceived common ground, shown in row 3 of Table 16.4. Female mediators believed that the negotiators were more cooperative with one another than did male mediators ($p = .10$; six-point scale, with 1 = extremely competitive and 6 = extremely cooperative).

Measures of mediator strategy were developed by counting the number of times each of the different types of messages was used across the five rounds of the negotiation. As shown in rows 6 through 9, males and females, as mediators, differed in the use of tactics. Row 6 shows that females were significantly more inactive than males: overall they sent fewer messages. Females were more likely to send integrative messages than males, although this was not a strong effect (row 7). Rows 8 and 9

Table 16.4. Means for Mediator Perceptions and Behavior
as a Function of Gender.

	Female Mediator	Male Mediator
Questionnaire Item		
1. Negotiators approve of recommendations	4.66	4.30[a]
2. Negotiators achieve good outcome	4.83	4.49[a]
3. Perceived negotiator cooperativeness	3.34	3.03[b]
4. Confidence in ability as a mediator	2.70	3.16[a]
5. Degree of influence on the parties	2.16	2.40[a]
Message		
6. Inaction (no message sent)	1.20	.75[a]
7. Integrating messages	1.80	1.50[b]
8. Pressing messages	1.00	1.50[a]
9. Compensating messages	.25	.50[a]

Note: See text for information on scale values.
[a] Difference between means statistically significant, $p < .05$.
[b] $p < .15$.

reveal that males used pressure tactics and compensation tactics significantly more than females.

Male and female mediators differed in their level of confidence in mediation. As can be seen in row 4 of Table 16.4, males were significantly more confident than females (measured on a five-point scale, with 1 = not at all confident, 3 = somewhat confident, 5 = extremely confident). This suggests that males may feel more comfortable in the role of mediator than females, at least in our simulated business setting. Male mediators also reported that their recommendations had a greater influence on the negotiators than those of female mediators (row 5). Male mediators, who were more forceful in mediation, were more confident in their ability to mediate and perceived themselves as more influential than females. It should be noted that there were no significant differences between male and female mediators for the overall quality of their recommendations.

Taken together, the results for the mediator strategy data are consistent with the interpretation that female mediators more than male mediators believe that there is common ground between disputants. But the picture is not so clear because the ratings on the questionnaire items indicated that female mediators had greater concern for the parties' aspirations than male mediators and thus, according to the model, should have used compensation more than male mediators. These findings may be reconciled if one accepts the proposition that females are less instrumental than males (Eagly and Crowley, 1986), and that compensation is a form of instrumental behavior. This suggests that other factors (such as socialization history) may directly influence a mediator's choice of strategy.

Summary

This chapter described a theoretical model of mediation that was inspired by firsthand observations of professional labor mediators and case analyses of organizational and international mediation. A series of laboratory studies tested the model, and extended it to time pressure in mediation, to the effects of mediator strategy on negotiator behavior, and to differences between male and female mediators. We believe that the model fared well in these laboratory tests. Future studies will examine the model's implications for other variables such as mediator expertise, mediator bias, and negotiator power (see Rubin, 1986).

Our first experiment (Carnevale and Henry, 1989) demonstrated that the mediator's concern for the parties' aspirations and the mediator's beliefs about the likelihood of a mutually acceptable agreement are useful for understanding the mediator's choice between integration, pressure, compensation, and inaction. Our second experiment (Carnevale and Conlon, 1988) demonstrated that time pressure caused mediators to increase their use of pressing and compensating, and this was caused by a reduction in the mediator's beliefs about the likelihood of a mutually acceptable agreement. Our third experiment (Harris and Carnevale, 1988) demonstrated that negotiators sometimes attempt to affect the mediator's choice of strategy. When the mediator could compensate and was also concerned for the negotiators' aspirations, negotiators reduced their concession making in an apparent effort to extract the compensation; and when the mediator could press and was also unconcerned for the negotiators' aspirations, negotiators increased their concession making in an apparent effort to avoid the pressure. Finally, the results from our fourth experiment (Hanisch and Carnevale, 1988) indicated that males and females differ in their approach to mediation, with males adopting a more forceful pressing and compensating strategy, and females preferring integration and inaction.

Much of the current research in mediation (in fact all but one of the other chapters in this volume) develop inferences and propositions about mediation based on observations of or reports about expert mediators in natural settings. But the research in this chapter is based on observations of university students mediating or negotiating with simulated others via computers in an artificial context in a brief time period. It is legitimate to wonder, therefore, how relevant our findings are to the "real world" of mediation.

There is insufficient room here to explicate the advantages and disadvantages of laboratory and field research (the interested reader is referred to Mook, 1983), but since our approach is so different from that taken by other authors in this volume, a few comments are in order.

Our experimental simulations were designed to test hypotheses about mediation in controlled circumstances. Our main concern was that the effects could be isolated and alternative explanations could be ruled out. Our time-pressure study (Carnevale and Conlon, 1988) was inspired by Kressel's observation (1972) that professional mediators are more likely to press as a deadline nears. But it was unclear why. The results of our study suggest why: a change in the mediator's perception of the likelihood of a mutually acceptable agreement. One benefit of experimental research is that it clarifies the mechanisms responsible for an effect, something that is often impossible to achieve in observations of natural settings or in survey studies.

One drawback of laboratory research is that it does not tell about the relative importance of different variables in natural settings. Our study of time pressure does not tell us how often and in what situations time pressure is important. It only tells us that time-pressure effects *can* occur in natural contexts in the manner that we have identified (Mook, 1983).

In addition, there are often difficulties in generalizing results from laboratory situations to natural situations. This problem is shared with field research, since natural settings differ from one another, but it can be more acute with laboratory research, since that tends to be done in simplified settings. An example might be our experiment for gender differences; the results may not apply to professional mediators, since the subjects in our studies were novices. Does expertise eliminate differences between male and female mediators? If so, the gender differences that we have found will not generalize to experts, but only to novices and to those who are just learning to mediate. This suggests an interesting follow-up laboratory study: in a laboratory context there should be no differences between experienced male and female mediators. (Note, however, that we have observed a similar gender difference in professional mediators' self-reports about their choice of tactics; see Chapter Ten, this volume.)

While there often are big differences between laboratory research settings and the field settings to which we wish to generalize, generalizability problems are not so great when we are doing theoretical research, as we are here. Our findings are relevant not because our procedures for collecting data correspond to natural settings, but because the theoretical processes on which they are based also occur in natural settings. We believe that the strategic-choice model, which predicts the strategies that mediators select in different circumstances and the manner in which negotiators react to mediation, applies to mediation in most contexts—regardless of whether the context is a natural one or an experimental psychologist's laboratory. This is the basis of our faith in the generality of our results.

References

Campbell, J. C. *Successful Negotiation: Trieste 1954*. Princeton, N.J.: Princeton University Press, 1976.

Carnevale, P. J. "Strategic Choice in Mediation." *Negotiation Journal*, 1986, *2*, 41–56.

Carnevale, P. J., and Conlon, D. "Time Pressure and Strategic Choice in Mediation." *Organizational Behavior and Human Decision Processes*, 1988, *42*, 111–133.

Carnevale, P. J., and Henry, R. A. "Determinants of Mediator Behavior: A Test of the Strategic Choice Model." *Journal of Applied Social Psychology*, 1989, *19*, 469–488.

Carnevale, P. J., and Lawler, E. J. "Time Pressure and the Development of Integrative Agreements in Bilateral Negotiation." *Journal of Conflict Resolution*, 1986, *30*, 636–659.

Carnevale, P. J., and Pegnetter, R. "The Selection of Mediation Tactics in Public-Sector Disputes: A Contingency Analysis." *Journal of Social Issues*, 1985, *41*, 65–81.

Eagly, A. H., and Crowley, M. "Gender and Helping Behavior: A Meta-Analytic Review of the Social Psychological Literature." *Psychological Bulletin*, 1986, *100*, 283–308.

Follett, M. P. "Constructive Conflict." In H. C. Metcalf and L. Urwick (eds.), *Dynamic Administration: The Collected Papers of Mary Parker Follett*. New York: Harper & Row, 1940.

Hanisch, K. A., and Carnevale, P. J. "Gender Differences in Mediation and Negotiation: Some General and Situation Specific Effects." Unpublished manuscript, 1988.

Harris, K. L., and Carnevale, P. J. "Chilling and Hastening Effects of Mediation: Implications of the Strategic Choice Model of Mediation for Negotiator Behavior." Unpublished manuscript, 1988.

Kressel, K. *Labor Mediation: An Exploratory Survey*. Albany, N.Y.: Association of Labor Mediation Agencies, 1972.

Kressel, K., and Pruitt, D. G. "Themes in the Mediation of Social Conflict." *Journal of Social Issues*, 1985, *41*, 179–198.

Mook, D. G . "In Defense of External Invalidity." *American Psychologist*, 1983, *38*, 379–387.

Pruitt, D. G. *Negotiation Behavior*. Orlando, Fla.: Academic Press, 1981.

Pruitt, D. G., and Rubin, J. Z. *Social Conflict: Escalation, Stalemate, and Resolution*. New York: Random House, 1986.

Raven, B. H., and Kruglanski, A. W. "Conflict and Power." In

P. Swingle (ed.), *The Structure of Conflict*. Orlando, Fla.: Academic Press, 1970.

Rubin, J. Z. "Experimental Research on Third-Party Intervention in Conflict: Toward Some Generalizations." *Psychology Bulletin*, 1980, *87*, 379–391.

Rubin, J. Z. (ed.). *Dynamics of Third Party Intervention: Kissinger in the Middle East*. New York: Praeger, 1981.

Rubin, J. Z. "Third Parties Within Organizations." In R. J. Lewicki, B. H. Sheppard, and M. H. Bazerman (eds.), *Research on Negotiation in Organizations*, Vol. 1. Greenwich, Conn.: JAI Press, 1986.

Schelling, T. C. "Strategies Analysis and Social Problems." *Social Problems*, 1965, *12*, 367–379.

Touval, S. *The Peace Brokers: Mediators in the Arab-Israeli Conflict 1948–1979*. Princeton, N.J.: Princeton University Press, 1982.

Young, O. R. "Intermediaries: Additional Thoughts on Third Parties." *Journal of Conflict Resolution*, 1972, *16*, 51–65.

SEVENTEEN

Process of Mediation in Dispute Settlement Centers

Dean G. Pruitt
Neil B. McGillicuddy
Gary L. Welton
William Rick Fry

Our research deals with how people—disputants and mediator—behave during mediation: what sorts of things determine
their behavior, and how it affects the flow of events. So far, we

Note: This research was supported by National Science Foundation Grants
BNS8309167 and SES 8520084. We wish to thank, for their advice and support
at many points in this project, Joyce Kowalewski, former executive director of
the Neighborhood Justice Project of Elmira, New York; Judith Peter, director
of the Dispute Settlement Center of Western New York; David Rynders,
executive director of the Neighborhood Justice Project; and Charles Under-
hill, president of the Better Business Foundation of Western New York, Inc.
The following staff members of the two centers were also very helpful: Mary
Beth Goris, James Meloon, David Polino, Brenda Ransom, and Beverly
Stearns. We are also indebted for intellectual guidance and data gathering to
Lynn Castrianno, Jill Dorfeld, Eldon K. Hutchinson, Carol Ippolito, Thomas
Nochajski, Helena Syna, Michael Van Slyck, and Josephine Zubek.

have done two studies involving direct observation of mediation sessions in dispute settlement centers.

The first study was designed to assess the effects of two forms of "med/arb," the procedure in which the dispute goes to arbitration if an agreement is not reached in mediation (see Pruitt, 1981b). This study also examined the stages in mediation and the nature and functions of caucus sessions (private meetings between the mediator and one of the disputants). The second study looked at caucusing in more detail.

There are more than 250 dispute settlement centers (DSCs) in the United States, conducting more than 230,000 hearings per year (Ray, 1986). Many, but by no means all, are funded by state and local governments. The main function of these centers is to help people in continuing relationships (friends, relatives, neighbors, spouses, former spouses, landlords and tenants, and so forth) reach a mutually acceptable resolution of their disputes. Many of the centers also deal with disputes about debts between people who do not have continuing relationships. Cases come from many sources, including judges, district attorneys, Legal Aid, court clerks, police, social workers, consumer protection agencies, and self-referrals. The mediators who hear these cases usually are trained volunteers from the ranks of schoolteachers, students, homemakers, and so on.

A typical hearing starts with the mediator explaining the procedure and assuring the disputants that he or she is neutral and that the hearing will be confidential. Then the disputants get a chance to ventilate, to tell their stories in turn. After that, the issues are analyzed, alternatives are developed, and the disputants, it is hoped, reach a decision. Caucus sessions are common at all points after the ventilation period. If and when a decision is made, the mediator writes it out for the disputants to sign. The resulting document ordinarily has the force of a contract.

Various rationales have been provided for the existence of DSCs. The most commonly cited is relief of pressure on the courts. Others include giving people an opportunity to develop win-win solutions to their controversies and cutting the costs of settlement for the disputants and the broader society (Kessler, 1978; McGillis, 1981; Ray, 1982). Evaluation studies have found evidence of high user satisfaction (Pearson and Thoennes, 1984; Roehl and Cook, 1985; Syna and others, 1983) and high levels of compliance with the decisions reached (McEwen and Maiman, 1984; Roehl and Cook, 1985; Syna and others, 1983). Hence, there is reason to believe that this form of mediation improves the quality of life for many of its users. Evidence about impact on the courts is less clear-cut (Roehl and Cook, 1985); but mediation is strongly endorsed by officers of the Buffalo City Court (including some judges), the jurisdiction we know best.

The Impact of Med/Arb on Mediation

We decided to study med/arb because of two controversies among leaders in the alternative dispute resolution movement. One concerns the advisability of using this procedure, as opposed to straight mediation. Proponents of med/arb argue that it encourages the disputants to try to reach agreement during mediation, because they fear loss of control over their outcomes in the event of arbitration. Indirect support for this argument is provided by a study of mediated public disputes (Kochan and Jick, 1978), in which it was found that disputants who expected arbitration if mediation failed (med/arb) were more likely to concede than those who expected fact finding. Other indirect support for this argument can be seen in two laboratory experiments (Bigoness, 1976; Johnson and Pruitt, 1972) that found that negotiators who expected arbitration if they failed to reach agreement conceded more rapidly than those who expected mediation. Another argument for med/arb is that it protects the referral agency from having to deal again with the case.

Opponents of med/arb argue that the second part of this procedure, arbitration, is an inferior form of dispute resolution, since it takes responsibility for the decision out of the hands of the disputants, who know the issues best.

The other controversy concerns the relative merits of two forms of med/arb, known by shorthand terminology: *med/arb (same)*, in which the mediator and the arbitrator are the same person, and *med/arb(diff)*, in which the mediator and arbitrator are different people. Proponents of med/arb(same) argue that having the power to arbitrate gives mediators enough prestige to persuade reluctant disputants to make concessions and engage in creative problem solving. Proponents of med/arb(diff) argue that having the power to arbitrate makes mediators too forceful, resulting in a decision that unduly reflects the mediator's own views. They also argue that mediation is a bad preparation for arbitration, for mediators may become partial to certain solutions, making them biased if they move into the role of arbitrator.

Method. Our first study, a true field experiment, was conducted at the Dispute Settlement Center in Buffalo, a branch of the Better Business Bureau Foundation of Western New York, Inc. Cases that came from Buffalo City Court were randomly assigned to three conditions: straight mediation, med/arb (same), and med/arb(diff). Our sample consisted of 36 cases, 12 in each condition. However, to get this number, it was necessary to assign 114 cases to the study. Forty were dropped from the sample by the agency or the researchers before the hearing, for varied reasons (such as the involvement of a juvenile or the fact that the case was assigned to a group that already had 12), and 38 cases were dropped because one or more subjects withdrew. Fortunately, there was no statistical relationship between the conditions and the number of subjects withdrawing. Hence, there is no reason to believe that the attrition in the sample disturbed the randomization.

On five separate occasions, disputants were told about the type of mediation they would experience (the condition they were in). Mediators were given this information on three separate occasions. Just before the hearing began, the mediator and both disputants were asked if they wanted to participate in the study. The hearings ranged from 20 to 160 minutes; the average was 75 minutes long.

The hearings were watched by two observers who were blind to the condition and who sat in a corner of the room, content-analyzing what was said. They recorded twenty-eight categories of mediator behavior and twenty-six categories of disputant behavior, using an electronic event recorder. The coding unit was a speaking turn: everything said by a person from the end of the prior person's remarks to the beginning of the next person's remarks. If a speaking turn lasted more than thirty seconds, a second unit was initiated, and so on for each thirty-second interval. A given unit could receive several different codes but never the same code twice. Intercoder reliability coefficients, calculated from earlier pilot data, were quite favorable. The median intercoder correlation coefficient across all the categories was .85. Using a criterion of .70 or better, forty-four of the fifty-four codes were reliable. Only these codes were used in the analysis.

At the end of the mediation session, the observers rated disputant motivation on three scales. They then asked the participants to fill out questionnaires about their perceptions of the session. All the mediators answered the questionnaire, but only forty-six of the seventy-two disputants were willing to do so.

The main data consisted of the relative frequency of each content code: the number of units in which this code was detected, divided by the total number of mediator or disputant units.

Results and Discussion. The results of this study are displayed in Table 17.1 (for a fuller report, see McGillicuddy, Welton and Pruitt, 1987). Those dealing with disputant behavior (rows 1 to 4) suggest that the mediation process was more favorable under med/arb(same) than under straight mediation. When the mediator had the power to arbitrate, disputants made fewer angry or hostile comments and fewer invidious comparisons. They also proposed more new alternatives for dealing with the issues — an indication of creative problem solving — and made (nonsignificantly) more concessions. On most of these measures, the med/arb(diff) procedure lay intermediate between med/arb(same) and straight mediation, though the differences between this condition and the others were usually not statistically significant. Med/arb(same) led to more agreements (row 9) than the other two conditions, though this result did not approach statistical significance.

A possible explanation for these results is suggested by the coder ratings of disputant motivation (rows 5 and 6). As

Table 17.1. Disputant and Mediator Behavior as a Function of Procedure.

	Straight Mediation	Med/Arb (Same)	Med/Arb (Diff.)
Disputant Behavior			
1. Angry or hostile comments	4.10_a	$.56_b$	$1.34_{a,\,b}$
2. Invidious comparisons between self and other	$.0093_a$	$.0013_b$	$.0003_b$
3. New alternatives for dealing with issues	$.0230_a$	$.0560_b$	$.0268_a$
4. Concessions	$.0040$	$.0075$	$.0053$
Observer Ratings of Disputant Motivation			
5. Desire to settle dispute	3.65_a	5.08_b	5.00_b
6. Desire to impress and follow mediator	3.48_a	5.01_b	$4.30_{a,\,b}$
Mediator Behavior			
7. Heavy pressure tactics	1.33_a	2.89_b	$1.78_{a,\,b}$
8. Involvement	3.09_a	2.63_a	$.26$
Outcome			
9. Number of agreements (out of 12)	8	10	8

Note: Means with different subscripts differ significantly at the .05 level by the Newman-Kuels test.

Lines 2, 3, and 4 present means of relative frequencies of content codes.

Lines 1 and 7 present means of indices constructed by averaging standard scores for several content codes and adding 2.00.

Lines 5 and 6 present means of ratings made on a seven-point scale.

Line 8 presents means of an index constructed by averaging standard scores of five questionnaire items and the number of mediator statements and adding 2.00.

postulated by the advocates of med/arb, disputants appeared to be more motivated to settle their dispute in the two med/arb conditions than in straight mediation. They also seemed especially anxious to follow the suggestions of and please the mediator in the med/arb(same) condition, perhaps because mediator prestige was greatest in this condition. These results imply that med/arb(same) produced at least one more motive favoring problem solving than did med/arb(diff). Hence, we might expect med/arb(same) to yield the most problem solving, med/arb(diff) the next most problem solving, and straight mediation the least problem solving—and this was found to be true.

Two elements of mediator behavior were also related to the conditions of this study. The use of heavy pressure tactics—threats and strong advocacy of a particular solution—was significantly greater in med/arb(same) than in straight mediation (row 7). Again med/arb(diff) was nonsignificantly intermediate between the other two conditions. This finding supports the criticism of med/arb(same) that it encourages forceful behavior from the mediator.

The other finding was that the mediators were less active and involved under med/arb(diff) than under the other two conditions (row 8). There are two possible explanations for this effect: (1) the mediators in med/arb(diff) may have felt less responsible for the case because another person could be relied upon to take it over, or (2) they may have become demoralized because they saw themselves as having lower power than the potential arbitrator.

Conclusions. Our results for med/arb(same) suggest the value of mediator power in dispute resolution. The mediators in these hearings had the power to make a binding decision, which apparently encouraged the disputants to be attentive to their wishes and anxious to reach agreement. As a result, the disputants moderated their tactics and aspirations and tended to engage in problem solving, developing creative ideas for solving their controversy.

Powerful mediators are very common in certain arenas, for example international mediation (Pruitt, 1981a), mediation in organizations (Chapter Eight, this volume), and mediation in the family. Community mediators in primitive societies are also frequently powerful figures (Gulliver, 1979; Chapter Four, this volume). Furthermore, there is evidence for the differential success of powerful mediators in one of these arenas—the international (Chapter Thirteen, this volume; Frei, 1976).

There is a flip side to mediator power: it may elicit authoritarian behavior from mediators, encouraging them to dictate terms. For example, in some settings, mediator/arbitrators may be tempted to become simple arbitrators. This can be a problem for two reasons. First, heavy-handed mediators may push the disputants into making premature and unnecessary concessions that interfere with the attainment of high joint benefit. Second, the disputants may not respect an agreement imposed by a mediator because they do not feel that they have participated in making it. These are real dangers; we have seen mediator/arbitrators in other dispute settlement centers succumb to the temptation to dictate terms, especially when they were in a hurry to finish the hearing.

There is a hint of these dangers in our data: the mediators in med/arb(same) used more pressure tactics than those in the other two conditions. However, we are convinced that most of the mediators in this condition were *not* highly directive. For one thing, their pressure tactics tended to be concentrated at the end of the sessions, suggesting a last-ditch effort to rescue a failing mediation rather than a policy of forceful advocacy. Furthermore, nonsignificant trends in the postquestionnaire data indicated that the disputants in med/arb(same) saw the mediator as *less* forceful and themselves as *more* involved in working out the terms of the agreement than those in the other two conditions.

The mediators in the Buffalo center are trained in the democratic tradition, with emphasis on helping the disputants find their own solutions. Furthermore, they are mostly idealistic volunteers, trying to provide a service rather than to finish a case as quickly as possible. In this context, giving them a little power appears to improve the quality of their sessions rather than to encourage the dictation of terms.

The endorsement of med/arb(same) implied by this study applies only to the mediation phase of the hearing. Arguments can be raised against this procedure if the hearing must go to arbitration. The biggest problem is that mediators often meet disputants in private caucus sessions from which the adversary is excluded. These sessions can be very useful for achieving progress in the hearing; but they may result in mediator bias because, as we will see, private sessions allow a disputant to make irresponsible charges that cannot be refuted by the other party.

If the mediator then becomes an arbitrator, he or she may make a biased judgment.

Opponents of med/arb(same) argue that the solution to this problem is med/arb(diff), that is, bringing in a separate arbitrator if mediation fails. However, our data point to problems with this procedure. One is that med/arb(diff) does not produce as much disputant problem solving as med/arb(same), though we must be cautious about this generalization because the differences were nonsignificant. The other is that med/arb(diff) appears to discourage mediator involvement with the case.

Perhaps the best solution is to use med/arb(same) and train the mediator/arbitrators in how to view the accusations they hear in caucus. Such accusations should be treated as potentially important information about the speaker's views, but they should not be believed unless the party accused has had an opportunity to refute them.

Stages in Mediation

Concepts of stages have been useful for analyzing social decision making in a number of settings, including problem-solving groups (Bales and Strodtbeck, 1951), labor negotiations (Douglas, 1962; Morley and Stephenson, 1977), and international negotiations (Druckman and Mahoney, 1977; Zartman, 1977). We tested two stage models of mediator behavior with data from our first study.

One was a three-stage model devised by Kressel (1972) on the basis of interviews with labor mediators. This model holds that mediators employ three distinct types of tactics in sequence. First come *reflexive* tactics, designed to establish rapport with the disputants and orient the mediator to the conflict. Then come *nondirective* tactics, designed to increase the likelihood that the disputants themselves will discover a mutually acceptable solution. Finally come *directive* tactics, designed to discover and put forward particular solutions and to encourage the parties to end the dispute.

The other was a five-stage decision-making model, which we devised. According to this model, mediators first gather *information* about what is going on. Second, they pose the *issues* for themselves and the disputants. Third, they facilitate, or if necessary undertake themselves, the generation and evaluation of *alternatives*. Fourth, they try to precipitate *decision making*. Finally, if a decision has been made, they facilitate planning for *implementation*.

Method. These models were tested with two types of data from our first study. One was responses to a checklist question-naire administered to mediators immediately after the end of the hearing. They were asked when in the mediation process they had mainly used twenty-six tactics: "early," "middle," "late," or "not at all." The second set of data came from the content analysis of mediator and disputant behavior. Each session was divided into three equal time intervals, and the relative frequency of each content code within each interval was then calculated.

Results and Discussion. Table 17.2 shows results from the mediator checklist. Only tactics reported by 40 percent or more of the mediators are included. The first column shows the percentage of mediators reporting the use of each tactic. The second column shows the average point in time (APT) when the tactic was used, on a scale running from 1 (used mainly in the first time period) to 3 (used mainly in the third time period).

The results support Kressel's model; reflexive tactics (numbers 1, 2, 3, and 12) were, with one notable exception, concentrated at the beginning of the session (mean APT = 1.56); nondirective tactics (4, 5, 8, 9, 14) primarily occurred in mid-session (mean APT = 1.97); and directive tactics (7, 10, 11, 13, 15, 16, 17, 18) were mainly encountered at the end (mean APT = 2.40). They also support our five-stage decision-making model, in that the tactics corresponding to the various phases of deci-sion making tended to appear in the predicted order:

	Mean APT
Information gathering (tactic number 3)	1.44
Posing issues (4, 9, 14)	2.02
Generating alternatives (7, 15)	2.23
Decision making (10, 11, 13, 16, 17)	2.44
Implementation (18)	2.57

Both models fit the data fairly well (except that tactic 6 did not seem to fit either), and each has certain advantages over the other. Our decision-making model has the advantage of providing more detail about the nature of the mediation process. But the Kressel model allows classification of more tactics, including those aimed at developing rapport (1, 2), enhancing social control (5, 8), and improving the atmosphere of the hearing (12)—important functions that are not envisioned by a strict decision-making analysis. Hence, it would appear that some combination of the two models is needed.

Table 17.2. Tactics Mediators Report Using: How Often, How Early.

Tactic	Percent Reporting Tactic	Average Point in Time*
1. Indicated that the session would be confidential	1.00	1.03
2. Indicated personal concern about settling dispute	.58	1.39
3. Asked for information about underlying goals or values	.75	1.44
4. Proposed agenda or order for discussing issues	.75	1.53
5. Criticized a disputant for improper behavior	.47	1.77
6. Met separately with the parties	.67	1.91
7. Questioned a petition, demand, assumption, or goal	.69	1.96
8. Attempted to cool a hostile interchange	.50	2.00
9. Summarized a party's position or interests	.94	2.09
10. Indicated cost of failing to reach agreement	.69	2.23
11. Urged one or both parties to move ahead	.64	2.38
12. Used humor or lightness	.42	2.38
13. Asked a party to react to own or other's proposal	.83	2.43
14. Tried to refocus attention from past to future	.61	2.45
15. Proposed a new solution to one or more issues	.56	2.50
16. Stated dissatisfaction with lack of progress	.58	2.57
17. Pressed one or both parties for concessions	.72	2.57
18. Suggested a method for implementing an agreement	.58	2.57

* Three time periods: early, middle, and late. Scale used: 1 = tactic used mainly in first time period, to 3 = used exclusively in third time period.

Table 17.3. Observed Mediator Tactics: How Frequent, How Soon.

Mediator Content Codes	Percent of Usage	Average Point in Time*
1. Attempts to cool a hostile interchange	.003	1.05
2. Asks for information	.155	1.64
3. Negative evaluation of behavior	.012	1.89
4. Positive evaluation of position	.007	1.97
5. Clarifies disputant position or interests	.103	1.98
6. Points out similarity or interdependence	.087	2.17
7. Attempts to build rapport or show expertise	.099	2.18
8. Tries to refocus attention from past to future	.010	2.19
9. Asks disputant for new ideas	.072	2.19
10. Suggests a procedure	.058	2.19
11. Negative evaluation of disputant position	.008	2.20
12. Urges taking a new perspective	.004	2.21
13. Requests reaction to a proposal	.120	2.29
14. Proposes order of discussing issues	.007	2.31
15. Urges movement toward agreement	.003	2.32
16. Uses humor or lightness	.009	2.33
17. Proposes a solution to one or more issues	.020	2.38
18. Positive evaluation of disputant behavior	.002	2.41
19. Threatens to withdraw from hearing	.004	2.69
20. Indicates costs of failing to reach agreement	.008	2.70
21. Argues for a proposal	.011	2.80

* Scale is 1 to 3, where 1 = earliest and 3 = latest.

Another interesting feature of these data is that the mediators said they used the heaviest, most directive tactics at the end of the session. They indicated that they had waited until the last minute to pose new solutions (15), state dissatisfaction with the disputants' lack of progress (16), and press for concessions (17).

Table 17.3 gives results from the content analysis of actual mediator behavior as it was observed by researchers on the spot. The first column shows the percentage of coding units (speaking turns) in which each tactic was detected. The second column again gives a number from 1 to 3 representing the average point in time (APT) at which the tactic was used.

The results of this analysis also provide support for the

Kressel model. Reflexive tactics (numbers 2, 7, and 16; mean APT = 2.05) occurred on the average earlier than nondirective tactics (1, 3, 5, 6, 8, 9, 10, 12, 14, 18; mean APT = 2.29), which occurred on the average earlier than directive tactics (4, 11, 13, 15, 17, 19, 20, 21; mean APT = 2.42). However, this support is weak; the means for the three groups of tactics are close together, reflecting considerable scatter in the location of the tactics in each group.

One problem with the Kressel model is that it shows mediator attempts to build rapport and show expertise as early phenomena, whereas our data indicate that they occur throughout the session.

A second problem with the Kressel model was encountered in the checklist data as well. Both sets of data suggest that mediators use humor and lightness toward the end of the session rather than toward the beginning as Kressel postulates. This discrepancy may reflect the special character of dispute settlement center hearings, in contrast to the labor-management sessions Kressel studied. These hearings usually begin with a period of "venting," in which the parties typically voice a series of accusations against each other. Early humor may well be counterproductive in such settings, implying that the mediator is making light of deeply felt concerns. On the other hand, late humor may be productive, because it can defuse tensions once a decision has been made and thus contribute to future solidarity between the disputants.

A third problem with the Kressel model is that he views mediator efforts to achieve social control ("attempts to cool a hostile interchange" and "negative evaluation of disputant behavior") as mid-session phenomena, whereas our data show that they occur quite early. Again, this may reflect the special character of hearings in dispute settlement centers, which commonly start with accusations. Resentful outbursts by the party being accused are quite common in this period and must usually be controlled to ensure an orderly hearing.

The results in Table 17.3 provide somewhat better support for our decision-making model. Tactics associated with the first four stages of decision making (implementation codes were not used) were employed in roughly the predicted order:

	Mean APT
Gathering information (2)	1.64
Posing issues (5, 8, 12, 14)	2.17
Generating alternatives (4, 9, 11, 13, 17)	2.21
Making decisions (15, 19, 20, 21)	2.63

Again, several of the tactics could not be classified in the decision-making scheme. These were either aimed at social control (1 and 3), at building rapport and credibility (7), or at improving the atmosphere of the hearing (6, 16, and 18). Also once again, the heaviest, most directive tactics (19 and 21) came at the end.

We also looked at the order of tactics used by the disputants. Table 17.4 shows these data. The earliest tactics used were critical and sarcastic remarks about the other party (1, 2, 6; mean APT = 1.85) and efforts to win (3, 4, 8, 10; mean APT = 1.96). These presumably arose primarily during venting and the period of argumentation that so often immediately follows venting. Providing information about the problem also came relatively early (7; APT = 1.95).

As time went on, conciliatory behavior began to appear. Disputants sometimes accepted responsibility for the problem (9), made concessions (11), acknowledged the other party's feelings (14), voiced new proposals (17), sought the other's reactions to these proposals (15), and asked the other for new proposals (16). We might call this a problem-solving phase (mean APT = 2.15).

Two aspects of the last time period are noteworthy in the behavior of the disputants. There were more general statements of care and concern (22; APT = 2.38), which presumably represent an effort at reconciliation with the other party. (These statements occurred mainly among disputants who were low in initial hostility.) There were also more heavy commitments, that

Table 17.4. Observed Disputant Tactics: How Frequent, How Soon.

Tactic	Percent of Usage	Average Point in Time*
1. Criticism of other's behavior	.077	1.78
2. Sarcastic remarks toward other	.005	1.84
3. Threatens other	.005	1.90
4. Persuasive arguments urging other to concede	.145	1.92
5. Asks a question	.001	1.94
6. Criticism of other's character	.010	1.94
7. Gives information	.346	1.95
8. Self-enhancing statements	.031	1.98
9. Takes responsibility for the problems	.011	1.99
10. Invidious comparison between self and other	.003	2.05
11. Concedes by lowering a demand	.004	2.06
12. Points out similarity or interdependence with other	.018	2.12
13. Swearing and angry displays	.013	2.13
14. Acknowledges other's feelings	.002	2.14
15. Requests reaction to a proposal	.006	2.23
16. Asks other party for a proposal	.002	2.24
17. Makes a proposal or offers a solution	.032	2.25
18. Agrees with mediator	.003	2.25
19. Asks an accusatory or hostile question	.005	2.25
20. Asks for information about other's perspective	.035	2.29
21. Warns about consequences of not making a concession	.002	2.32
22. Expresses care and concern about other	.005	2.38
23. Heavy commitment to a demand	.016	2.60

* Scale is 1 to 3, where 1 = earliest and 3 = latest.

is, strong statements of unwillingness to make further concessions (23; APT = 2.60). Such commitments are risky at earlier stages because disputants do not have information about each other's limits of tolerance and hence may commit themselves to a position the other cannot accept. They are useful at later stages because they can end a dispute or, if it does not end, can provide guidance to a subsequent arbitrator about the terms that must be included in a judgment for it to be workable.

Conclusions. Combining the two models and the data from

both sources, we have developed a three-stage model of mediator behavior (numbers preceded by an "A" refer to the items in Table 17.2; those preceded by a "B" refer to the items in Table 17.3):

	Mean APT
Stage 1. Setting the Stage	
Clarifying the ground rules (A1, 2)	1.21
Gathering information (A3, B2)	1.54
Exerting social control (A5, 8, B1, 3)	1.68
Stage 2. Problem Solving	
Posing issues (A4, 9, 14, B5, 8, 12, 14)	2.10
Generating alternatives (A7, 15, B4, 9, 11, 13, 17)	2.22
Trying to improve the interpersonal atmosphere (A12, B6, 16)	2.29
Stage 3. Achieving a Workable Agreement	
Urging agreement (A10, 11, 13, B15, 20)	2.40
Pressing heavily for agreement (A16, 17, B19, 21)	2.66
Suggesting implementation methods (A18)	2.57

We put "suggesting implementation methods" at the end for reasons of logic, even though its APT score was slightly lower than the preceding tactic. Note that rapport building and the display of expertise, important elements of Kressel's reflexive stage, are missing from the first stage of our model. Our evidence is that these are continuing phenomena, found at all stages of the hearing.

It is interesting to note that the middle period, in which the mediator is trying to improve the atmosphere and encourage problem solving, is also characterized by maximal disputant efforts at problem solving (see Table 17.4). Hence, it appears that many mediators are successful in this effort. The new model also suggests that mediators first urge the parties to reach agreement and then, if this does not work, begin to press heavily for the same objective.

Given the similarity between the order of events listed in

Tables 17.2 and 17.3, we might expect a close correspondence between what mediators said they did on the mediator checklist and what they actually did in the hearing. To test this hypothesis, we identified nine tactics that appeared in both lists (A4–B13, A5–B3, A7–B10, A8–B1, A10–B19, A11–B14, A12–B15, A14–B7, and A15–B16) and computed, for each tactic, a phi coefficient (the proper correlation coefficient for this purpose) between the reported and actual use of that tactic. Only three of these coefficients were statistically significant, and the average of all nine coefficients was a low .256. Hence, there was little consistency between what the mediators did and what they said they had done. This raises some doubt about the value of retrospective accounts for identifying what has actually happened in a hearing, a concern also voiced by Kressel and Pruitt (1985).

If mediators do not accurately report what they did, how can there be such a close correspondence in the order of events shown in Tables 17.2 and 17.3? Conceivably, in filling out the checklist, our mediators were reporting *stereotypes* about the events that occur in mediation sessions, based on their own general experience and that of other mediators. These stereotypes (whose means are shown in Table 17.2) might well describe average mediator behavior (as shown in Table 17.3) but not reflect what actually happened in the session just mediated.

Caucusing

Caucusing—meeting separately with a disputant—is a very common mediator maneuver (Kressel, 1972). However, there is considerable controversy about whether it *should* be used, especially among community and divorce mediators (Markowitz and Engram, 1983; Silbey and Merry, 1986).

Some mediators feel that caucus sessions should be called during difficult hearings, when the disputants are taking a contentious rather than a problem-solving approach. This policy is evident in our data. The mediators in our studies were especially likely to call caucuses when the disputants displayed hostility toward each other and generated few new alternatives.

There are four characteristics of caucus sessions that

make them useful in difficult hearings. First, the other party is not present as a stimulus, so the disputant in a caucus session should be less tense, angry, and defensive, and thus more flexible and creative (Carnevale, Beckman, and Bona, 1984). Second, the other party is not present to hear the disputant. Hence, the disputant should feel freer to provide information about underlying interests and assumptions, and to throw out tentative new ideas for possible solutions (Kerr, 1954; Kolb, 1983; Pruitt, 1981b).

Third, the other party is not present to see and hear the mediator. This allows the mediator to interact intimately with the disputant without appearing partial, thus encouraging increased rapport and sharing of information (see Vallone, Ross, and Lepper, 1985). It also allows the mediator to make positive remarks about the other party without emboldening or seeming to curry favor with that party (Bercovitch, 1984; Blades, 1984; Kolb, 1983; Pruitt, 1981b). Fourth, the other party is not available as a target for the diffusion of responsibility, so the mediator can be more effective at challenging the disputant to take personal responsibility for solving the problem.

Other mediators reject caucusing. Some do so because they believe that joint problem solving (by the two disputants) is essential for developing a solution to the present problem and for fostering skills that can be used in future controversies when the mediator is not around. Others fear that caucusing will backfire in one or more of the following ways: (1) disputants will become suspicious of the mediator when he or she is caucusing with the other side, (2) they will mislead the mediator by making inaccurate statements in caucus sessions, because the opponent is not there to correct them, or (3) disputants not in caucus may be meeting with friends, relatives, or other supporters, and this may cause them to become more committed to their positions.

Method. The impact of caucusing was examined with data from both studies. The second study differed from the first in that no variables were manipulated and the two observers transcribed the hearings for later coding rather than coding them on sight. Data were gathered in both the Buffalo Dispute Settlement Center and the Neighborhood Justice Project of Elmira,

New York. Seventy-three cases were observed in all. The data again consisted of relative frequencies of the codes used in the content analysis of mediator and disputant behavior.

Results and Discussion. A synthesis of the results from the two studies will be presented here (for more results on the first study, see Welton, Pruitt, and McGillicuddy, 1988). Approximately 35 percent of the time was spent in caucus, 65 percent in joint session.

Direct, emotion-laden hostility—swearing, angry displays, and hostile questions—was less frequent in caucus than in joint sessions, no doubt because the opponent was not present as a stimulus to emotion. This probably accounts for the fact that two mediator tactics associated with social control were also less frequent in caucus: negative evaluation of a party's behavior and efforts to reduce the level of hostility.

Though direct hostility was diminished in caucus sessions, indirect types of hostility were on the increase. Criticisms of the opponent's behavior and character assassination occurred more frequently, and caucus sessions were also used to point out the merits of one's own person and case. In short, disputants in caucus tended to praise themselves and criticize their adversary, presumably because that adversary could not hear and refute what they had to say.

Though we cannot be certain, it seems likely that many of the self-enhancing and other-critical statements made in caucus were inaccurate. If they are not careful, mediators may be misled by what they hear in caucus.

A variety of results suggest that problem solving was more likely to occur in caucus than in joint sessions. Disputants provided more information about underlying feelings, values, and goals. Also mediators were more likely to ask disputants to generate new ideas to resolve the conflict, and (in Buffalo but not Elmira) disputants obliged by actually doing so. Mediators also generated more ideas for solutions in caucus than in joint sessions.

There are three possible reasons why problem solving should be more prominent in caucus than in joint sessions: (1) tension is reduced; (2) the mediator has an easier time persuading an individual disputant to take responsibility for solving the problem; and (3) the opponent is not there to hear a disputant's underlying rationale, tentative new ideas, or candid reaction to a mediator proposal.

Of course, we are not talking about joint problem solving but about problem-solving discussions between disputant and mediator. There is some evidence in our data that the mediator often takes the part of the other side in such discussions. We found that mediators were more likely in caucus than in joint sessions to talk positively about the other party, argue for the other party's position, and explain the other party's interests and needs.

Other findings were that mediators in caucus were more likely to resonate with a disputant by restating his or her viewpoint and to criticize disputant proposals. These forms of behavior, which can be milestones on the way to effective agreements, might well contribute to perceptions of bias if enacted in front of the other party.

Conclusions. These results suggest both strengths and weaknesses of caucusing. On the positive side, caucus sessions can be used to quiet angry disputants and generate new ideas by both disputant and mediator. On the negative side, there is good reason to believe that disputants will voice more self-serving falsehoods in caucus than in joint sessions. It follows that mediators should (and our evidence suggests that they do) shift to caucusing if joint problem solving fails. However, they must also be careful to treat much of what they hear in caucus sessions as disputant opinion rather than accurate information unless it is confirmed by the other party.

Additional Findings

A few other findings from the second study are especially interesting. Some concern disputant hostility, which we measured in two ways: prior hostility, a rating of the severity of the worst incident that was reported to have occurred before the hearing, and in-session hostility, an index composed of such behaviors as swearing, hostile questions, and character assassination. Both hostility measures were related to the absence of joint problem solving as rated by our observers, to immediate postsession disputant dissatisfaction with the agreement, and to failure to resolve the issues of importance to the disputants as rated by later coders. Clearly, hostility disrupts the quality of the hearing and its outcome.

Disputant concern about principles (for example, thieves should not benefit from their crimes) appeared to have a similar impact. In hearings where principles were often mentioned, hostility was greater, joint problem solving was reduced, disputants were less satisfied with the agreement, and there was less resolution of issues of importance to the disputants.

We were also able to identify mediator strategies that reduced hostility and enhanced the likelihood that the final agreement would deal with the issues of greatest importance to the disputants. Direct efforts to stem hostility were unavailing, but mediators were successful when they identified issues, proposed agendas, and challenged the disputants to come up with new ideas.

In line with findings on experiences with the police and the courts (Tyler, 1987a), disputants were more satisfied with both the conduct of the hearing and the final agreement if they felt that the mediator understood what they had said. This finding was somewhat stronger for complainants than respondents, perhaps because complainants are more aggrieved and hence more concerned about getting their points across.

In follow-up phone calls, four to eight months after the hearing, disputants were asked about their current satisfaction with the agreement and about whether the other party had complied with the agreement. The answers to these questions were correlated with the responses to an interview that had occurred immediately after the hearing. Follow-up satisfaction with the agreement was unrelated to immediate postsession satisfaction. However, it was related to postsession reports of satisfaction with the conduct of the hearing and postsession reports that the true underlying problems had come out. Complainant reports that the respondent had complied with the terms of the agreement were also unrelated to the respondent's postsession satisfaction with the agreement. Instead they were related to the respondent's immediate postsession report that the true underlying problems had come out in the hearing and that he or she had received a fair hearing. (Respondent reports of complainant compliance were unrelated to complainant statements in the postsession interview.) These findings confirm Tyler's assertion (1987b) that procedural matters are of crucial importance in the long-term success of an agreement.

Overall Conclusions

Our studies suggest a number of conclusions about mediation. One is that med/arb(same) discourages contentious behavior and encourages problem solving on the part of the disputants. This procedure, or some other that gives mediators a comparable level of power, has merit if the ideology and circumstances of the mediators lead them to encourage the disputants to reach their own agreement. Second, mediators follow a logical series of steps, starting with clarification of the ground rules, moving to efforts to gain information and keep order, then to efforts to pose and solve the issues, and finally to implementation. A third finding is that mediators tend to call caucuses when the disputants are behaving hostilely toward each other and not developing new ideas for solving their problems. Fourth, caucusing reduces angry displays and encourages problem-solving discussions between the mediator and each disputant. In discussions of mediation this kind of problem solving must be considered, in addition to joint problem solving by the two disputants of the kind stressed by Walton and McKersie (1965). Fifth, disputant hostility and concern about principles disrupt both the process and outcome of mediation.

Two other findings show the importance of mediator conduct of the hearing. One is that disputant satisfaction is closely linked to perceptions of whether the mediator understood what the disputants said. The other is that long-term satisfaction and compliance with the agreement are a function of satisfaction with the conduct of the hearing and a sense that important issues were aired.

We have also reached a tentative conclusion about research on the process of mediation: it is best to observe the hearings directly. We found that a checklist of tactics that the mediators filled out after the hearings provided inadequate information about how they actually had behaved.

A final technical issue needs to be raised: to what extent does the presence of observers in a mediation session affect the process? This question is hard to answer definitively, but we have some observations. Disputants only occasionally seemed to take note of the observers. Indeed, in one hearing that was not in our sample, a husband and wife frankly discussed changes in their strategy while the mediator was caucusing with their opponent in another room, completely ignoring an observer who sat a few feet away. Some *mediators*, on the other hand, seemed nervous about our presence, especially at first. One possible explanation for this difference is that we were in the mediators' but not the disputants' line of sight. (We had to be in somebody's line of sight because the room was not equipped with one-way mirrors.) Another is that for the mediator, we were a novel intrusion in an accustomed environment, whereas for most disputants, we were one of many elements in a totally novel setting.

It is not clear how the nervousness we observed affected the data. But we suspect that this impact was not very large, since both mediators and disputants tended to become heavily absorbed in the hearings.

References

Bales, R. F., and Strodtbeck, F. L. "Phases in Group Problem Solving." *Journal of Abnormal and Social Psychology*, 1951, *46*, 485–495.

Bercovitch, J. *Social Conflicts and Third Parties: Strategies of Conflict Resolution.* Boulder, Colo.: Westview, 1984.

Bigoness, W. J. "The Impact of Initial Bargaining Position and Alternative Modes of Third Party Intervention in Resolving Bargaining Impasses." *Organizational Behavior and Human Performance*, 1976, *17*, 185–198.

Blades, J. "Mediation: An Old Art Revisited." *Mediation Quarterly,* 1984, *3,* 59–95.

Carnevale, P. J. D., Beckman, S., and Bona, S. "Cognitive Elements of Cooperation and Competition: Categorization and Functional Fixedness." Unpublished manuscript, Department of Psychology, University of Illinois, Urbana–Champaign, 1984.

Douglas, A. *Industrial Peacemaking.* New York: Columbia University Press, 1962.

Druckman, D., and Mahoney, R. "Processes and Consequences of International Negotiations." *Journal of Social Issues,* 1977, *33,* 60–87.

Evarts, W. R., and others. *Winning Through Accommodation: The Mediator's Handbook.* Dubuque, Iowa: Kendall/Hunt, 1983.

Frei, D. "Conditions Affecting the Effectiveness of International Mediation." *Peace Science Society Papers,* 1976, *26,* 67–84.

Gulliver, P. H. *Disputes and Negotiations: A Cross-Cultural Perspective.* Orlando, Fla.: Academic Press, 1979.

Haynes, J. M. *Divorce Mediation: A Practical Guide for Therapists and Counselors.* New York: Springer-Verlag, 1981.

Johnson, D. F., and Pruitt, D. G. "Preintervention Effects of Mediation Versus Arbitration." *Journal of Applied Psychology,* 1972, *56,* 1–10.

Kerr, C. "Industrial Conflict and Its Mediation." *American Journal of Sociology,* 1954, *60,* 230–245.

Kessler, S. *Creative Conflict Resolution: Mediation.* Atlanta, Ga.: Society of Professionals, 1978.

Kochan, T. A., and Jick, T. "The Public Sector Mediation Process: A Theory and Empirical Examination." *Journal of Conflict Resolution,* 1978, *22,* 209–240.

Kolb, D. M. *The Mediators.* Cambridge, Mass.: MIT Press, 1983.

Kressel, K. *Labor Mediation: An Exploratory Survey.* Albany, N.Y.: Association of Labor Mediation Agencies, 1972.

Kressel, K., and Pruitt, D. G. "Themes in the Mediation of Social Conflict." *Journal of Social Issues,* 1985, *41,* 179–198.

McEwen, C. A., and Maiman, R. J. "Mediation in Small Claims Court: Achieving Compliance Through Consent." *Law & Society Review,* 1984, *18,* 11–50.

McGillicuddy, N. B., Welton, G. L., and Pruitt, D. G. "Third Party Intervention: A Field Experiment Comparing Three Different Models." *Journal of Personality and Social Psychology*, 1987, *53*, 104–112.

McGillis, D. "Conflict Resolution Outside the Courts." In L. Bickman (ed.), *Applied Social Psychology Annual*. Vol. 2. Beverly Hills, Calif.: Sage, 1981.

Markowitz, J. R., and Engram, P. S. "Mediation in Labor Disputes and Divorces: A Comparative Analysis." *Mediation Quarterly*, 1983, *2*, 67–78.

Morley, I. E., and Stephenson, G. M. *The Social Psychology of Bargaining*. London: Allen & Unwin, 1977.

Pearson, J., and Thoennes, N. "A Preliminary Portrait of Client Reactions to Three Court Mediation Programs." *Mediation Quarterly*, 1984, *3*, 21–40.

Pruitt, D. G. "Kissinger as a Traditional Mediator with Power." In J. Z. Rubin (ed.), *Dynamics of Third Party Intervention*. New York: Praeger, 1981a.

Pruitt, D. G. *Negotiation Behavior*. Orlando, Fla.: Academic Press, 1981b.

Ray, L. *Dispute Resolution Program Directory*. Washington, D.C.: American Bar Association, 1986.

Ray, L. "The Alternative Dispute Resolution Movement." *Peace and Change*, 1982, *8*, 117–128.

Roehl, J. A., and Cook, R. F. "Issues in Mediation: Rhetoric and Reality Revisited." *Journal of Social Issues*, 1985, *41*, 161–178.

Silbey, S. S., and Merry, S. E. "Mediator Settlement Strategies." *Law and Policy*, 1986, *8*, 7–32.

Syna, H., and others. "Effectiveness of Community Mediation for Conflict Resolution: An Evaluation." Paper presented at the annual meeting of the American Psychological Association, Anaheim, California, 1983.

Tyler, T. R. "Conditions Leading to Value-Expressive Effects in Judgments of Procedural Justice: A Test of Four Models." *Journal of Personality and Social Psychology*, 1987a, *52*, 333–344.

Tyler, T. R. "The Psychology of Disputant Concerns in Mediation." *Negotiation Journal*, 1987b, *3*, 367–374.

Vallone, R. P., Ross, L., and Lepper, M. R. "The Hostile Media

Phenomenon: Biased Perception and Perceptions of Media Bias in Coverage of the Beirut Massacre." *Journal of Personality and Social Psychology*, 1985, *49*, 577–585.

Walton, R. E., and McKersie, R. B. *A Behavioral Theory of Labor Negotiations*. New York: McGraw-Hill, 1965.

Welton, G. L., Pruitt, D. G., and McGillicuddy, N. B. "An Exploratory Examination of Caucusing: Its Role in Community Mediation." *Journal of Conflict Resolution*, 1988, *32*, 181–202.

Witty, C. J. *Mediation and Society: Conflict Management in Lebanon*. Orlando, Fla.: Academic Press, 1980.

Zartman, I. W. "Negotiation as a Joint Decision-making Process." *Journal of Conflict Resolution*, 1977, *21*, 619–638.

EIGHTEEN

Conclusion:
A Research Perspective
on the Mediation
of Social Conflict

Kenneth Kressel
Dean G. Pruitt

The research reported in this volume represents some of the best work currently available on the systematic study of the mediation of social conflict. Since our first endeavor as chroniclers of this growing field of inquiry (Kressel and Pruitt, 1985a), new methods have been introduced, new areas opened to investigation, and new theoretical vistas suggested. Research projects or areas of investigation represented in our earlier effort have expanded.

It is still evident, however, that we are in the relative infancy of sustained study of the mediation process. This concluding chapter may be viewed as a continuation of our earlier assessment (Kressel and Pruitt, 1985b): summarizing what is currently known and pointing out major conceptual and methodological issues. We have weighted our discussion most heavily on the chapters in this volume, but have also drawn on other relevant work.

Our summarizing discussion here is organized around seven major questions:

1. Does mediation work?
2. Under what conditions is it most effective?
3. What factors determine whether mediation will be used as a means of dispute resolution?
4. What do mediators do in attempting to resolve conflict, and under what conditions are these various efforts effective?
5. What is the impact of mediator power?
6. How do mediators decide which strategies and tactics to use?
7. How do mediators cope with the stresses of the role?

Needless to say, there are no definitive answers to any of these queries, but, on the whole, matters are further advanced than they were four or five years ago.

The Question of Effectiveness: Does Mediation Work?

The rapid rise of mediation programs and the threats they pose to established procedures, particularly legal ones, have lent a polemical air to discussions of the effectiveness of mediation. There is both a good side and a bad side to this polemical climate. The good side is that research has been encouraged. The bad side is that empirical questions tend to become oversimplified when they are shaped by practical controversies. A case in point: the question of whether mediation "works" assumes that "mediation" is a uniform intervention, both within and across dispute settings. In a more tranquil atmosphere this dubious assumption would be treated as an empirical issue in its own right.

The Outcomes of Mediation

User Satisfaction. User satisfaction with mediation is typically 75 percent or higher, even for those who fail to reach a

mediated agreement (see Chapters One, Two, and Twelve). There
is also evidence that mediation is more satisfying to disputing
parties than adjudication (Chapters One and Two) or arbitration (Brett and Goldberg, 1983).

These are generally comforting results, but their precise
meaning is unclear. On the positive side, we have some evidence
that they reflect disputant perceptions that mediation affords
them a measure of control and privacy (Chapters One and Two)
and, at least for complainants, gratification at being able to state
their own position (Chapter Seventeen). On the other hand,
disputant satisfaction should not be confused with an objective
evaluation of the quality of services rendered. We also note that,
at least in the area of divorce mediation, as many as 45 to 50
percent of those surveyed have significant complaints about the
mediation experience, regardless of their overall level of satisfaction (Chapter One).

Rates of Compliance. The evidence on rates of compliance
with mediated agreements is generally favorable. Roehl and
Cook (Chapter One) report 67 to 87 percent compliance with
agreements reached in neighborhood justice centers. In the
small claims area, McEwen and Maiman (Chapter Three) report
full compliance in 81 percent of the mediated cases compared
to 48 percent under adjudication. While *some* of the advantage to
mediation in such cases can be explained by degree of admitted
liability before intervention (Vidmar, 1985), McEwen and
Maiman argue convincingly that such factors do not explain
away all of mediation's more favorable impact. Mediation has
also been associated with greater compliance in divorce (Chapter One) but not in criminal cases (Davis, Tichane, and Grayson,
1980).

If we use relitigation data as a criterion of compliance, the
positive outcomes with mediation generally continue but there
are occasionally exceptions (Chapter One). In no studies, however, are the data on relitigation *less* favorable with mediation.

McEwen and Maiman (Chapter Three) explore a number
of reasons why compliance is generally higher in mediation,
including a greater satisfaction and sense of fairness, the greater
specification of details about how the mediation agreement is to

be implemented, and the fact that financial settlements are generally smaller and represent a smaller proportion of the original claim. McEwen and Maiman also argue that, compared to adjudication, mediation is much more likely to set in motion a variety of constructive psychological events and dynamics, including the opportunity for the parties to gain emotional support from the mediator and to explore a range of moral and interpersonal reasons for reaching agreement.

Rates of Settlement. There is little consistency in findings about the rate of settlement in mediation. Across domains of mediation, a conservative estimate would place the median settlement rate at somewhere around 60 percent, with a range typically between 20 and 80 percent (Chapter Thirteen; Kressel, 1985; Kressel and Pruitt, 1985b).

There has probably been an overemphasis on settlement rates as an indication of success. Kelly and Gigy (Chapter Twelve) found that a significant minority of their sample of divorcing couples who did not reach a mediated settlement nevertheless valued the process because it accomplished other things, such as improving communication or reconciliation. Conversely, in the Delaware child support mediation program (see Chapter One), settlement rates were high, but so too were levels of user dissatisfaction.

The Nature of Agreements. There is some evidence that mediated agreements involve more compromise and more equal sharing of resources than adjudicated agreements. Thus, in divorce mediation, Pearson and Thoennes (Chapter One) report that mediation produced more joint (as opposed to sole) custody agreements, a finding replicated by Emery and Wyer (1987). In small claims mediation, McEwen and Maiman (Chapter Three) report that lopsided awards going entirely to the plaintiff occurred in nearly 50 percent of the adjudicated cases, but in only 17 percent of the mediated ones.

This pattern is hardly uniform, however. Thus, while Pearson and Thoennes found that mediated settlements involved child support awards that represented more reasonable proportions of the fathers' income than adjudicated ones, Emery and Wyer (1987) found no such difference. In the Delaware mediation study (Chapter One), child support awards in mediation actually fell below the levels achieved through adjudication — and without compensatory improvements in payment patterns or relitigation. Days of visitation, which may be taken as another rough index of degree of "sharing," also show an equivocal pattern: Pearson and Thoennes report significantly more days of visitation in mediated settlements, but no such difference was found in the field experiment of Emery and Wyer (1987).

We also note that "compromise" is not an unassailable virtue. For example, in a study of small claims mediation, Vidmar (1985) noted that many respondents felt obligated to settle because of the strong-arm tactics used by the mediator and that they deeply resented the "compromise" settlement they reached. Similar complaints of mediator pressure or bias, on the order of 25 to 50 percent of those sampled, have been reported in divorce mediation (see Chapter One).

Efficiency Issues: Speed of Settlement, Costs, and Court Backlogs. There is evidence that cases that get to mediation reach settlement more quickly than comparable cases that follow the traditional adversarial approach (Chapter Two; Emery and Wyer, 1987). There is also some evidence that divorce mediation is less costly, both to the parties and to society, than traditional adjudication (Pearson and Thoennes, 1984). On the other hand, Roehl and Cook's review of neighborhood justice centers (Chapter Two) suggests that cost effectiveness is difficult to measure and that the case for mediation is not yet proved on such grounds. Bingham (1986), reviewing a decade's experience with environmental mediation, reached a similar conclusion.

 There is also little evidence that mediation has had any appreciable effect in reducing court backlogs (Chapter Two). Pearson (1983) has identified several reasons for this limited impact. She notes that many mediation programs attract cases that would not have been filed with the courts in the first place; that others that would have been filed would have been quickly dismissed or resulted in rapid settlements; and that a sizable percentage of cases fail to settle in mediation and therefore end up in court anyway.

Another important reason for the meager impact of mediation on court case loads is that mediation is typically refused by between one-third and two-thirds of those to whom it is offered, even on a low-cost or no-cost basis (Chapters One and Two). This suggests that mediation programs will probably have a bigger impact on the efficiency of the justice system if courts more vigorously press disputants to mediate. However, mandatory mediation has raised fears about coercion. Several chapters offer reassurance in that regard. Pearson and Thoennes, for example (Chapter One), find that the likelihood of agreement and user satisfaction are equal for elective and compulsory mediation, and many disputants apparently feel free to discontinue the process, even if it was initially imposed on them (Chapters Three and Twelve).

Improvement in the Postdispute Climate. An important argument made by proponents of mediation is that the procedure can penetrate below the surface details of a dispute and improve long-term relationships between the disputants. However, evidence from community justice centers (Chapter Two), divorce mediation programs (Chapter One), and international conflict (Chapter Six) suggests that mediation is usually unable to alter dysfunctional patterns of relating. Mediation might fail on this score because it is too brief, the problems too deep, and the postmediation context so stressful and complex that it "swamps" any positive benefits mediation might confer (Chapter One).

The concern has also been raised that mediation disadvantages the less powerful by exposing them to intimidation and coercion while simultaneously depriving them of rights and protection they maintain in adjudicatory forums. However, the evidence on this matter is fragmentary and contradictory.

In divorce mediation, where this concern has mainly been raised, there is evidence both for and against the notion that women, typically the less powerful of the parties from an economic perspective, are disadvantaged by the mediation experience. Kelly and Gigy's data (Chapter Twelve) show no evidence that women are more dissatisfied with mediation than men or feel forced into unfair agreements by it. Indeed, two-thirds or more of both sexes judged the economic terms of their agreements fair and satisfying, and more than 80 percent of the women felt that the mediator had helped them stand up for their rights. A less optimistic picture emerges in the Emery and Wyer field experiment (1987), in which women in the mediation group showed more postsettlement depression and the adversarial women felt that they had won more and lost less.

In nonindustrial societies, as Merry makes abundantly clear (Chapter Four), the purpose of mediation is *avowedly* to preserve existing status inequalities. In her words, "Mediated settlements between unequals are unequal." The "mediation between unequals is unequal" school of thought may also be found in contemporary labor mediation, where a realistic acceptance that power discrepancies will win out is often presented as the greater part of wisdom (McCarthy, 1985).

Methodological Issues in the Evaluation of Mediation

The evidence on mediation's effects suffers from a number of methodological problems common to most new areas of inquiry. One problem is the absence of controls for placebo effects. People often draw benefit from a novel, intriguing, and enthusiastically administered form of treatment when the treatment itself has no inherent merit. This placebo effect is especially likely to contaminate attitudinal measures, such as general satisfaction, which are precisely the ones on which the evidence in favor of mediation is most impressive.

A second difficulty is the usual absence of controls for pretreatment differences between mediated cases and the nonmediated comparison cases. In investigations of both voluntary and mandatory mediation, it appears that the more cooperatively oriented and less severely disturbed people end up in the mediation group, while the more conflictual cases are found in the comparison or "control" conditions (Kressel and Pruitt, 1985b). When pretreatment differences are held constant through various statistical and analytic stratagems, the advantages for mediation remain (Chapters One and Three). Nonetheless, the best solution to the pretreatment difference problem is true experimental designs, where cases are randomly assigned to treatment conditions. Only two such studies have been reported in the literature (Emery and Wyer, 1987; Pearson and Thoennes, 1984), and their results generally support the value of mediation compared to adjudication. Where feasible, more field experimental designs are sorely needed.

A third difficulty is that most investigations fail to provide details about the specific mediation and control procedures under study. Yet a multitude of different procedures can be accommodated under the "mediation" label, including some that do not differ from those employed by lawyers or the courts. Hence it is often not clear just what is being evaluated in these studies.

The Effectiveness of Mediation: Conclusion

What are we to conclude from the accumulating but methodologically and conceptually diverse research literature on mediation's efficiency?

It seems evident that mediation is a helpful and satisfying procedure for many people in a wide variety of disputes. However, the degree of effectiveness has probably been inflated in the available studies, for various methodological reasons. Furthermore, there are a number of important outcome variables on which evidence about the usefulness of mediation is equivocal, and others that have been neglected. Among the latter are the impact of the mediation experience on the mediator's immediate and long-range satisfactions with the third-party role. The outcome literature is also dominated by studies of *contractual* mediation, in which the mediator is an outsider. The effectiveness of *emergent* mediation, in which the mediator is closely related to the disputing parties and not a formal dispute resolver (as in the case of parental intervention in conflicts between children), may need to be judged by substantially different criteria. The goals of emergent mediation may differ in important ways. Kolb, for example, points out that in the modern organization the primary function of the emergent mediator may not be so much to resolve disputes as to give legitimacy and focus to conflicts that would otherwise be buried; see Chapter Five. (We shall discuss the contractual-emergent distinction in more detail later.)

In defense of mediation it must be pointed out that evidence on its value comes largely from studies of relatively inexperienced mediators, given the hastiest of training, working under severe constraints of time (a session or two) and significant ambiguities of practice. As the field of mediation becomes better established and more confident in its methods, research evaluations are likely to yield more positive results. It is also worth noting that research on mediation, for all its shortcomings, is much further along than research on the inadequately labeled "adversary" system. As we begin to have more systematic evidence on the roles that lawyers and the courts play in the resolution of disputes, we will have a more adequate context by which to judge mediation's strengths and weaknesses.

A broad critique of the evaluation literature is that such traditional questions as "Does mediation work?" or "Is mediation better than adjudication?" are oversimplifications. In the next sections we will try to pose more attractive and useful questions.

Under What Conditions Is Mediation Effective?

Moderate Levels of Conflict. In the research on the effects of mediation, one finding stands out: The worse the state of the parties' relationship with one another, the dimmer the prospects that mediation will be successful (Kressel and Pruitt, 1985b). Several of the chapters in this volume strengthen that general conclusion.

The measures of conflict intensity that correlate negatively with settlement include the severity of prior conflict between the parties (Chapters Thirteen and Seventeen); the level of hostility during the hearing (Chapters Eleven and Seventeen); the existence of ideological or cultural differences (Chapter Thirteen); and a perception that the other is untrustworthy, unreasonable, or angry (Chapter Twelve) and impossible to communicate with (Chapter One).

Motivation to Reach Agreement. In industrial mediation,

mediator perceptions that the parties have low motivation to resolve the conflict has been found to have a negative association with the probability of settlement (Carnevale and Pegnetter, 1985; Chapter Eleven; Kochan and Jick, 1978). We may also infer the motivational issue in Hiltrop's finding (Chapter Eleven) that settlement is more likely when mediation occurs under strike conditions than when there is no strike. Presumably, experience with a strike produces what Touval and Zartman (Chapter Six) call a "hurting stalemate," leading to an especially strong commitment to resolve the dispute. In divorce mediation, the negative impact of a low motivation to settle may be discerned in the finding that mediation tends to fail when one spouse has a high level of continuing psychological attachment to the other or refuses to accept the decision to divorce (Chapter Twelve; Sprenkle and Storm, 1983). Note, however, that in environmental mediation, Bingham (1986) found no relationship between the existence of a negotiation deadline and the likelihood of settlement, and Thoennes and Pearson (1985) did not corroborate the relationship between lingering marital attachment and success in divorce mediation.

Commitment to Mediation. In labor mediation, Hiltrop reports (Chapter Eleven) that settlement rates are highest when mediation is requested by both sides rather than only one or by the mediation agency. Conversely, settlement rates are lower when the chief negotiators are unenthusiastic about mediation or do not trust the mediator. Similarly, Carnevale and his coworkers report (Chapter Ten) that receptivity to mediation and trust in the mediator (as perceived by the mediator) are positively related to settlement. All these findings suggest that commitment to the process encourages settlement.

Available Resources. Mediation is especially unlikely to succeed under conditions of resource scarcity. Thus, the inability of the employer to pay (as judged by the mediator) has been found negatively correlated with successful intervention in two studies of labor mediation (Carnevale and Pegnetter, 1985; Kochan and Jick, 1978). Also, low income or great financial strain is negatively related to success in divorce mediation (Doyle and Caron, 1979; Kressel and others, 1980; Pearson, Thoennes, and Vanderkooi, 1982). The simplest explanation for these findings is that resource scarcity reduces, sometimes to zero, the number of mutually acceptable solutions. In so doing it may also diminish the amount of perceived common ground (see Chapter Sixteen; Pruitt and Rubin, 1986) and hence the motivation of the parties to join with the mediator in problem solving for mutual gain.

Absence of Issues of "Principle." Several chapters in this volume support the idea, long cherished by experienced mediators, that disputes involving issues of "principle" are especially difficult to resolve. Both Hiltrop for labor mediation (Chapter Eleven) and Bercovitch for international conflict (Chapter Thirteen) marshal evidence that issues of principle (of union recognition or ideological differences between countries) are more difficult to resolve than more mundane — and "compromisable" — disputes (over wages or "security" concerns). Pruitt and his colleagues also report (Chapter Seventeen) that issues of principle make it harder to reach agreement in community mediation, and Bingham (1986) notes that in environmental mediation site-specific disputes are nearly twice as likely to get resolved as those involving differences over general policy.

There is a good rationale for the proposition that issues of principle make it hard to agree. For one thing, they are deeply felt. For another, they are either-or propositions that do not admit of compromise. Ideology seldom embraces such wishy-washy concepts as "partial justice," which are nevertheless the basis for many successful agreements. All of this notwithstanding, several studies of labor mediation, including Chapter Ten in this volume, find no evidence for the proposition (Carnevale and Pegnetter, 1985; Kochan and Jick, 1978).

Parties of Equal Power. It is widely felt by practitioners that disputes in which one side is much more powerful than the other (more articulate, more self-confident, better able to withstand the economic consequences of a strike) are among the most difficult to mediate. Although Pearson and Thoennes (Chapter One) find no impact of what we might call the psychological balance of power in divorce mediation, Kelly and Gigy's data (Chapter Twelve) do give a measure of support to the proposition. Divorcing couples who were able to reach full agreements in mediation were more likely than those who could reach only a partial settlement to have more nearly equal self-appraisal of their financial knowledge. Bercovitch (Chapter Thirteen) also cites numerous studies on international mediation in which smaller power differentials between the disputants have been consistently and positively associated with settlement.

The Absence of Severe Internal Discord. We can add one final popular notion for which the empirical literature seems to lend a modicum of support: the higher the level of *intraparty* conflict and divisiveness, the greater the mediator's headaches and the less probable a mediated settlement. In international conflict, for example, mediation is more successful when the disputants are internally united and clearly identifiable and there are no strong factions for the mediator — and the chief negotiators — to contend with (Chapter Thirteen). Similarly, divorce mediation has a higher probability of success when clients' lawyers accept the mediation process (Irving, Bohm, MacDonald, and Benjamin, 1979; Pearson and Thoennes, 1982) and hence do not question their clients' commitment to it. In environmental mediation, the single most predictive factor of settlement was whether those with authority to implement a decision were represented at the bargaining table; if the chief negotiators were limited to making recommendations to a constituency with ultimate authority, that is, if they had to deal with a powerful "faction," settlement was less likely (Bingham, 1986).

The one nonconfirmatory finding is that of Carnevale and his associates (Chapter Ten), who report that "internal problems" (as perceived by their labor mediator sample) were not related to outcomes.

Summary: Dispute Characteristics and Mediated Settlement

Intensely conflicted disputes involving parties of widely disparate power, with low motivation to settle, fighting about matters of principle, suffering from discord or ambivalence within their own camps, and negotiating over scarce resources are likely to defeat even the most adroit mediators. Even in isolation, these factors are bound to cause serious mediator headaches. Combine a few of them, and we are talking major mediator migraine.

These findings may serve as a useful antidote for mediators who are victimized by the unrealistically high expectation that they can achieve settlement under virtually any conditions. "Settlement mania" certainly appears to be an occupational hazard in the burgeoning area of divorce mediation (Kressel, Butler-DeFreitas, Forlenza, and Wilcox, forthcoming); even staid labor mediation pros are not immune to this malady, to judge by Carnevale and Pegnetter's report (1985) that the experienced mediators in their sample seemed to woefully underestimate the magnitude of obstacles to settlement.

The findings just described may also reflect dispute characteristics that complicate *all* forms of negotiation, not just those involving mediation. None of our studies address this issue; but it has been found that in divorce disputes, scarcity of resources and intense conflict are as fatal in lawyer-orchestrated negotiations as they are in mediated ones (Hochberg and Kressel, 1983).

How Does Mediation Get Started?

Despite the adulation of its advocates and the research favoring it, mediation is not a highly popular vehicle for conflict resolution. As we have already observed, in interpersonal disputes of all kinds, one-third to two-thirds of those given the option to use mediation decline it (Chapters One and Two). Nation-states appear to have much in common with individual people. It takes very special levels of distress (such as the "hurting stalemate") to motivate them to seek out or accept a mediator (Chapters Six and Thirteen).

It is also apparent that mediators are often reluctant participants, drawn into a dispute more by felt necessity than by desire (Chapters Five and Six). According to Kolb's account in Chapter Five, experience as a mediator is likely to be so chastening to people in organizations that they frequently take steps to avoid the role in the future!

We can only sketch some of the variables that appear to

determine whether mediation will occur. They fall into three distinct but interrelated categories: characteristics of the social context in which mediation is embedded; characteristics of the disputants; and characteristics of the would-be mediator.

Characteristics of the Social Context Related to Entering Mediation

Contractual Versus Emergent Mediation. In *contractual* mediation the mediator is an outsider with whom the parties contract for the specific purpose of helping them resolve their dispute. In *emergent* mediation the parties and the mediator are part of a continuing relational set, with enduring and encompassing ties to one another. Emergent mediation is found in families, friendship groups, organizations of all kinds, and international relations.

These two forms of mediation differ in the way they get started. All that is usually required for beginning contractual mediation is that the disputants (or a party such as the courts that controls their interests) decide on mediation. They then turn or are directed to a mediation facility or individual to mediate their conflict. In emergent mediation, by contrast, potential mediators are free to decline to serve, making it uncertain whether mediation will occur even if the disputants want it. Chapters Five, Six, and Eight devote considerable attention to the kinds of decisions likely to be involved here. When the parties do not want mediation, or are skeptical, they must be persuaded. This may be a task of considerable proportions, particularly since the disputants may correctly perceive that the mediator has his or her own interests at stake (Chapter Six; Susskind and Ozawa, 1985).

The Availability of an Institutional Structure. By definition, emergent mediation is devoid of formal rules and procedures for beginning the mediation process. In many forms of contractual mediation, on the other hand, a well-defined institutional structure determines the onset of mediation. For example, in labor mediation, mediation may be mandated when a bargaining impasse lasts sixty days or longer. In some forms of contractual mediation this institutional structure may be fully or partially hidden from the disputants, as when the parties appear for a small claims hearing only to have the judge "suggest" mediation.

An exception to the normally well-institutionalized procedures for beginning contractual mediation may be seen in multiparty disputes such as those that occur in many environmental and public resource conflicts (Chapter Seven). Here the mediator is typically recruited by one or a partial set of the interested parties and must locate the others and persuade them to participate, just as if he or she were an emergent mediator (Susskind and Ozawa, 1985). To increase the prospects for mediation and to reduce the headaches of cranking the process up anew for each dispute, proponents of mediation in such domains have begun to try their hand at institutionalization. Alas, from Brock and Cormick's analysis (Chapter Seven), it would appear that building such structures is an arduous and uncertain task.

Pressures from the Social Environment. The parties' motivation to mediate may be increased or decreased by the way the broader social environment views social conflict and the process of mediation. The clearest example comes from Chapter Four on mediation in nonindustrial societies. There Merry indicates that mediation is most likely to occur when the warring factions have many cross-cutting kinship ties and the broader community is unwilling to tolerate the disruption in social life that a continuation or escalation of the conflict would entail. In such cases, much social pressure is brought to bear on the principals to mediate. Important community leaders are likely to be involved in recruiting the mediator, pushing the disputants into mediation, urging them to follow the mediator's suggestions, and enforcing the final agreements.

"Coercion" into mediation is less intense in American mediation, but pressure to mediate does occur. Where powerful others, such as judges, legislatures, or other agents of social control may want mediation to occur, it can be made to happen, with or without the full volition of the parties. That such coercion does not appear to decrease the effectiveness of mediation is one of the interesting and important findings reported in this book (Chapters One, Two, and Three).

It would also appear that judges and attorneys in the northeastern and western United States look much more favorably on judicial mediation than the legal community in the southern and northcentral parts of the country, suggesting contrasting social norms on the mediation role for judges (Chapter Nine). In divorce, the adversarial culture of many attorneys may dissuade clients from choosing to mediate (Chapter One).

We may also infer from Chapters Five and Eight that organizational environments may work both for and against the mediational role. Support for mediation comes from the increasingly nonhierarchical nature of organizational life, where task forces are often composed of individuals or groups who have no common superior but are of equal standing. Such a context is ripe soil for the ambitious manager with conflict-resolving skills, who emerges to mediate the issues and then relinquishes the mediation role when the task force has attained its objectives.

On the other hand, the modern organization has an ambivalent stance toward internal conflict. Kolb notes (Chapter Five) that managers often take their lead from this uncertain climate, preferring conflict-avoidant strategies (reorganization and firing) to mediation, and that they are highly inclined to bolster these approaches by defining conflicts as rooted in the parties' personalities and thus not amenable to resolution. She also cites the plight of the organizational ombudsmen, charged with both helping people and protecting the organization. Since the helping role often requires acknowledging conflicts that are not supposed to exist, ombudsmen often resolve their dilemma by adopting strategies that appear motivated by "a desire to keep disputes quiet and avoid confrontation."

Characteristics of the Disputants Related to Entering Mediation

Relationship Dynamics. Several chapters suggest that disputants are more responsive to mediation when their conflict has become so intense that they can no longer ignore it (Chapter Sixteen). Nevertheless, a degree of goodwill is still also necessary to instigate a move toward mediation, just as it is usually necessary for success once mediation has started. For example, divorce mediation necessarily emerges from the breakup of a relationship. Yet mediation, as opposed to adjudication, is more likely to be chosen by those with more positive views of their spouse, more optimism about the prospects for cooperation (at least in regard to the children), and a greater willingness to accept blame for the marital discord (Chapters One and Twelve).

Appraisal of the Alternatives. Mediation is often chosen as a lesser of two evils. Thus, resort to mediation frequently emerges from the disputants' despair about what they can achieve by unaided discussion. In addition, much of the impetus for divorce mediation appears to come from the very high levels of public disenchantment with the traditional legal approach to divorce (Chapter One). In Kelly and Gigy's study (Chapter Twelve), more than 80 percent of those who chose divorce mediation did so to reduce contact with lawyers and court proceedings and the costs associated with them.

Perceptions of Mediation or Would-Be Mediators. A common view is that acceptance of mediation hinges on the parties' belief that the mediator is utterly neutral and unbiased. While there is some evidence that mediator effectiveness declines with perceived bias (Chapter Eleven; Welton and Pruitt, 1987), in the international sphere, Touval and Zartman argue convincingly (Chapter Six) that impartiality is not as crucial as whether the mediator is perceived as capable of getting the disputants what they want. Indeed, one party's acceptance of mediation may even hinge on a perception of the mediator as aligned with (and hence wielding influence over) *the adversary*. The classic example is Egypt's eagerness to have its 1974 dispute with Israel mediated by Henry Kissinger, the Jewish representative of a state closely aligned with Israel (Rubin, 1981).

The same phenomenon may help explain Bercovitch's report (Chapter Thirteen) that as the power of the parties increase, the likelihood of international mediation decreases. This presumably results because it is difficult for the disputants to find a still more powerful mediator having the requisite leverage with the other side to make mediation worth the gamble.

The lubricating value of perceived mediator power over the adversary is not limited to international conflict. Industrial mediators report that management sometimes prefers a labor-oriented mediator when they perceive that the union is being inflexible (Kressel, 1972).

Returning to less exalted if no less tempestuous arenas of conflict, there is also tantalizing evidence that divorcing men and women may have contrasting perceptions of when and for what purposes mediation is desirable. Kelly and Gigy report (Chapter Twelve) that men were not only more positive than women about entering mediation (82 compared to 67 percent), but also differed in their reasons for favoring mediation. Husbands were more likely to mediate when they had a desire for reconciliation or when they perceived the marital climate as badly strained. In contrast, for wives, willingness to start mediation was associated with perceptions that the husband was honest and trustworthy and that the marital climate was cooperative. Pearson and Thoennes report (Chapter One) that wives rejected mediation because of mistrust, fear, or a desire to avoid the husband. These data hint that for men the mediation choice is perceived in terms of attaining an instrumental goal—keeping the marriage afloat or getting help with a difficult partner—while for women the choice is more weighted by judgments about whether the marital climate is safe. These differences in receptivity to mediation are consistent with the broader literature on psychological differences associated with gender, where the task preoccupations of men and the more socioemotional orientation of women have long been noted (Ashmore and Del Boca, 1986; Rubin and Brown, 1975). They may also reflect the more vulnerable economic and social situation of women in divorce (Kressel, 1985; Weitzman, 1985).

Finally, Peachey notes (Chapter Fourteen) that receptivity to mediation is often a function of the justice motivations of the disputants and those who refer people to mediation. One central justice motivation is what he calls *retributive justice*—the desire for revenge through the exaction of retribution. Mediation is an unappealing vehicle when such motivation prevails because it is based on notions of compromise and joint responsibility for the conflict, and hence by its nature excludes retribution.

Characteristics of the Mediator Related to Entering Mediation

As we have noted, mediator decision making is an important antecedent of emergent (as opposed to contractual) mediation. Hence mediator characteristics are especially important in determining whether emergent mediation will occur. Third parties typically choose to mediate to achieve important ends of their own. These include conserving time and energy (Chapter Nine), reaching important agreements (Chapter Five), reducing disruption caused by conflict (Chapter Four), and protecting or extending the mediators' sphere of influence (Chapter Six). Powerful mediators with self-interested motives for mediating a particular conflict are more likely than less powerful ones to be able to convince (or oblige) the disputants to make use of their services (Frei, 1976; Chapter Four). (A more extended discussion of mediator power will be found in a later section.)

Several of our contributors also note that emergent mediators tend to have strong ties to both sides (Chapter Four, Five, and Six). Such ties may motivate potential mediators to act because conflict between one's associates is usually distasteful or disruptive. A prior relationship with the disputants also makes it easier for would-be mediators to intrude themselves into a controversy, making them more likely to try to do so.

There is an equally impressive list of third-party goals and motives that can *deter* mediation. Chapter Five suggests that managers will avoid playing a mediational role when they perceive that doing so is not valued by the organziation. Such a perception is likely to develop when mediation activities are not highly visible to the would-be mediator's superiors and therefore seem unlikely to produce rewards. The experimental studies by Carnevale and his associates (Chapter Sixteen) also suggest that third parties will tend to reject mediation when they feel that the disputants have little common ground or when they are not very concerned about whether the parties attain their aspirations.

The research by Sheppard and his colleagues (Chapter Eight) starts with the assumption that emergent third parties have a choice among various approaches, including mediation and arbitration. Their data suggest that third parties tend to prefer mediation over arbitration when they see the dispute as complex and important, view it as resulting from a personality clash, or expect future interaction between the disputants. They tend to prefer arbitration over mediation when they will be held directly accountable for the outcome, believe that the outcome will establish an important precedent, or are in a position of authority over the disputants.

What Mediators Do, and with What Effect

The virtually limitless array of actions that mediators can take may be grouped under four major headings: (1) establishing a working alliance with the parties; (2) improving the climate between the parties; (3) addressing the issues; and (4) applying pressure for settlement.

Establishing a Working Alliance

Although establishing a trusting relationship with the parties is a central dogma in the practitioner literature, it has received little attention from researchers. Chapter Ten strengthens the case for rapport-building ("reflexive") interventions. Such mediator behaviors were associated with favorable outcomes when hostility between the parties was high, when there were internal conflicts within the parties, and when there was initial resistance to mediation. Pruitt and his associates (Chapter Seventeen) also report that an important correlate of disputant satisfaction with the mediation experience in a community justice center was a feeling that the mediator had been fair and had understood them. The finding is in line with the research on procedural justice, which demonstrates that people's satisfaction with dispute resolution mechanisms is as much a function of feeling fairly treated as of "winning" (Tyler, 1987).

Improving the Climate Between the Parties

Interventions aimed at improving the climate between the disputants are the clearest embodiment of the traditional view that mediators are catalysts and facilitators, not arm twisters or proponents of this or that solution. Two climate-changing strategies dominate the work reported in this volume: facilitating communication between the parties and making timely use of the caucus.

Facilitating Communication. Touval and Zartman (Chapter Six) describe one of the primary functions of the mediator of international conflicts as that of "communicator." The aim of a communicator is to ease dialogue between the disputants by "tact, palatable wording, and sympathetic presentation" of each side's position to the other. Kolb's concept of the "orchestrator" style of labor mediation (Chapter Five) touches on a similar point, and Silbey and Merry (1986) have identified a nearly identical "person-oriented" style among mediators of family disputes. Peachey's review of neighborhood dispute centers (Chapter Fourteen) suggests that one important value of fostering understanding between the disputants is that it dampens the wish for retribution, a common motive among the casually acquainted people who make up much of the case load of such centers.

What can be said for the effectiveness of mediator efforts to improve communication and understanding? Pearson and Thoennes (Chapter One) report that in divorce mediation, the parties' assessment that the mediator had facilitated communication and had provided clarification and insight were the most important correlates of settlement. Similarly, Hiltrop finds (Chapter Eleven) that "acting as a communication link" and "helping the parties understand the other side's position" were positively associated with settlement, particularly under inauspicious circumstances as when hostility was high, motivation to settle was low, and the parties were far apart in their positions.

The Use of the Caucus. Of all the tactics described in practitioner manuals as aids to "climate control," caucusing (meeting with each party separately) is perhaps the most commonly invoked.

The observational data of Pruitt and his co-workers (Chapter Seventeen) support the value of the caucus for the harried mediator and throw useful light on the dynamics of the caucus. Caucusing was a frequent activity of their community mediators, who spent approximately one-third of the mediation in private sessions. Mediators tended to call a caucus "when the disputants displayed hostility toward each other and generated few new alternatives." The result of caucusing was an immediate reduction of "emotion-laden hostility," although indirect hostility — in the form of criticizing the opponent to the mediator — tended to increase. The key value of the caucus, however, was an increase in problem-solving activities between the disputants and the mediator, with the mediator often presenting the other party's position in a sympathetic way.

We must note, however, that the pattern of findings reported by Hiltrop (Chapter Eleven) suggests that mediating *exclusively* through the caucus actually works best under relatively benign conditions of conflict (when positional differences are small or motivation to settle is high). On the other hand, under strained circumstances — when the parties were unmotivated to settle, hostility was high, and positional differences large — mediators fared better either by eschewing the caucus entirely or combining it with joint meetings.

Addressing the Issues

All mediators deal with the issues in one way or another. Some are very gentle and nondirective, leaving the bulk of the substantive work to the disputants. Others grapple directly with the issues, developing ideas and advocating them vigorously. The evidence on mediator attention to the issues falls into four distinct if overlapping categories: issue identification and agenda setting, proposal shaping, proposal making, and face saving.

Issue Identification and Agenda Setting. Helping the parties identify issues and develop an agenda emerges as an important mediator activity in the chapters on divorce mediation (Chapters One and Fifteen), community mediation (Chapter Seventeen), labor mediation (Chapters Ten and Eleven), international mediation (Chapter Six), and mediation within organizations (Chapter Five). Since the lack of a clear and relevant agenda often creates considerable tension between the parties, agenda-setting behaviors could well be classified under strategies for improving the climate. The same mediator behaviors can serve multiple purposes.

The effect of mediator efforts to identify and order issues on the outcomes of mediation are generally positive.

Pruitt and his co-workers (1989) report that posing issues and proposing an agenda are predictive of high-quality outcomes in community mediation. Hiltrop (Chapter Eleven) reports that arranging preliminary meetings with the parties to explore the issues was one of the two mediator strategies most reliably correlated with settlement. Mediators can apparently also provide a useful service by directing the parties to start working on the easier issues first (as implied by Huber, Pruitt, and Welton, 1986) and by discouraging them from starting with the more difficult ones (Chapter Eleven).

Carnevale and his colleagues also report (Chapter Ten) that agenda-oriented activities were positively correlated with successful agreements and improved relations between the disputants. Such tactics were especially effective when there was conflict within the parties and were also helpful when hostility was low and when there was a single important issue. Donohue's analysis of divorce mediation transcripts (Chapter Fifteen) indicates that, compared to mediators who deadlock, mediators who reach agreement concentrate on identifying the key issues much earlier in the dispute. These findings are consistent with Pruitt's evidence from community mediation (Chapter Seventeen) that the parties' satisfaction with mediation was positively related to a sense that the underlying issues had come out.

Proposal Shaping. Mediators often attempt to move the parties closer to agreement by tactics designed to give shape to the ultimate agreement without openly suggesting specific terms. Thus, Peachey (Chapter Fourteen) believes that encouraging the disputants to seek outcomes other than retribution is a central task of the community mediator. The "shaping" role is also evident in the "paternalistic" strategy of the mediator-judge, which includes such tactics as informing the lawyers about ways similar cases have been settled and channeling discussion to areas that have the highest probability of settlement (Chapter Nine).

There is evidence that proposal-shaping tactics are positively associated with settlement, although the pattern is not uniform. In his first study, Hiltrop (Chapter Eleven) found no significant relationship between settlement and mediator reports that they had discussed the strengths and weaknesses of each party's case in closed meetings. However, in his later investigation two proposal-shaping tactics — "identifying specific points of agreement and disagreement" and "suggesting the use of step-by-step implementation" — were both predictive of agreement under an array of inhospitable circumstances. Donohue (1985) reports that, relative to divorce mediators who deadlocked, mediators who settled used a much more varied set of reframing tactics. While the reframing strategy includes direct proposals by the mediator, it is also heavily laden with less direct substantive activities that are closer to our sense of proposal shaping (such as recasting disputants' remarks as proposals and negatively evaluating disputant proposals).

Proposal Making. Despite a persistent ideology that mediators ought to refrain from pushing their own ideas, it is quite evident that they are often a primary source of settlement proposals and that they are not at all shy about playing such a role. Thus, Pearson and Thoennes report that in divorce mediation the mediator was the source of most of the proposed solutions (Chapter One). Studies of both labor mediation (Chapters Five and Ten) and judicial mediation (Chapter Nine) identify forceful suggestion making as a central dimension of mediator behavior.

Evidence from divorce and judicial mediation indicates that there is value in the mediator taking an active lead in throwing out substantive ideas (Chapters One and Nine). However, studies on labor mediation present a more complex and less favorable picture. Hiltrop (Chapter Eleven) finds that "suggesting solutions for resolving the issues" is a highly effective tactic under favorable conditions (low hostility, small differences in disputant positions, high motivation to solve) but is worse than useless under unfavorable conditions (high hostility, large differences in disputant positions, low motivation to solve). Carnevale and his associates, on the other hand, report that proposal making was ineffective under most conditions (Chapter Ten).

Face Saving. One common cause for deadlocked negotiations is the pressure to take extreme positions exerted on negotiators by their constituents. An important part of the mediator's function, therefore, is to make proposals that help negotiators beat graceful retreats from positional posturing (Chapters Nine, Ten, and Eleven).

Carnevale and his associates report that the face-saving strategy was positively associated with outcomes, particularly when the parties were perceived by the mediator as being beset by "internal" problems (rival constituents), or were unreceptive to mediation (Chapter Sixteen). Hiltrop (Chapter Eleven) reports a very similar pattern of results for the tactic of "asking negotiators to recommend a possible agreement to their constituents"—a move commonly aimed at helping the negotiators save face by having the mediator shoulder the responsibility for unpalatable ideas.

Applying Pressure for Settlement

Pressure tactics are efforts to push the disputants toward agreement. A prevailing ideology, especially in community and family mediation, views such tactics as alien to good mediation. Instead, so this view goes, the mediator's principal tools are reason and compassion. Ideology notwithstanding, the research in this volume clearly shows that most mediators regard pressure tactics as an essential ingredient of their kit bag. Nearly every chapter makes this point.

Perhaps the most pungent illustration is Merry's account of mediation in nonindustrial societies (Chapter Four). For example, of the mediator in Nuer society she writes: "His authority rests on his control over supernatural power and the ability to curse." Of the Ifuago *monkalun* she writes, "In the event of a failure to reach an agreement his reputation as a headhunter becomes salient." Her report is all the more revealing because American community mediation has drawn its inspiration from an altogether different idea of the nature of mediation in such societies.

The likelihood that a mediator will use pressure tactics seems to increase when the mediator's own interests or values are at stake (Rubin, 1981; Susskind and Ozawa, 1985; Chapter Six); when the dispute involves very high levels of hostility (Chapters Ten and Eleven; Gerhart and Drotning, 1980); when the mediator is exposed to strong institutional pressures to avoid the costs of adjudication (Chapters Three and Nine; Vidmar, 1985); and when the mediator is invested with much formal authority (Chapters Four, Six, Nine, Thirteen, and Seventeen). There is also evidence from experimental simulations that the use of mediator pressure tactics is associated with an increase in negotiation deadlines and with male, as opposed to female, mediators (Chapter Sixteen).

What is the impact of mediator pressure tactics? The picture is decidedly mixed. Bercovitch (Chapter Thirteen) finds that such tactics lead to more settlements in international mediation than milder approaches involving facilitating communication and formulating issues. Unfortunately his results on this issue fall short of statistical significance. Hiltrop's analysis of labor mediation in Great Britain (Chapter Eleven) suggests that there is no straightforward relationship between mediator pressure and outcome. Thus, while "threatening to quit" and "emphasizing the need to make concessions" were effective under inhospitable circumstances, "suggesting the use of arbitration" seemed to backfire under conditions of high hostility in his most recent data, while "pointing out the implications of continued

disagreement" was associated with settlement only when conditions were relatively favorable. Carnevale and his associates
report even less efficacy for mediator pressure tactics in their
study of American labor mediators (Chapter Ten). While pressure tactics had a positive relationship with general settlement
under a few circumstances, the prevailing association was negative. Pressure tactics had even more dubious effects when the
measure of outcome was the parties' relationship with one
another.

It is also important to note that, because longitudinal
designs are rare in mediation research, the *long-term* consequences of mediator pressure tactics are unknown. It is often
asserted that such tactics reduce the parties' sense of psychological ownership of the settlement and thus ultimately produce
noncompliance. There is, as yet, no direct evidence for this
assertion; but Kolb, in her detailed study of labor mediators
(1983), notes that mediator aggressiveness in one case can negatively affect the mediator's acceptability to the same parties in
subsequent cases.

Mediator Power and Its Impact

Mediator power can take a number of forms: authority
over the disputants, the capacity to provide rewards, or the
capacity to threaten punishments. But whatever form it takes, it
is likely to affect the probability that mediation will occur, the
mediator's behavior, and the course and outcome of mediation.

Earlier we noted that would-be emergent mediators are
more likely to gain acceptance the greater their status and
power. This can be explained in at least three ways. First, more
powerful individuals are harder to resist in anything they suggest. Second, more powerful mediators seem more likely to have
influence over the other disputant, increasing the likelihood
that they can precipitate an agreement (Chapter Six). Third, this
power may be helpful in overcoming mediators' ambivalence
about intervening by suggesting to them that they have the where-
withal to overcome whatever obstacles may be encountered.

While high levels of third-party power are likely to encourage recourse to mediation, they are also likely to lead to the use of rather heavy-handed interventions. Thus Pruitt and colleagues (Chapter Seventeen) found that mediators who had the power to arbitrate tended to employ heavier pressure tactics than those who did not; Sheppard and his associates (Chapter Eight) found that third parties with authority over the disputants were especially likely to identify solutions for them; and Wall and Rude (Chapter Nine) found that judges frequently adopt strong-arm tactics that in the hands of less powerful mediators might well be unacceptable and unworkable.

What is the effect of mediator power on the course and outcome of mediation? The conventional wisdom on this subject holds, in Fisher's picturesque language (1981), that the mediator should be a "eunuch from Mars," totally unbiased and powerless. A good deal more study of this central issue is clearly needed, but the evidence in this volume suggests that mediator power has some decided benefits.

Bercovitch (Chapter Thirteen) argues that, in international mediation, "leverage, resources, power, and influence are at the heart of successful mediation," and he is supported in this assertion by the report of Touval and Zartman (Chapter Six).

On the domestic scene, the main evidence on the effects of mediator power comes from the study by Pruitt and his colleagues of community mediation (Chapter Seventeen). They found that disputant problem solving was encouraged when mediators had the power to arbitrate if mediation failed. Disputants made fewer angry or hostile comments, voiced fewer invidious comparisons, and devised more alternatives for dealing with the issues than when the mediator did not have this power. Two explanations for these effects were supported by the data: first, that a desire to avoid the mediator's exercise of power strengthened the disputants' motivation to resolve their conflict, and second, that the disputants were more motivated to impress and follow a more powerful mediator. The power to arbitrate also increased the number of agreements, but this effect was not statistically significant.

These results corroborate the positive findings about mediator power in international relations. However, Pruitt and colleagues argue that they should be viewed with some caution. Powerful mediators tend to act like arbitrators, dictating solutions instead of seeking a consensus. The result is likely to be an "agreement" that is unsatisfactory to one or both parties and may therefore fail to be implemented. Power probably works best in the hands of mediators who have a strong democratic ideology that allows them to resist the temptation to simply dictate a solution.

How Do Mediators Decide What to Do?

Effective mediation requires more than an arsenal of intervention strategies and tactics. There must be some basis for determining which interventions to use. One such basis is the mediator's active monitoring of the unfolding conflict; another is the mediator's often unarticulated preference for a particular style of mediation.

Coordinating Interventions to Perceptions of the Conflict

Carnevale and others' study of labor mediators (Chapter Ten) provides evidence that mediators attempt to link their interventions to their perceptions of the underlying obstacles to agreement. For example, when the parties had unrealistic expectations, mediators reported using pressure tactics designed to change the expectations and induce compromise. Donohue's analysis of divorce mediation (Chapter Fifteen) suggests that in successful mediation, rising levels of conflict are likely to trigger a flurry of mediator activity designed to reduce hostilities while declining tensions lead to a recession of mediator activity.

Carnevale's strategic-choice model (Chapter Sixteen) attempts to predict several common forms of mediator activity from two underlying conditions: the degree to which the mediator believes that the parties have overlapping interests ("perceived common ground") and the mediator's level of concern that the parties attain their aspirations. The results of the experimental tests of the model are promising. With high concern, mediators chose strategies aimed at finding a mutually acceptable solution. If high concern was coupled with low perceived common ground, they also tended to compensate the parties for concessions. A combination of low concern and low perceived common ground encouraged them to adopt pressure tactics.

It is also a favorite theme of practitioners that mediation proceeds in distinctive stages (Folberg and Taylor, 1984; Haynes, 1981). Chapters Fifteen and Seventeen support the broad assertion that mediators organize their interventions according to the stage that mediation is in, while calling into question certain common assumptions about the precise nature of the stages, such as those summarized by Kressel (1972).

Thus, Pruitt and his colleagues (Chapter Seventeen) note that tactics directed at keeping hostility within manageable bounds tend to come *early*, not in mid-session; humor and "lightness" tend to come at the *end*, rather than at the beginning of sessions; and rapport building and shows of expertise occur more or less continuously, rather than being confined to the opening period. Donohue's data (Chapter Fifteen) indicate that in mediations that proceed to settlement, mediators are much quicker to identify disputed issues and to solicit and process proposals than has frequently been recommended in formal manuals of mediation.

The Influence of Mediator Stylistic Preferences

Mediators are not always self-conscious diagnosticians. The literature is beginning to suggest that mediators often lean toward either a task-oriented or socioemotional style regardless of the specific dispute before them.

The task-oriented style involves active grappling with the issues — that is, proposal shaping and proposal making — and it makes liberal use of pressure tactics. This style is often combined with skepticism about the parties' abilities to deal with each other and a corresponding sense of necessity for the mediator to do the lion's share of the work, often through caucusing. Kolb's "deal makers" epitomize this schema in labor mediation (Chapter Five). The "bargaining" stance described by Silbey and

Merry (1986) provides a nearly identical account for small claims and family mediation.

The socioemotional style, by contrast, emphasizes the need of the parties to work through to their own solutions. Mediators with this orientation tend to be more optimistic about the parties' ability to manage their own affairs if conditions are "right." This orientation is ordinarily combined with an emphasis on improving the long-term relations between the parties. The mediator's role is correspondingly less active and more focused on opening direct lines of communication. Kolb's "orchestrators" (Chapter Five) and Silbey and Merry's (1986) "person-oriented" style of mediation exemplify this approach.

Other evidence for a division between the task-oriented and socioemotional approaches may be found in Vanderkooi and Pearson (1983) for divorce mediation and Susskind and Ozawa (1985) for the mediation of public policy disputes. Interestingly enough, the distinction also fits the negotiating style of lawyers (Kressel, 1985; Williams, 1983).

The determinants of mediator styles are matters much in need of elucidation. There may be circumstances in which the mediator's enactment of the role is largely dictated by the context in which the mediator functions. Thus, Kolb (1983) has reported that labor mediators employed by a state agency were uniformly deal makers, while the federal mediators she studied were all orchestrators. Kolb argues that adherence to the deal-maker role reflects the difficult circumstances confronting the state labor mediator (including the necessity to work with inexperienced negotiators, the lack of a strike deadline by which to motivate negotiators to make concessions, and the multiple constituencies on both sides, which limit negotiator flexibility). These hazards, she contends, constrain the mediator to take charge in a highly directive manner and preclude the more nondirective orchestrating style that federal labor mediators can use because of much more congenial negotiating circumstances.

It is also clear, however, that mediators may vary their styles from one dispute to another or even within the same dispute (Silbey and Merry, 1986). We know very little about the factors and dynamics influencing these choices or the way that the mediator's stylistic leanings may affect the process and outcome of mediation.

As a final note to the topic of mediator choice of tactics, we observe that, despite the fruitful beginnings under review, the research record shows no connection yet between mediator tactical behavior and any coherent theories of conflict. Mediators appear influenced by an immediate stimulus (such as rising hostility) and perhaps by a generalized preference for a particular style of mediation, but not by any integrated perspective about the proper response to various underlying dysfunctional dynamics. The situation seems much more primitive in this regard than what prevails in psychotherapy—another type of "conflict" intervention—in which therapist behavior is typically rooted in theories of personality development or family dynamics.

How Do Mediators Cope with the Stresses of Their Role?

It is becoming increasingly clear that whatever mediation's calming potential may be for disputants, it can be an extremely stressful experience for mediators (Kressel, 1981, 1985).

The Sources of the Problems

Some of these stresses result from disputant characteristics. It would be helpful if mediators were typically welcomed into disputes by parties sophisticated about the process. More often, however, their services are either rejected out of hand or distrusted by ignorant, misinformed, or suspicious disputants (Chapters One, Two, Six, and Seven). To complicate matters, the parties' antipathy for each other can make it hazardous for the mediator to empathize with either one, and the disputants also frequently have great power to resist the mediator's substantive initiatives (Chapters Five and Six). They may be abetted in these efforts by knowledge that the mediator is at least as dependent on them as they are on the mediator (Chapters Five, Six, and Seven).

Other mediator headaches derive from the normative definitions of the role or the institutional contexts in which the role is embedded. For example, mediators are supposed to produce settlements. Yet the norms that govern their behavior often enjoin them to do so without pressuring the parties or injecting too much of their own thinking on the terms of settlement. In many cases this is an impossible combination of requirements. Mediators caught in such a bind sometimes forgo settlements or suggest terms that are too vague to be meaningful (Kressel, 1985; Merry, 1982; Silbey and Merry, 1986). More often, they prefer to abandon the mantle of nondirectiveness in favor of the liberal use of pressure. When they do so they are often resented (Vidmar, 1985) or suspected of unethical behavior (Chapter Nine)—all the more so because such tactics tend to fall more heavily on one party than the other (Chapter Six).

Mediating a dispute is also fundamentally different from fixing a carburetor or removing a gall bladder; there are no precise guidelines for proceeding and the result of intervention is by no means self-evident. Mediators are deprived of straightforward means of demonstrating their competence and, as Kolb has shown (1985), may feel compelled to establish their credentials with tactics that may, ironically, give them an untrustworthy and unreliable appearance (such as name dropping to establish their expertise or inventing "facts" to convey their "knowledge").

The mediation role also often lacks institutional support. Organizations often provide little encouragement to ombudsmen or other third parties, denying the importance or even the existence of conflict (Chapter Five). In other cases, there may be institutional expectations and conditions that are antithetical to the standard mediation role. For example, court-connected mediation programs, especially in the family area, are likely to press their mediators to process large numbers of cases as rapidly as possible, forcing them to apply more pressure than they wish or to make other compromises with their role.

The ambivalence and demoralization resulting from all these problems may be surmised from the large proportion of third parties who forswear the mediation role when given the opportunity (North Carolina Bar Association, 1987; Chapters Five and Eight).

Mediator Coping Responses

It is entirely premature for a comprehensive statement about the variety of strategies that mediators may employ to manage the stresses of their role. Here we simply note several of the more obvious candidates.

Denial. There are various indications that tactics of denial are used by mediators to shield themselves from the stresses of their work. This may explain why labor mediators in Carnevale and Pegnetter's sample (1985) tended to systematically underestimate the difficulty of the cases they had handled. The same mechanism may also account for the discrepancy between the use of highly aggressive tactics by mediators and their tendency to downplay this side of their work (Kressel, 1972, 1981).

"Economizing" Strategies. Given the parties' high level of ambivalence about mediation, the more frequently mediators intervene the more likely they are to stimulate resistance and damage their authority. On the other hand, it is often necessary to intervene actively lest the mediator lose control of the conflict. A solution to this dilemma may be for mediators to intervene frequently enough to maintain control but not too frequently to stimulate resentment. This may be one explanation for Donohue's finding (Chapter Fifteen) that while mediators who failed to get agreement interrupted the parties' exchanges either very rarely or a great deal, successful mediators interrupted the parties at an intermediary rate.

Adopting a Preferred Mediation Style. As Sheppard notes (Chapter Eight), cognitive schemata help organize a complex world and simplify understanding and action. We may speculate that one way mediators strive to reduce their role problems is to adopt a particular schema and the tactics associated with it. The task-oriented and socioemotional styles of mediation we have previously described may be thought of as being built around such schema. Their prominence in the literature may reflect the fact that each is responsive to somewhat different but equally important aspects of the role headache. The task orientation heeds the pressures on mediators to arrange settlements efficiently and to steer clear of the murky relationship waters that they may have neither the time nor training to manage; the socioemotional stance is responsive to the press to respect the parties' autonomy, to remain impartial, and to foster enduring, not merely expedient, settlements.

Clearly we have not exhausted the variety of ways in which the stresses of the mediation role may be handled. Other identifiable mechanisms include the use of humor, cathartic outbursts to relieve tension, a self-conscious rejection of responsibility for getting settlements, and the development of professional support groups and organizations.

Finally, it must also be noted that the mechanisms that mediators adopt for lessening the stresses of their role are likely to have consequences for the disputants as well. That is, some solutions will work better than others, in the sense of both helping mediators maintain their morale and in producing a process the parties experience as helpful. The intersection of mediator efforts to solve their own role problems with mediator efforts to help solve the problems of the parties remains to be explored.

Whither Research on Mediation?

Like mediation itself, research on mediation is an extremely heterogeneous activity, not only in terms of the home disciplines of its investigators and its underlying goals, but also in its methods. This diversity is undoubtedly a source of strength, but it may also work to retard a sense of a shared arena of discourse.

We are prompted to make certain suggestions about method which grow out of the cumulative impressions made on us in the course of editing this volume. Five things are needed:

1. *The need for a contingency approach to understanding the effects of intervention.* Questions about whether mediation works and what kinds of mediator behavior are desirable should be

answered from a contingency perspective. Under what conditions is mediation advisable? Under what circumstances are different mediator tactics effective?

There are numerous methods suitable to a contingency approach. One of the most useful is experimental methodology, which allows us to isolate the conditions of interest and thus make more precise comparisons than can be done in field research. Three of our chapters (Nine, Fourteen, and Sixteen) illustrate the use of experimental methodology of one kind or another. The well-known dangers of artificiality associated with the experiment can be offset by a variety of complementary approaches, including field experiments (see Chapter Seventeen), the use of expert mediators rather than naive subjects in laboratory simulations, and the decision to proceed to the experiment only after direct, in-depth observation in the field has clarified the issues of moment.

2. *The need for a holistic approach.* The study of mediator behavior has tended to emphasize frequency counts of discrete mediator acts. While such an approach has simplicity on its side, it ignores the organic quality of the mediation process.

Thus, *when* a tactic is used may be more important than *how often* it is used. This is the issue of timing of which practitioners are rightly enamored and that was studied by Donohue in this volume (Chapter Fifteen). Disputes have an internal developmental course. Coordinating interventions to the waxing and waning of such psychological forces as trust, suspicion, and the need for a solution is a crucial part of the mediator's skill. It is appropriate, we believe, to speak of *critical moments* in any dispute, during which mediators must be ready to alter their strategy. A frequency count of mediator activities misses this crucial aspect of the mediation process.

We note, in this connection, that it is important to measure not only what the mediator does, but what *the parties* are doing when the mediator intervenes and what they are doing after an intervention. Mediation is a situation of reciprocal influence. Focusing exclusively on the mediator violates this reality and may well retard our understanding of the mediation process. Focusing on the mediator-disputant *system* may also help us learn about the psychological *processes* of conflict resolution.

The success of mediator efforts also depends on *skill*. This is an obvious cliché but one that nevertheless needs to be grappled with. Current approaches tend to skirt the issue of skill. We count *what* mediators did (or say they did) rather than *how* they did it. However, while any fool can separate the parties, only a skillful mediator knows when to do so and what to say to the parties once they are apart. Likewise, it is clear that strategies and tactics are not used separately but are bundled together in strategic thrusts. Skillful mediators know how to construct such bundles.

3. *The need for observational studies.* Two of the chapters in this volume (Fifteen and Seventeen) involve direct observation of mediators at work rather than retrospective accounts. This is a new development aimed at solving some of the problems connected with the subjective recollections provided by mediators or disputants. The most notable of these problems is an often weak correspondence between retrospective accounts and what actually happened in mediation (Chapter Seventeen). Checklists of mediator activity (see Kochan and Jick, 1978; Chapters Nine, Eleven, and Ten), a very popular self-report approach, seem particularly vulnerable to such distortions since they evoke few memory clues (compared, say, to the vignette typology employed by Sheppard and his associates [Chapter Eight]). They also tend to encourage idealized responses (what I *should* have done rather than what I did).

Observed mediator behavior also has its own problems, of course. It can be much more time-consuming and arduous than using self-report methods, and in three instances reported in this volume (Chapters Five, Eleven, and Seventeen) it was forbidden in whole or in part by authorities sensitive to the confidential nature of the mediation process. We believe resistance of this kind will begin to lessen as familiarity between researchers and mediation agencies increases. Observation may also become a more common research tool if the field of conflict management continues to move toward a stronger alliance with universities, where the norms of objective scrutiny tend to compete on at least an equal footing with the requirements of privacy. We are beginning to see the emergence of university-based "laboratories" for studying conflict, a development perhaps analogous to the emergence of research-oriented psychotherapy clinics at universities in the 1950s, which did so much to place psychotherapy research on a more objective footing.

4. *The need for case-study methodology and other systematic approaches to self-report data.* In spite of our cautions, it is clear that self-reports have an important place in the study of mediation. In this volume a variety of self-report methods are illustrated, including the checklist of mediator behavior, conflict vignettes, and case studies built around open-ended interviews. Each has its strengths and weaknesses. When used with sophisticated statistical techniques, such as path analysis, self-report data allow the fleshing out of intricate relationships between dispute characteristics and third-party activities, a point illustrated in Chapter Eight.

Self-reports are also the backbone of the much-maligned case study. Social scientists are beginning to reassess the value of the case study, and methods for conducting them in a systematic way are beginning to be described (Yin, 1984). In-depth, systematic case studies are very much in order for the study of mediation. They can convey the richness, headaches, and complexities of the mediation process better than any other method, can help us formulate models of clinical practice for more refined testing, and can suggest unanticipated hypotheses about social conflict (Kressel, Butler-DeFreitas, Forlenza, and Wilcox, forthcoming).

5. *The need for scholar-practitioners.* We are coming to believe that research on mediation will be enriched in direct proportion to the degree to which those who study the process have direct experience as mediators. Such a scholar-practitioner model has proved valuable in clinical psychology and all branches of medicine. It is in line with Mark Twain's dictum that in holding up a cat by the tail you learn things that you can learn in no other way. Or, to paraphrase Kurt Lewin on a more serious level, if there is nothing so practical as a good theory, there may be nothing so theoretical as good practice.

References

Ashmore, R. D., and Del Boca, F. K. (eds.). *The Social Psychology of Female-Male Relations: A Critical Analysis of Central Concepts.* Orlando, Fla.: Academic Press, 1986.

Bingham, G. *Resolving Environmental Disputes: A Decade of Experience.* Washington, D.C.: Conservation Foundation, 1986.

Brett, J. M., and Goldberg, S. B. "Mediator-Advisors: A New Third-Party Role." In M. H. Bazerman and R. J. Lewicki (eds.), *Negotiating in Organizations.* Beverly Hills, Calif.: Sage, 1983.

Carnevale, P., and Pegnetter, R. "The Selection of Mediation Tactics in Public-Sector Disputes: A Contingency Analysis." *Journal of Social Issues,* 1985, *41,* 65–81.

Davis, R., Tichane, M., and Grayson, D. *Mediation and Arbitration as Alternatives to Prosecution in Felony Arrest Cases: An Evaluation of the Brooklyn Dispute Resolution Center.* New York: Vera Institute of Justice, 1980.

Donohue, W. A., Allen, M., and Burrell, N. "Communication Strategies in Mediation." *Mediation Quarterly,* 1985, *10,* 75–89.

Doyle, P., and Caron, W. "Contested Custody Intervention: An Empirical Assessment." In D. H. Olson (ed.), *Child Custody: Literature Review and Alternative Approaches.* Minneapolis: Department of Family Social Sciences, University of Minnesota, 1979.

Emery, R. E., and Wyer, M. M. "Child Custody Mediation and Litigation: An Experimental Evaluation of the Experience of Parents." *Journal of Consulting and Clinical Psychology,* 1987, *55,* 179–186.

Fisher, R. "Playing the Wrong Game?" In J. Z. Rubin (ed.), *Dynamics of Third Party Intervention: Kissinger in the Middle East.* New York: Praeger, 1981.

Folberg, J., and Taylor, A. *Mediation: A Comprehensive Guide to Resolving Conflicts Without Litigation.* San Francisco: Jossey-Bass, 1984.

Frei, D. "Conditions Affecting the Effectiveness of International Mediation." *Peace Science Society Papers,* 1976, *26,* 67–84.

Gerhart, P. F., and Drotning, J. E. "Dispute Settlement and the

Intensity of Mediation." *Industrial Relations*, 1980, *19*, 352–359.

Haynes, J. M. *Divorce Mediation: A Practical Guide for Therapists and Counselors.* New York: Springer-Verlag, 1981.

Hochberg, A. M., and Kressel, K. "Determinants of Successful and Unsuccessful Divorce Settlement Negotiation." Paper presented at the meeting of the American Psychological Association, Anaheim, California, Aug. 1983.

Huber, E. L., Pruitt, D. C., and Welton, G. L. "The Effect of Prior Negotiation Experience on the Process and Outcome of Later Negotiation." Paper presented at the annual meeting of the Eastern Psychological Association, New York, April 1986.

Irving, H., Bohm, P., MacDonald, G., and Benjamin, M. *A Comparative Analysis of Two Family Court Services: An Exploratory Study of Conciliation Counseling.* Toronto: Department of National Health and Welfare and the Ontario Ministry of the Attorney General, 1979.

Kochan, T. A., and Jick, T. "The Public Sector Mediation Process: A Theory and Empirical Examination." *Journal of Conflict Resolution*, 1978, *22*, 209–240.

Kolb, D. M. *The Mediators.* Cambridge, Mass.: MIT Press, 1983.

Kolb, D. M. "To Be a Mediator: Expressive Tactics in Mediation." *Journal of Social Issues*, 1985, *41*, 1–25.

Kressel, K. *Labor Mediation: An Exploratory Survey.* Albany, N.Y.: Association of Labor Mediation Agencies, 1972.

Kressel, K. "Kissinger in the Middle East: An Exploratory Analysis of Role Strain in International Mediation." In J. Z. Rubin (ed.), *Dynamics of Third Party Intervention: Kissinger in the Middle East.* New York: Praeger, 1981.

Kressel, K. *The Process of Divorce: How Professionals and Couples Negotiate Settlements.* New York: Basic Books, 1985.

Kressel, K., Butler-DeFreitas, F., Forlenza, S. G., and Wilcox, C. "Research in Contested Custody Mediations: An Illustration of the Case Study Method." *Mediation Quarterly*, forthcoming.

Kressel, K., and Pruitt, D. G. (eds.). "The Mediation of Social Conflict." A special issue of the *Journal of Social Issues*, 1985a, *41* (2).

Kressel, K., and Pruitt, D. G. "Themes in the Mediation of Social Conflict." *Journal of Social Issues*, 1985b, *41*, 179–198.

Kressel, K., and others. "A Typology of Divorcing Couples: Implications for Mediation and the Divorce Process." *Family Process*, 1980, *19*, 101–116.

McCarthy, W. "The Role of Power and Principle in *Getting to Yes*." *Negotiation Journal* 1985, *1*, 59–66.

Merry, S. E. "Defining Success in the Neighborhood Justice Movement." In R. Tomasic and M. Feeley (eds.), *Neighborhood Justice: As Assessment of an Emerging Idea*. New York: Longman, 1982.

North Carolina Bar Association. *Mandatory Child Custody Mediation Program in Mecklenburg County: A Study and Evaluation*. Raleigh: North Carolina Bar Association, 1987.

Pearson, J. "An Evaluation of Alternatives to Court Adjudication." Unpublished paper, Denver: Center for Policy Research, 1983.

Pearson, J., and Thoennes, N. "Mediation and Divorce: The Benefits Outweigh the Costs." *The Family Advocate*, 1982, *4*, 26–32.

Pearson, J., and Thoennes, N. "Mediating and Litigating Custody Disputes: A Longitudinal Evaluation." *Family Law Quarterly*, 1984, *17*, 497–524.

Pearson, J., Thoennes, N., and Vanderkooi, L. "The Decision to Mediate: Profiles of Individuals Who Accept and Reject the Opportunity to Mediate Contested Child Custody and Visitation Issues." *Journal of Divorce*, 1982, *6*, 17–35.

Pruitt, D. G., and Rubin, J. Z. *Social Conflict: Escalation, Stalemate, and Settlement*. New York: Random House, 1986.

Pruitt, D. G., and others. "The Process of Mediation: Caucusing, Control, and Problem Solving." In M. A. Rahim, (ed.), *Managing Conflict: Interdisciplinary Perspectives*. New York: Praeger, 1989.

Rubin, J. Z. (ed.). *Dynamics of Third Party Intervention: Kissinger in the Middle East*. New York: Praeger, 1981.

Rubin, J. Z., and Brown, B. R. *The Social Psychology of Bargaining and Negotiation*. Orlando, Fla.: Academic Press, 1975.

Silbey, S. S., and Merry, S. E. "Mediator Settlement Strategies," *Law and Policy*, 1986, *8*, 7–32.

Sprenkle, D. H., and Storm, C. L. "Divorce Therapy Outcome Research: A Substantive and Methodological Review." *Journal of Marital and Family Therapy*, 1983, *9*, 239–258.

Susskind, L., and Ozawa, C. "Mediating Public Disputes: Obstacles and Possibilities." *Journal of Social Issues*, 1985, *41*, 145–159.

Thoennes, N., and Pearson, J. "Predicting Outcomes in Divorce Mediation: The Influence of People and Process." *Journal of Social Issues*, 1985, *41*, 115–126.

Tyler, T. R. "The Psychology of Disputant Concerns in Mediation." *Negotiation Journal*, 1987, *3*, 367–374.

Vanderkooi, L., and Pearson, J. "Mediating Divorce Disputes: Mediator Behaviors, Styles, and Roles." *Family Relations*, 1983, *2*, 557–566.

Vidmar, N. "An Assessment of Mediation in a Small Claims Court." *Journal of Social Issues*, 1985, *41*, 127–144.

Weitzman, L. J. *The Divorce Revolution: The Unexpected Consequences for Women and Children in America.* New York: Free Press, 1985.

Welton, G. L., and Pruitt, D. G. "The Mediation Process: The Effects of Mediator Bias and Disputant Power." *Personality and Social Psychology Bulletin*, 1987, *13*, 123–133.

Williams, G. R. *Legal Negotiation and Settlement.* St. Paul, Minn.: West, 1983.

Yin, R. K. *Case Study Research: Design and Methods.* Beverly Hills, Calif.: Sage, 1984.

Name Index

Subject Index

A

Achenbach-Edelbrock Behavior Checklist, 23

Acton Investments, emergent managerial mediation case at, 100–103, 106, 109

Adjudication, by informal mediators, 169–170, 173–174, 186

Administration for Children, Youth and Families, 10

Advisory, Conciliation, and Arbitration Service (ACAS) (United Kingdom), and labor mediation studies, 241–260

Affective-cognitive behaviors, by mediators, 217–219

Afghanistan, mediation in, 69, 74–77, 80, 81, 82, 84

Africa: international mediation in, 116, 117, 119, 120, 122, 123, 124, 126, 131, 133, 135, 286, 410; mediation in, 69, 70–72, 81, 84, 419

Agreement. *See* Settlement

Alaska, and fishing rights case, 141

Algeria, and international mediation, 116, 119, 122, 135

Alternate dispute resolution (ADR),

in public policy and regulatory conflicts, 138–165

American Bar Association, Committee on Dispute Resolution of, 37

Angola, and international mediation, 131, 133

Arab countries, and international mediation, 116, 120, 286

Arab League, mediation by, 121, 286

Arbitration. *See* Mediation/arbitration

Argentina, and international mediation, 120

Arusha (Tanzania), mediation by, 69, 80, 81

Asia: international mediation in, 116, 119, 120, 122–123, 131, 135, 286; mediation in, 69, 74–77, 79, 80, 81, 82, 84

Aspirations of disputants, in strategic-choice model, 347–348, 350–351, 355–356, 357–358, 359, 361

Association of Counties (Wisconsin), 158

Association of Family and Conciliation Courts, 326

Association of Manufacturers and Commerce, 156